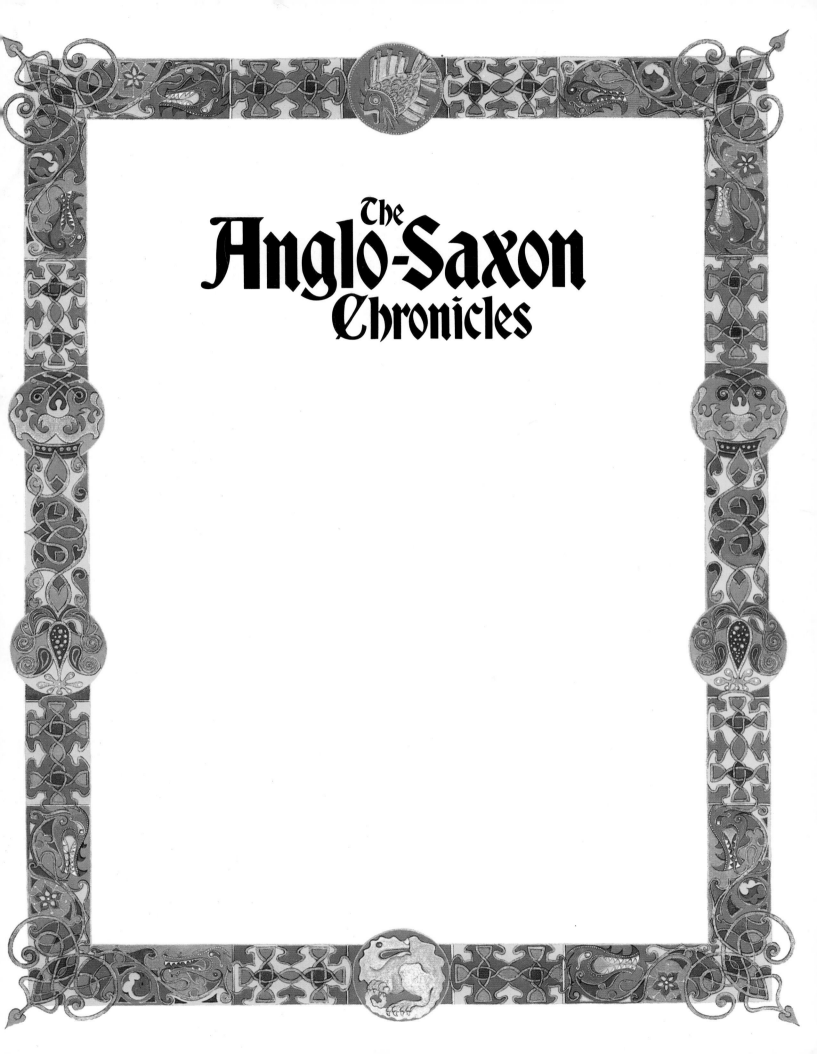

The Anglo-Saxon Chronicles

Illustrated Material

Editor: Christopher Pick
Historical and Picture Researcher: Phyllis Hunt
Consultant: S. A. Bradley, Senior Lecturer in
English at the University of York
Designer: Lorraine Johnson

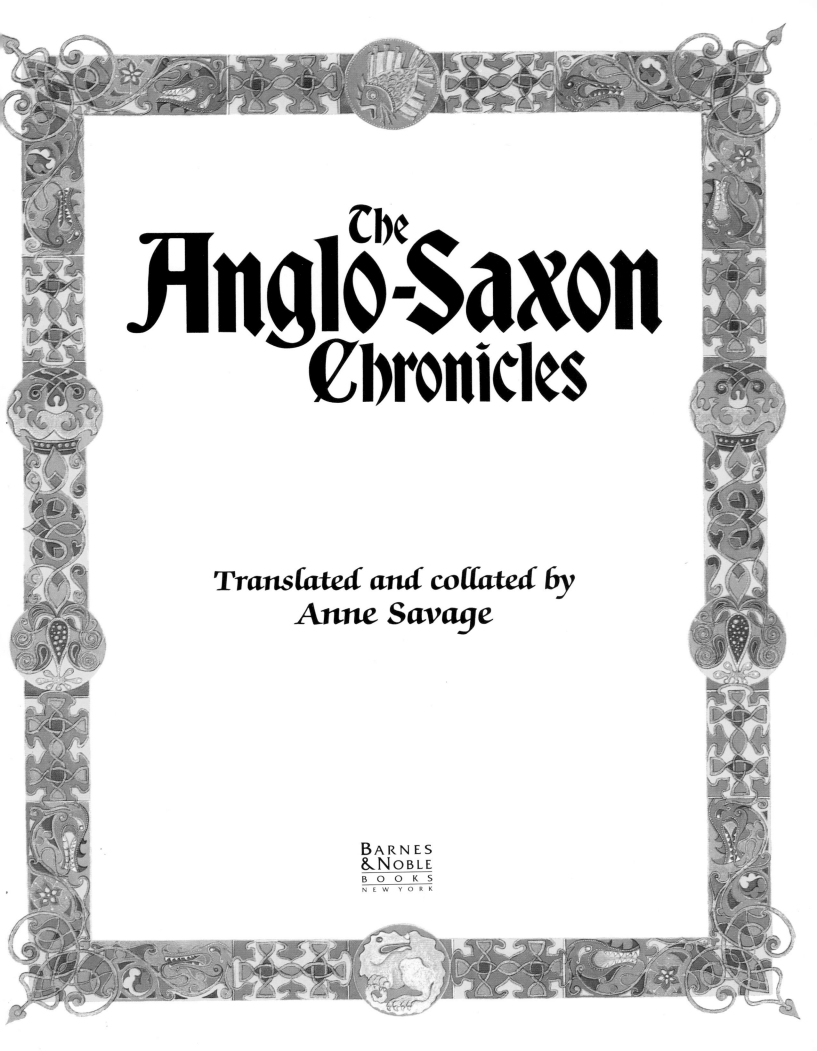

The Anglo-Saxon Chronicles

Translated and collated by
Anne Savage

BARNES
&NOBLE
BOOKS
NEW YORK

This edition published by Barnes & Noble Inc.,
by arrangement with Salamander Books Ltd
8, Blenheim Court
Brewery Road
London N7 9NT

A member of the Chrysalis Group plc

Printed and bound in Spain

ISBN 0 7607 2263 3
M 10 9 8 7 6 5 4 3 2 1

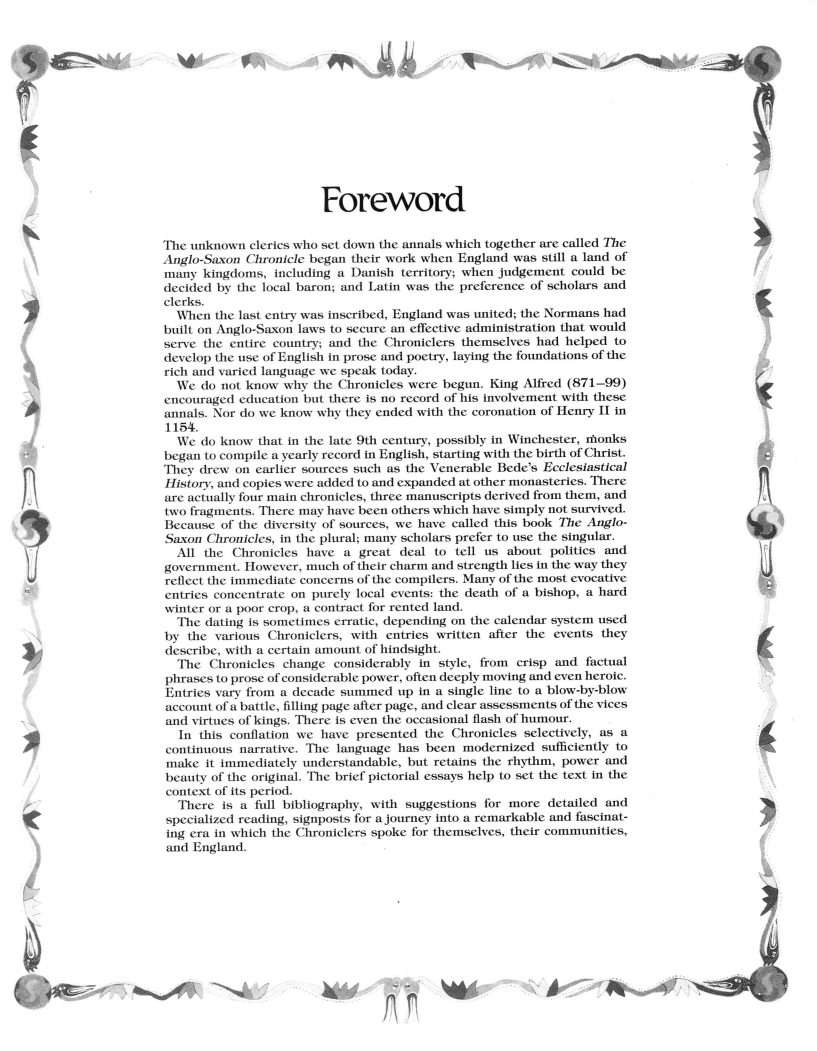

Foreword

The unknown clerics who set down the annals which together are called *The Anglo-Saxon Chronicle* began their work when England was still a land of many kingdoms, including a Danish territory; when judgement could be decided by the local baron; and Latin was the preference of scholars and clerks.

When the last entry was inscribed, England was united; the Normans had built on Anglo-Saxon laws to secure an effective administration that would serve the entire country; and the Chroniclers themselves had helped to develop the use of English in prose and poetry, laying the foundations of the rich and varied language we speak today.

We do not know why the Chronicles were begun. King Alfred (871–99) encouraged education but there is no record of his involvement with these annals. Nor do we know why they ended with the coronation of Henry II in 1154.

We do know that in the late 9th century, possibly in Winchester, monks began to compile a yearly record in English, starting with the birth of Christ. They drew on earlier sources such as the Venerable Bede's *Ecclesiastical History*, and copies were added to and expanded at other monasteries. There are actually four main chronicles, three manuscripts derived from them, and two fragments. There may have been others which have simply not survived. Because of the diversity of sources, we have called this book *The Anglo-Saxon Chronicles*, in the plural; many scholars prefer to use the singular.

All the Chronicles have a great deal to tell us about politics and government. However, much of their charm and strength lies in the way they reflect the immediate concerns of the compilers. Many of the most evocative entries concentrate on purely local events: the death of a bishop, a hard winter or a poor crop, a contract for rented land.

The dating is sometimes erratic, depending on the calendar system used by the various Chroniclers, with entries written after the events they describe, with a certain amount of hindsight.

The Chronicles change considerably in style, from crisp and factual phrases to prose of considerable power, often deeply moving and even heroic. Entries vary from a decade summed up in a single line to a blow-by-blow account of a battle, filling page after page, and clear assessments of the vices and virtues of kings. There is even the occasional flash of humour.

In this conflation we have presented the Chronicles selectively, as a continuous narrative. The language has been modernized sufficiently to make it immediately understandable, but retains the rhythm, power and beauty of the original. The brief pictorial essays help to set the text in the context of its period.

There is a full bibliography, with suggestions for more detailed and specialized reading, signposts for a journey into a remarkable and fascinating era in which the Chroniclers spoke for themselves, their communities, and England.

Contents

Kings of Wessex and England: 6th to 9th Centuries

Cerdic 519–34

Cynric 534–60

Ceawlin 560–92

Ceola 592–7

Ceolwulf 597–611

Cynegils 611–42

Cenwalh 642–72

Aescwine 673–6

Centwine 676–86

Ceadwalla 686–8

Ine 688–726

Aethelheard 726–40

Cuthred 740–56

Sigebryht 756–7

Cynewulf 757–86

Brihtric 786–802

Ecgbryht 802–39

Aethelwulf 839–58

Aethelbald 858–60

Aethelberht 860–6

Aethelred 866–71

Alfred the Great 871–99

Edward the Elder 899–924

Aethelstan 924–39

Edmund 939–46

Eadred 946–55

Eadwig the All-Fair 955–9

Edgar the Peacable 959–75

Edward the Martyr 975–8

Aethelred Evil-Council 978–1016

Svein 1013–14
King of Denmark c.988–1014

Edmund Ironside 1016

Cnut 1016–35
King of Denmark 1018–35

Harold Harefoot 1035–1040

Harthacnut 1040–2

Edward the Confessor 1042–66

Harold Godwinesson 1066

William the Conqueror 1066–87

William II Rufus 1087–1100

Henry I 1100–35

Stephen 1135–54

Henry II 1154–89

The Scandinavian Kings: 9th to 11th Centuries

Norway

Harald Fairhair   c.872–c.930

Olaf Tryggvason   995–1000

St Olaf   1014–30

Magnus   1035–47

Harald Sigurdsson (Hardrada)   1047–66

Magnus   1066–9

Olaf   1067–93

Denmark

Harold Bluetooth   c.988

Svein Forkbeard   c.988–1014
(King of England   1013–14)

Harald 1014–c.1018

Cnut   1018–35
(King of England   1016–35)

Svein   1047–74

Sweden

Eric the Victorious   c.980–95

Olaf Svenski   995–1022

Anund (James)   1022–56

Edmund Gamul   1056–60

Introduction

The annals contained in the seven manuscripts and two fragments known as *The Anglo-Saxon Chronicle* start by recounting events which took place in pre-Roman Britain; they were compiled in the 9th century, and documentation continues for almost a century after the Battle of Hastings. The Chronicle is unusual in its continuity over such a long period, punctuated as it was by wars and invasions which repeatedly left the monasteries, with their libraries and *scriptoria*, in ruins. Its use of the vernacular rather than Latin is also remarkable; only in the Irish annals and an early Russian chronicle is the vernacular employed in the recording of history at a comparable date. Although the Norman Conquest marked a revival of the use of Latin in England, the language of the manuscript extending furthest into the 12th century ('E', the Laud or Peterborough Chronicle) is still Old English. The resurgence of Latin is reflected in the bilingual chronicle ('F' – see page 12).

The decline of Latin in 9th-century Anglo-Saxon England necessitated the use of the vernacular as a *written* language. The translation of scholarly works into Old English and its employment in learning and letters contributed much to the development and refinement of English as a language both literary and dialectical. This process can be followed in the Chronicle itself, in which a wide range of styles is covered: the brief recording of single events; the complete story of Cynewulf and Cyneheard in 757; later analyses of the Danish invasions, Norman Conquest and reign of king Stephen; the merging of charters and direct speech with narrative. The poetry of the Chronicle is also varied, including a metrical calendar (the *Menologium*), gnomic verse, battle and occasional poems, as well as rhythmic prose of an oratorical kind.

Time-units of days and months were marked in the ecclesiastical calendar of saints' days, other holy days, and the rhythm of the seasons. Within such a relatively undifferentiated flow of time, the earliest function of the historical chronicle was not analysis, or the recording of events for their own sake, but 'to *characterise* the receding series of years, each by a mark and sign of its own, so that the years might not be confused in the retrospect of those who had lived and acted in them.'* The different prefaces to some of the Chronicle manuscripts express some of the levels of awareness of time for the Anglo-Saxons: the *Menologium* reckons the days of the church-calendar in relation to one another and the seasons, with the names of each month; the gnomic verses which follow it in the C-text, within descriptions of landscape, aspects of man-made objects, animal life and codes of human behaviour, express a concept of time as cruel, mysterious, yet part of the beauty of Creation. See page 275.

The Parker Chronicle begins with a genealogical preface, emphasising the importance of the kings of Wessex and their descent from Cerdic; D, E and F begin with a passage based on Bede's *Ecclesiastical History* giving the dimensions and languages of Britain, and describing the arrival of the Picts. Both prefaces are included before the start of the chronicles.

The dating system followed in this translation is that of Whitelock's *The Anglo-Saxon Chronicle, A Revised Translation*. The manuscripts often differ from one another in the date for a given event, not only because later scribes

---

* *Two of the Saxon Chronicles Parallel*, ed. Charles Plummer, on the basis of an edition by John Earle; Earle's introduction, p. xix.

have altered existing dates by accident, or in an attempt to correct them, but because of the different calendar systems in use at the time. The earlier chronicles and *Menologium* begin the year at Christmas, but another calendar also employed at this time begins the year in the autumn, being the time of the Caesarian Indiction. By the 11th century it was common to begin the year at the Annunciation, 25 March. However, by 1094, it is evident in the reported order of the times during which king William held his court that the Christmas-reckoning is being employed again. The dates given by the annalists for the arrivals of the Angles, Saxons and Jutes, along with their kingships, are relatively conjectural, and may have been supplied from an oral tradition of mnemonic verse.

Proper names have been regularised to some extent for the sake of clearness, as spellings in the text often vary even when reference is made to the same person, usually for the reason that manuscripts were written in areas with different dialects, such as Wessex and Northumbria. Modern place-names have been given where possible; but the term 'Scots' was employed until king Alfred's time in reference to the Irish Scots or the Irish of Argyll. Genealogies follow this introduction. Titles have for the most part been left in the original: *eorl* can have the general meaning of 'brave man, warrior, chief,' as well as the originally Danish title of a local *ealdorman*. In the Chronicle manuscripts, the differentiation between English *eorl* and Danish *jarl* is not made, and therefore it is not made in translation here. *Ealdorman* could be translated 'ruler, chief,' although it is often used more specifically in reference to the superior officer of a shire, or a high civil or religious officer. *Aetheling*, given here in its later form, 'atheling', refers to a man of royal blood, nobleman, prince or chief. *Cild*, also given in its later form, 'child', has, in addition to its usual meaning, that of 'a young man of noble birth.' *Hold* is a Danish title, specifically referring to one who holds his own land, not subject to a superior.

The Chronicle Manuscripts
Sometime in the last decade of the 9th century, a number of copies of a chronicle manuscript were compiled and sent out to various locations in England. Some were eventually recopied, new material being added from written sources, and events of international, national or local interest recorded. Written sources were earlier Latin annals, Bede's *Ecclesiastical History*, genealogies, lists of episcopal appointments and charters.

The manuscripts containing the annals are actually *four* chronicles, since each of Ā, C, D, and E exists in its own right as an independent document. This translation is a conflation of the four main chronicles, with additional information from the others. No labelling of particular manuscripts has been done in this translation, the object of which is to provide chronicle information in sequential rather than parallel form; readers are directed to the Garmonsway or the Whitelock translation, both of which keep the texts separate. The other manuscripts, A, B and F, were derived from original versions of the four main chronicles. The surviving manuscripts and fragments, containing the chronicles alongside other works, are as follows:

Ā, Corpus Christi College Cambridge MS 173, the Parker Chronicle.
This was probably begun at Winchester and carried on there until the 11th century. Possibly sometime after the Norman Conquest it was taken to Christchurch, Canterbury. It is the oldest manuscript, the first hand having been dated as that of the late 9th or early 10th century. Dates covered: 60 BC–AD 1070.

A, British Museum Cotton MS Otho B.xi.

This was a copy made of Ā before it left Winchester. It was destroyed by fire in 1731, leaving only a few fragments. Previously, an edition of it had been made by Abraham Wheloc, upon which modern editors rely for the text, along with information supplied from the fragments.

B, British Museum Cotton MS Tiberius A.vi and C, British Museum Cotton MS Tiberius B.i, The Abingdon Chronicles.

These are both 11th-century copies twice removed from an original, now lost, which was probably sent to Abingdon after the abbey there was refounded in the middle of the 10th century. Both manuscripts have incorporated the 'Mercian Chronicle', or 'The Annals of Athelflaed' in the years 902–924. Dates covered: AD 1–977 and 60 BC–AD 1066.

D, British Museum Cotton MS Tiberius B.iv, the Worcester Chronicle.

This is a mid-11th century manuscript taken from a lost original, which was probably located at Ripon or York. The compilers not only copied material, but verified it and added their own from other sources; for example, material from the 'Mercian Chronicle' has been integrated into the text, rather than incorporated whole. Dates covered: AD 1–1079, plus one entry dated 1080, the events of which belong to 1130.

E, Bodleian MS Laud 636, the Laud or Peterborough Chronicle; F, British Museum Cotton MS Domitian A.viii.

E was written in the 11th to 12th centuries at Peterborough, initially copied from a chronicle sent from St Augustine's, Canterbury, based on D or a version of D. It contains many interpolations, such as charters, events concerning the monastery, and also some Latin entries about foreign and local affairs.

F is a bilingual chronicle based on the same lost Kentish chronicle from which E and Ā were copied. Each annal is written out in Latin and English, indicating the revival of Latin as the language of historical documentation. Dates covered: AD 1–1153; AD 1–1058.

H, British Museum Cotton MS Domitian A.ix.

This is a fragment, probably from a Winchester manuscript. Dates covered: AD 1113–1114.

I, British Museum Caligula A.xv, written on an Easter table; it is from Christchurch, Canterbury. Dates covered: AD 988–1268.

For further history and a more detailed description of manuscripts, see *Two of the Saxon Chronicles Parallel*, and the introductions to the translations by Garmonsway and Whitelock.

A note on the translation

The choice faced by a translator of Old English is a difficult one, that between a completely natural-sounding modern English rendering, and one which is slightly out of the ordinary in sound and rhythm. I have opted for the latter; though it introduces the paradox that the Chronicle language would have sounded completely natural to its writers, and a rendering of some of its basic qualities does not to the modern reader, I hope to convey a sense of the original language.

ANNE SAVAGE

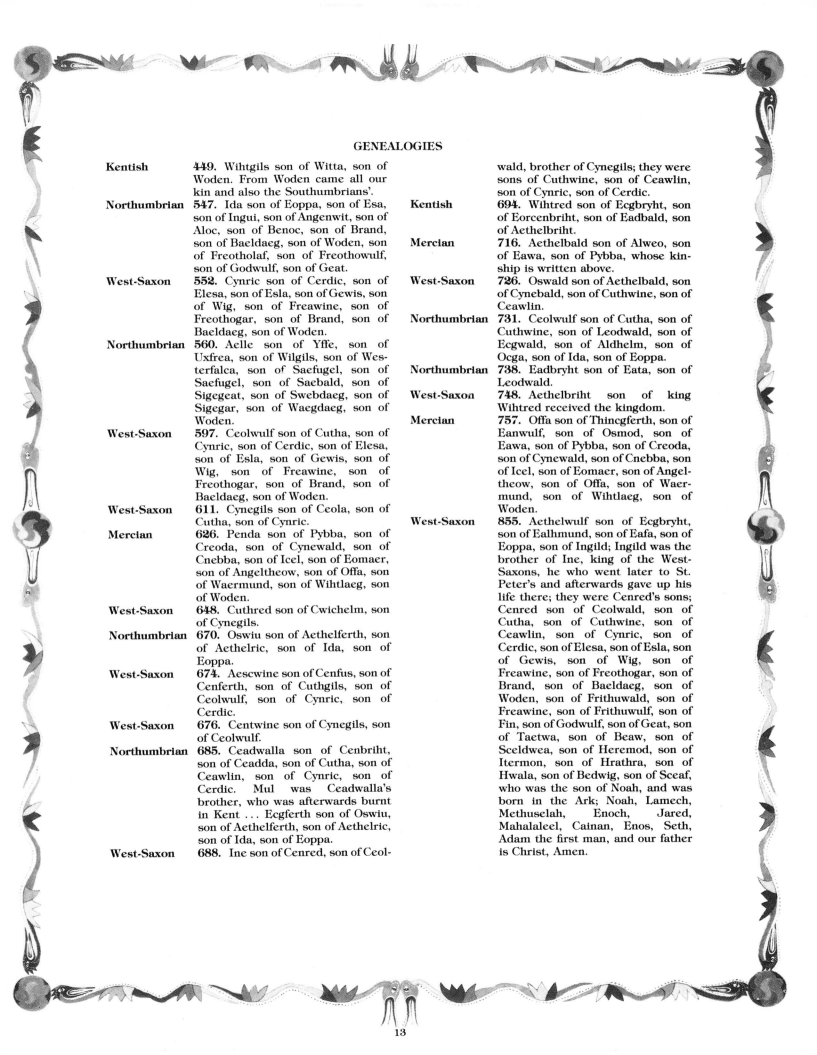

GENEALOGIES

Kentish 449. Wihtgils son of Witta, son of Woden. From Woden came all our kin and also the Southumbrians'.

Northumbrian 547. Ida son of Eoppa, son of Esa, son of Ingui, son of Angenwit, son of Aloc, son of Benoc, son of Brand, son of Baeldaeg, son of Woden, son of Freotholaf, son of Freothowulf, son of Godwulf, son of Geat.

West-Saxon 552. Cynric son of Cerdic, son of Elesa, son of Esla, son of Gewis, son of Wig, son of Freawine, son of Freothogar, son of Brand, son of Baeldaeg, son of Woden.

Northumbrian 560. Aelle son of Yffe, son of Uxfrea, son of Wilgils, son of Westerfalca, son of Saefugel, son of Saefugel, son of Saebald, son of Sigegeat, son of Swebdaeg, son of Sigegar, son of Waegdaeg, son of Woden.

West-Saxon 597. Ceolwulf son of Cutha, son of Cynric, son of Cerdic, son of Elesa, son of Esla, son of Gewis, son of Wig, son of Freawine, son of Freothogar, son of Brand, son of Baeldaeg, son of Woden.

West-Saxon 611. Cynegils son of Ceola, son of Cutha, son of Cynric.

Mercian 626. Penda son of Pybba, son of Creoda, son of Cynewald, son of Cnebba, son of Icel, son of Eomaer, son of Angeltheow, son of Offa, son of Waermund, son of Wihtlaeg, son of Woden.

West-Saxon 648. Cuthred son of Cwichelm, son of Cynegils.

Northumbrian 670. Oswiu son of Aethelferth, son of Aethelric, son of Ida, son of Eoppa.

West-Saxon 674. Aescwine son of Cenfus, son of Cenferth, son of Cuthgils, son of Ceolwulf, son of Cynric, son of Cerdic.

West-Saxon 676. Centwine son of Cynegils, son of Ceolwulf.

Northumbrian 685. Ceadwalla son of Cenbriht, son of Ceadda, son of Cutha, son of Ceawlin, son of Cynric, son of Cerdic. Mul was Ceadwalla's brother, who was afterwards burnt in Kent ... Ecgferth son of Oswiu, son of Aethelferth, son of Aethelric, son of Ida, son of Eoppa.

West-Saxon 688. Ine son of Cenred, son of Ceolwald, brother of Cynegils; they were sons of Cuthwine, son of Ceawlin, son of Cynric, son of Cerdic.

Kentish 694. Wihtred son of Ecgbryht, son of Eorcenbriht, son of Eadbald, son of Aethelbriht.

Mercian 716. Aethelbald son of Alweo, son of Eawa, son of Pybba, whose kinship is written above.

West-Saxon 726. Oswald son of Aethelbald, son of Cynebald, son of Cuthwine, son of Ceawlin.

Northumbrian 731. Ceolwulf son of Cutha, son of Cuthwine, son of Leodwald, son of Ecgwald, son of Aldhelm, son of Ocga, son of Ida, son of Eoppa.

Northumbrian 738. Eadbryht son of Eata, son of Leodwald.

West-Saxon 748. Aethelbriht son of king Wihtred received the kingdom.

Mercian 757. Offa son of Thincgferth, son of Eanwulf, son of Osmod, son of Eawa, son of Pybba, son of Creoda, son of Cynewald, son of Cnebba, son of Icel, son of Eomaer, son of Angeltheow, son of Offa, son of Waermund, son of Wihtlaeg, son of Woden.

West-Saxon 855. Aethelwulf son of Ecgbryht, son of Ealhmund, son of Eafa, son of Eoppa, son of Ingild; Ingild was the brother of Ine, king of the West-Saxons, he who went later to St. Peter's and afterwards gave up his life there; they were Cenred's sons; Cenred son of Ceolwald, son of Cutha, son of Cuthwine, son of Ceawlin, son of Cynric, son of Cerdic, son of Elesa, son of Esla, son of Gewis, son of Wig, son of Freawine, son of Freothogar, son of Brand, son of Baeldaeg, son of Woden, son of Frithuwald, son of Freawine, son of Frithuwulf, son of Fin, son of Godwulf, son of Geat, son of Taetwa, son of Beaw, son of Sceldwea, son of Heremod, son of Itermon, son of Hrathra, son of Hwala, son of Bedwig, son of Sceaf, who was the son of Noah, and was born in the Ark; Noah, Lamech, Methuselah, Enoch, Jared, Mahalaleel, Cainan, Enos, Seth, Adam the first man, and our father is Christ, Amen.

In the first centuries after the Romans left Britain, political and cultural dominance was established by the Northumbrian centres around Jarrow and Lindisfarne. Later, the Mercian kingdom gradually gained control over most of central England and East Anglia. Under Aethelbald (716–57) and Offa (757–96), self-confident and aggressive monarchs who were able to achieve political unity, the Mercians improved their rather strained relations with Rome, and increased foreign trade. Offa in particular was interested and active in securing trading routes; his silver pennies were the first standard coins issued in England, and remained in use until the Norman Conquest.

As coastal settlements and river ports in the east became vulnerable to Viking raids, Wessex grew in importance. From the time when Alfred (871–99) came to the throne it dominated the Anglo-Saxon kingdoms almost up to the Norman Conquest.

As the map shows, there were many other kingdoms during the early and middle Anglo-Saxon period. However, the Chronicles are concerned mainly with the parts of the country where the major manuscripts were kept: Kent, the North, Peterborough. It is possible that similar annals were written in other regions, and subsequently lost or destroyed; there is no definite evidence one way or the other. What can be stated is that the Chronicle manuscripts often vary in political bias as well as in content; and that so far it is accepted that no particular one can be considered the definitive authority.

The
Anglo-Saxon
Kingdoms

DALRIADA

GODODDIN
● Lindisfarne
● Bamburgh
● Yeavering

BERNICIA

RHEGED

● Monkwearmouth
● Jarrow

DEIRA

ISLE OF MAN

● York

ELMET
● Sancton
● Brough

Anglesey

● Lincoln

GWYNEDD

LINDSEY

R. Trent

MERCIA

MIDDLE ANGLIA

● Leicester
● Crowland

● Burgh Castle

EAST
ANGLIA

POWYS

● Oundle

● Sutton Hoo

● Cambridge

DYFED

● Gloucester

St Albans ●

Kelvedon ●
● Colchester

● Cirencester

R. Thames

ESSEX

● London
● Mucking

● Bath

● Silchester

● Rochester

● Canterbury

● Glastonbury

● Winchester

SUSSEX

● Chichester

WESSEX

R. Tamar

DUMNONIA

ISLE OF WIGHT

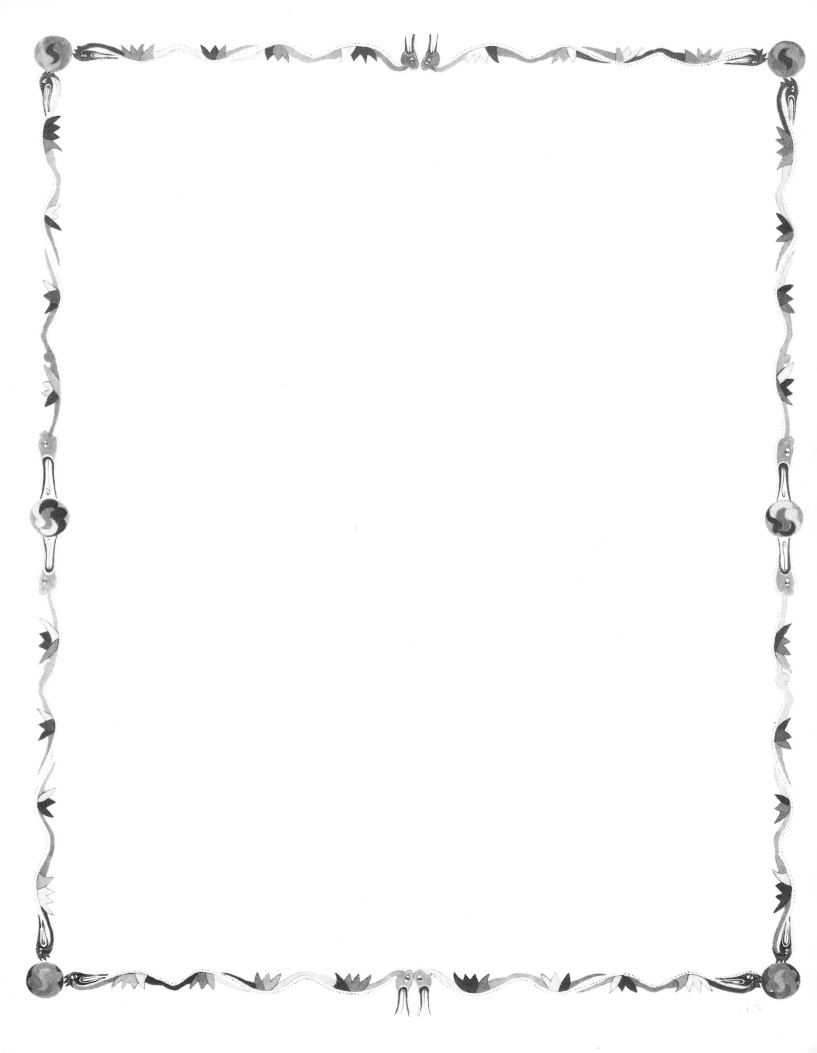

Part One

1~800

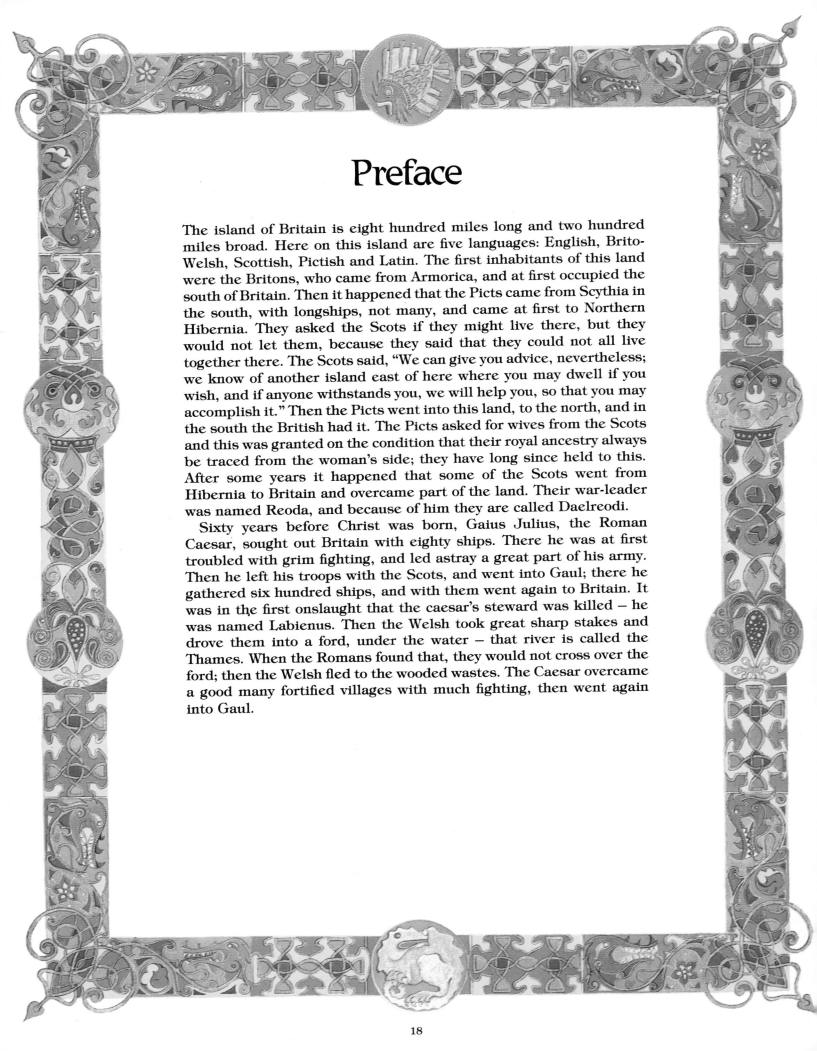

Preface

The island of Britain is eight hundred miles long and two hundred miles broad. Here on this island are five languages: English, Brito-Welsh, Scottish, Pictish and Latin. The first inhabitants of this land were the Britons, who came from Armorica, and at first occupied the south of Britain. Then it happened that the Picts came from Scythia in the south, with longships, not many, and came at first to Northern Hibernia. They asked the Scots if they might live there, but they would not let them, because they said that they could not all live together there. The Scots said, "We can give you advice, nevertheless; we know of another island east of here where you may dwell if you wish, and if anyone withstands you, we will help you, so that you may accomplish it." Then the Picts went into this land, to the north, and in the south the British had it. The Picts asked for wives from the Scots and this was granted on the condition that their royal ancestry always be traced from the woman's side; they have long since held to this. After some years it happened that some of the Scots went from Hibernia to Britain and overcame part of the land. Their war-leader was named Reoda, and because of him they are called Daelreodi.

Sixty years before Christ was born, Gaius Julius, the Roman Caesar, sought out Britain with eighty ships. There he was at first troubled with grim fighting, and led astray a great part of his army. Then he left his troops with the Scots, and went into Gaul; there he gathered six hundred ships, and with them went again to Britain. It was in the first onslaught that the caesar's steward was killed – he was named Labienus. Then the Welsh took great sharp stakes and drove them into a ford, under the water – that river is called the Thames. When the Romans found that, they would not cross over the ford; then the Welsh fled to the wooded wastes. The Caesar overcame a good many fortified villages with much fighting, then went again into Gaul.

Preface

In the year that was 494 years past the birth of Christ, Cerdic and his son Cynric came up to *Cerdicesora* with five ships; this Cerdic was the son of Elesa, son of Esla, son of Gewis, son of Wig, son of Freawine, son of Freothogar, son of Brand, son of Baeldaeg, son of Woden. Within about six years of their coming they overcame the West-Saxon kingdom, and they were the first kings of Wessex who overcame the Welsh. He had that kingdom for sixteen years; when he passed away, his son Cynric received the kingdom and held it for twenty-six years. When he passed away, his son Ceawlin received it and held it for seventeen years. When he passed away, Ceol received it and held it for six years. When he passed away, his brother Ceolwulf received it and reigned for seventeen years; and their kin go back to Cerdic. Then Cynegils, Ceolwulf's brother's son, received the kingdom and reigned for thirty-one years; and he accepted baptism, the first of the West-Saxon kings. Then Cenwalh received it and he held it for thirty-one years; Cenwalh was Cynegils' son. Seaxburg his queen held the kingdom for one year after him. Aescwine, whose kin go back to Cerdic, received the kingdom and held it for two years. Then Centwine, son of Cynegils, received the West-Saxon kingdom and reigned for seven years. Then Ceadwalla, whose kin go back to Cerdic, received the kingdom and held it for three years. Then Ine, whose kin go back to Cerdic, received the West-Saxon kingdom and held it for twenty-seven years. Then Aethelheard, whose kin go back to Cerdic, held it for fourteen years. Then Cuthred, whose kin go back to Cerdic, received it and held it for seventeen years. Then Sigebryht, whose kin go back to Cerdic, received it for one year. Then Cynewulf, whose kin go back to Cerdic, received it and held it for thirty-one years. Then Brihtric, whose kin go back to Cerdic, received the kingdom and held it for sixteen years. Then Ecgbryht received the kingdom and held it for thirty-seven years and seven months. His son Aethelwulf received it and held it for eighteen years. Aethelwulf was the son of Ecgbryht, son of Ealhmund, son of Eafa, son of Eoppa, son of Ingild, son of Cenred; Ine, Cuthburh and Cwenburh were children of Cenred, son of Ceolwald, son of Cuthwulf, son of Cuthwine, son of Ceawlin, son of Cynric, son of Cerdic. This his son Aethelbald received the kingdom and held it for five years; then his brother Aethelberht received it, and held it for five years. Then their brother Aethelred received the kingdom and held it for five years, then their brother Alfred received the kingdom; twenty-three years of his age passed, three hundred and ninety-six since his ancestors first took Wessex from the Welsh.

1. Octavian reigned for fifty-six years, and in the forty-second year of his reign, Christ was born.

2. The astrologers from the east came in order to worship Christ, and the children in Bethlehem were killed because of the persecution of Christ by Herod.

3. Herod died through stabbing himself, and his son Archelaus received the kingdom. The child Christ was brought back from Egypt.

6. From the origin of the world until this year, there had passed five thousand two hundred years.

11. Herod Antipas received the kingdom in Judaea.

12. Philippus, Herod and Lysianus divided Judaea into four kingdoms.

16. Tiberius received the kingdom.

26. Pilate received the government of Judaea.

30. Christ was baptized; Peter, Andrew, James, John and Phillip were converted, and the twelve apostles.

33. Christ was crucified; from the origin of the world, about five thousand two hundred and twenty-six years had passed.

34. St. Paul was converted, and St. Stephen stoned.

35. The blessed apostle Peter occupied the bishop's seat in Antioch.

38. Pilate was killed by his own hand.

39. Gaius received the kingdom.

40. Matthew began to write his gospel in Judaea.

44. The blessed apostle Peter occupied the bishop's seat in Rome.

45. Agrippa died, he who had killed James one year before his own death.

47. Claudius, king of the Romans, went with an army into Britain and overcame that island, and subdued all the Picts and Welsh to the rule of the Romans. This fight was completed in the fourth year of his reign, in the year of the great famine in Syria which was foretold in the Acts of the Apostles by Agabus the sage. Then Nero received the kingdom after Claudius, he who nearly lost the island of Britain through his idleness. Mark the Evangelist in Egypt begins to write the gospel.

48. There was very harsh famine this year.

49. Nero began to reign.

50. Paul was sent to Rome.

62. James, the brother of the Lord, suffered martydom.

63. Mark the Evangelist passed away.

69. Peter suffered death on a cross, and Paul was beheaded.

70. Vespasian received the kingdom.

71. Titus, Vespasian's son, killed one hundred and eleven thousand Jews in Jerusalem.

81. Titus received the kingdom, he who said that he lost the day on which he did no good.

83. Domitian, brother of Titus, received the kingdom.

85. John the Evangelist, on the island of Patmos, wrote *The Book of the Apocalypse.*

100. Simon the Apostle was crucified, and John the Evangelist found rest in Ephesus.

101. Pope Clement passed away.

110. Bishop Ignatius suffered martyrdom.

116. Adrianus caesar began to reign.

137. Antoninus began to reign.

155. Marcus Antoninus and Aurelius his brother received the kingdom.

Although the Chroniclers begin their account with the birth of Christ, the history of Britain during the Roman occupation and the next two centuries receives scant attention. There were few sources available, and the Chroniclers relied mainly on Bede's *Ecclesiastical History* of Britain between the Roman occupation and 731, a book which is still an important historical source. Only when they reached the late 8th century, when the events they were describing had happened little more than 100 years earlier, did the Chroniclers begin to write in more detail.

From 43 AD (the Chroniclers, perhaps following Bede, date it somewhat later), when the Emperor Claudius began to invade, to the first years of the 5th century, Britain was a peripheral colony of the great Roman Empire. Settlers came, built their villas, baths and libraries, enriched them with mosaics and sculptures, farmed the land, engaged in trade – and finally, in the early 5th century, withdrew to the further side of the Channel. Magnificent though the remains of Roman rule are in Britain, their splendour is far outshone by those of France (Roman Gaul) and the mother-country itself.

As in other colonies, control was ensured by a substantial military presence and facilitated by a complex network of Roman roads, built ruler-straight across country. In the north, Hadrian's Wall defined the limits of Roman rule, and in the west conquest went no further than Exeter. Settlement largely took place south of the Wash, and most of the thousands of villas constructed were further south still.

Opposite: Roundel from the magnificent mosaic pavement found at Hinton St Mary, Dorset.

Below: The Roman road across Wheeldale Moor, North Yorkshire, part of a route running from Malton to Whitby. Several thousand miles of road were built in Britain, part of a much larger network with its hub at the imperial capital.

Above: Roman soldiers crossing a pontoon bridge on campaign. (Detail from Trajan's Column, Rome.)

Below: 3rd-century Roman bowl, made from green glass.

167. Eleutherius received the bishopric in Rome, and held it worthily for fifteen years. To him Lucius, king of the Britons, sent men with letters, asking that he be baptized, and he soon sent back to him; after this they remained in the true faith until Diocletian's time.

189. Severus received the kingdom, and fared with an army to Britain. With force he overcame the greatest part of the island, and built a dike with turves and a broad wall on top of it from sea to sea as protection against the Britons. He reigned for seventeen years, and died at York. Bassanius his son received the kingdom. His second son was called Geta, he who perished.

200. The Holy Cross was found.

286. Here suffered St. Alban, martyr.

343. St. Nicholas passed away.

379. Gratian received the kingdom.

381. Maximus caesar received the kingdom. He was born in Britain; he went from there to Gaul and killed the caesar, Gratian. His brother he drove from the land; he was called Valentinian, and this Valentinian gathered a host again, killed Maximus and received the kingdom. In these times the Pelagian heresy arose throughout the world.

410. The Goths broke into Rome, and never since has a Roman ruled in Britain. In all they had reigned for four hundred and seventy years since Gaius Julius first sought out that island.

418. The Romans gathered all the gold-hords there were in Britain; some they hid in the earth, so that no man might find them, and some they took with them to Gaul.

423. Theodosius the Younger received the kingdom.

430. Bishop Palladius was sent by Pope Celestine to preach baptism to the Scots.

444. St. Martin passed away.

446. The British sent men over the sea to Rome, and asked for help against the Picts, but they never had it, because they were on an expedition against king Attila the Hun. They sent then to the Angles, and the Anglian athelings, with the same request.

A magnificent hoard of 34 silver bowls, platters, goblets and spoons was found at Mildenhall, Suffolk, in the 1940s. It probably belonged to Lupicinus, a Roman general, whose family hid it in about 360 after he had been arrested. This is the Great Dish. In the centre is the bearded mask of the sea-god Neptune. The inner frieze shows Nereids revelling with sea-creatures, the outer frieze a Bacchic revel, with Bacchus triumphant over Hercules.

All three motifs are typical of pre-Christian decoration.

From about 350 AD, Roman power and prosperity declined at home as well as throughout the Empire, and the Chronicles record that in 410 'the Goths broke into Rome'. In Britain, there were repeated raids by Scots and Picts from the north, and by Angles and Saxons from Denmark and northern Germany. Defences were strengthened and a chain of shore forts was constructed. Despite these, the Romans found it increasingly difficult to maintain their presence in Britain, especially after Hadrian's Wall was overwhelmed in 367.

Too much spending on defence and too little on trade led to a general disintegration of Roman civilization, both in Britain and on the continent. Inscriptions were poorly lettered, roads badly maintained, and the comfortable villa life abandoned. After 409, Roman rule in Britain officially ended, and the remaining garrisons gradually departed, burying their treasure 'so that no man might find it'. Usually no man did, although a few hoards have been recovered, more often than not found by chance.

Thrown back on their own resources, the Britons could not maintain the economic and political structures developed by the Romans. Coinage was debased and became smaller; the quality of the craftwork declined still more, the pottery and glass industries ceased production. In despair at ever bolder raids by the Picts and Scots (the young St Patrick was carried off during a foray by the latter), the Britons asked Rome for help. The request was refused: Briton had to find its own salvation, military and religious. In these years, Christianity, which had become the official religion of the entire Empire in the mid-4th century, flourished in Britain. British missionaries travelled abroad and British bishops attended continental councils.

Multangular tower at York, one of several added to the fortress walls soon after 300 AD to serve as launching-platforms for projectiles. The upper part of the stonework is a medieval addition.

Left: Plan of the coastal forts erected to guard against a Saxon invasion. Under the command of an officer, known as the Count of the Saxon Shore, stationed at Richborough, each fort was manned by 500 to 1000 men. A single garrison of this size might not have been adequate to repulse a determined attack, but the fact that these forts were built shows how seriously the Saxon threat was taken. (Illustration from a 1436 copy of a lost copy of a lost original Notitia Dignitatum, a handbook for the defence of Roman Britain.)

Below: Burgh Castle, Norfolk, one of the surviving forts of the Saxon Shore. Exterior bastions were added to the old walls to strengthen them. The graves of Saxon mercenaries have been found here.

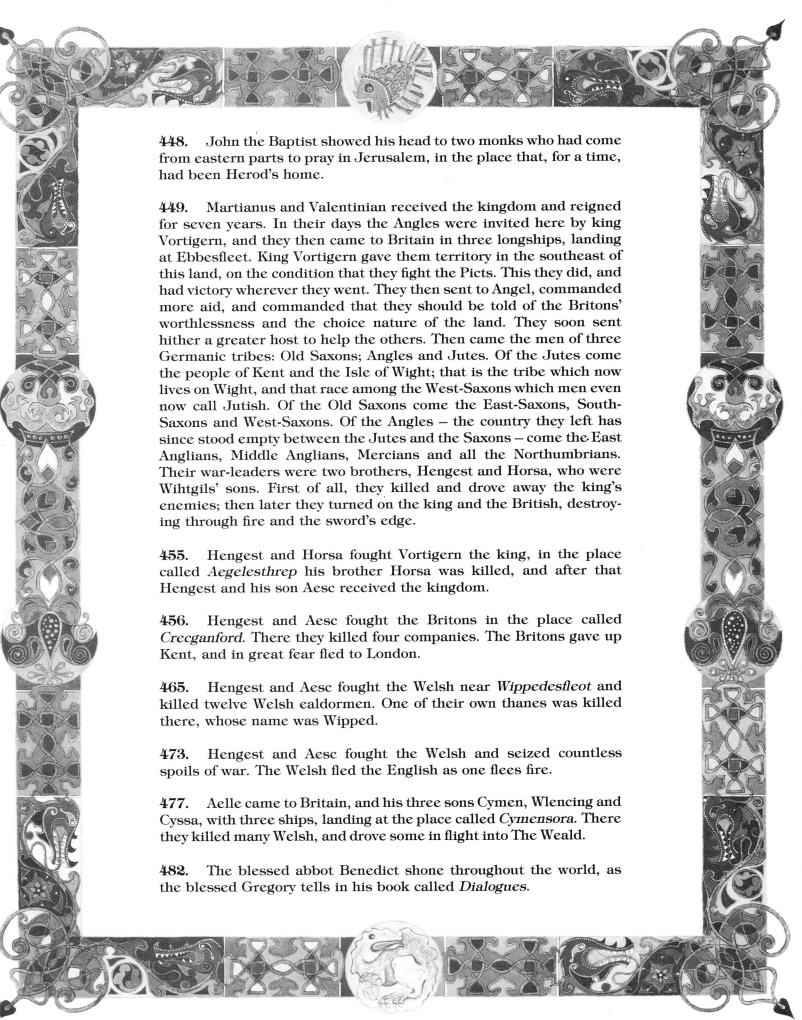

448. John the Baptist showed his head to two monks who had come from eastern parts to pray in Jerusalem, in the place that, for a time, had been Herod's home.

449. Martianus and Valentinian received the kingdom and reigned for seven years. In their days the Angles were invited here by king Vortigern, and they then came to Britain in three longships, landing at Ebbesfleet. King Vortigern gave them territory in the southeast of this land, on the condition that they fight the Picts. This they did, and had victory wherever they went. They then sent to Angel, commanded more aid, and commanded that they should be told of the Britons' worthlessness and the choice nature of the land. They soon sent hither a greater host to help the others. Then came the men of three Germanic tribes: Old Saxons; Angles and Jutes. Of the Jutes come the people of Kent and the Isle of Wight; that is the tribe which now lives on Wight, and that race among the West-Saxons which men even now call Jutish. Of the Old Saxons come the East-Saxons, South-Saxons and West-Saxons. Of the Angles – the country they left has since stood empty between the Jutes and the Saxons – come the East Anglians, Middle Anglians, Mercians and all the Northumbrians. Their war-leaders were two brothers, Hengest and Horsa, who were Wihtgils' sons. First of all, they killed and drove away the king's enemies; then later they turned on the king and the British, destroying through fire and the sword's edge.

455. Hengest and Horsa fought Vortigern the king, in the place called *Aegelesthrep* his brother Horsa was killed, and after that Hengest and his son Aesc received the kingdom.

456. Hengest and Aesc fought the Britons in the place called *Crecganford*. There they killed four companies. The Britons gave up Kent, and in great fear fled to London.

465. Hengest and Aesc fought the Welsh near *Wippedesfleot* and killed twelve Welsh ealdormen. One of their own thanes was killed there, whose name was Wipped.

473. Hengest and Aesc fought the Welsh and seized countless spoils of war. The Welsh fled the English as one flees fire.

477. Aelle came to Britain, and his three sons Cymen, Wlencing and Cyssa, with three ships, landing at the place called *Cymensora*. There they killed many Welsh, and drove some in flight into The Weald.

482. The blessed abbot Benedict shone throughout the world, as the blessed Gregory tells in his book called *Dialogues*.

It is more than likely that the Britons, deserted by the Roman legions and at the mercy of the Picts and Scots, had the good sense to invite foreign mercenaries to bolster their forces, as the Chronicle entry for 449 reports. The newcomers, given land in return for military service, attracted further settlers, who were tempted by the fertile soil and the Britons' military vulnerability.

The first wave of immigrants probably came from the coast of Germany and the Netherlands. Their leaders, Hengest and Horsa, are possibly legendary, although a 'Hengest', who may be the same person, does appear in *Beowulf*. More settlers came after the mercenaries turned against the British in the mid-450s, and strong communities established themselves.

Three main groups are mentioned by the Chroniclers: the Saxons, the Angles and the Jutes. The Jutes settled in Kent, prospered and imported wine, ornaments and other luxuries from Europe. They developed their own art and culture, a mixture of continental and British elements, now mainly known through jewellery and other objects found in graves. The other invaders dispersed through East Anglia, the Midlands and Sussex. The Anglo-Saxon advance was halted early in the 6th century, and there were 50 years of relative peace, until they won a decisive victory in 571. Soon most of the West Country had been taken, and by the end of the century the indigenous Britons had been pushed back to the Celtic fringes and a distinctive Anglo-Saxon England had emerged.

The Chroniclers were writing three centuries later and knew little of the detailed sequence of events. Their main source was Bede, whose general reliability recent archaeological excavations have confirmed. But there is now much evidence to suggest that large numbers of Anglo-Saxons had settled in England well before the dates given in the Chronicles. The rapid invasion portrayed there was in fact a gradual process of settlement.

Opposite top: 7th-century Anglo-Saxon drinking horn. It was found in a barrow, probably the grave of a chief, at Taplow, Buckinghamshire, in 1883, along with many other items. The mounts are silver and gilt.

Below left: A Scot as portrayed in the Book of Kells, probably written in Ireland in about 800. The Scots moved north-east from Ireland during Roman rule, giving the name of their tribe to Scotland.

Below: Picts depicted on the 9th-century Aberlemno Stone. Pictish raids were a constant annoyance first to the Britons, then to the Anglo-Saxons, of the south. The English finally defeated the Picts in 711, the Scots only in 850.

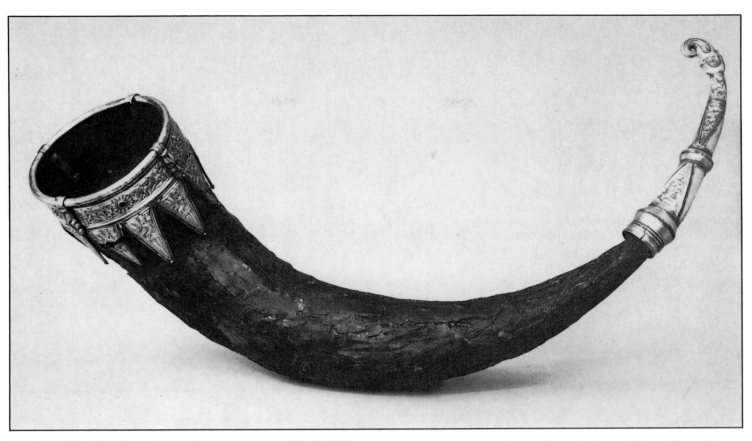

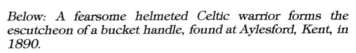
Left: 6th-century square-headed brooch from Empingham, Mercia.

Below: A fearsome helmeted Celtic warrior forms the escutcheon of a bucket handle, found at Aylesford, Kent, in 1890.

Opposite page top: Oak vessels like this reconstruction of the Nydam boat may have carried the Anglo-Saxons across the stormy North Sea to Britain. The Nydam boat is 77 feet long and less than 11 wide, with 14 oars on each side. Afloat it would have been fast but unstable and difficult to manoeuvre. It had neither sail nor mast.

Opposite page bottom: Some of the Nydam finds.

Right: Weapons found alongside the Nydam boat in a peat bog in South Jutland in 1859–63.

Below: Pevensey Castle, Sussex. The outer wall is from the original fort of the Saxon Shore. The rest of the castle was rebuilt by the Normans after 1066. It was here that Aelle, who became king of Sussex, landed and massacred the native Britons in 491.

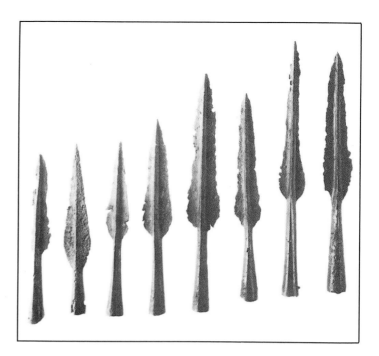

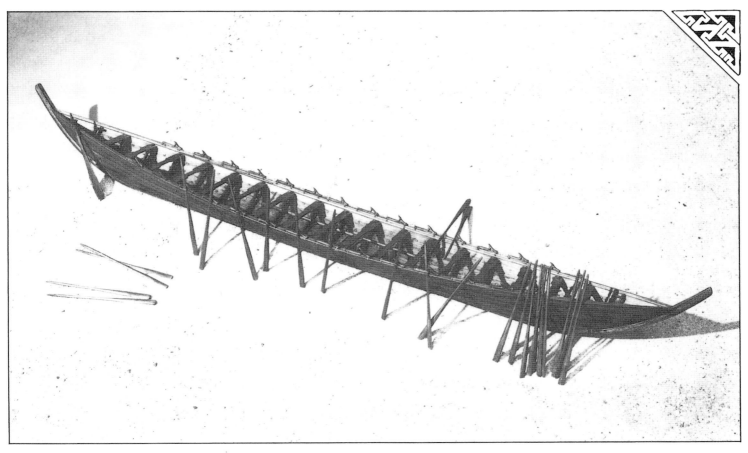

Above: Anglo-Saxon pendant.

Right: 6th-century square-headed brooch from Howletts, near Canterbury.

Below: Kentish jewelled brooches made between about 575 and 625. Because of the area's close contacts with the continent, the most splendid Anglo-Saxon jewellery was produced in east Kent. Although imported gems, glass and bronze were used, local workmanship surpassed continental work of the same period. The extensive Roman remains may also have provided inspiration.

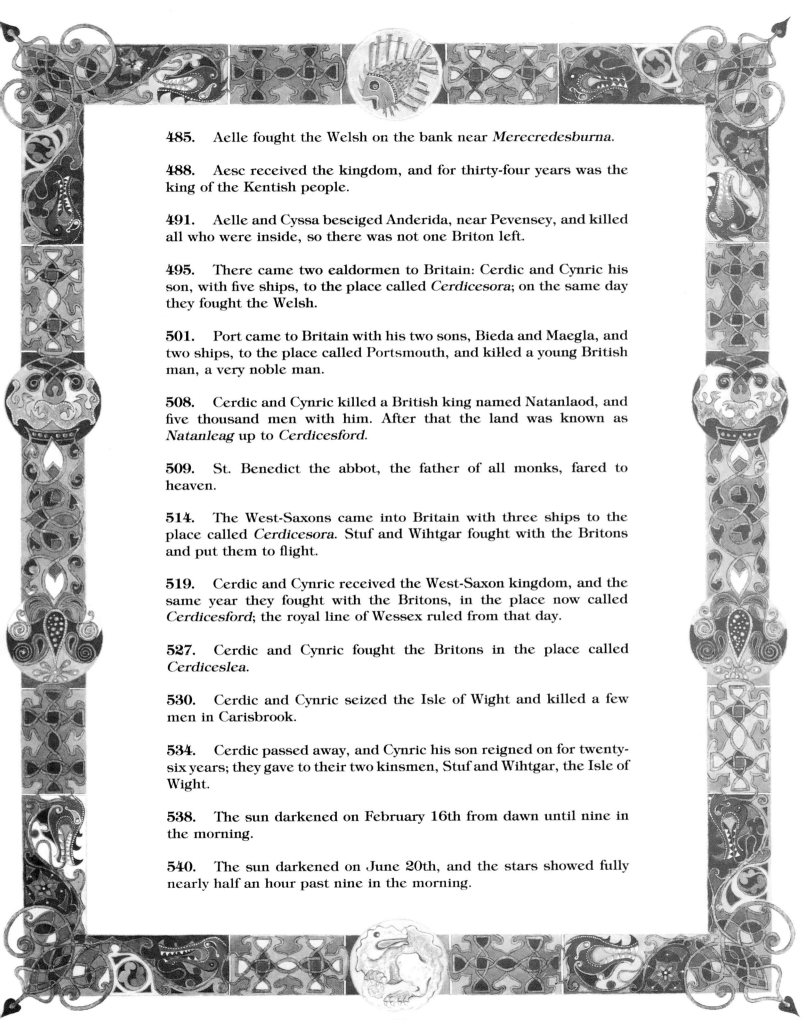

485.   Aelle fought the Welsh on the bank near *Merecredesburna*.

488.   Aesc received the kingdom, and for thirty-four years was the king of the Kentish people.

491.   Aelle and Cyssa beseiged Anderida, near Pevensey, and killed all who were inside, so there was not one Briton left.

495.   There came two ealdormen to Britain: Cerdic and Cynric his son, with five ships, to the place called *Cerdicesora*; on the same day they fought the Welsh.

501.   Port came to Britain with his two sons, Bieda and Maegla, and two ships, to the place called Portsmouth, and killed a young British man, a very noble man.

508.   Cerdic and Cynric killed a British king named Natanlaod, and five thousand men with him. After that the land was known as *Natanleag* up to *Cerdicesford*.

509.   St. Benedict the abbot, the father of all monks, fared to heaven.

514.   The West-Saxons came into Britain with three ships to the place called *Cerdicesora*. Stuf and Wihtgar fought with the Britons and put them to flight.

519.   Cerdic and Cynric received the West-Saxon kingdom, and the same year they fought with the Britons, in the place now called *Cerdicesford*; the royal line of Wessex ruled from that day.

527.   Cerdic and Cynric fought the Britons in the place called *Cerdiceslea*.

530.   Cerdic and Cynric seized the Isle of Wight and killed a few men in Carisbrook.

534.   Cerdic passed away, and Cynric his son reigned on for twenty-six years; they gave to their two kinsmen, Stuf and Wihtgar, the Isle of Wight.

538.   The sun darkened on February 16th from dawn until nine in the morning.

540.   The sun darkened on June 20th, and the stars showed fully nearly half an hour past nine in the morning.

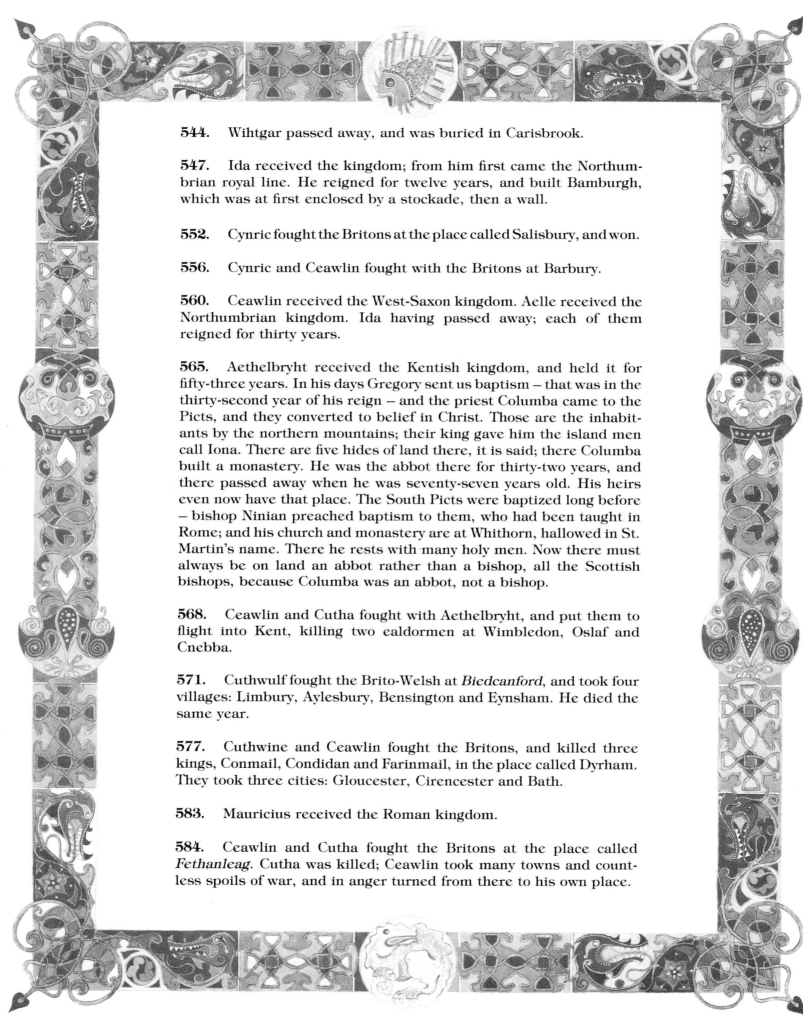

544. Wihtgar passed away, and was buried in Carisbrook.

547. Ida received the kingdom; from him first came the Northumbrian royal line. He reigned for twelve years, and built Bamburgh, which was at first enclosed by a stockade, then a wall.

552. Cynric fought the Britons at the place called Salisbury, and won.

556. Cynric and Ceawlin fought with the Britons at Barbury.

560. Ceawlin received the West-Saxon kingdom. Aelle received the Northumbrian kingdom. Ida having passed away; each of them reigned for thirty years.

565. Aethelbryht received the Kentish kingdom, and held it for fifty-three years. In his days Gregory sent us baptism – that was in the thirty-second year of his reign – and the priest Columba came to the Picts, and they converted to belief in Christ. Those are the inhabitants by the northern mountains; their king gave him the island men call Iona. There are five hides of land there, it is said; there Columba built a monastery. He was the abbot there for thirty-two years, and there passed away when he was seventy-seven years old. His heirs even now have that place. The South Picts were baptized long before – bishop Ninian preached baptism to them, who had been taught in Rome; and his church and monastery are at Whithorn, hallowed in St. Martin's name. There he rests with many holy men. Now there must always be on land an abbot rather than a bishop, all the Scottish bishops, because Columba was an abbot, not a bishop.

568. Ceawlin and Cutha fought with Aethelbryht, and put them to flight into Kent, killing two ealdormen at Wimbledon, Oslaf and Cnebba.

571. Cuthwulf fought the Brito-Welsh at *Biedcanford*, and took four villages: Limbury, Aylesbury, Bensington and Eynsham. He died the same year.

577. Cuthwine and Ceawlin fought the Britons, and killed three kings, Conmail, Condidan and Farinmail, in the place called Dyrham. They took three cities: Gloucester, Cirencester and Bath.

583. Mauricius received the Roman kingdom.

584. Ceawlin and Cutha fought the Britons at the place called *Fethanleag*. Cutha was killed; Ceawlin took many towns and countless spoils of war, and in anger turned from there to his own place.

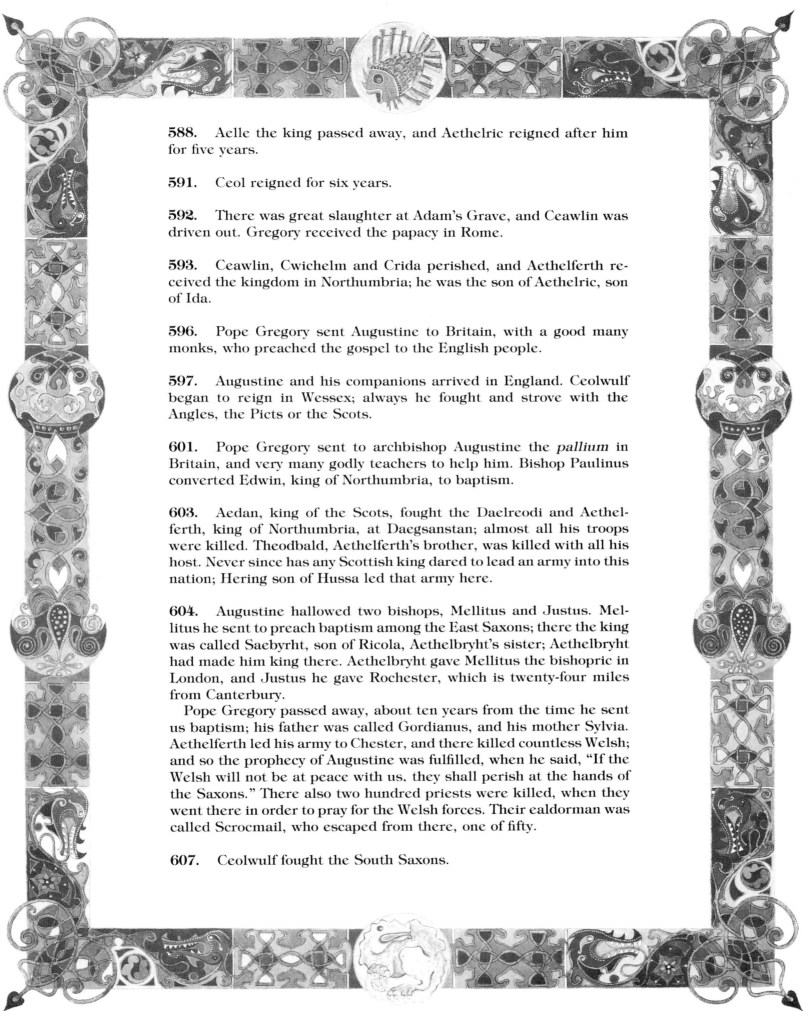

588.   Aelle the king passed away, and Aethelric reigned after him for five years.

591.   Ceol reigned for six years.

592.   There was great slaughter at Adam's Grave, and Ceawlin was driven out. Gregory received the papacy in Rome.

593.   Ceawlin, Cwichelm and Crida perished, and Aethelferth received the kingdom in Northumbria; he was the son of Aethelric, son of Ida.

596.   Pope Gregory sent Augustine to Britain, with a good many monks, who preached the gospel to the English people.

597.   Augustine and his companions arrived in England. Ceolwulf began to reign in Wessex; always he fought and strove with the Angles, the Picts or the Scots.

601.   Pope Gregory sent to archbishop Augustine the *pallium* in Britain, and very many godly teachers to help him. Bishop Paulinus converted Edwin, king of Northumbria, to baptism.

603.   Aedan, king of the Scots, fought the Daelreodi and Aethelferth, king of Northumbria, at Daegsanstan; almost all his troops were killed. Theodbald, Aethelferth's brother, was killed with all his host. Never since has any Scottish king dared to lead an army into this nation; Hering son of Hussa led that army here.

604.   Augustine hallowed two bishops, Mellitus and Justus. Mellitus he sent to preach baptism among the East Saxons; there the king was called Saebyrht, son of Ricola, Aethelbryht's sister; Aethelbryht had made him king there. Aethelbryht gave Mellitus the bishopric in London, and Justus he gave Rochester, which is twenty-four miles from Canterbury.
   Pope Gregory passed away, about ten years from the time he sent us baptism; his father was called Gordianus, and his mother Sylvia. Aethelferth led his army to Chester, and there killed countless Welsh; and so the prophecy of Augustine was fulfilled, when he said, "If the Welsh will not be at peace with us, they shall perish at the hands of the Saxons." There also two hundred priests were killed, when they went there in order to pray for the Welsh forces. Their ealdorman was called Scrocmail, who escaped from there, one of fifty.

607.   Ceolwulf fought the South Saxons.

During the 6th and 7th centuries, the Anglo-Saxon kingdoms struggled to achieve military supremacy. Success depended on the ability of their leaders, kings who led their armies into battle. The Chronicles for these years record the major battles and also trace the gradual reconversion of the country to Christianity.

Augustine's arrival from Rome in 597 was a momentous event. He converted Aethelbryht, king of Kent, and established the first English archbishopric, at Canterbury. More missionaries came after him, and a hierarchical Church on the Roman pattern, with monasteries and bishoprics, was established. In Northumbria and Mercia, the Celtic Church founded in the 6th century by St Columba and based on remote, self-contained monastic communities was strong. At the synod held at Whitby in 664 (but not mentioned in the Chronicles), the differences between the two traditions were resolved in Rome's favour, and Canterbury's pre-eminent position in English Christianity was consolidated as a result.

Missionary work depended on the support of strong, receptive monarchs, and there were frequent setbacks. Often several generations of royalty reverted to paganism; Aethelbryht's son nearly ended the Christian mission in Kent.

Above: Remains of the ramparts and defences of the monastery established by St Columba on the island of Iona, on the west coast of Scotland, in 563. Iona became the focal point of a large number of monastic communities in both Ireland and Scotland.

Below left and right: Pages from the Book of Durrow (c.650), the earliest known example of the new Christian art inspired by the return of Celtic Christianity to England. The style of the figure of St Matthew is wholly secular and may have been inspired by Roman mosaics and metalwork.

Below centre: Page from St Augustine's Gospel. The book is written in a 6th-century Italian hand and may have been sent to Augustine by Pope Gregory the Great, who sponsored Augustine's mission to England.

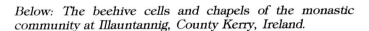

Above: The monastic church at Reculver, Kent, depicted in a late 18th-century engraving. The church, founded by Ecgbryht, king of Kent, in the 7th century survived until 1805. The towers are Norman.

Below left: Interior of the chapel of St Peter-on-the-Wall, Bradwell-on-Sea, Essex, built c.674. Bede says that St Cedd built the church. Re-used Roman materials and sophisticated stoneworking suggest Italian influence or craftsmen. A Roman gate can still be seen in the fabric.

Below: The beehive cells and chapels of the monastic community at Illauntannig, County Kerry, Ireland.

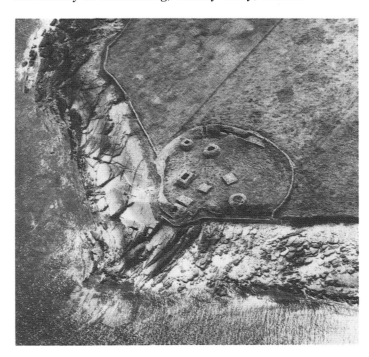

611. Cynegils received the kingdom in Wessex, and held it for thirty-one years.

614. Cynegils and Cwichelm fought at *Beandun* and killed two thousand and sixty-five Welsh.

616. Aethelbryht king of Kent passed away, the first of the English kings to receive baptism – he was the son of Eormenric – who has reigned for fifty-three years. After him his son received the kingdom, he who forsook his baptism and lived in heathenish custom such that he had his father's widow for his wife. Then Laurentius, who was then archbishop of Kent, had in mind that he would go south over the sea, and forsake all that; but in the night the apostle Peter came to him, and beat him violently, because he meant to forsake God's flock. He commanded him to go to that king and preach the true faith to him; so he did, and the king converted and was baptized. In this king's days, archbishop Laurentius, who was then in Kent after Augustine, passed away on February 2nd, and was buried next to Augustine. The holy Augustine, when well, had hallowed him bishop, so that the Christian church, which was yet new in England, should at no time after his death be without an archbishop. Then after him, Mellitus received the archbishopric, who had been bishop of London. Then the Londoners turned heathen, where Mellitus had been, and five years later, when Eadbald was reigning, Mellitus went to Christ. Then after him Justus received the archbishopric, and hallowed Romanus to Rochester, where he has been bishop.

617. Aethelferth, king of Northumbria, was killed by Raedwald, king of East Anglia. Edwin, son of Aelle, received the kingdom, and overcame all of Britain except Kent alone; he drove out the othelings, Aethelferth's sons, first Eanfrith, then Oswald, Oswiu, Oslac, Oswudu, Oslaf and Offa.

624. Archbishop Mellitus passed away.

625. Archbishop Justus hallowed Paulinus bishop of the Northumbrians on July 21st.

626. Eomer came from Cwichelm, the West-Saxon king; he thought to stab to death king Edwin, but he stabbed Lilla, his thane, and Forthere, and wounded the king. The same night, a daughter was born to Edwin; she was called Eanflaed. Then the king promised Paulinus that he would give his daughter to God, if he would accomplish, by praying to God, that he might strike down his enemy, who had sent the assassin there. He then went into Wessex with troops, struck down five kings and killed many people. Paulinus

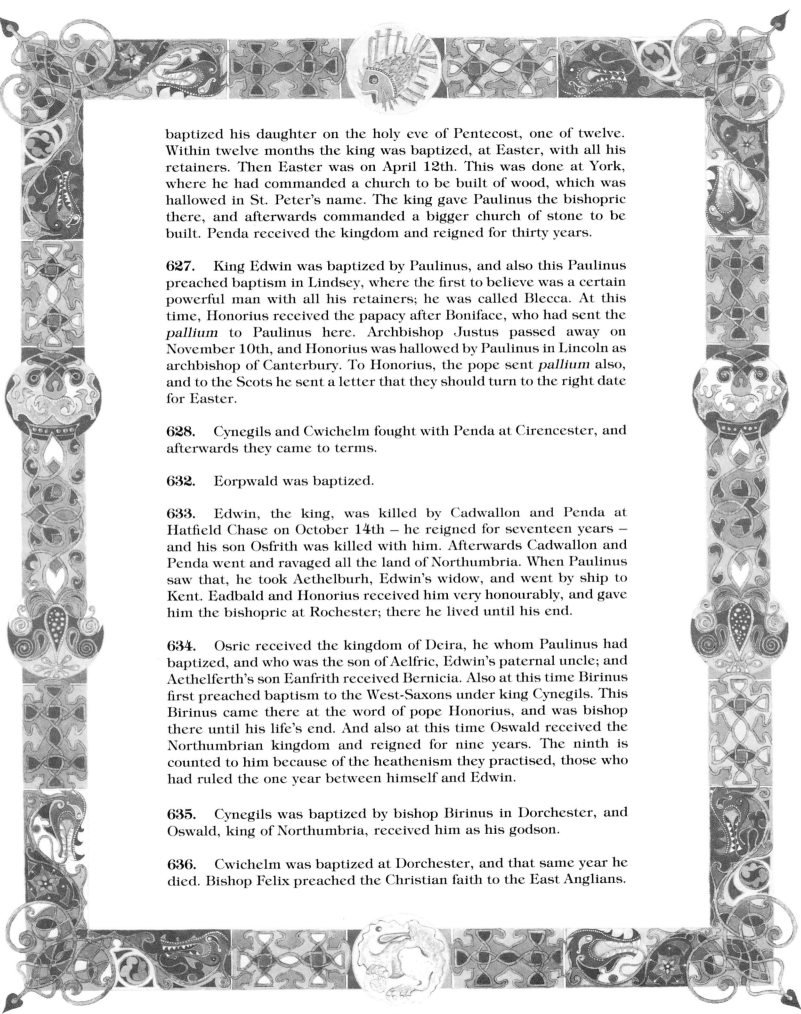

baptized his daughter on the holy eve of Pentecost, one of twelve. Within twelve months the king was baptized, at Easter, with all his retainers. Then Easter was on April 12th. This was done at York, where he had commanded a church to be built of wood, which was hallowed in St. Peter's name. The king gave Paulinus the bishopric there, and afterwards commanded a bigger church of stone to be built. Penda received the kingdom and reigned for thirty years.

627. King Edwin was baptized by Paulinus, and also this Paulinus preached baptism in Lindsey, where the first to believe was a certain powerful man with all his retainers; he was called Blecca. At this time, Honorius received the papacy after Boniface, who had sent the *pallium* to Paulinus here. Archbishop Justus passed away on November 10th, and Honorius was hallowed by Paulinus in Lincoln as archbishop of Canterbury. To Honorius, the pope sent *pallium* also, and to the Scots he sent a letter that they should turn to the right date for Easter.

628. Cynegils and Cwichelm fought with Penda at Cirencester, and afterwards they came to terms.

632. Eorpwald was baptized.

633. Edwin, the king, was killed by Cadwallon and Penda at Hatfield Chase on October 14th – he reigned for seventeen years – and his son Osfrith was killed with him. Afterwards Cadwallon and Penda went and ravaged all the land of Northumbria. When Paulinus saw that, he took Aethelburh, Edwin's widow, and went by ship to Kent. Eadbald and Honorius received him very honourably, and gave him the bishopric at Rochester; there he lived until his end.

634. Osric received the kingdom of Deira, he whom Paulinus had baptized, and who was the son of Aelfric, Edwin's paternal uncle; and Aethelferth's son Eanfrith received Bernicia. Also at this time Birinus first preached baptism to the West-Saxons under king Cynegils. This Birinus came there at the word of pope Honorius, and was bishop there until his life's end. And also at this time Oswald received the Northumbrian kingdom and reigned for nine years. The ninth is counted to him because of the heathenism they practised, those who had ruled the one year between himself and Edwin.

635. Cynegils was baptized by bishop Birinus in Dorchester, and Oswald, king of Northumbria, received him as his godson.

636. Cwichelm was baptized at Dorchester, and that same year he died. Bishop Felix preached the Christian faith to the East Anglians.

In the summers of 1938 and 1939, as the clouds of war gathered over Europe, excavators working in Suffolk uncovered one of the richest and most significant archaeological discoveries ever made in England: the Sutton Hoo ship burial. Of the ship, a large open rowing boat, 89 feet long and 14 feet at its widest, nothing remained but the iron rivets and a series of stains in the sand to indicate where she had lain. But there was treasure in staggering profusion: jewellery, coins, silver plate, weapons and armour, utensils, textiles, leather, cups, drinking-horns, all where they had been deposited 1300 years before.

The grave is almost certainly that of Raedwald, king of East Anglia until his death in 624 or 625, a monarch whose status as Bretwalda (high king) gave him considerable authority over other Anglo-Saxon kingdoms. His resting place was among his ancestors in what may have been a traditional royal family burial ground (forthcoming excavations will investigate this guess), where he was lain after an elaborate ceremony. The funeral ship was first dragged a third of a mile from the estuary of the river Deben, and lowered carefully into a trench. A wooden cabin was then constructed amidships. Here the body was lain. Jewellery was worn by the corpse, and other items were held in its hand or placed by its side. The trench was filled and a mound built up over the ship.

For the Anglo-Saxon community burial goods had two purposes. They were practical items that the dead man could use in his next life, and they also demonstrated his status as king. His journey to the next life would be in his ship, as a great monarch. Although this is an unquestionably pagan form of burial, some of the individual objects have strong Christian associations. According to Bede, Raedwald had converted to Christianity, probably at Aethelbryht's court in Kent, but he never rejected his nation's traditional gods.

Opposite: Detail of a ceremonial sceptre surmounted by a bronze stag.

Above right: Helmet made of iron and covered with tinned bronze decorative plates. The features of the mask are gilded. This is a reconstruction made in 1971 from small, corroded and fragile pieces discovered in the burial.

Right: Bronze plaque with enamel decoration.

639. Birinus baptized king Cuthred at Dorchester, and received him as his godson.

640. Eadbald, king of the Kentish people, passed away, who was king for twenty-four years. He had two sons, Ermenred and Ercenberht. His son Ercenberht received the kingdom, he who threw down all the idolatry in his kingdom, and, the first of all the English kings, he established the observance of the Easter fast. His daughter was called Ercongota, a holy virgin and wondrous person, whose mother was Seaxburh, daughter of Anna, king of the East Anglians. Ermenred begot two sons, who were aftwerwards martyred by Thunor.

641. Oswald, king of Northumbria, was killed by Penda in Southumbria, of *Maserfeld*, on August 5th; his body was buried at Bardney, of which holiness and wonders were afterwards manifold, told throughout this island. His hands are uncorrupted at Bamburgh. Cenwalh received the West-Saxon kingdom, and held it for twenty-one years. This Cenwalh ordered the church at Winchester to be built; he was the son of Cynegils. The same year in which Oswald was killed, his brother Oswiu received the Northumbrian kingdom, and ruled for two years less than thirty.

644. Bishop Paulinus passed away in Rochester on October 10th; he was bishop for one year less than two months and twenty-one days. Oswine, the son of Edwin's cousin, the son of Osric, received the kingdom of Deira and reigned for seven years.

645. Cenwalh was driven from his kingdom by king Penda.

646. Cenwalh was baptized.

648. Cenwalh gave his kinsman Cuthred three thousand hides of land by Ashdown. The church at Winchester was completed, which Cenwalh the king had built in St. Peter's name, and hallowed.

650. Aegelbriht of Gaul, received the bishopric of Wessex, after Birinus the Roman bishop.

651. King Oswiu commanded king Oswine killed on August 20th. Twelve nights after, bishop Aidan passed away on August 31st.

652. Cenwalh fought at Bradford on Avon.

653. The Middle Angles, under ealdorman Penda, received the true faith. King Anna was killed, and Botulf began to build the church at *Icanho*.

Opposite top: Golden shoulder clasp, decorated with cloissonné garnets and millefiori glass. The fastening pin has been withdrawn.

Opposite bottom: Gold purse lid, restored since its discovery; the mounts are decorated with garnets and millefiori glass. Thirty-seven gold coins were found lying on top of the lid, together with three unstruck circular blanks and two small ingots. The coins themselves are not of exceptional value. Their number (40 in all) is, however, important since it has been suggested that their purpose was to pay the 40 ghostly oarsmen who would have taken the ship and her royal passenger to their final destination in the after life.

Top right: Ornamental bird decorating the shield.

Right: Gilt-bronze winged dragon, part of the fittings from the front of the large circular shield.

Below: Gold buckle decorated with interlacing animal ornament.

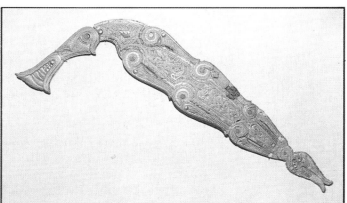

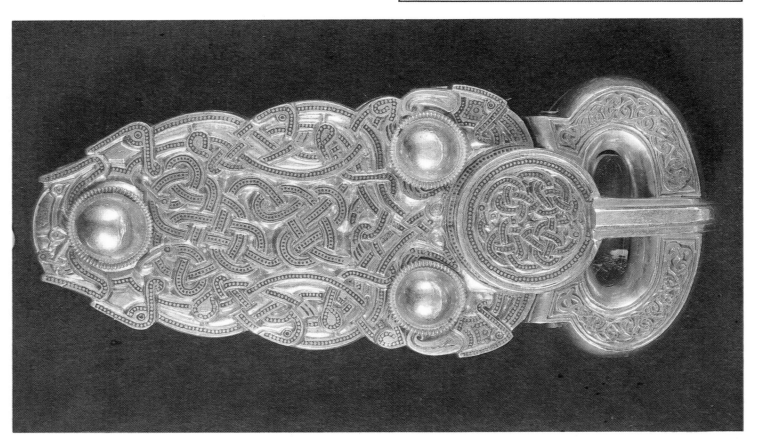

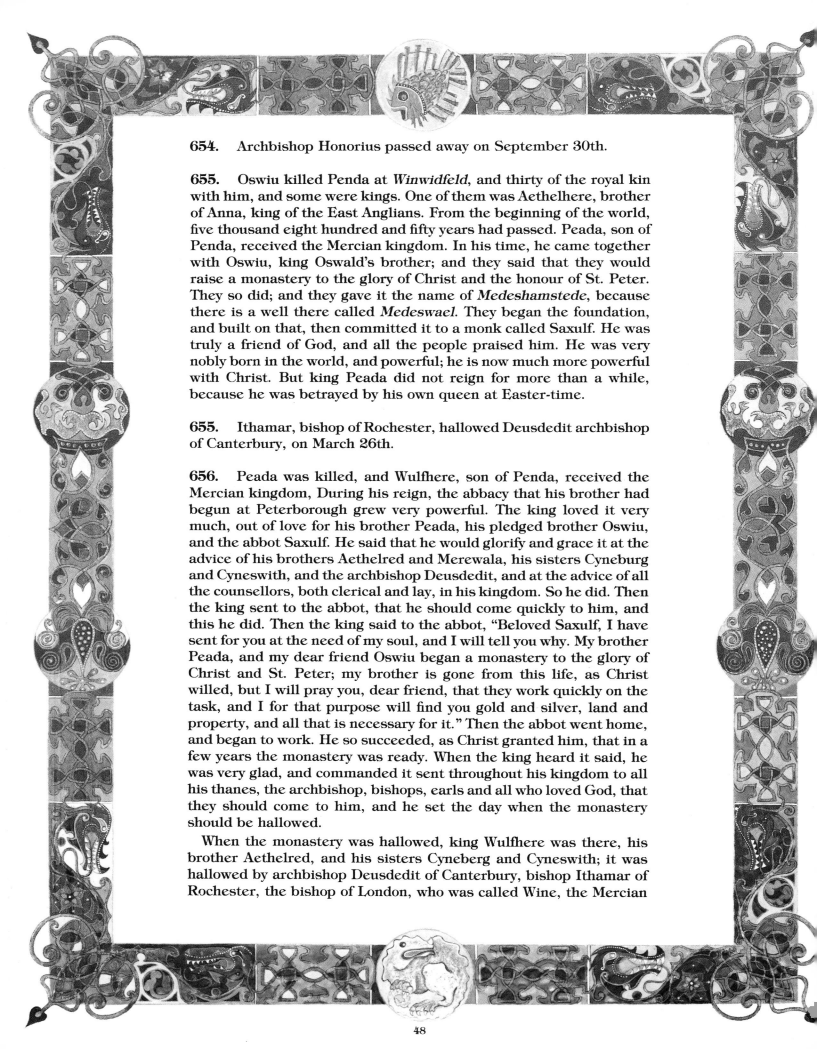

654. Archbishop Honorius passed away on September 30th.

655. Oswiu killed Penda at *Winwidfeld*, and thirty of the royal kin with him, and some were kings. One of them was Aethelhere, brother of Anna, king of the East Anglians. From the beginning of the world, five thousand eight hundred and fifty years had passed. Peada, son of Penda, received the Mercian kingdom. In his time, he came together with Oswiu, king Oswald's brother; and they said that they would raise a monastery to the glory of Christ and the honour of St. Peter. They so did; and they gave it the name of *Medeshamstede*, because there is a well there called *Medeswael*. They began the foundation, and built on that, then committed it to a monk called Saxulf. He was truly a friend of God, and all the people praised him. He was very nobly born in the world, and powerful; he is now much more powerful with Christ. But king Peada did not reign for more than a while, because he was betrayed by his own queen at Easter-time.

655. Ithamar, bishop of Rochester, hallowed Deusdedit archbishop of Canterbury, on March 26th.

656. Peada was killed, and Wulfhere, son of Penda, received the Mercian kingdom, During his reign, the abbacy that his brother had begun at Peterborough grew very powerful. The king loved it very much, out of love for his brother Peada, his pledged brother Oswiu, and the abbot Saxulf. He said that he would glorify and grace it at the advice of his brothers Aethelred and Merewala, his sisters Cyneburg and Cyneswith, and the archbishop Deusdedit, and at the advice of all the counsellors, both clerical and lay, in his kingdom. So he did. Then the king sent to the abbot, that he should come quickly to him, and this he did. Then the king said to the abbot, "Beloved Saxulf, I have sent for you at the need of my soul, and I will tell you why. My brother Peada, and my dear friend Oswiu began a monastery to the glory of Christ and St. Peter; my brother is gone from this life, as Christ willed, but I will pray you, dear friend, that they work quickly on the task, and I for that purpose will find you gold and silver, land and property, and all that is necessary for it." Then the abbot went home, and began to work. He so succeeded, as Christ granted him, that in a few years the monastery was ready. When the king heard it said, he was very glad, and commanded it sent throughout his kingdom to all his thanes, the archbishop, bishops, earls and all who loved God, that they should come to him, and he set the day when the monastery should be hallowed.

When the monastery was hallowed, king Wulfhere was there, his brother Aethelred, and his sisters Cyneberg and Cyneswith; it was hallowed by archbishop Deusdedit of Canterbury, bishop Ithamar of Rochester, the bishop of London, who was called Wine, the Mercian

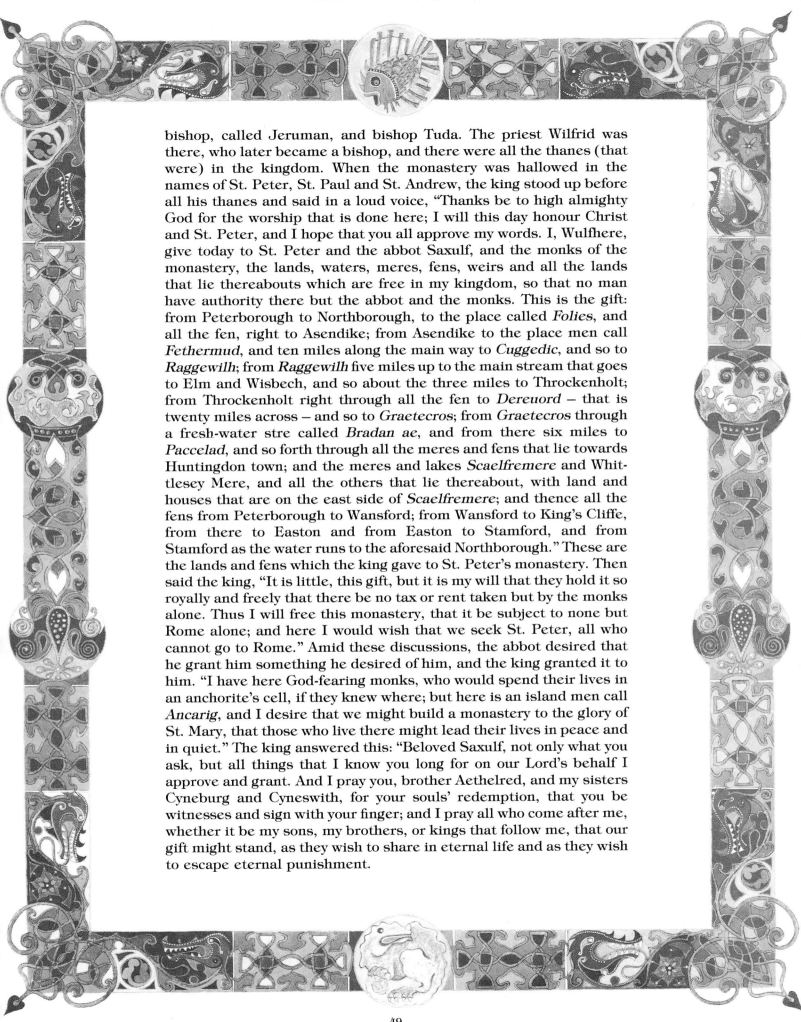

bishop, called Jeruman, and bishop Tuda. The priest Wilfrid was there, who later became a bishop, and there were all the thanes (that were) in the kingdom. When the monastery was hallowed in the names of St. Peter, St. Paul and St. Andrew, the king stood up before all his thanes and said in a loud voice, "Thanks be to high almighty God for the worship that is done here; I will this day honour Christ and St. Peter, and I hope that you all approve my words. I, Wulfhere, give today to St. Peter and the abbot Saxulf, and the monks of the monastery, the lands, waters, meres, fens, weirs and all the lands that lie thereabouts which are free in my kingdom, so that no man have authority there but the abbot and the monks. This is the gift: from Peterborough to Northborough, to the place called *Folies*, and all the fen, right to Asendike; from Asendike to the place men call *Fethermud*, and ten miles along the main way to *Cuggedic*, and so to *Raggewilh*; from *Raggewilh* five miles up to the main stream that goes to Elm and Wisbech, and so about the three miles to Throckenholt; from Throckenholt right through all the fen to *Dereuord* – that is twenty miles across – and so to *Graetecros*; from *Graetecros* through a fresh-water stre called *Bradan ae*, and from there six miles to *Paccelad*, and so forth through all the meres and fens that lie towards Huntingdon town; and the meres and lakes *Scaelfremere* and Whittlesey Mere, and all the others that lie thereabout, with land and houses that are on the east side of *Scaelfremere*; and thence all the fens from Peterborough to Wansford; from Wansford to King's Cliffe, from there to Easton and from Easton to Stamford, and from Stamford as the water runs to the aforesaid Northborough." These are the lands and fens which the king gave to St. Peter's monastery. Then said the king, "It is little, this gift, but it is my will that they hold it so royally and freely that there be no tax or rent taken but by the monks alone. Thus I will free this monastery, that it be subject to none but Rome alone; and here I would wish that we seek St. Peter, all who cannot go to Rome." Amid these discussions, the abbot desired that he grant him something he desired of him, and the king granted it to him. "I have here God-fearing monks, who would spend their lives in an anchorite's cell, if they knew where; but here is an island men call *Ancarig*, and I desire that we might build a monastery to the glory of St. Mary, that those who live there might lead their lives in peace and in quiet." The king answered this: "Beloved Saxulf, not only what you ask, but all things that I know you long for on our Lord's behalf I approve and grant. And I pray you, brother Aethelred, and my sisters Cyneburg and Cyneswith, for your souls' redemption, that you be witnesses and sign with your finger; and I pray all who come after me, whether it be my sons, my brothers, or kings that follow me, that our gift might stand, as they wish to share in eternal life and as they wish to escape eternal punishment.

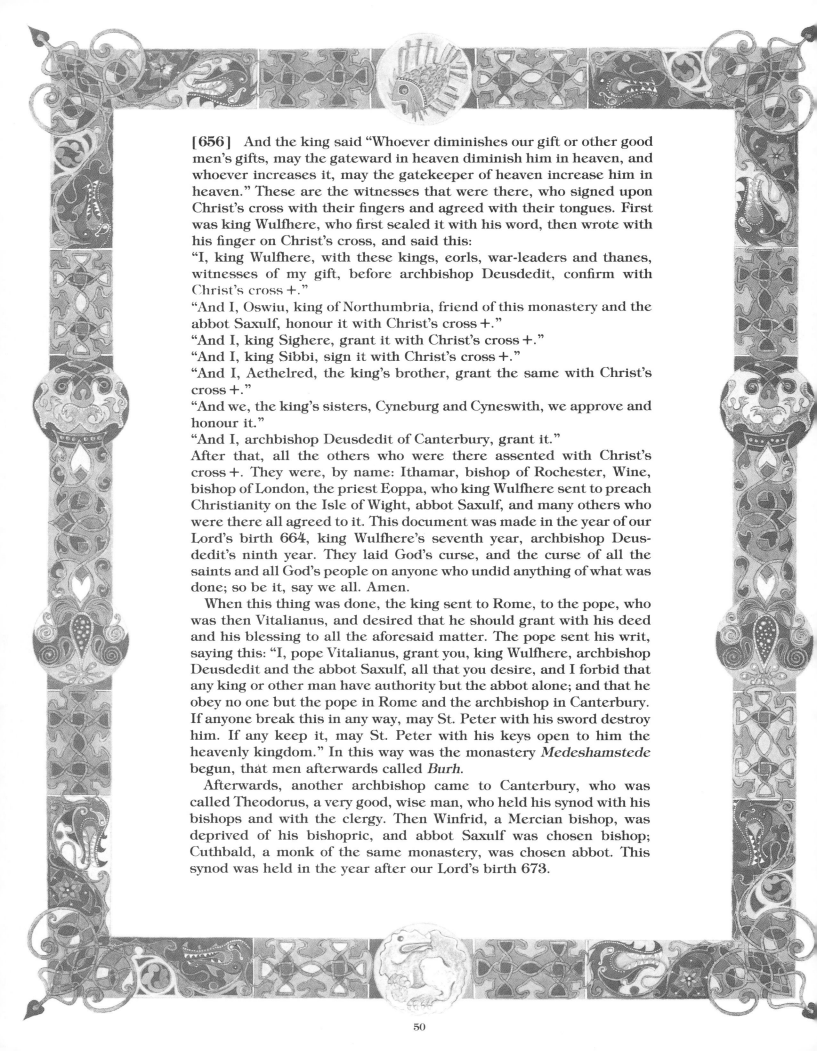

[656] And the king said "Whoever diminishes our gift or other good men's gifts, may the gateward in heaven diminish him in heaven, and whoever increases it, may the gatekeeper of heaven increase him in heaven." These are the witnesses that were there, who signed upon Christ's cross with their fingers and agreed with their tongues. First was king Wulfhere, who first sealed it with his word, then wrote with his finger on Christ's cross, and said this:

"I, king Wulfhere, with these kings, eorls, war-leaders and thanes, witnesses of my gift, before archbishop Deusdedit, confirm with Christ's cross +."

"And I, Oswiu, king of Northumbria, friend of this monastery and the abbot Saxulf, honour it with Christ's cross +."

"And I, king Sighere, grant it with Christ's cross +."

"And I, king Sibbi, sign it with Christ's cross +."

"And I, Aethelred, the king's brother, grant the same with Christ's cross +."

"And we, the king's sisters, Cyneburg and Cyneswith, we approve and honour it."

"And I, archbishop Deusdedit of Canterbury, grant it."

After that, all the others who were there assented with Christ's cross +. They were, by name: Ithamar, bishop of Rochester, Wine, bishop of London, the priest Eoppa, who king Wulfhere sent to preach Christianity on the Isle of Wight, abbot Saxulf, and many others who were there all agreed to it. This document was made in the year of our Lord's birth 664, king Wulfhere's seventh year, archbishop Deusdedit's ninth year. They laid God's curse, and the curse of all the saints and all God's people on anyone who undid anything of what was done; so be it, say we all. Amen.

When this thing was done, the king sent to Rome, to the pope, who was then Vitalianus, and desired that he should grant with his deed and his blessing to all the aforesaid matter. The pope sent his writ, saying this: "I, pope Vitalianus, grant you, king Wulfhere, archbishop Deusdedit and the abbot Saxulf, all that you desire, and I forbid that any king or other man have authority but the abbot alone; and that he obey no one but the pope in Rome and the archbishop in Canterbury. If anyone break this in any way, may St. Peter with his sword destroy him. If any keep it, may St. Peter with his keys open to him the heavenly kingdom." In this way was the monastery *Medeshamstede* begun, that men afterwards called *Burh*.

Afterwards, another archbishop came to Canterbury, who was called Theodorus, a very good, wise man, who held his synod with his bishops and with the clergy. Then Winfrid, a Mercian bishop, was deprived of his bishopric, and abbot Saxulf was chosen bishop; Cuthbald, a monk of the same monastery, was chosen abbot. This synod was held in the year after our Lord's birth 673.

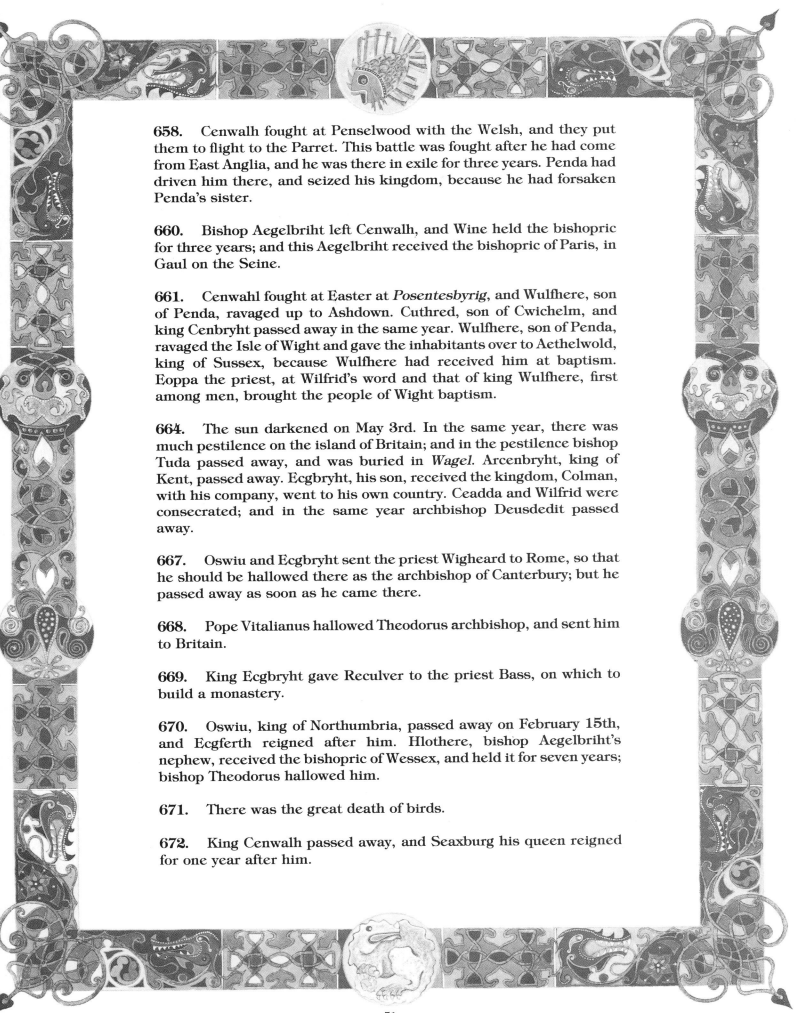

658. Cenwalh fought at Penselwood with the Welsh, and they put them to flight to the Parret. This battle was fought after he had come from East Anglia, and he was there in exile for three years. Penda had driven him there, and seized his kingdom, because he had forsaken Penda's sister.

660. Bishop Aegelbriht left Cenwalh, and Wine held the bishopric for three years; and this Aegelbriht received the bishopric of Paris, in Gaul on the Seine.

661. Cenwahl fought at Easter at *Posentesbyrig*, and Wulfhere, son of Penda, ravaged up to Ashdown. Cuthred, son of Cwichelm, and king Cenbryht passed away in the same year. Wulfhere, son of Penda, ravaged the Isle of Wight and gave the inhabitants over to Aethelwold, king of Sussex, because Wulfhere had received him at baptism. Eoppa the priest, at Wilfrid's word and that of king Wulfhere, first among men, brought the people of Wight baptism.

664. The sun darkened on May 3rd. In the same year, there was much pestilence on the island of Britain; and in the pestilence bishop Tuda passed away, and was buried in *Wagel*. Arcenbryht, king of Kent, passed away. Ecgbryht, his son, received the kingdom, Colman, with his company, went to his own country. Ceadda and Wilfrid were consecrated; and in the same year archbishop Deusdedit passed away.

667. Oswiu and Ecgbryht sent the priest Wigheard to Rome, so that he should be hallowed there as the archbishop of Canterbury; but he passed away as soon as he came there.

668. Pope Vitalianus hallowed Theodorus archbishop, and sent him to Britain.

669. King Ecgbryht gave Reculver to the priest Bass, on which to build a monastery.

670. Oswiu, king of Northumbria, passed away on February 15th, and Ecgferth reigned after him. Hlothere, bishop Aegelbriht's nephew, received the bishopric of Wessex, and held it for seven years; bishop Theodorus hallowed him.

671. There was the great death of birds.

672. King Cenwalh passed away, and Seaxburg his queen reigned for one year after him.

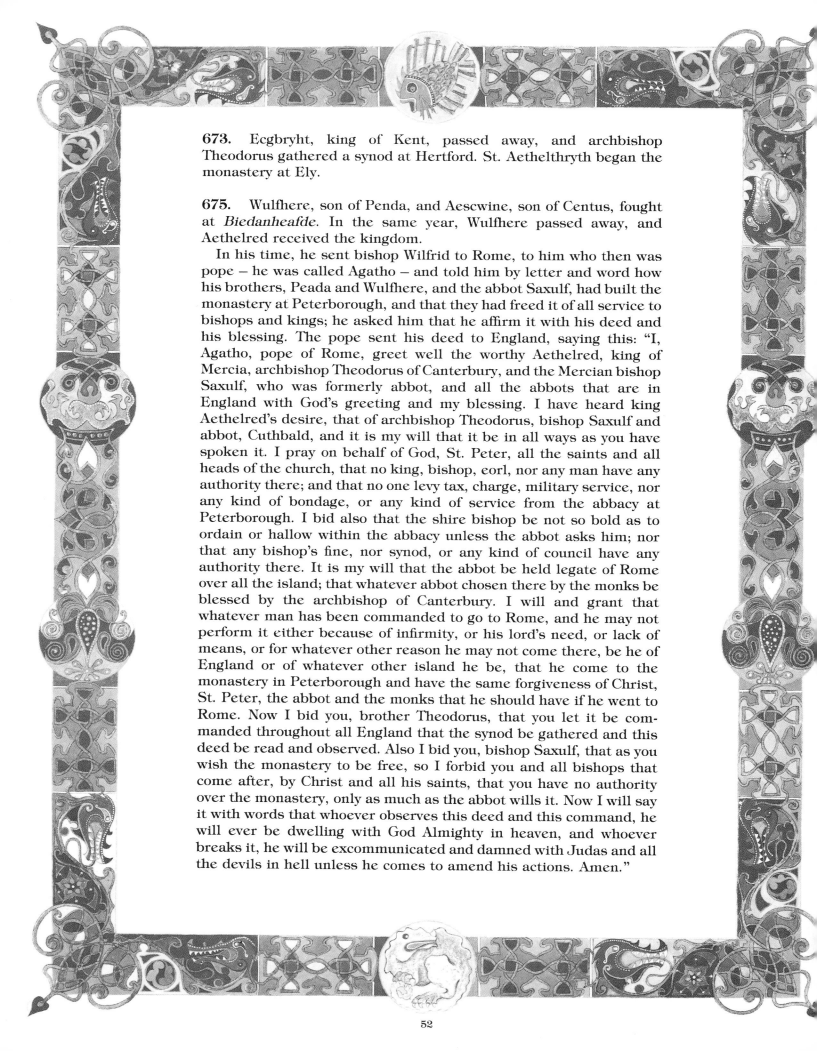

673. Ecgbryht, king of Kent, passed away, and archbishop Theodorus gathered a synod at Hertford. St. Aethelthryth began the monastery at Ely.

675. Wulfhere, son of Penda, and Aescwine, son of Centus, fought at *Biedanheafde*. In the same year, Wulfhere passed away, and Aethelred received the kingdom.

In his time, he sent bishop Wilfrid to Rome, to him who then was pope – he was called Agatho – and told him by letter and word how his brothers, Peada and Wulfhere, and the abbot Saxulf, had built the monastery at Peterborough, and that they had freed it of all service to bishops and kings; he asked him that he affirm it with his deed and his blessing. The pope sent his deed to England, saying this: "I, Agatho, pope of Rome, greet well the worthy Aethelred, king of Mercia, archbishop Theodorus of Canterbury, and the Mercian bishop Saxulf, who was formerly abbot, and all the abbots that are in England with God's greeting and my blessing. I have heard king Aethelred's desire, that of archbishop Theodorus, bishop Saxulf and abbot, Cuthbald, and it is my will that it be in all ways as you have spoken it. I pray on behalf of God, St. Peter, all the saints and all heads of the church, that no king, bishop, eorl, nor any man have any authority there; and that no one levy tax, charge, military service, nor any kind of bondage, or any kind of service from the abbacy at Peterborough. I bid also that the shire bishop be not so bold as to ordain or hallow within the abbacy unless the abbot asks him; nor that any bishop's fine, nor synod, or any kind of council have any authority there. It is my will that the abbot be held legate of Rome over all the island; that whatever abbot chosen there by the monks be blessed by the archbishop of Canterbury. I will and grant that whatever man has been commanded to go to Rome, and he may not perform it either because of infirmity, or his lord's need, or lack of means, or for whatever other reason he may not come there, be he of England or of whatever other island he be, that he come to the monastery in Peterborough and have the same forgiveness of Christ, St. Peter, the abbot and the monks that he should have if he went to Rome. Now I bid you, brother Theodorus, that you let it be commanded throughout all England that the synod be gathered and this deed be read and observed. Also I bid you, bishop Saxulf, that as you wish the monastery to be free, so I forbid you and all bishops that come after, by Christ and all his saints, that you have no authority over the monastery, only as much as the abbot wills it. Now I will say it with words that whoever observes this deed and this command, he will ever be dwelling with God Almighty in heaven, and whoever breaks it, he will be excommunicated and damned with Judas and all the devils in hell unless he comes to amend his actions. Amen."

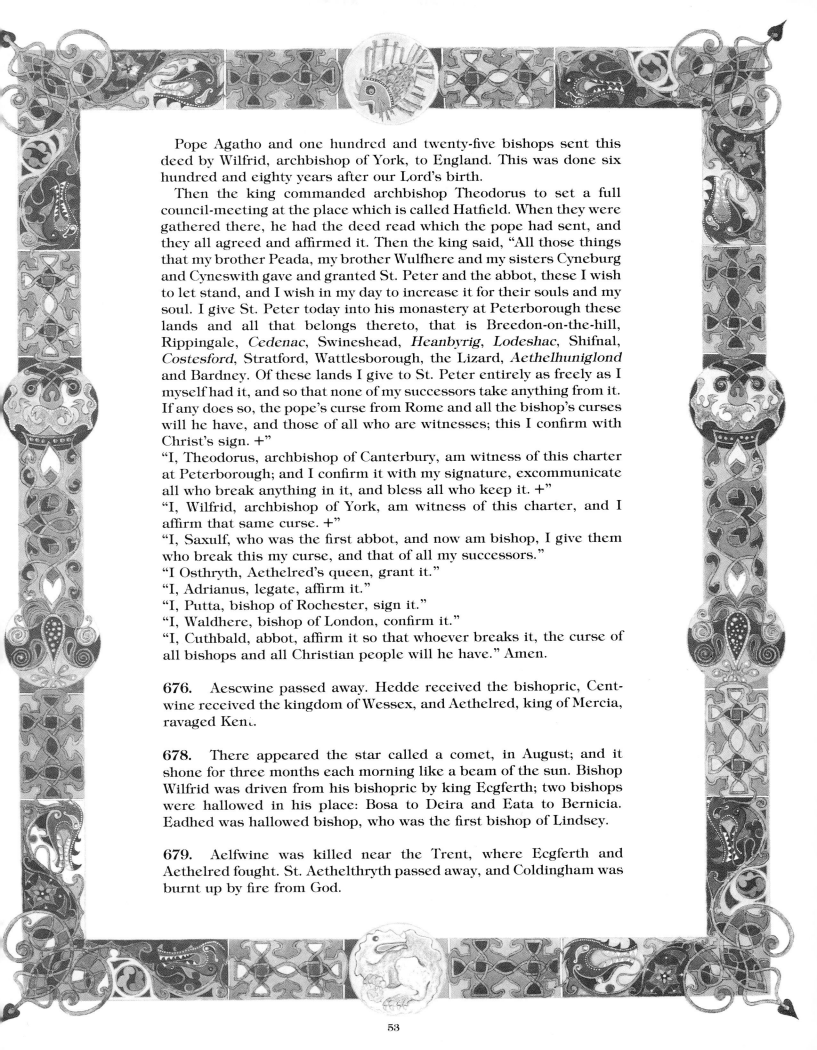

Pope Agatho and one hundred and twenty-five bishops sent this deed by Wilfrid, archbishop of York, to England. This was done six hundred and eighty years after our Lord's birth.

Then the king commanded archbishop Theodorus to set a full council-meeting at the place which is called Hatfield. When they were gathered there, he had the deed read which the pope had sent, and they all agreed and affirmed it. Then the king said, "All those things that my brother Peada, my brother Wulfhere and my sisters Cyneburg and Cyneswith gave and granted St. Peter and the abbot, these I wish to let stand, and I wish in my day to increase it for their souls and my soul. I give St. Peter today into his monastery at Peterborough these lands and all that belongs thereto, that is Breedon-on-the-hill, Rippingale, *Cedenac*, Swineshead, *Heanbyrig*, *Lodeshac*, Shifnal, *Costesford*, Stratford, Wattlesborough, the Lizard, *Aethelhuniglond* and Bardney. Of these lands I give to St. Peter entirely as freely as I myself had it, and so that none of my successors take anything from it. If any does so, the pope's curse from Rome and all the bishop's curses will he have, and those of all who are witnesses; this I confirm with Christ's sign. +"

"I, Theodorus, archbishop of Canterbury, am witness of this charter at Peterborough; and I confirm it with my signature, excommunicate all who break anything in it, and bless all who keep it. +"

"I, Wilfrid, archbishop of York, am witness of this charter, and I affirm that same curse. +"

"I, Saxulf, who was the first abbot, and now am bishop, I give them who break this my curse, and that of all my successors."

"I Osthryth, Aethelred's queen, grant it."

"I, Adrianus, legate, affirm it."

"I, Putta, bishop of Rochester, sign it."

"I, Waldhere, bishop of London, confirm it."

"I, Cuthbald, abbot, affirm it so that whoever breaks it, the curse of all bishops and all Christian people will he have." Amen.

676. Aescwine passed away. Hedde received the bishopric, Centwine received the kingdom of Wessex, and Aethelred, king of Mercia, ravaged Kent.

678. There appeared the star called a comet, in August; and it shone for three months each morning like a beam of the sun. Bishop Wilfrid was driven from his bishopric by king Ecgferth; two bishops were hallowed in his place: Bosa to Deira and Eata to Bernicia. Eadhed was hallowed bishop, who was the first bishop of Lindsey.

679. Aelfwine was killed near the Trent, where Ecgferth and Aethelred fought. St. Aethelthryth passed away, and Coldingham was burnt up by fire from God.

quim multa ag̃ cūr solẽ tia lũx q̄ mi hi ꝓ bre q̄ ī comẽ ꞇ ꞇ an hũr
illi ꞇ ꞇ o op̃ ator u ẽr bi ꞇ ꞇ ꞇ at ꝑ eſ cr̃ ebat hrath̃ ꝛeligioꞃ uꝛ
ꞇ bon uꝛ uir loŋ e lation̄ omnia ꝓ uo catuꝛ ꞇ ꝓ ꝰim ꞇ ꝛ egi ꝼꝛ ꞇ ꝑati
ad uiam luſtitiae ꝛ edi poꝛ at adeo uꝛ ꝑ eli citꝛꝛ ꝼ iuede ſtrucꞇꝛ ꝼ aŋ ꞇ
aꝯꝛꝓ quar ꝼ actꝼ anꞇ ap ꞇ r̃ mẽ ꞇ ꞇ clar̃ ac nꝛꝛ xꝑi cui ꞇ ꞇr̃ adi xꞇꝼ aꝑ
Iꝼ teꝛ ꝛ ga udeꞇ ꞇ ꞇ r̃ it ma giꝛ cum ꝼ id eꝛ ꞇ uꝛꝛ r̃ ꞇ d omꝛ ꞇ r̃ i llo moꝛ i

Inlib ꝛ m̃ hiꝼ ꞇ ꞇ ꞇ
ı Uꞇ d eꝼ ꝛ nꞇ o d
miꝛ ꝼ uꝛ ꝛ ed illoꝛꝛ
hadꝛ iano ab baꞇꞇ
angloꝛꝛ ꞇ ꞇ ꞇ cl ꞇ ꞇ cꝛꝛ
ꝛ ꝛ ꞇ ln b ꝛ m̃ ꞇ ꞇ ꞇ ꝛ
ıı Uꞇ ꞇ ꞇ ad da d eꝼ ꝼ
ꞇ ꞇ ꝛ ꝑ ultu r̃ aꝛꝛ ꞇ
da um iꝼꝼ ꞇ ꞇ ꞇꝛ a
oꝛ ꝛ n̄ u ꞇ ꞇ ꞇ b eꝛꝛ
ꝼ ꝛ i de bat arch ꞇ e
ac ceꝑ iꞇꝛ ꞇ ꞇ ꞇ ar̄
aꝼ ꝼ ꞇ ꞇ ꞇ o b eꝼ ꞇ ꞇ ꞇ e
ꝼ ꞇ luce mon ꝼ ꞇ ꞇ
uꝛ ꝛ g i nꝛ uꝼ q̄ꝛꝛ ꝛ ꝛ ed
ra ſam ꝑ aꝛ ticul̄ ſ iꞇ ꞇ r̄ r̄ i ꞇ lu c iꝛ aꝼ ꝼ ꝓ ꝛ iꞇꞇꞇ ıx Q̄ua e ſ int oꝼ ꞇ r̄ ꞇ a c eꝼ ꝼ
tur ſ ig na cum ꞇ ꞇ ꝓ ꝛ ia m ꞇ ꞇ iꝼ gr̃ ega tion iꝼ illi uꝛ ꞇ mundo ꞇ ꝛ anſ iꞇ ꝛ̄
x Uꞇ ad er̃ m ꞇ ꞇ ꝓ ꝛ um̃ ꞇꞇ mon aꝼ ꞇ r̃ ıı oꝛ anꞇ ca da lu ca m̃ ꝓ ꝼ ꞇ ꞇ ꝑꝛꞇꞇ x ı Uꞇ ꞇ ꝑꝛꞇ
ꞇ d em̃ ꝑ um geꝛꝛ e b bı ln m̃ ꝛꝛ ch au n ꞇ ꞇ a u eꝛꝛ ꝼ ati on̄ ſ in iꞇꝼ x ıı Uꞇ ꞇ ꝑ ıꝛꞇ ꝓꝑ aꝛꝛ
occ ide ꞇ ꞇ al ıı ꝛꝛ r̄ ꝛꝛ leu ꞇ ꞇ rꝓ ꝛ i o h ꞇ ꞇ diꝛ ꞇ ꞇ ꝑ ı mꝓ ſ ꝼ r̄ ꝼ r̄ ꞇ ꞇ ꝑꝑꞇ ꞇ a c y ch e ꝛꝛ m̃
ꞇ ꝑ ꝑ ꝛ ꞇ ꝛ em̃ m̃ da cc eꝼ ꞇ ꞇ r̄ ꞇ ꞇ ꞇ ꞇꞇ nor dan hꝛꝛ m bꝛ oꝛꝛ ꝼ uꝛ ꝼ in ꞇ ꞇ ꝑꝛꞇ x ıı ıı Uꞇ ꞇ u ꞇ ꞇ ıl
ꝼ r̄ ıd eꞇ ꞇꝛ ꝼꝛꝛ nꝯ ã au ꝼ ꞇ ꞇ ꝛ al ıı ꝛꝛ r̄ ꝛꝛ ad xꝑ m̃ ıu cꞇ ꞇ r̄ iꞇꝼ x ı ıı ı Uꞇ ꞇ u eꝛꞇ al nꝼ uł a xꝑꞇꞇꝛꝛı

70

qui multa agebat solercia luxq̇ mihi ꝓ brē qui comes tan·hir
illi & eo operator uǰ biscitat at ꝑescebat hꝗach ꝑeligiosur
&bonur uir longelateq. omnia puagatur & ꝓꝑm & ꝑegem̄ ꝑpatu
aduiam lusticiaeredigit adeo utꝑelicit sue destructr san̄
aꝑisq. quar fcr antaꝑ sir ōt ɔclar ac n̄ xp̄i cui tꝯpadixchr
Jꝛcꝯgaudetur magir cum fider sur ꝑccdonir in llomor·
q. Im pideꝯr·m uh lꝛ dal a·ur e·ur es. quib· lꝛagestur

In libr·n̄ h

I Utdesir cta
misur ꝑediu
hadꝛianoab
anglor̄ &cue
isiIn buis &
III Utoeadda de
&sepultura
dauiurisꝯr
osuiu &cꝯq̇
sspidebat are
accꝑsr̄ crē
aꝑscꝛiobesic
ꝑtlucemon
uirginem qꝛ
ꝑa lamparticula sutur ueluciraꝑsꝗ̄t· IV Quaesintorscnꝛa cel
tursigna cum &ipsamatis grꝛegaronir illuer emundoꝑransrꝑt
V Utadcr̄imcꝗⁱum·ē·monasceꝛ·ii oransꝛata lucam ꝑcꝯꝑsr̄t· VI Utꝯꝑꝓx̄
adenꝑuingꝛeobbi luiⁿ ꝛꝛchauⁱtauꝗesꝗoⁿesm̄nscꝛt· XII Utꝯꝑiꝛcꝯꝑ au·
occidꝯtalⁱuꝛꝛꝛ leucheꝛio h꜄dⁱcꝗ mꝛpꝯ a h ꝛoꝑsⁱsꝛꝯ꜁ꝯꝑꝑꝛ ⁱtta cyche·ⁱⁱ
&ꝑisꝑꝛoꝛcꝑmuⁿ accꝯꝑsr̄t ꝯꝗ̄t nordan hꝛꝛmbror sucꝯⁱⁿtcꝑⁱ XIII Utꝯⁱul
fridꝯr̄t ꝑynꝓꝗ̄ausꝛaⁱⁱuꝛꝛꝛ adⁱꝑꝗ̄m ⁱucꝯsꝛt· XIIII Utuꝯꝗⁱalⁱⁿꜱula xꝑꝛⁱꝗⁿꝛⁱ

The Chronicles mention the three major figures of Northumbrian Christianity – St Cuthbert, Wilfrid and the Venerable Bede – only briefly. St Cuthbert (c.625–87), the ascetic prior of Lindisfarne, reluctantly accepted the bishopric of Hexham in 685 but soon returned to the lonely cell he had built for himself on Farne island off Bamburgh. His shrine on Lindisfarne was venerated and when in 875 the monks of Lindisfarne had to flee a Danish invasion they carried his coffin on their shoulders.

Unlike Cuthbert, Wilfrid (634–709), bishop of Northumbria, was aggressive and worldly. The leading spokesman for the Roman cause at the Synod of Whitby, he built splendid stone churches 'in the Roman manner' at Ripon and Hexham. Expelled from his see in 678 after a quarrel about the division of his diocese, he spent the last 30 years of his life in exile, fighting for his rights. A difficult man, he none the less contributed a great deal to the international sophistication of English Christianity, importing architects, sculptors and craftsmen to build his churches. He made many conversions and founded new monasteries organized upon the firm regime of devotion, study and labour embodied in the Rule of St Benedict.

The reputation and achievements of the Venerable Bede (c.673–735) tower high above those of his fellow churchmen. He spent his entire life at the monasteries of Monkwearmouth and Jarrow, studying – everything from the classical languages to astronomy and medicine – teaching and writing. His output was prodigious – no less than 36 works of theology, grammar, history and biblical commentary – and his manuscripts were widely distributed. His *Ecclesiastical History* formed the basis of the Chronicles compiled in the late 9th century, the first Chroniclers adopting his year-by-year approach and copying much of his information about early English history.

Page 54: Page from the Moore Manuscript, the oldest of the five surviving manuscripts of Bede's Ecclesiastical History, probably copied c.737, after the author's death. Inset: Bede at his writing-desk, from a late 12th-century version of the Life and Miracles of St Cuthbert.

Page 55: Page from the Moore Manuscript. Inset: Illustration from Bede's Life of St Cuthbert, showing the saint returning from Scotland by boat with two companions. This is a version of the traditional story of three men in an oarless boat (see the Chronicle entry for 891).

Opposite left and top right: St Cuthbert's stole, originally ordered by Aelfleda, queen of King Edward the Elder, for Frithstan, bishop of Winchester before 916. In 934 king Aethelstan presented the vestments to St Cuthbert's shrine. The acanthus leaves and solid figures (seen here are Peter the Deacon and John the Baptist) show Byzantine influence. The splendour of English embroidery was known throughout Europe in the Anglo-Saxon and Norman periods.

Opposite bottom: St Cuthbert's cross, found when the saint's tomb was opened in 1827. The cross is of gold inset with garnets: a Christian object made according to secular Anglo-Saxon techniques.

Below: The crypt of Hexham Abbey, built by Wilfrid in 674 and one of the few surviving remains of a pre-10th-century English cathedral church. Wilfrid brought back from Rome ornaments and vestments for his church, which was remembered as a magnificent building. The windows were glazed and the roof covered with lead.

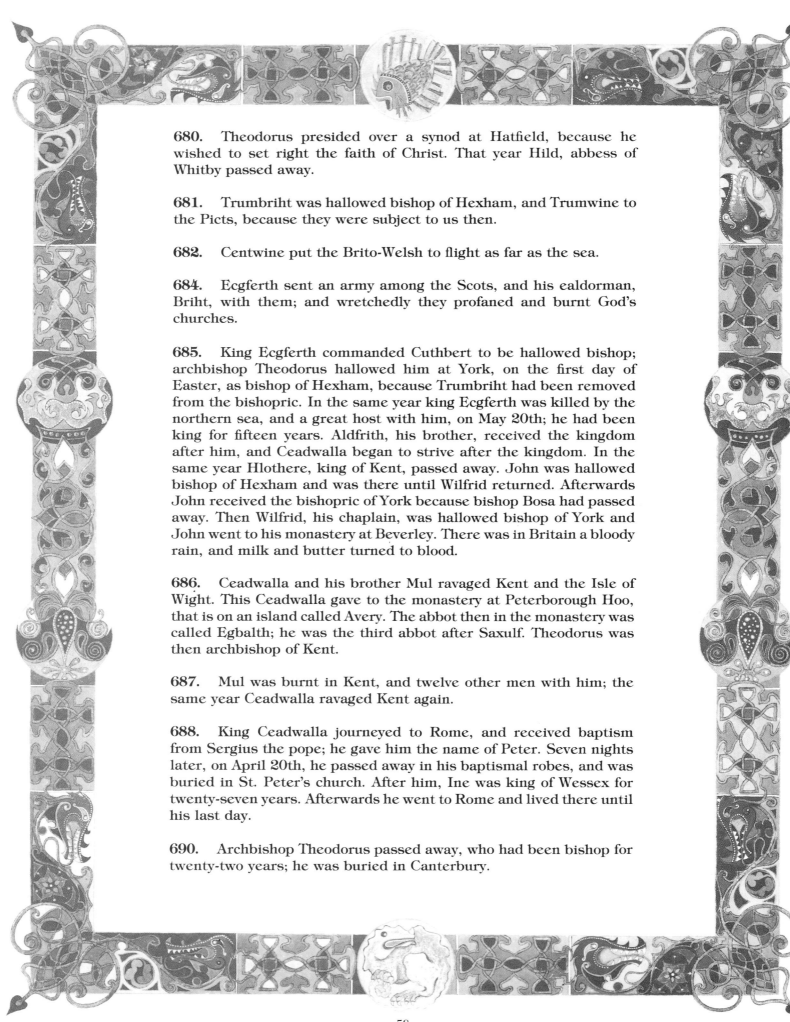

680. Theodorus presided over a synod at Hatfield, because he wished to set right the faith of Christ. That year Hild, abbess of Whitby passed away.

681. Trumbriht was hallowed bishop of Hexham, and Trumwine to the Picts, because they were subject to us then.

682. Centwine put the Brito-Welsh to flight as far as the sea.

684. Ecgferth sent an army among the Scots, and his ealdorman, Briht, with them; and wretchedly they profaned and burnt God's churches.

685. King Ecgferth commanded Cuthbert to be hallowed bishop; archbishop Theodorus hallowed him at York, on the first day of Easter, as bishop of Hexham, because Trumbriht had been removed from the bishopric. In the same year king Ecgferth was killed by the northern sea, and a great host with him, on May 20th; he had been king for fifteen years. Aldfrith, his brother, received the kingdom after him, and Ceadwalla began to strive after the kingdom. In the same year Hlothere, king of Kent, passed away. John was hallowed bishop of Hexham and was there until Wilfrid returned. Afterwards John received the bishopric of York because bishop Bosa had passed away. Then Wilfrid, his chaplain, was hallowed bishop of York and John went to his monastery at Beverley. There was in Britain a bloody rain, and milk and butter turned to blood.

686. Ceadwalla and his brother Mul ravaged Kent and the Isle of Wight. This Ceadwalla gave to the monastery at Peterborough Hoo, that is on an island called Avery. The abbot then in the monastery was called Egbalth; he was the third abbot after Saxulf. Theodorus was then archbishop of Kent.

687. Mul was burnt in Kent, and twelve other men with him; the same year Ceadwalla ravaged Kent again.

688. King Ceadwalla journeyed to Rome, and received baptism from Sergius the pope; he gave him the name of Peter. Seven nights later, on April 20th, he passed away in his baptismal robes, and was buried in St. Peter's church. After him, Ine was king of Wessex for twenty-seven years. Afterwards he went to Rome and lived there until his last day.

690. Archbishop Theodorus passed away, who had been bishop for twenty-two years; he was buried in Canterbury.

692. Brihtwold was chosen archbishop on July 1st; he had been abbot in Reculver. Before this there were Roman archbishops, and after, they were English. There were two kings in Kent then, Wihtred and Waebheard.

693. Brihtwold was hallowed archbishop by Godwine, bishop of Gaul, on July 3rd; bishop Gifemund died, and Tobias was hallowed in his stead. Drythelm was led out of this life in a vision.

694. The people of Kent held council with Ine, and gave him 'thirty thousands' because they had burnt Mul. Wihtred received the kingdom of Kent, and held it for twenty-three years.

697. The Mercians killed Osthryth, Aethelred's queen.

698. The Picts killed ealdorman Brihtred.

702. Cenred received the kingdom of Mercia.

703. Bishop Hedde passed away; he held the bishopric for twenty-seven years in Winchester.

704. Aethelred, son of Penda, who had been king of Mercia for twenty-nine years before Cenred, received monkhood.

705. Aldfrith, king of Northumbria, passed away on December 14th at Driffield, and his son Osred received the kingdom.

709. Bishop Aldhelm passed away, who was bishop west of the wood, in Selwood. The bishopric of Wessex was formerly, in Daniel's day, divided in two, before it was one; Daniel held one, bishop Aldhelm the other. After Aldhelm, Forthere received it. Ceolred received the kingdom of Mercia, and Cenred went to Rome, Offa with him. Cenred was there until his life's end. The same year, bishop Wilfrid passed away in Oundle and his body was taken to Ripon. He was bishop for forty-five years, whom king Ecgferth had earlier driven to Rome.

710. Acca, Wilfrid's chaplain, received the bishopric which he had held. The same year, ealdorman Beorhtfrith fought with the Picts between the Avon and the Carron. Ine and Nun, his kinsman, fought with Geraint, the Welsh king. The same year, Sygbald was killed.

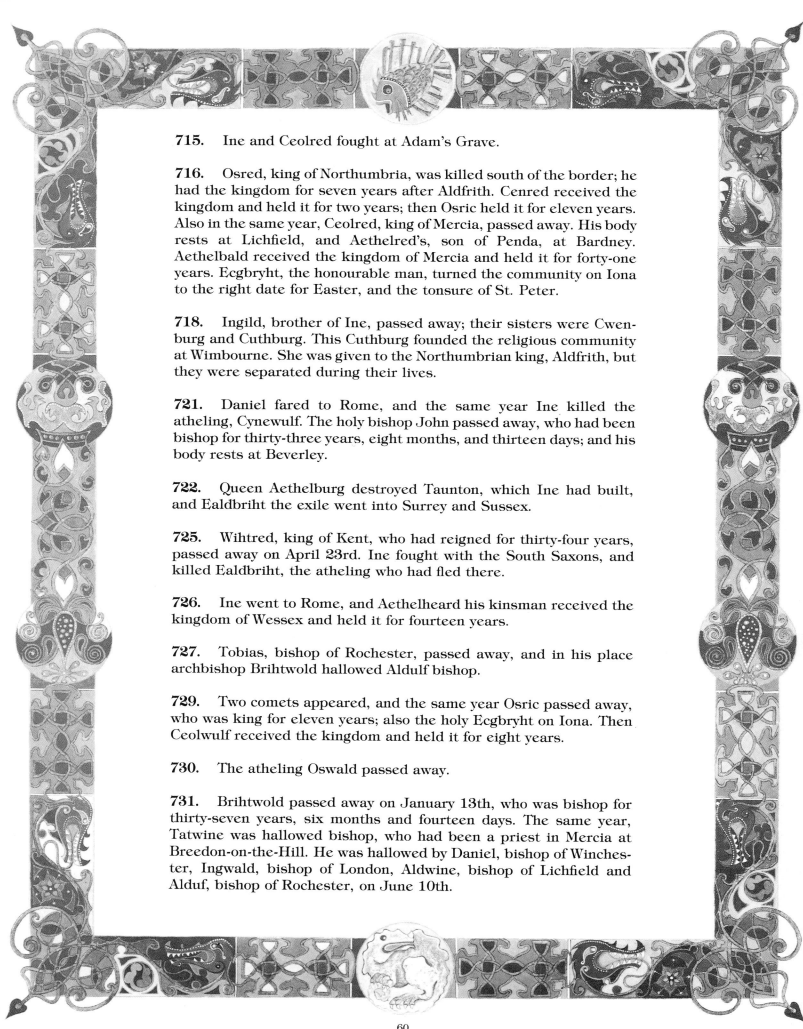

715. Ine and Ceolred fought at Adam's Grave.

716. Osred, king of Northumbria, was killed south of the border; he had the kingdom for seven years after Aldfrith. Cenred received the kingdom and held it for two years; then Osric held it for eleven years. Also in the same year, Ceolred, king of Mercia, passed away. His body rests at Lichfield, and Aethelred's, son of Penda, at Bardney. Aethelbald received the kingdom of Mercia and held it for forty-one years. Ecgbryht, the honourable man, turned the community on Iona to the right date for Easter, and the tonsure of St. Peter.

718. Ingild, brother of Ine, passed away; their sisters were Cwenburg and Cuthburg. This Cuthburg founded the religious community at Wimbourne. She was given to the Northumbrian king, Aldfrith, but they were separated during their lives.

721. Daniel fared to Rome, and the same year Ine killed the atheling, Cynewulf. The holy bishop John passed away, who had been bishop for thirty-three years, eight months, and thirteen days; and his body rests at Beverley.

722. Queen Aethelburg destroyed Taunton, which Ine had built, and Ealdbriht the exile went into Surrey and Sussex.

725. Wihtred, king of Kent, who had reigned for thirty-four years, passed away on April 23rd. Ine fought with the South Saxons, and killed Ealdbriht, the atheling who had fled there.

726. Ine went to Rome, and Aethelheard his kinsman received the kingdom of Wessex and held it for fourteen years.

727. Tobias, bishop of Rochester, passed away, and in his place archbishop Brihtwold hallowed Aldulf bishop.

729. Two comets appeared, and the same year Osric passed away, who was king for eleven years; also the holy Ecgbryht on Iona. Then Ceolwulf received the kingdom and held it for eight years.

730. The atheling Oswald passed away.

731. Brihtwold passed away on January 13th, who was bishop for thirty-seven years, six months and fourteen days. The same year, Tatwine was hallowed bishop, who had been a priest in Mercia at Breedon-on-the-Hill. He was hallowed by Daniel, bishop of Winchester, Ingwald, bishop of London, Aldwine, bishop of Lichfield and Alduf, bishop of Rochester, on June 10th.

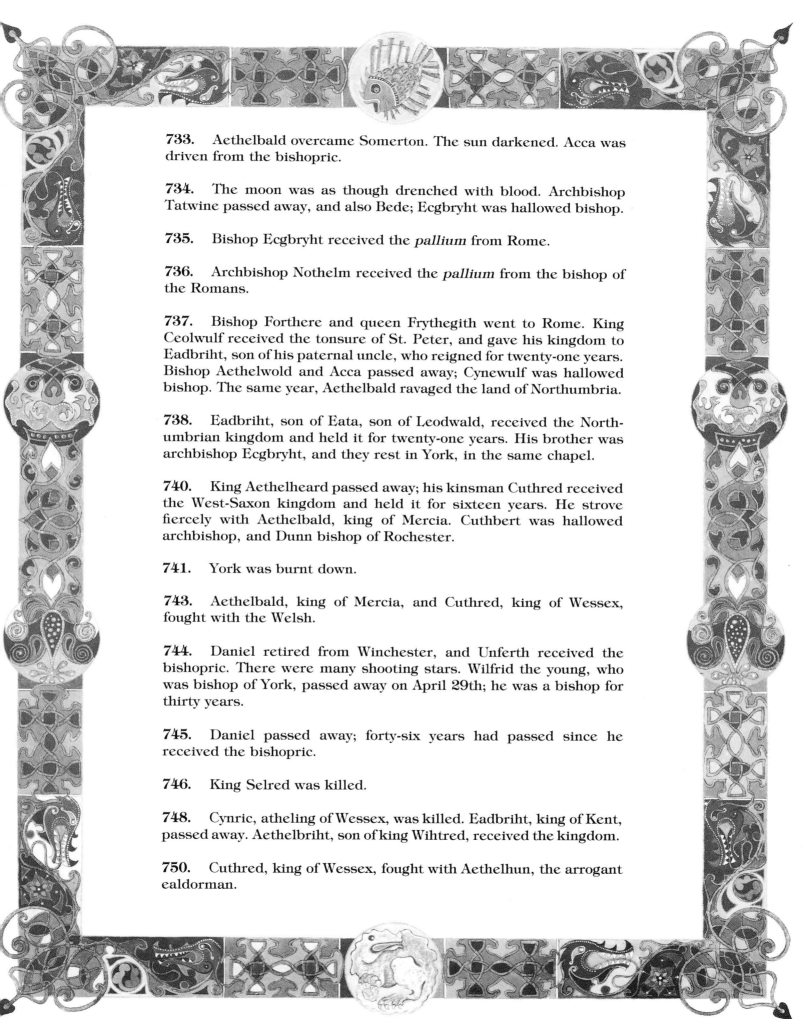

733. Aethelbald overcame Somerton. The sun darkened. Acca was driven from the bishopric.

734. The moon was as though drenched with blood. Archbishop Tatwine passed away, and also Bede; Ecgbryht was hallowed bishop.

735. Bishop Ecgbryht received the *pallium* from Rome.

736. Archbishop Nothelm received the *pallium* from the bishop of the Romans.

737. Bishop Forthere and queen Frythegith went to Rome. King Ceolwulf received the tonsure of St. Peter, and gave his kingdom to Eadbriht, son of his paternal uncle, who reigned for twenty-one years. Bishop Aethelwold and Acca passed away; Cynewulf was hallowed bishop. The same year, Aethelbald ravaged the land of Northumbria.

738. Eadbriht, son of Eata, son of Leodwald, received the Northumbrian kingdom and held it for twenty-one years. His brother was archbishop Ecgbryht, and they rest in York, in the same chapel.

740. King Aethelheard passed away; his kinsman Cuthred received the West-Saxon kingdom and held it for sixteen years. He strove fiercely with Aethelbald, king of Mercia. Cuthbert was hallowed archbishop, and Dunn bishop of Rochester.

741. York was burnt down.

743. Aethelbald, king of Mercia, and Cuthred, king of Wessex, fought with the Welsh.

744. Daniel retired from Winchester, and Unferth received the bishopric. There were many shooting stars. Wilfrid the young, who was bishop of York, passed away on April 29th; he was a bishop for thirty years.

745. Daniel passed away; forty-six years had passed since he received the bishopric.

746. King Selred was killed.

748. Cynric, atheling of Wessex, was killed. Eadbriht, king of Kent, passed away. Aethelbriht, son of king Wihtred, received the kingdom.

750. Cuthred, king of Wessex, fought with Aethelhun, the arrogant ealdorman.

Below left and right: The almost unaltered church at Escomb, County Durham, has been used continuously (except for one four-year break) as a place of worship since the late 8th century. The large square stones of the chancel arch were almost certainly taken from an earlier Roman building, and five original windows remain, four in the nave. The window jambs are typically Anglo-Saxon; the technical description is now 'Escomb fashion'.

As befitted some of the most important buildings of Anglo-Saxon England, churches were often built of stone so that some survived longer than contemporary wooden houses and fortifications, in spite of additions and conversions. Such churches and monastic buildings are clear evidence of the skills of Anglo-Saxon builders and craftsmen. In the south, imported Italian masons brought to England during and soon after Augustine's mission designed buildings like small Roman basilicas, with a central room and a smaller room or apse beyond it. The north was more influenced by Frankish architecture: the churches were very narrow in proportion to their height, the walls were thin, the few windows high and narrow and the interior walls were probably painted.

Opposite top: New Testament scenes decorate the Wirksworth slab, a typical example of the crude but vigorous sculpture being done in Mercia at the time of Offa.

Below: St Lawrence, Bradford-on-Avon. The lower part of the walls dates from the early 8th century, but the rest of the church was built three centuries later. The church was rediscovered a century ago, when the chancel was being used as a cottage and the chapel as a school.

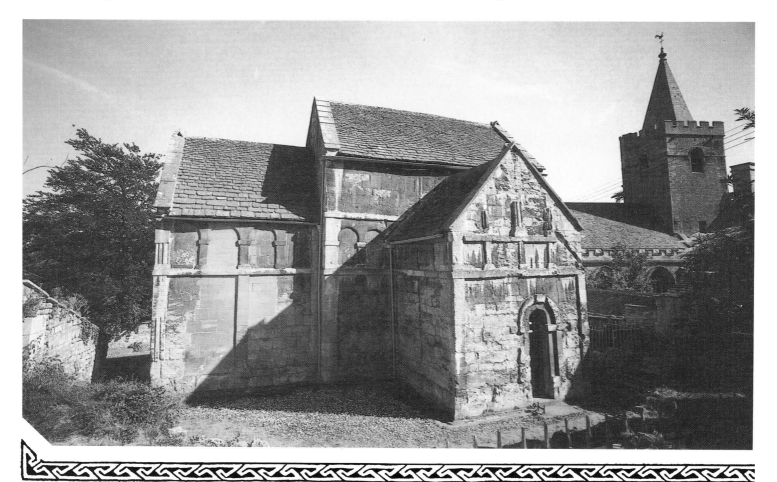

Mercia was the central kingdom of Anglo-Saxon England and remained independent until almost the end of the 9th century, developing its own distinctive and vigorous styles. Among the best examples are these three carvings from a frieze in the church of St Mary and St Hardulph at Breedon-on-the-Hill, Leicestershire. The birds are full of life, the foliage twines, the figures are well modelled with flowing drapery, and the animals are particularly vivid and lifelike.

752. Cuthred, king of Wessex, fought in the twenty-second year of his reign, at *Beorford* with Aethelbald, king of Mercia, and put him to flight.

753. Cuthred, king of Wessex, fought with the Welsh.

756. Cuthred, king of Wessex, passed away, and Cyneheard received the bishopric after Unferth in Winchester. Canterbury burnt the same year. Sigebryht, Cuthred's kinsman, received the kingdom of Wessex and held it for one year.

757. In this year Cynewulf and the West-Saxon counsellors deprived his kinsman Sigebryht of the kingdom, because of his unjust actions; except Hampshire, and he had that when he killed the eorl who had been with him the longest. Then Cynewulf drove him into the Weald, where he lived until a swineherd stabbed him to death at Privett-stream, and so avenged the eorl, Cumbra.

Cynewulf often fought great fights with the Britons; and in the thirty-first year that he had the kingdom he wanted to drive out an atheling who was called Cyneheard. This Cyneheard was Sigebryht's brother. He discovered that the king, with few companions, was in the company of a woman at *Merantun*. He overtook him there and surrounded the chamber before the king's men were aware of it. When the king realized this, he went to the door and defended himself courageously until he saw the atheling, whom he rushed upon and seriously wounded; then they all fought the king until they killed him. Then the crying out of the woman roused the king's men to the disturbance, and then whoever was best prepared and fastest ran there.

The prince offered each of them wealth and life, and none of them would accept it; but they all kept fighting until they all lay dead, except for one British hostage, and he was badly wounded.

When in the morning the king's thanes, whom he had left behind, found out that the king had been killed, they rode there with his ealdorman Osric, his thane Wiferth and the men he had left behind him. They met the atheling in the town where the king lay killed. He and his men had locked the gates against them; to that place they went. He offered them their own choice of wealth and land if they would grant him the kingdom; and he said that their kinsmen were with him, and would not go from him. They replied then that no kinsman was dearer to them than their lord, and that they would never follow his killer. They offered to their kinsmen that they come out safely from there. They replied that the same terms were offered to their own companions, who had been with the king; they replied that they took no heed of that, "any more than your own men, who were killed with the king".

65

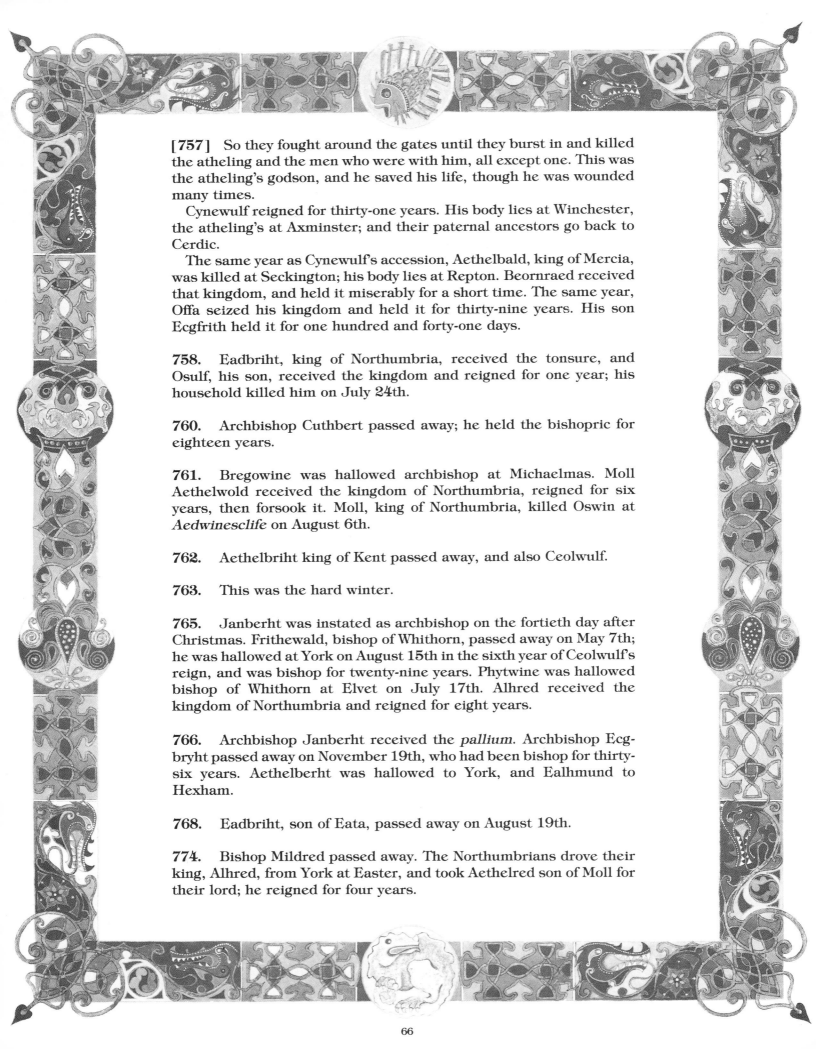

[757] So they fought around the gates until they burst in and killed the atheling and the men who were with him, all except one. This was the atheling's godson, and he saved his life, though he was wounded many times.

Cynewulf reigned for thirty-one years. His body lies at Winchester, the atheling's at Axminster; and their paternal ancestors go back to Cerdic.

The same year as Cynewulf's accession, Aethelbald, king of Mercia, was killed at Seckington; his body lies at Repton. Beornraed received that kingdom, and held it miserably for a short time. The same year, Offa seized his kingdom and held it for thirty-nine years. His son Ecgfrith held it for one hundred and forty-one days.

758. Eadbriht, king of Northumbria, received the tonsure, and Osulf, his son, received the kingdom and reigned for one year; his household killed him on July 24th.

760. Archbishop Cuthbert passed away; he held the bishopric for eighteen years.

761. Bregowine was hallowed archbishop at Michaelmas. Moll Aethelwold received the kingdom of Northumbria, reigned for six years, then forsook it. Moll, king of Northumbria, killed Oswin at *Aedwinesclife* on August 6th.

762. Aethelbriht king of Kent passed away, and also Ceolwulf.

763. This was the hard winter.

765. Janberht was instated as archbishop on the fortieth day after Christmas. Frithewald, bishop of Whithorn, passed away on May 7th; he was hallowed at York on August 15th in the sixth year of Ceolwulf's reign, and was bishop for twenty-nine years. Phytwine was hallowed bishop of Whithorn at Elvet on July 17th. Alhred received the kingdom of Northumbria and reigned for eight years.

766. Archbishop Janberht received the *pallium*. Archbishop Ecgbryht passed away on November 19th, who had been bishop for thirty-six years. Aethelberht was hallowed to York, and Ealhmund to Hexham.

768. Eadbriht, son of Eata, passed away on August 19th.

774. Bishop Mildred passed away. The Northumbrians drove their king, Alhred, from York at Easter, and took Aethelred son of Moll for their lord; he reigned for four years.

Northumbria, which covered the area between Hadrian's Wall, the Humber and the Pennines, emerged as a powerful state towards the end of the 8th century. This was the setting for the golden age of the early English Church and of early English art. Ruled by strong kings, the land prospered, and between the late 8th century and the middle of the 9th the new monasteries and schools produced a truly remarkable flowering of art and scholarship.

The chief artistic inspiration was continental — mainly from Italy and the Frankish Empire of Charlemagne. Men such as Benedict Biscop travelled to Italy — Biscop no less than six times — and brought back manuscripts, paintings, relics, and craftsmen who taught their English counterparts to carve in stone. (Biscop founded the monasteries at Monkwearmouth and Jarrow and used his knowledge of monastic life in Rome and Canterbury to make them model foundations.) Links with the Carolingian Empire were a two-way affair. While Northumbrian artists took in Carolingian styles, they also went abroad as missionaries, exporting art and spiritual scholarship. But indigenous local influences were not ignored, and Celtic themes and motifs also appear in manuscripts and on sculpture, producing a unique mixture of traditional secular and Christian themes.

The most spectacular examples of Northumbrian art of this period are the Lindisfarne Gospels. Their rich and elaborate style, and their remarkable fusion of Roman, Celtic and Anglo-Saxon influences, sets them among the greatest works of art ever produced. The Gospels were written in Latin and illuminated in about 698 at the island monastery of Lindisfarne by a monk named Eadfrith, who afterwards became bishop of Lindisfarne. His successor Aethelwold (whose death the Chronicles record in 737) pressed and bound the Gospels, and in the 10th century a priest named Aldred added an Anglo-Saxon translation.

Each of the four Gospels is prefaced by a portrait of the Evangelist, an elaborate abstract design known as a 'carpet page' and an initial page. The manuscripts of the late classical world provided the inspiration for the portraits of the Evangelists, who appear as naturalistic figures. The ornamental pages and borders are wonderfully contrived, with skilful and complex designs of animals and birds and intricate patterns. While each page is a testament to Eadfrith's skill and intelligence, he often left some tiny detail unfinished, no doubt to demonstrate his humility.

The most impressive sculptures of the artists of Northumbria are the large standing crosses, raised to commemorate an event or to mark the place where people gathered to hear monks sent on preaching tours throughout the countryside. Like the monks and scribes who created the magnificent illuminated manuscripts, the stonemasons and

Previous page: Initial page at the beginning of St Luke's Gospel.

Below: The west side of the Bewcastle Cross, Cumbria, displays three full-length figures, of John the Baptist, Christ and John the Evangelist. The runic inscriptions on this face of the cross date it to about 700. The east face is covered with a completely abstract vinescroll decoration in which the animals have lost their identity and become patterns only.

carvers employed on these crosses drew on both native and continental sources. The stately figures and folded drapery are interpretations of Greek and Roman art, while the scrolls, interlace and animal ornament were also adapted from foreign styles. Raised in the north of England from the 8th century until Norman times, the crosses were decorated with biblical scenes.

Right: The Stonyhurst Gospels, found lying on the lid of the coffin in St Cuthbert's tomb when it was opened in 1104. The manuscript is either Italian or an Anglo-Saxon copy of an Italian original, but the leather binding is native Northumbrian work of the 7th century and thus the oldest surviving English book-binding.

Below: One of the sources for details of 8th-century weapons, dress and social life is this whalebone box, possibly a reliquary, known as the Franks Casket, after Sir Augustus Franks, Keeper of British Antiquities at the British Museum in the 19th century. He discovered it being used as a workbox by a French family. The casket depicts the Epiphany and a variety of scenes from Germanic and Roman legend and history.

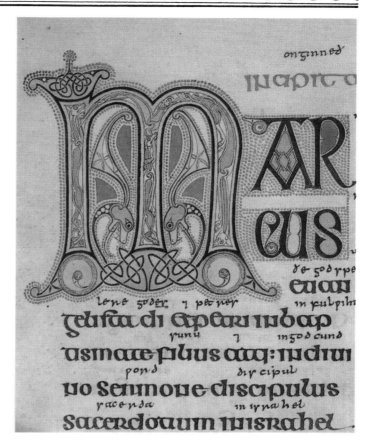

Opposite: 'Carpet page' at the opening of St Matthew's Gospel.

Right: Initial M at the beginning of the argumentum (short introduction) to St Mark's Gospel.

Below: The Ormside Bowl, found in a Viking grave in Cumbria, survives as a tribute to the talents of Northumbrian craftsmen. Made of silver lined with gilt copper, it has gilt copper jewels inside and out. There are glass inlays on the rim, and the decoration consists of imaginary animals and rich foliage.

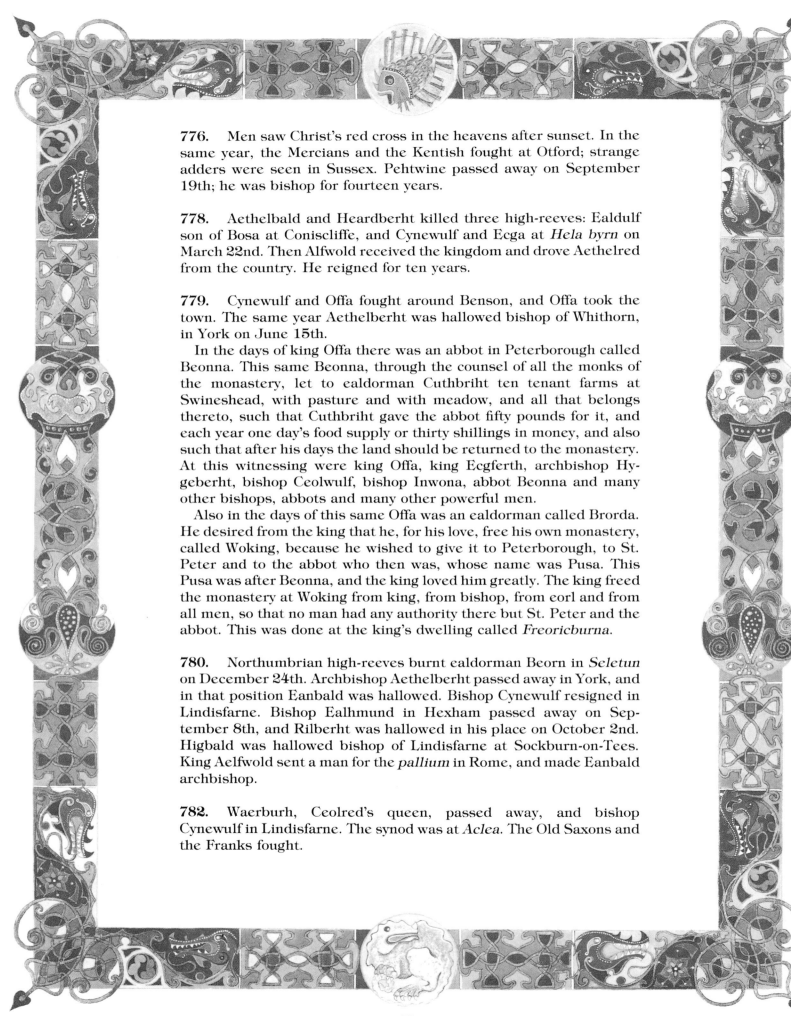

776. Men saw Christ's red cross in the heavens after sunset. In the same year, the Mercians and the Kentish fought at Otford; strange adders were seen in Sussex. Pehtwine passed away on September 19th; he was bishop for fourteen years.

778. Aethelbald and Heardberht killed three high-reeves: Ealdulf son of Bosa at Coniscliffe, and Cynewulf and Ecga at *Hela byrn* on March 22nd. Then Alfwold received the kingdom and drove Aethelred from the country. He reigned for ten years.

779. Cynewulf and Offa fought around Benson, and Offa took the town. The same year Aethelberht was hallowed bishop of Whithorn, in York on June 15th.

In the days of king Offa there was an abbot in Peterborough called Beonna. This same Beonna, through the counsel of all the monks of the monastery, let to ealdorman Cuthbriht ten tenant farms at Swineshead, with pasture and with meadow, and all that belongs thereto, such that Cuthbriht gave the abbot fifty pounds for it, and each year one day's food supply or thirty shillings in money, and also such that after his days the land should be returned to the monastery. At this witnessing were king Offa, king Ecgferth, archbishop Hygeberht, bishop Ceolwulf, bishop Inwona, abbot Beonna and many other bishops, abbots and many other powerful men.

Also in the days of this same Offa was an ealdorman called Brorda. He desired from the king that he, for his love, free his own monastery, called Woking, because he wished to give it to Peterborough, to St. Peter and to the abbot who then was, whose name was Pusa. This Pusa was after Beonna, and the king loved him greatly. The king freed the monastery at Woking from king, from bishop, from eorl and from all men, so that no man had any authority there but St. Peter and the abbot. This was done at the king's dwelling called *Freoricburna*.

780. Northumbrian high-reeves burnt ealdorman Beorn in *Seletun* on December 24th. Archbishop Aethelberht passed away in York, and in that position Eanbald was hallowed. Bishop Cynewulf resigned in Lindisfarne. Bishop Ealhmund in Hexham passed away on September 8th, and Rilberht was hallowed in his place on October 2nd. Higbald was hallowed bishop of Lindisfarne at Sockburn-on-Tees. King Aelfwold sent a man for the *pallium* in Rome, and made Eanbald archbishop.

782. Waerburh, Ceolred's queen, passed away, and bishop Cynewulf in Lindisfarne. The synod was at *Aclea*. The Old Saxons and the Franks fought.

786. Cyneheard killed king Cynewulf; he himself was killed, and eighty-four men with him. Then Brihtric received the kingdom of Wessex and reigned for sixteen years; his body lies at Wareham, and his direct paternal ancestors go back to Cerdic.

787. There was a contentious synod at Chelsea; archbishop Janberht gave up a share of his bishophric, and king Offa chose Hygebriht for it. Ecgfrith was hallowed king. In these times messages were sent from Rome, from pope Adrian to England, to renew the faith and the peace which St. Gregory sent us through bishop Augustine; they received with honour and sent back with peace. A synod was gathered in Northumbria.

788. Aelfwold, king of Northumbria, was killed by Sicga on September 23rd, and a heavenly light was often seen there where he was killed; he was buried at Hexham in the church. The synod was gathered at *Aclea*. Osred, Alhred's son, received the kingdom after him; he was his nephew.

789. Brihtric took Offa's daughter Eadburg for his wife. In his days came the first three ships of the Northmen from Hörthaland. The reve rode there, and meant to force them to the king's dwelling, because he did not know what they were; and then he was killed. Those were the first ships of Danish men to seek out the land of the English.

790. Osred, king of Northumbria, was betrayed and driven from the kingdom, and Aethelred son of Aethelwold, received the kingdom again.

791. Baldulf was hallowed bishop of Whithorn on July 17th by archbishop Eanbald and bishop Aethelberht.

792. Archbishop Janberht passed away, and the same year abbot Aethelheard was chosen archbishop.

793. In this year fierce, foreboding omens came over the land of Northumbria, and wretchedly terrified the people. There were excessive whirlwinds, lightning storms, and fiery dragons were seen flying in the sky. These signs were followed by great famine, and shortly after in the same year, on January 8th, the ravaging of heathen men destroyed God's church at Lindisfarne through brutal robbery and slaughter; and Sicga died on February 2nd.

Above and right: Details of woodcarving on items found in the Oseberg ship burial, Norway.

Below: 6th-century Swedish three-ringed gold collar. There is delicate use of filigree, and the collar is set with minute figures. Such items were probably made from melted-down objects looted from remaining Roman outposts.

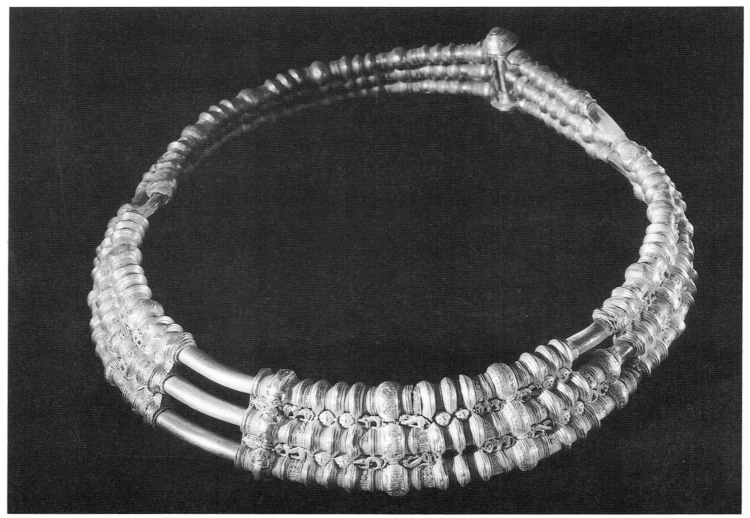

The basic element of Scandinavian art of the 5th to 9th centuries was animal ornament: both whole animals and parts of animals stretched, flattened, twisted, looped and otherwise stylized to suit a pattern and fill a space. Between the 4th and 6th centuries artists and craftsmen throughout Europe had employed these designs. But while elsewhere other motifs and techniques gradually took over, in Scandinavia animal ornament persisted. Stylistic embellishments were developed, and influences and motifs from foreign work absorbed; but these were all adapted to the traditional interlace. Much of this work was done in wood, which is why so little survives.

Naturalistic art chiefly consisted of human beings, animals and mythological scenes carved on memorial picture stones and on household goods. Narrative scenes were often combined with, or framed by, more abstract patterns of animal origin.

Ornamented with filigree, outlined in silver, painted in bright colours, the art of these centuries was rich and vigorous, often full of action and drama. The planning and execution of tangled animals and mythological scenes reveals the high level of skill of individual craftsmen.

Right: Swedish helmet of the Vendel period (555–800) decorated with bronze panels portraying warriors.

Below left and right: 8th-century Swedish picture stones: narrative detail combined with decorative ornament.

794. Offa, king of Mercia, commanded Aethelberht's head to be struck off. Osred, who was king of Northumbria, after coming home from exile, was taken and killed on September 14th; his body lies at Tynemouth. King Aethelred took a new wife, who was called Aelflaed, on September 29th.

Ealdorman Aethelheard passed away on August 1st. The heathens in Northumbria ravaged and robbed Ecgfrith's monastery at Jarrow. There some of their war-leaders were killed; also some of their ships were broken up in bad weather, and many drowned. Some came alive to shore and were quickly killed at the river's mouth.

796. Pope Adrian and king Offa passed away, and Aethelred, king of Northumbria, was killed by his own people on April 19th. Bishop Ceolwulf and bishop Eadbald went from the land. Ecgferth received the Mercian kingdom and passed away the same year. Eadbriht, whose other name was Praen, received the kingdom in Kent. The moon was darkened between cock-crow and dawn on March 28th. Eardwulf received the Northumbrian kingdom on May 14th, and was afterwards blessed and enthroned on May 26th in York by archbishop Eanbald, Aethelberht, Higbald and Baldulf. Archbishop Eanbald died on August 10th, and his body lies at York. The same year, bishop Ceolwulf passed away, and another Eanbald was hallowed in the other's place on August 14th.

797. Eanbald received the *pallium* on September 8th, and bishop Aethelberht passed away on November 16th. Heardred was hallowed in his stead on October 30th.

798. Cenwulf, king of Mercia, ravaged the Kentish people and the people of Romney Marsh; their king, Praen, was taken, and they led him bound into Mercia, and had his eyes put out and his hands cut off. Bishop Alfhun passed away in Sudbury and was buried in Dunwich, and Tidfrith was chosen after him. Siric, king of Essex, went to Rome. In the same year, the body of Wihtburg, sister of St. Aethelthryth, was found to be all whole and uncorrupted at Dereham, fifty-five years after she went from this life.

There was a great battle in Northumbria during the spring, on April 2nd, at Whalley. Alric son of Heardberht was killed, and many other men with him.

799. The Romans cut out pope Leo's tongue, put out his eyes and banished him from his see. Then soon afterwards through God's help he could see and speak, and was pope again as he was before.

800. The moon was darkened during the second hour of the night on January 16th.

After 800, when Ecgbryht (ruled 802–39) became king of Wessex, the Chroniclers begin to fill out events in some detail. In 827 they describe him as 'Bretwalda', or ruler, of Britain, a title merited in many ways. Ecgbryht expanded his own kingdom, uniting it with Kent and defeating a coalition of Welsh and Vikings in 835. During his reign the centre of power shifted from Mercia to Wessex, where it remained for the next century. Under pressure from the Viking invaders, and with Ecgbryht's leadership and diplomacy, the English kingdoms slowly moved towards a single monarchy, which eventually achieved its strongest leader in Alfred, Ecgbryht's grandson. Aethelwulf (ruled 839–58) was probably the most pious of the Wessex dynasty. In 853 he sent his four-year-old son Alfred to Rome and pledged a tenth of his land to the Church. He himself then spent a year in Rome. However, Aethelwulf was not above political manoeuvring, and on the journey home from Rome he married the 13-year-old daughter of Charles the Bald, king of the Franks, a diplomatic gesture that did not please his sons.

Below: One of the few surviving pieces of early 9th-century sculpture, this carving shows a dancing man raising a branch. The style is a mixture of Frankish influence and native Anglo-Saxon exuberance, a precursor of the maturer Anglo-Saxon art of the Winchester school.

Below: Aethelwulf's ring, of gold inlaid with niello, found at Laverstock, Wiltshire. It is inscribed with his name.

Together with ornaments, weapons and domestic utensils, ships were sometimes buried in elaborate graves. Stones were also used instead of a real ship to outline the shape of a vessel. These are on a grave in the Isle of Man.

By the late 8th century, there had been no significant attacks from the sea for 200 years, and none were expected. Once the Anglo-Saxons had settled in Britain, they concentrated on internal struggles for supremacy. Coastal defences were not built, nor was a fleet of warships maintained. The new monasteries were deliberately built on islands or the coast as sanctuaries of learning.

The sudden appearance of the Vikings in 793 was violent. Lindisfarne and the monastery at Jarrow were sacked: 'the ravaging of heathen men destroyed God's church at Lindisfarne through brutal robbery and slaughter'. Alcuin of York, now established at Charlemagne's court, wrote of the tragedy as a just punishment for the extravagances of the rich Northumbrian princes; the 'fierce foreboding omens' mentioned by the Chroniclers had been ignored – 'whirlwinds, lightning storms and fiery dragons . . . seen flying in the sky.' He also forecast correctly, in powerful rhetoric, that the raid might not be an isolated event.

Shocking though the devastation was, the Vikings did not come again for a generation, concentrating their raids instead on the Irish and continental coasts. But their forays on to the English shore resumed in 835. In most cases these were hit-and-run raids: a landing was made, villages pillaged, the local armies fought and defeated, and the

(Continued on page 86)

Below: Longships like this brought the Viking raiders across the North Sea to England, and further afield still, to southern Europe and to North America. Designed for rapid manoeuvrability, especially in confined coastal waters, they were narrow, shallow and pointed at both ends. They were equipped with a large, heavy square sail and with about ten oars on each side and probably carried about 40 soldiers. This vessel, known as the Gokstad ship, was discovered in a burial mound in Norway; a replica was sailed across the Atlantic from Norway to the USA in 1893.

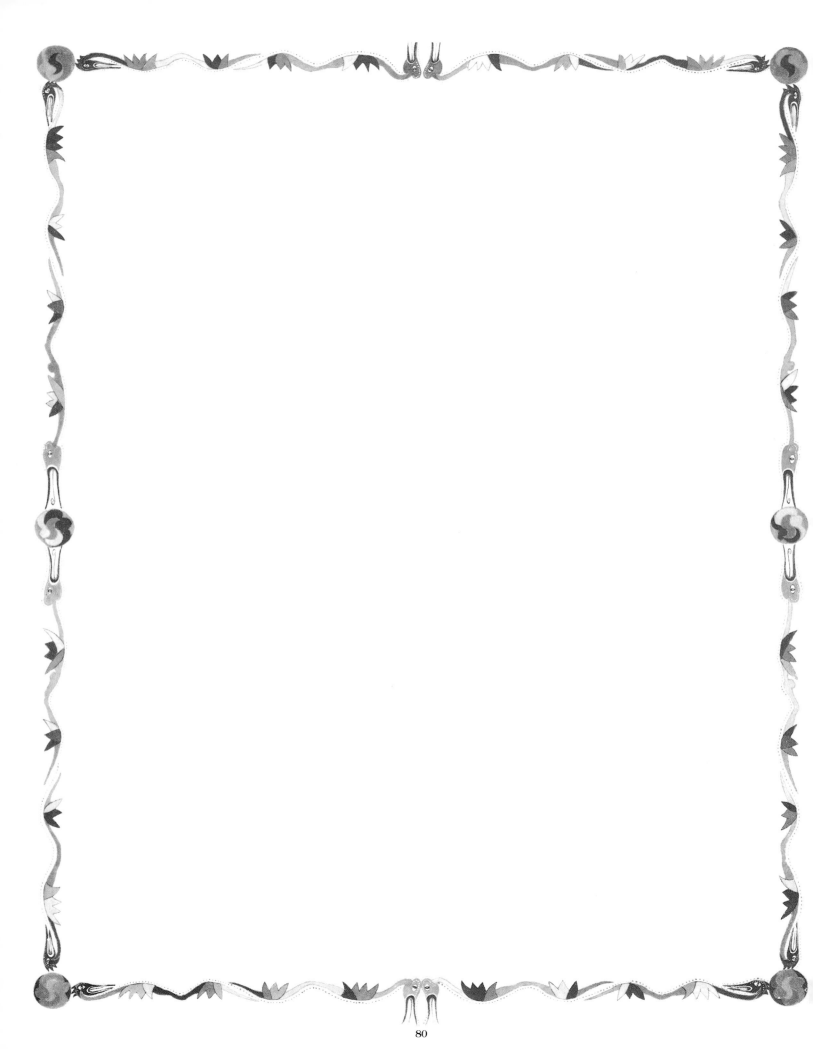

Part Two

801~963

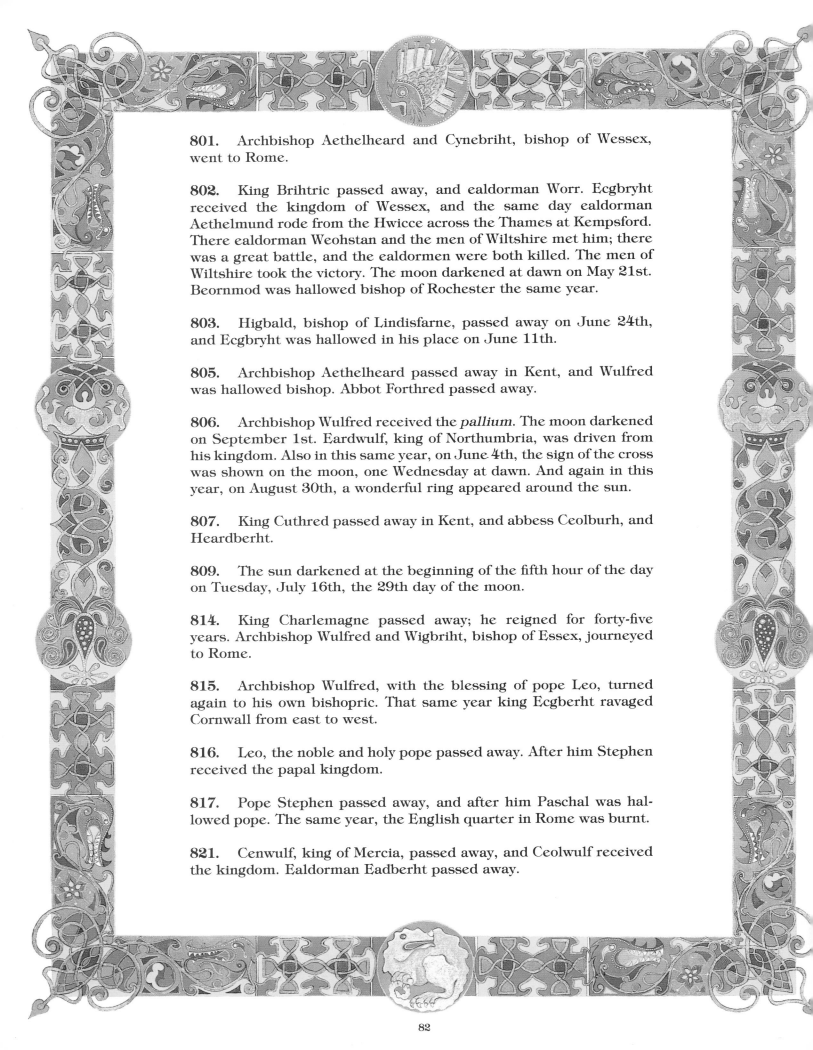

801. Archbishop Aethelheard and Cynebriht, bishop of Wessex, went to Rome.

802. King Brihtric passed away, and ealdorman Worr. Ecgbryht received the kingdom of Wessex, and the same day ealdorman Aethelmund rode from the Hwicce across the Thames at Kempsford. There ealdorman Weohstan and the men of Wiltshire met him; there was a great battle, and the ealdormen were both killed. The men of Wiltshire took the victory. The moon darkened at dawn on May 21st. Beornmod was hallowed bishop of Rochester the same year.

803. Higbald, bishop of Lindisfarne, passed away on June 24th, and Ecgbryht was hallowed in his place on June 11th.

805. Archbishop Aethelheard passed away in Kent, and Wulfred was hallowed bishop. Abbot Forthred passed away.

806. Archbishop Wulfred received the *pallium*. The moon darkened on September 1st. Eardwulf, king of Northumbria, was driven from his kingdom. Also in this same year, on June 4th, the sign of the cross was shown on the moon, one Wednesday at dawn. And again in this year, on August 30th, a wonderful ring appeared around the sun.

807. King Cuthred passed away in Kent, and abbess Ceolburh, and Heardberht.

809. The sun darkened at the beginning of the fifth hour of the day on Tuesday, July 16th, the 29th day of the moon.

814. King Charlemagne passed away; he reigned for forty-five years. Archbishop Wulfred and Wigbriht, bishop of Essex, journeyed to Rome.

815. Archbishop Wulfred, with the blessing of pope Leo, turned again to his own bishopric. That same year king Ecgberht ravaged Cornwall from east to west.

816. Leo, the noble and holy pope passed away. After him Stephen received the papal kingdom.

817. Pope Stephen passed away, and after him Paschal was hallowed pope. The same year, the English quarter in Rome was burnt.

821. Cenwulf, king of Mercia, passed away, and Ceolwulf received the kingdom. Ealdorman Eadberht passed away.

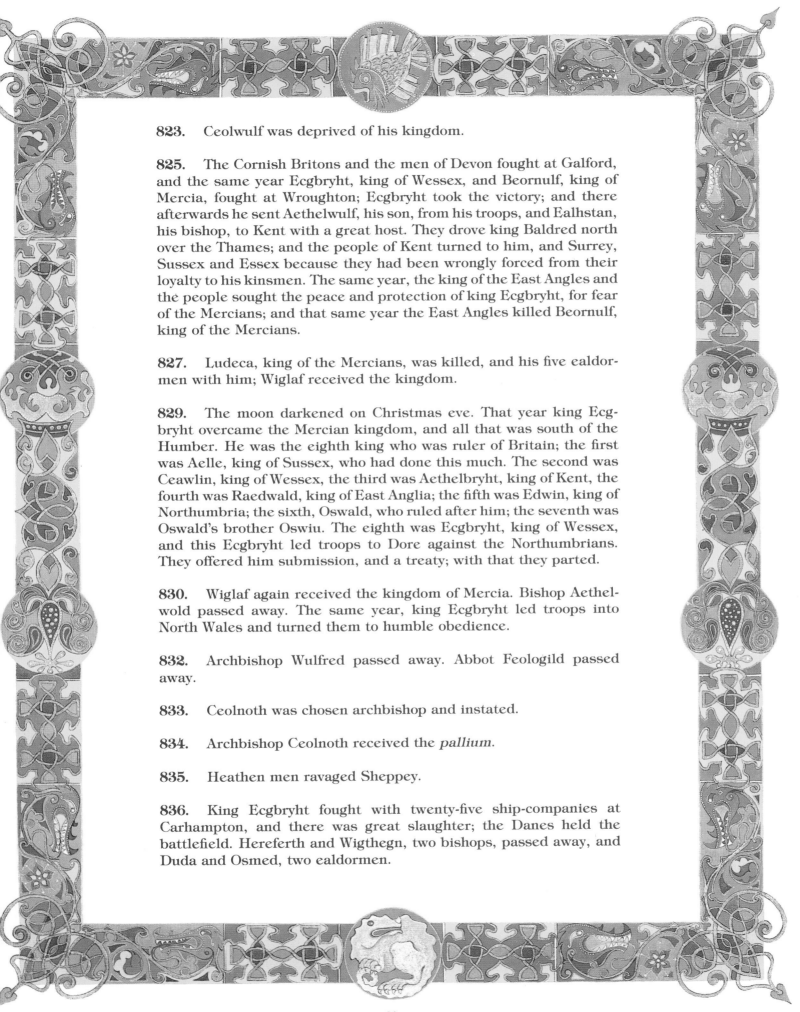

823. Ceolwulf was deprived of his kingdom.

825. The Cornish Britons and the men of Devon fought at Galford, and the same year Ecgbryht, king of Wessex, and Beornulf, king of Mercia, fought at Wroughton; Ecgbryht took the victory; and there afterwards he sent Aethelwulf, his son, from his troops, and Ealhstan, his bishop, to Kent with a great host. They drove king Baldred north over the Thames; and the people of Kent turned to him, and Surrey, Sussex and Essex because they had been wrongly forced from their loyalty to his kinsmen. The same year, the king of the East Angles and the people sought the peace and protection of king Ecgbryht, for fear of the Mercians; and that same year the East Angles killed Beornulf, king of the Mercians.

827. Ludeca, king of the Mercians, was killed, and his five ealdormen with him; Wiglaf received the kingdom.

829. The moon darkened on Christmas eve. That year king Ecgbryht overcame the Mercian kingdom, and all that was south of the Humber. He was the eighth king who was ruler of Britain; the first was Aelle, king of Sussex, who had done this much. The second was Ceawlin, king of Wessex, the third was Aethelbryht, king of Kent, the fourth was Raedwald, king of East Anglia; the fifth was Edwin, king of Northumbria; the sixth, Oswald, who ruled after him; the seventh was Oswald's brother Oswiu. The eighth was Ecgbryht, king of Wessex, and this Ecgbryht led troops to Dore against the Northumbrians. They offered him submission, and a treaty; with that they parted.

830. Wiglaf again received the kingdom of Mercia. Bishop Aethelwold passed away. The same year, king Ecgbryht led troops into North Wales and turned them to humble obedience.

832. Archbishop Wulfred passed away. Abbot Feologild passed away.

833. Ceolnoth was chosen archbishop and instated.

834. Archbishop Ceolnoth received the *pallium*.

835. Heathen men ravaged Sheppey.

836. King Ecgbryht fought with twenty-five ship-companies at Carhampton, and there was great slaughter; the Danes held the battlefield. Hereferth and Wigthegn, two bishops, passed away, and Duda and Osmed, two ealdormen.

In the first decades of the 9th century, the Vikings' occasional forays onto the English coast became a recurrent harassment; the spectacular raid on Lindisfarne, which is so graphically described in the Chronicles entry for 793, was followed sporadically by other assaults and in 835 the Viking invasions began in earnest.

Longships arrived from many northern areas, and the men they carried are usually referred to in the Chronicles as 'the force', with little indication as to whether they were Norwegian, Swedish or Danish. 'The force' was the enemy. Today our view of this pagan army is gradually changing as we begin to understand the Vikings' achievements throughout the known world as well as in England.

In many ways there had always been a considerable northern influence on Britain. Much of Northumbria and Scotland were frequently under Danish influence, or made treaties with kings of Denmark (see page 9). However, by the mid-9th century the pattern of individual war-lords had changed; instead there was a well-organized and unified intention to conquer and settle, under royal leaders who were prepared to stay through the winter, with land defences and, later, permanent settlements.

The influence of the Vikings on the Anglo-Saxon people as a whole has still to be assessed. It is certainly true to say that during the whole of the 9th century their presence, or simply the threat of their arrival, had a considerable effect on individual kingdoms, and on the political balance within England, as the country united to defeat them.

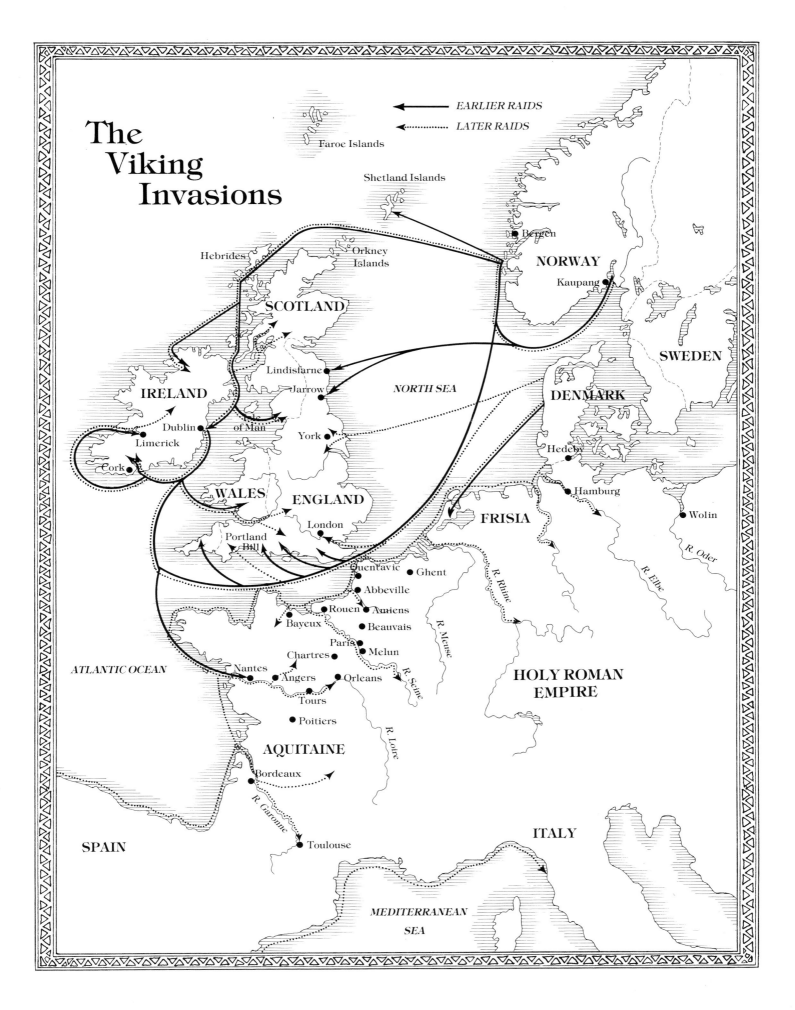

The Viking
Invasions

EARLIER RAIDS
LATER RAIDS

Faroe Islands

Shetland Islands

NORWAY

Bergen

Hebrides

Orkney
Islands

Kaupang

SCOTLAND

NORTH SEA

SWEDEN

IRELAND

Lindisfarne

Jarrow

DENMARK

Dublin

of Man

Limerick

York

Hedeby

Cork

WALES

ENGLAND

Hamburg

Wolin

London

FRISIA

R. Oder

Portland
Bill

R. Elbe

Quentavic

Ghent

R. Rhine

Abbeville

ATLANTIC OCEAN

Rouen

Amiens

Bayeux

Beauvais

R. Meuse

Nantes

Paris

Chartres

Melun

Angers

Orleans

R. Seine

HOLY ROMAN
EMPIRE

Tours

Poitiers

R. Loire

AQUITAINE

Bordeaux

R. Garonne

ITALY

SPAIN

Toulouse

*MEDITERRANEAN
SEA*

85

raiders left with their plunder. Then, after a few weeks, certainly no more than a summer, the Vikings sailed home, having seldom penetrated more than about 15 miles inland. But in 851 they stayed over the winter. That year, according to the Chronicles, 350 ships appeared in the Thames estuary and the raiders 'ruined Canterbury', put the king of Mercia to flight and 'made the greatest carnage of a heathen army that we ever heard of'.

Who were these Vikings? The word is a generic term for Scandinavians, inhabitants of what are now Sweden, Denmark and Norway. Danes predominated in the raids on southern England, while

Left: Raiders, axes raised, rush to attack the monastery at Lindisfarne, one of the jewels of the early English Church.

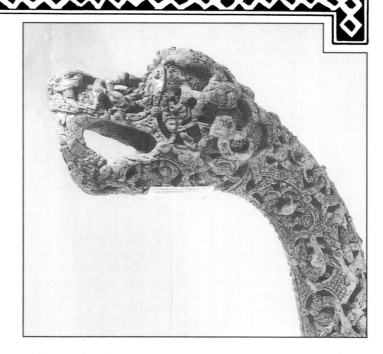

Norsemen took greater part in attacks on Northumbria, Scotland, the Isle of Man and Ireland and established a capital at York. The Vikings were ready to travel, and England was just one of the regions they reached. They crossed the Atlantic to Iceland, Greenland and North America; they marched overland through Russia to Byzantium; raided the coast of the Low Countries and Normandy, and even got as far south as Spain.

A number of different reasons impelled them to leave home. Particularly important were the pressure of a growing population on an inhospitable and unproductive land, political instability and the lure of richer, more fertile and lightly defended lands.

Opposite bottom: The wealth gathered in raids throughout Europe was put to good use in developing the best weaponry that contemporary craftsmen could fashion.

Right: One of the best sources of information about Viking ships are the funerary picture stones erected by roadsides or near burial grounds on the Swedish island of Gotland in the Baltic. Usually they depict a combination of mythological scenes and real events from the life of the warrior whom they commemorate. The detail is vivid, especially of ships' rigging and military equipment. Originally the stones were painted. Some 375 stones survive from the period between 400 and 1000; the best specimens, including this, date from the 8th century.

Above left and right: Dragon heads, similar to these found on vehicles at Oseberg, Norway, in 1904, reared up from the prow.

838. A great ship-force came to Cornwall; united with the Cornish and turned, fighting with Ecgbryht, king of Wessex. Then he marched against them and fought them at Hingston Down; there he put them to flight together, the Britons and the Danes.

839. King Ecgbryht passed away; King Offa of Mercia and Brihtric of Wessex had driven him for three years from England to the land of the Franks, before he was king. Brihtric had helped him because Offa had his daughter as queen. This Ecgbryht had reigned for thirty-seven years and seven months. His son Aethelwulf received the kingdom of Wessex; and his son Aethelstan received the kingdoms of Kent, Surrey and Sussex.

840. Ealdorman Wulfheard fought at Southampton against thirty-seven ship-companies, made great slaughter and took the victory. The same year, Wulfheard passed away, and ealdorman Aethelhun fought with the Danes at Portland, with the men of Dorset; this ealdorman was killed, and the Danes held the battlefield.

841. Ealdorman Herebryht was killed by heathen men, and many of the people of Romney Marsh with him. That year again, in Lindsey, East Anglia and Kent, many men were killed by that force.

842. There was great slaughter in London, Quentavic and Rochester.

843. King Aethelwulf fought at Carhampton against the companies of thirty-five ships, and the Danes had the power of the battlefield.

845. Ealdorman Eanulf, with the men of Somerset, bishop Ealhstan and ealdorman Osric, with the men of Dorset, fought at the mouth of the Parret with a Danish army there made great slaughter, and took the victory.

851. Ealdorman Ceorl, with the men of Devon, fought with heathen men at *Wicgeanbeorg*, made great slaughter and took the victory. The heathen men stayed over the winter, and that year three hundred and fifty ships came to the mouth of the Thames; they ruined Canterbury, put to flight Brihtwulf the Mercian king with his troops. They then went south over the Thames into Surrey, and King Aethelwulf and his son Aethelbald, with the West-Saxon troops, fought them at *Acled*, and there made the greatest carnage of a heathen army that we ever heard of; and they took the victory. That year, king Aethelstan and ealdorman Ealhere fought in ships and destroyed a great force at Sandwich; they took nine ships and put the others to flight.

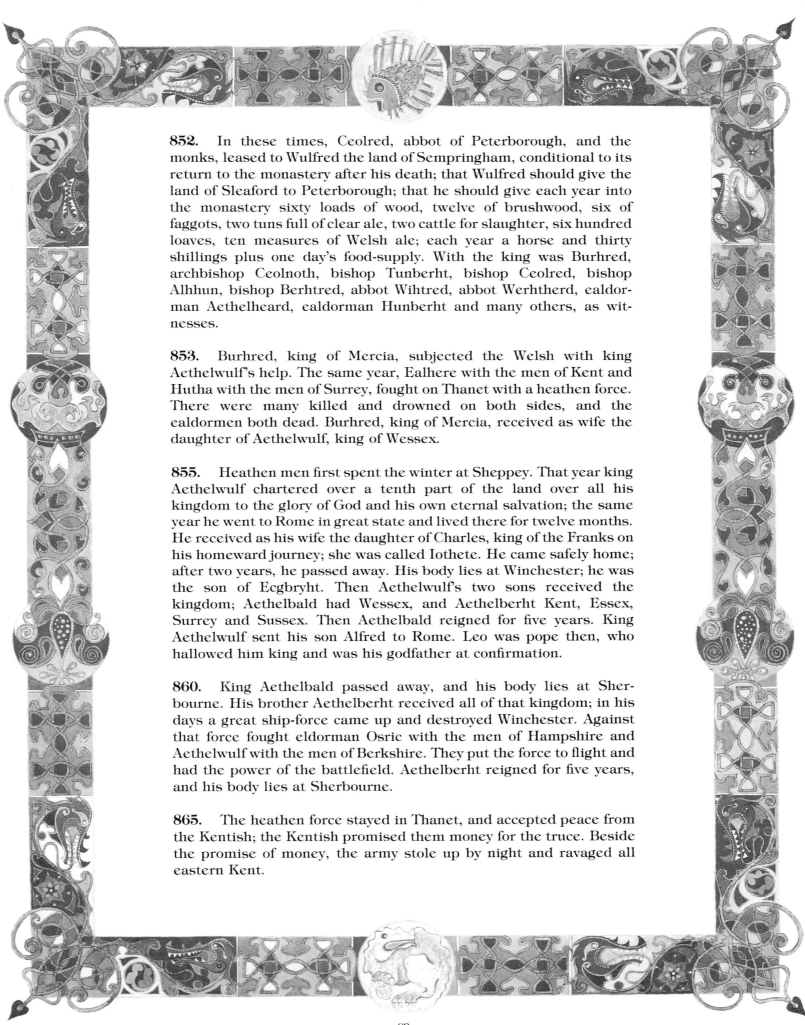

852. In these times, Ceolred, abbot of Peterborough, and the monks, leased to Wulfred the land of Sempringham, conditional to its return to the monastery after his death; that Wulfred should give the land of Sleaford to Peterborough; that he should give each year into the monastery sixty loads of wood, twelve of brushwood, six of faggots, two tuns full of clear ale, two cattle for slaughter, six hundred loaves, ten measures of Welsh ale; each year a horse and thirty shillings plus one day's food-supply. With the king was Burhred, archbishop Ceolnoth, bishop Tunberht, bishop Ceolred, bishop Alhhun, bishop Berhtred, abbot Wihtred, abbot Werhtherd, ealdorman Aethelheard, ealdorman Hunberht and many others, as witnesses.

853. Burhred, king of Mercia, subjected the Welsh with king Aethelwulf's help. The same year, Ealhere with the men of Kent and Hutha with the men of Surrey, fought on Thanet with a heathen force. There were many killed and drowned on both sides, and the ealdormen both dead. Burhred, king of Mercia, received as wife the daughter of Aethelwulf, king of Wessex.

855. Heathen men first spent the winter at Sheppey. That year king Aethelwulf chartered over a tenth part of the land over all his kingdom to the glory of God and his own eternal salvation; the same year he went to Rome in great state and lived there for twelve months. He received as his wife the daughter of Charles, king of the Franks on his homeward journey; she was called Iothete. He came safely home; after two years, he passed away. His body lies at Winchester; he was the son of Ecgbryht. Then Aethelwulf's two sons received the kingdom; Aethelbald had Wessex, and Aethelberht Kent, Essex, Surrey and Sussex. Then Aethelbald reigned for five years. King Aethelwulf sent his son Alfred to Rome. Leo was pope then, who hallowed him king and was his godfather at confirmation.

860. King Aethelbald passed away, and his body lies at Sherbourne. His brother Aethelberht received all of that kingdom; in his days a great ship-force came up and destroyed Winchester. Against that force fought eldorman Osric with the men of Hampshire and Aethelwulf with the men of Berkshire. They put the force to flight and had the power of the battlefield. Aethelberht reigned for five years, and his body lies at Sherbourne.

865. The heathen force stayed in Thanet, and accepted peace from the Kentish; the Kentish promised them money for the truce. Beside the promise of money, the army stole up by night and ravaged all eastern Kent.

In 865, a 'great heathen force' of Vikings arrived in East Anglia – not to carry out summer coastal raids, as its predecessors had, but as a permanent army of occupation. After a year spent preparing for campaign, gathering horses and assembling supplies from their defeated hosts, the army quickly marched on York. On 1 November 866 the city, caught unawares in the midst of a civil war, was taken.

When, five months later, the defeated Northumbrians finally united and assembled a rival army, it proved no match for the powerful and disciplined Vikings and was soundly defeated. The Vikings burnt churches, villages and crops within a wide radius of York. Of the library and school there, nothing remained. The brilliant cultural life of the north was obliterated, and the province was devastated, its history for the remainder of the century known only from chronicles kept elsewhere.

After a year, the Vikings moved on Nottingham, where the Mercians were forced to sue for peace.

Their next campaign, in 870, took them back to East Anglia. King Edmund was slain and the region was laid waste, churches, monasteries and all written records of the early history of the kingdom being destroyed.

Below left: Vikings attacking a burh, probably at Thetford in East Anglia. The wall has battlements and a tower. The upper part of the page shows defenders and attackers. Beneath, the Vikings are shown entering the town and slaying its inhabitants.

Below: Legend suggests that king Edmund was killed in a particularly brutal fashion and that he met death heroically. Both Danes and English quickly came to regard him as a saint; his shrine was much visited by pilgrims, and he was placed in the calendar of the Church.

(Both illustrations from a 12th-century manuscript written and illuminated at Bury St Edmunds.)

Right: This stone, and the foundations of one wall, are all that remains of the monastery at Peterborough, burnt by the Vikings in 870: 'they made that which was very great such that it became nothing.' The figures on the stone represent Christ, Mary, St Peter and other Apostles; above the figures there is typical Anglo-Saxon ornamentation.

Bottom: These Scandinavian warriors have outsized boar ornaments on their heads – symbol of bravery in their own and Celtic and Anglo-Saxon tradition.

Immediately below: Memorial penny commemorating the martyrdom of Edmund, issued in about 900 by the Christianized Danes of East Anglia.

866. Aethelred, Aethelberht's brother, received the kingdom of Wessex. That year a great heathen force came into English land, and they took winter-quarters in East Anglia; there they were horsed, and they made peace with them.

867. The army went from East Anglia over the Humber's mouth to York in Northumbria. There was great discord in this people amongst themselves; they had overthrown their king, Osbriht, and had taken an unnatural king, Aelle. They decided late in the year that they were going to fight the others, yet they gathered a great army and sought the force at York, then broke into the fort; some went in and there was immeasurable slaughter among the Northumbrians, some inside and some outside. The kings were both killed, and the survivors made peace with the force. The same year, bishop Ealhstan died; he had the bishopric at Sherbourne for fifty years, and his body lies there in the churchyard.

868. The same force went into Mercia to Nottingham, and there took winter quarters. Burhred, king of Mercia, and his counsellors asked Aethelred, king of Wessex, and Alfred his brother that they help them, that they fight against the force. Then they went with the West-Saxon troops into Mercia to Nottingham, and the force met them at the fortifications. They besieged them. There was no heavy fighting, and Mercia made peace with the force.

869. The force went again to York, and stayed there for a year.

870. The force went over Mercia to East Anglia, and took winter quarters at Thetford. In that year, St. Edmund the king fought against them and the Danes took the victory, killed the king, and overcame all the land. They destroyed all the churches they came to; the same time they came to Peterborough, they burned and broke, killed the abbot and monks, and all they found there. They made that which was very great such that it became nothing. That year, archbishop Ceolnoth died.

871. The force rode to Reading in Wessex, and the third day, the two Danish eorls rode up-country. Ealdorman Aethelwulf met them at Englefield; he fought with them there and took the victory. There the second was killed, whose name was Sidrac. Four days later, king Aethelred and his brother Alfred led a great troop to Reading and fought the force, there was much slaughter on both sides. Ealdorman Aethewulf was killed, and the Danes had the power of the battlefield. Four days later, king Aethelred and his brother Alfred fought the whole force at Ashdown. They were in two groups: in one were Basecg and Halfdane, the heathen kings, and in the other were the eorls.

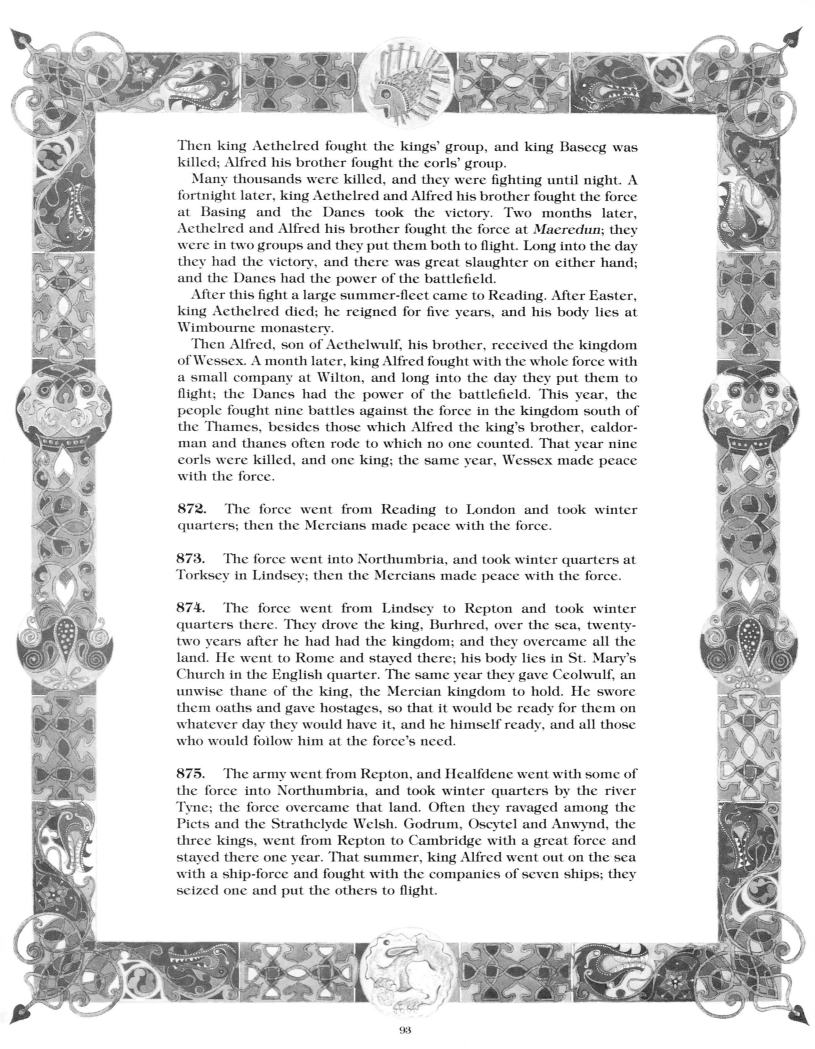

Then king Aethelred fought the kings' group, and king Basecg was killed; Alfred his brother fought the eorls' group.

Many thousands were killed, and they were fighting until night. A fortnight later, king Aethelred and Alfred his brother fought the force at Basing and the Danes took the victory. Two months later, Aethelred and Alfred his brother fought the force at *Maeredun*; they were in two groups and they put them both to flight. Long into the day they had the victory, and there was great slaughter on either hand; and the Danes had the power of the battlefield.

After this fight a large summer-fleet came to Reading. After Easter, king Aethelred died; he reigned for five years, and his body lies at Wimbourne monastery.

Then Alfred, son of Aethelwulf, his brother, received the kingdom of Wessex. A month later, king Alfred fought with the whole force with a small company at Wilton, and long into the day they put them to flight; the Danes had the power of the battlefield. This year, the people fought nine battles against the force in the kingdom south of the Thames, besides those which Alfred the king's brother, ealdorman and thanes often rode to which no one counted. That year nine eorls were killed, and one king; the same year, Wessex made peace with the force.

872. The force went from Reading to London and took winter quarters; then the Mercians made peace with the force.

873. The force went into Northumbria, and took winter quarters at Torksey in Lindsey; then the Mercians made peace with the force.

874. The force went from Lindsey to Repton and took winter quarters there. They drove the king, Burhred, over the sea, twenty-two years after he had had the kingdom; and they overcame all the land. He went to Rome and stayed there; his body lies in St. Mary's Church in the English quarter. The same year they gave Ceolwulf, an unwise thane of the king, the Mercian kingdom to hold. He swore them oaths and gave hostages, so that it would be ready for them on whatever day they would have it, and he himself ready, and all those who would follow him at the force's need.

875. The army went from Repton, and Healfdene went with some of the force into Northumbria, and took winter quarters by the river Tyne; the force overcame that land. Often they ravaged among the Picts and the Strathclyde Welsh. Godrum, Oscytel and Anwynd, the three kings, went from Repton to Cambridge with a great force and stayed one year. That summer, king Alfred went out on the sea with a ship-force and fought with the companies of seven ships; they seized one and put the others to flight.

Left: Portrait of Alfred from Matthew Paris' Historia Major. Paris (c. 1200–59), a Benedictine monk who trained at St Albans and who became the best 13th-century chronicler, described Alfred as the first king to reign over all England and as a great scholar.

The accounts of the reign of Alfred (871–99) mark a change in the Chronicles. For the first centuries the Chroniclers provided no more than a catalogue of isolated events. As they came nearer their own time, they became more circumstantial and expansive. Alfred emerges as a more complex and forceful king than any earlier ruler, and his devotion to his subjects and his innovative abilities are made very evident. There is no evidence that Alfred himself ordered the Chronicles to be compiled, but his well-known interest in learning and history would certainly have stimulated such a project. The story of the Scandinavian invasions in the early 9th century was written during Alfred's reign, and the account of Alfred's own battles makes skilful propaganda for the royal house of Wessex.

Alfred came to the throne of Wessex in 871 on the death of his brother Aethelred, at a moment when English fortunes were low. Throughout his reign, his chief preoccupation was to ward off Danish invasions. Even though much of Wessex was taken in 878, by the late 890s a balance of power had been achieved. The Danes held the Danelaw, the area east of Watling Street (the Roman road running from London to Chester); Alfred held Mercia, where he was recognized as overlord, and his own Wessex kingdom.

Below: The Pastoral Care was a manual of guidance for bishops, produced by Pope Gregory the Great (c. 540–604). In a prefatory poem to his edition, Alfred explained that he had translated the work, and sent copies throughout the kingdom, 'for those who know only a little Latin'. He laments the decline of English learning and announces his intention of reviving interest in learning and books. This page is from the copy of the Pastoral Care sent to Worcester.

Above: Coin of Alfred as king of the English, minted in about 880. 'England' then meant the land to the south and west of Watling Street.

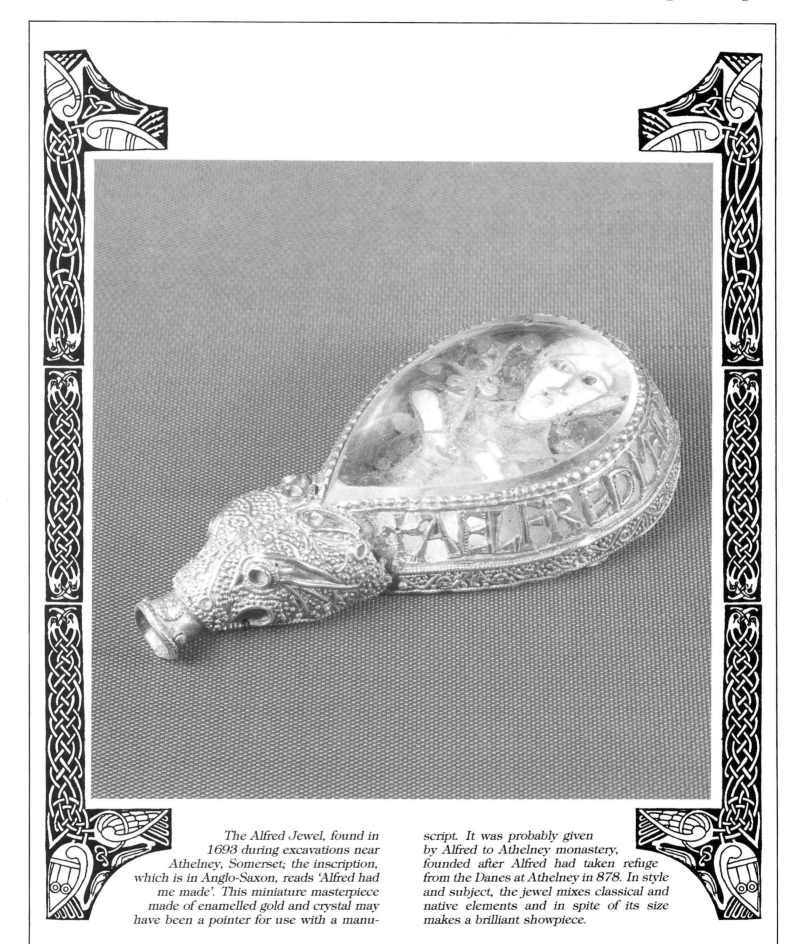

The Alfred Jewel, found in 1693 during excavations near Athelney, Somerset; the inscription, which is in Anglo-Saxon, reads 'Alfred had me made'. This miniature masterpiece made of enamelled gold and crystal may have been a pointer for use with a manuscript. It was probably given by Alfred to Athelney monastery, founded after Alfred had taken refuge from the Danes at Athelney in 878. In style and subject, the jewel mixes classical and native elements and in spite of its size makes a brilliant showpiece.

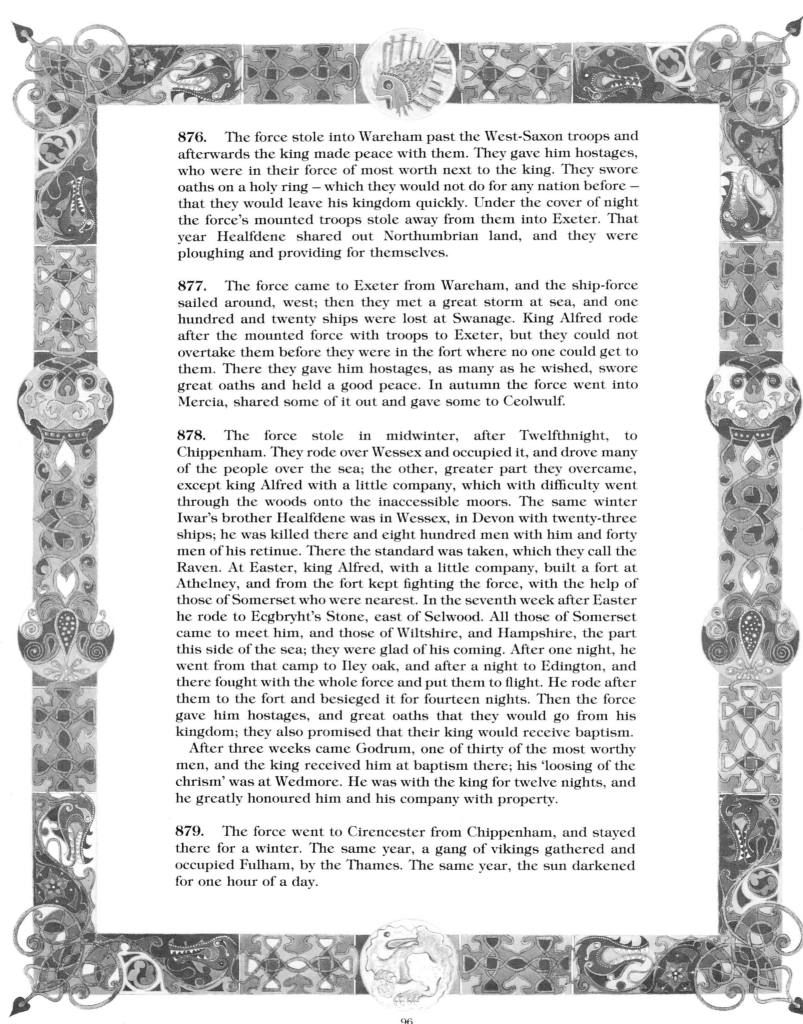

876. The force stole into Wareham past the West-Saxon troops and afterwards the king made peace with them. They gave him hostages, who were in their force of most worth next to the king. They swore oaths on a holy ring – which they would not do for any nation before – that they would leave his kingdom quickly. Under the cover of night the force's mounted troops stole away from them into Exeter. That year Healfdene shared out Northumbrian land, and they were ploughing and providing for themselves.

877. The force came to Exeter from Wareham, and the ship-force sailed around, west; then they met a great storm at sea, and one hundred and twenty ships were lost at Swanage. King Alfred rode after the mounted force with troops to Exeter, but they could not overtake them before they were in the fort where no one could get to them. There they gave him hostages, as many as he wished, swore great oaths and held a good peace. In autumn the force went into Mercia, shared some of it out and gave some to Ceolwulf.

878. The force stole in midwinter, after Twelfthnight, to Chippenham. They rode over Wessex and occupied it, and drove many of the people over the sea; the other, greater part they overcame, except king Alfred with a little company, which with difficulty went through the woods onto the inaccessible moors. The same winter Iwar's brother Healfdene was in Wessex, in Devon with twenty-three ships; he was killed there and eight hundred men with him and forty men of his retinue. There the standard was taken, which they call the Raven. At Easter, king Alfred, with a little company, built a fort at Athelney, and from the fort kept fighting the force, with the help of those of Somerset who were nearest. In the seventh week after Easter he rode to Ecgbryht's Stone, east of Selwood. All those of Somerset came to meet him, and those of Wiltshire, and Hampshire, the part this side of the sea; they were glad of his coming. After one night, he went from that camp to Iley oak, and after a night to Edington, and there fought with the whole force and put them to flight. He rode after them to the fort and besieged it for fourteen nights. Then the force gave him hostages, and great oaths that they would go from his kingdom; they also promised that their king would receive baptism.

After three weeks came Godrum, one of thirty of the most worthy men, and the king received him at baptism there; his 'loosing of the chrism' was at Wedmore. He was with the king for twelve nights, and he greatly honoured him and his company with property.

879. The force went to Cirencester from Chippenham, and stayed there for a winter. The same year, a gang of vikings gathered and occupied Fulham, by the Thames. The same year, the sun darkened for one hour of a day.

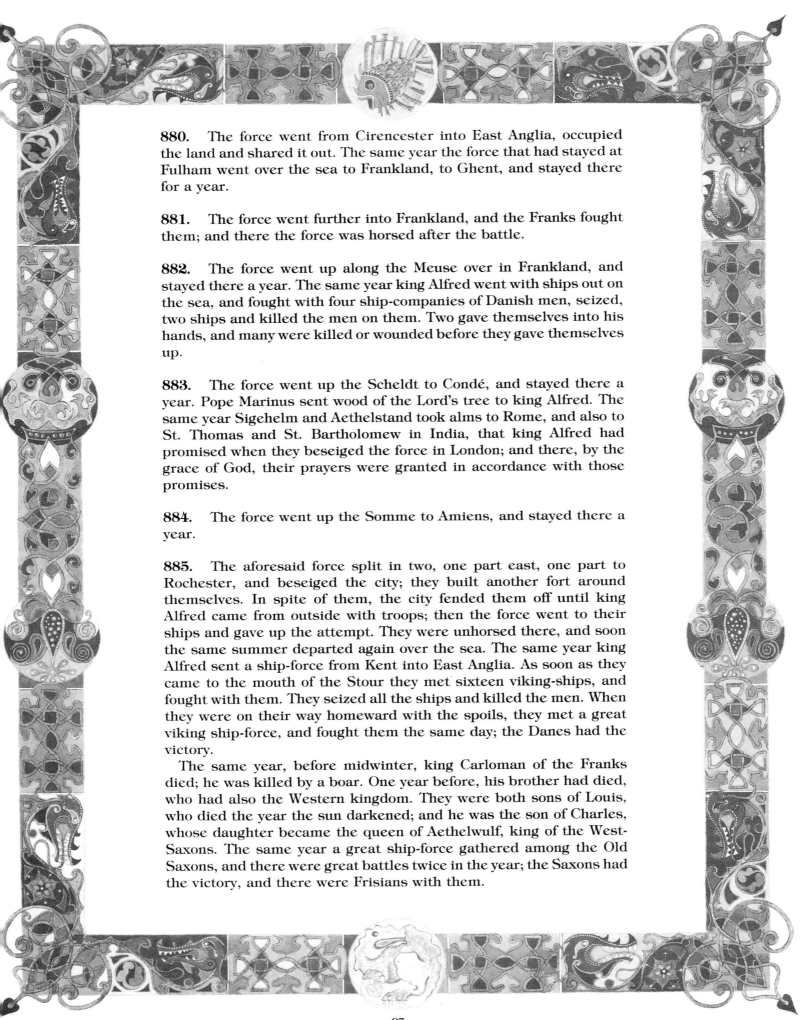

880. The force went from Cirencester into East Anglia, occupied the land and shared it out. The same year the force that had stayed at Fulham went over the sea to Frankland, to Ghent, and stayed there for a year.

881. The force went further into Frankland, and the Franks fought them; and there the force was horsed after the battle.

882. The force went up along the Meuse over in Frankland, and stayed there a year. The same year king Alfred went with ships out on the sea, and fought with four ship-companies of Danish men, seized, two ships and killed the men on them. Two gave themselves into his hands, and many were killed or wounded before they gave themselves up.

883. The force went up the Scheldt to Condé, and stayed there a year. Pope Marinus sent wood of the Lord's tree to king Alfred. The same year Sigehelm and Aethelstand took alms to Rome, and also to St. Thomas and St. Bartholomew in India, that king Alfred had promised when they beseiged the force in London; and there, by the grace of God, their prayers were granted in accordance with those promises.

884. The force went up the Somme to Amiens, and stayed there a year.

885. The aforesaid force split in two, one part east, one part to Rochester, and beseiged the city; they built another fort around themselves. In spite of them, the city fended them off until king Alfred came from outside with troops; then the force went to their ships and gave up the attempt. They were unhorsed there, and soon the same summer departed again over the sea. The same year king Alfred sent a ship-force from Kent into East Anglia. As soon as they came to the mouth of the Stour they met sixteen viking-ships, and fought with them. They seized all the ships and killed the men. When they were on their way homeward with the spoils, they met a great viking ship-force, and fought them the same day; the Danes had the victory.

The same year, before midwinter, king Carloman of the Franks died; he was killed by a boar. One year before, his brother had died, who had also the Western kingdom. They were both sons of Louis, who died the year the sun darkened; and he was the son of Charles, whose daughter became the queen of Aethelwulf, king of the West-Saxons. The same year a great ship-force gathered among the Old Saxons, and there were great battles twice in the year; the Saxons had the victory, and there were Frisians with them.

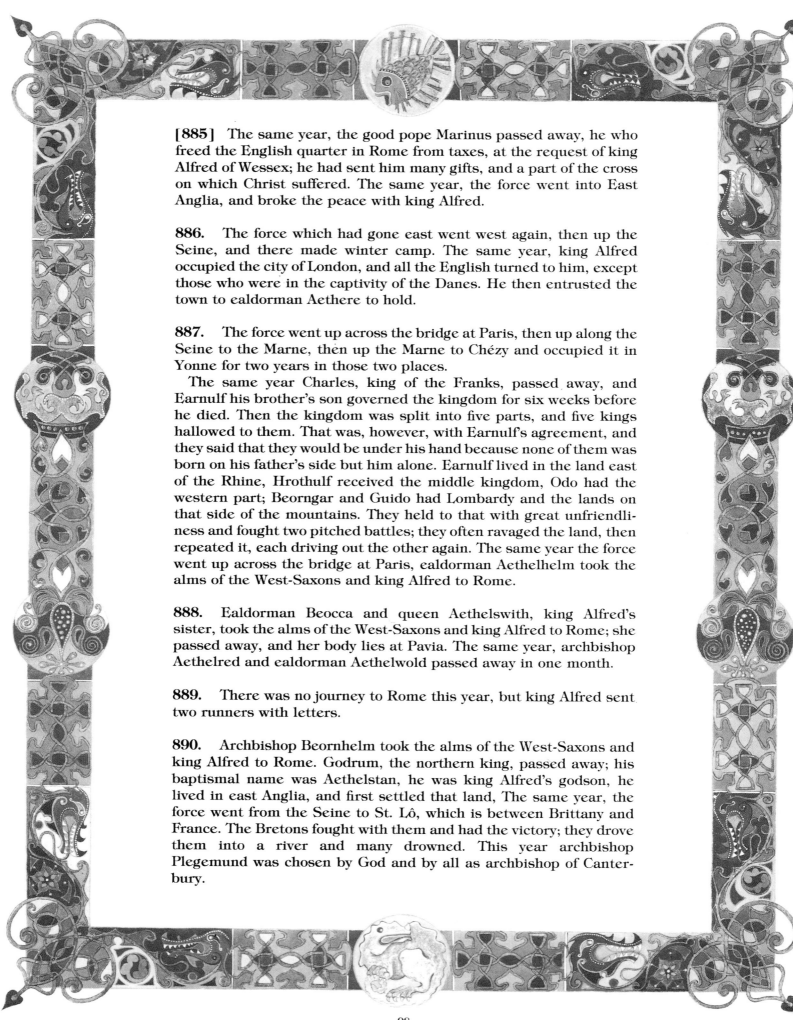

[885] The same year, the good pope Marinus passed away, he who freed the English quarter in Rome from taxes, at the request of king Alfred of Wessex; he had sent him many gifts, and a part of the cross on which Christ suffered. The same year, the force went into East Anglia, and broke the peace with king Alfred.

886. The force which had gone east went west again, then up the Seine, and there made winter camp. The same year, king Alfred occupied the city of London, and all the English turned to him, except those who were in the captivity of the Danes. He then entrusted the town to ealdorman Aethere to hold.

887. The force went up across the bridge at Paris, then up along the Seine to the Marne, then up the Marne to Chézy and occupied it in Yonne for two years in those two places.

The same year Charles, king of the Franks, passed away, and Earnulf his brother's son governed the kingdom for six weeks before he died. Then the kingdom was split into five parts, and five kings hallowed to them. That was, however, with Earnulf's agreement, and they said that they would be under his hand because none of them was born on his father's side but him alone. Earnulf lived in the land east of the Rhine, Hrothulf received the middle kingdom, Odo had the western part; Beorngar and Guido had Lombardy and the lands on that side of the mountains. They held to that with great unfriendliness and fought two pitched battles; they often ravaged the land, then repeated it, each driving out the other again. The same year the force went up across the bridge at Paris, ealdorman Aethelhelm took the alms of the West-Saxons and king Alfred to Rome.

888. Ealdorman Beocca and queen Aethelswith, king Alfred's sister, took the alms of the West-Saxons and king Alfred to Rome; she passed away, and her body lies at Pavia. The same year, archbishop Aethelred and ealdorman Aethelwold passed away in one month.

889. There was no journey to Rome this year, but king Alfred sent two runners with letters.

890. Archbishop Beornhelm took the alms of the West-Saxons and king Alfred to Rome. Godrum, the northern king, passed away; his baptismal name was Aethelstan, he was king Alfred's godson, he lived in east Anglia, and first settled that land, The same year, the force went from the Seine to St. Lô, which is between Brittany and France. The Bretons fought with them and had the victory; they drove them into a river and many drowned. This year archbishop Plegemund was chosen by God and by all as archbishop of Canterbury.

891. The force went east, and king Earnulf fought with the mounted troops, before the ships came, with the East Franks, Saxons and Bavarians, and put it to flight. Three Scots came to king Alfred, in a boat without oars from Ireland, from whence they had stolen away because for the love of God they wished to be in exile, they did not care where. The boat in which they came was worked from two and a half hides; they took with them food for seven days. They came to land on the seventh night in Cornwall, and went soon to king Alfred. Thus were they called: Dubslane, Macbeth, and Maelinmum. Swiftneh, the best scholar among the Scots, passed away. The same year, after Easter, during the Rogation days or before, the star appeared which men call in latin *cometa*; some men say in English that it is a hairy star, because long beams stand out, sometimes on one side, sometimes on every side.

892. In this year, the great force of which we spoke before went again from the east kingdom westward to Boulogne, and there got ships, so that in one trip they set out with horses and all, then came up the mouth of the Lympne with two hundred and fifty ships. This rivermouth is in East Kent at the east end of the great wood we call Andred, The Weald. This wood is by east and west one hundred and twelve miles long, or longer, and thirty miles broad. The river of which we have spoken runs out of these woods, and on the river they took their ships up to the forest four miles from the outward mouth, and there broke into a fort; in the stronghold there were only a few peasants staying, and it was half-built. Soon after that came Haesten with eighty ships, up in the mouth of the Thames. He built himself a fort at Milton Royal, and the other force at Appledore.

893. This year, twelve months since they had built the fort in the eastern kingdom, the Northumbrians and East Anglians had given oaths, and the East Anglians six chief hostages. Yet contrary to that treaty, as often as the other armies went out with all their forces, they went out, either with one of them or on their own behalf, alone. Then king Alfred gathered his troops and went so that he camped between the two forces, near to the fort in the woods and the one by the water, and so that he might reach either if they meant to seek open country. Then they went along in the woods in bands and mounted troops, on whichever side was then without an army. Other bands, from the army or the towns, sought they day and night. The king had split his troops in two, so that half the men were always home, and half out, except those who had to hold the boroughs. The force did not come out in full of those two camps more than twice, once when they first came to the land, before the troops were gathered, and the other time when they wished to leave the camps. They took much plunder, then started north over the Thames into Essex to meet the ships.

Above: Sword that may have been used in Alfred's campaigns, found at Abingdon.

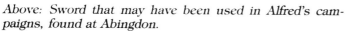

Right: At the Battle of Reading in 871 the Wessex forces tried, unsuccessfully, to attack the Danish fortifications. This sword was found on the site in 1831, together with the skeleton of a warrior, possibly the sword owner, and his horse.

By 870, the Vikings had taken all England bar Wessex. The next year, Alfred 'made peace' with them, providing a large payment or Danegeld. The Viking army divided. One part settled in Yorkshire, began to farm the land and gradually became integrated with the existing inhabitants. The other followed Godrum to Cambridge, from where, in 876, yet another assault was launched on Wessex. Having lost 5000 men at sea, the Vikings were forced to retreat to Mercia, but in January 878, 'after Twelfthnight', they surprised Alfred's army as it was celebrating the holy feast at Chippenham. Central and western Wessex were immediately occupied, and Alfred fled into the Somerset fen country. In May, however, he gathered a large army, marched to meet Godrum and finally won a decisive battle at Edington, 15 miles from Chippenham.

By the terms of the Peace of Wedmore which followed, Godrum converted to Christianity and withdrew his army, first to Cirencester and then, the following year, over the Wessex border to East Anglia, where they 'occupied the land and shared it out'. There an Anglo-Danish England gradually emerged from the devastation of war, its character shaped by the surprisingly peaceful mingling of former enemies.

Above and below left: Alfred built a fort on this site at Athelney, Somerset, in 878, from which he rallied his forces for his successful attack on Godrum at Edington on the northern ridge of Salisbury Plain.

Right: The Peace of Wedmore defined the borders of the Danelaw and established the position and monetary worth of various ranks of Danish and Saxon citizens.

[893] The army rode in front and fought them at Farnham, put the force to flight and seized the plunder. The Danes fled over the Thames where there was no ford, and up the Colne onto an island. The army besieged them for as long as they had food; but they had done their term of army service and used up their provisions. The king was on his way there with the shire then doing him service. When he was going towards them, they were going home. The Danish stayed behind because their king was wounded in the fighting, so that they could not move him.

The Danes who lived in Northumbria and East Anglia gathered some hundred ships and went around the south, and some forty ships went around the north and besieged a fort in Devonshire by the north coast. Those who went south besieged Exeter. When the king heard that he went west towards Exeter with the whole army, but for a very inconsiderable part of the people from the east. They went on till they came to London, then with the city-dwellers and the aid that came from the west, went east to Benfleet. Haesten had arrived there with his army, which had occupied Milton Royal, and also that great force had come that had stayed in the mouth of the Lympne at Appledore. Haesten had earlier built that fort at Benfleet; he had gone out plundering, and the great force was at home. The English went to them, put the force to flight, broke into the fort and seized all that was inside, in property, women, also children, and brought all to London, and broke up all the ships, or burnt them up, or brought them either to London or Rochester. Haesten's wife and two sons were brought to the king, and he gave them back to him, because one was his godson and the other ealdorman Aethelred's. They had received them as such before Haestan came to Benfleet, and he had given them hostages and oaths, and the king had given him much property; so he did again when he gave back the boy and the woman. But as soon as they came to Benfleet and built the fort, he ravaged in the kingdom, the same area which his son's godfather Aethelred had to hold; again, this other time he was plundering in that same kingdom was when his fort was stormed.

Then the king went west with the army to Exeter, as I said before, and the force had then besieged the town; when he had arrived there, they went to their ships. When he was busy with the force there in the west, the two other forces were both gathered at Shoebury in Essex, and they made forts there. Together they went up the Thames, and many reinforcements came to them from both East Anglia and Northumbria. They went up the Thames until they reached the Severn, then up the Severn. Then gathered ealdorman Aethelred, ealdorman Aethelhelm, ealdorman Aethelnoth and the king's thanes who were then staying at the forts, from each town east of the Parret, both west of Selwood and east, north of the Thames, and west of the Severn; and also some part of the North Welsh.

Left: Alfred's boats were probably like this, a little too large to manoeuvre comfortably in coastal waters but successful on the open sea. His new ships were manned by Frisian crews, since English sailors and shipbuilders had as yet little experience of warships. (Boat-building from an early 11th-century English manuscript.)

Bottom: One of the burhs Alfred built was at Wallingford, where the Ridgeway crosses the Thames. It covered the site now occupied by the modern town and had a rampart 3300 yards long.

Below: Soldiers manning a burh, as depicted in an early 11th-century manuscript.

Alfred learnt from his enemies. Following the Danish example, he constructed burhs, or defensive strongholds, along the borders of his kingdom after the new peace treaty. Some were in rebuilt Roman sites, others, such as the one at Oxford, were new. The burhs were permanent defensive units and were designed to hold provisions and provide shelter for local citizens, who were required to man them.

Later, in the entry for 896, the Chronicles describe the new ships designed by Alfred. He went to sea three times to fight the Danes and was the first English king to understand the importance of creating a fleet to engage the enemy before it reached land, although he had little success in naval engagements.

Threats to Wessex did not completely stop after the Peace of Wedmore, and a new band of Vikings reached the Thames in 880, although they turned back almost immediately and spent several years campaigning in France, as the Chronicles relate in some detail. There were further attacks in 885, and a major invasion in 892 took several years to repel. After that, disturbances continued throughout the last years of Alfred's reign.

Within England, Alfred made sure of a friendly and strong Mercia between the Danelaw and his own lands by marrying his daughter to Aethere, ealdorman of Mercia. The marriage cemented the alliance between Wessex and Mercia, and in 886 Alfred was able to drive the Danes out of London and, with Aethere as governor, rebuild, fortify and repopulate it. The city now became a centre of trade and defence for the whole of England.

Opposite: The Codex Aureus, an 8th-century copy of the four Gospels, written and illuminated at Canterbury. During Alfred's reign it was ransomed from the Danes by an ealdorman named Alfred and his wife and presented to Christ Church monastery at Canterbury. To commemorate their gift, the couple had an inscription placed around one of the manuscript's pages.

Below left: The Vikings landed at Appledore, Devon, in 892 and were not repulsed for more than a year. The unsettled state of Wessex must have led many people to hide their precious objects, and it was not until 1774 that this silver scourge was found in Cornwall, at Trewhiddle.

Below: In the Danelaw, pagan and Christian styles and beliefs soon mixed. On the early 10th-century Middleton Cross, from North Yorkshire, a pagan warrior with sword, shield, helmet and axe is depicted on a Christian artefact.

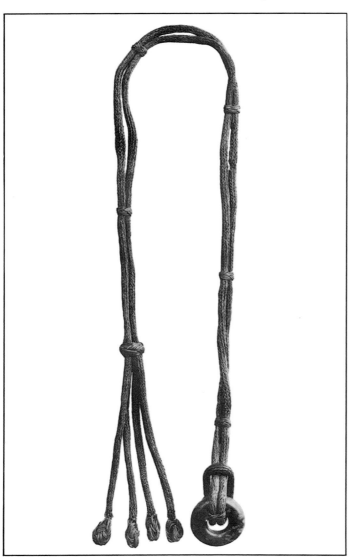

[893] When they were all gathered together, they went up behind the force at Buttington on Severn shore, and surrounded them on every side in a stronghold. When they had camped for many weeks on the banks of the river, and the king was in the west, in Devon with the shipforce, they were weighed down by want of food and had eaten a great number of their horses. Others were dead of hunger. They went out to those men camped on the east side of the river, and fought with them; the Christians had the victory. Ordheh, the king's thane, was killed, and many other king's thanes; of the Danes there was made much slaughter, and the part that came away were saved by flight. When those in Essex came to their fort and to their ships, they gathered what was left of their force from East Anglia and Northumbria in a great force before winter, made safe their women, their ships and their property in East Anglia, and went in one stretch, by day and night, till they came to an empty town in the Wirral, which is called Chester. Then the army could not come up behind them before they were in the fort. They besieged the fort outside nevertheless, for some two days, seized all the cattle there were outside, killed the men they cut off outside the fort, and burnt the corn — or their horses ate it in every field. That was twelve months after they had come here over the sea.

894. Soon after that, this year, the force went from the Wirral into North Wales, because they could not stay there; that was because they were deprived of both corn and cattle, which had been ravaged. When they went out of North Wales again with the plunder they had taken there, they went over the land of Northumbria, and East Anglia, so that the army could not overtake them, until they came to east Essex, on an island out in the sea that is called Mersea. Then the force which had besieged Exeter turned homewards again, ravaged up in Sussex near Chichester, and the town-dwellers put them to flight, killed many hundreds of them, and seized some of their ships.

Then, the same year before winter, the Danish who sat out on Mersea pulled their ships up in the Thames, then up the Lea. That was two years after they had come over the sea.

895. In the same year the aforesaid force built a fort by the Lea twenty miles above the city of London. Later in the summer went a great number of the city-dwellers and also other people, till they reached the Danish fort; there they were put to flight, and some four of the king's thanes were killed. Later in the autumn the king camped near the town while they reaped their corn so that the Danes could not prevent the reaping. One day the king rode up along the river, and saw where one might block the river, so that they could not bring out their ships; so they did, and built two forts, on boths sides of the river.

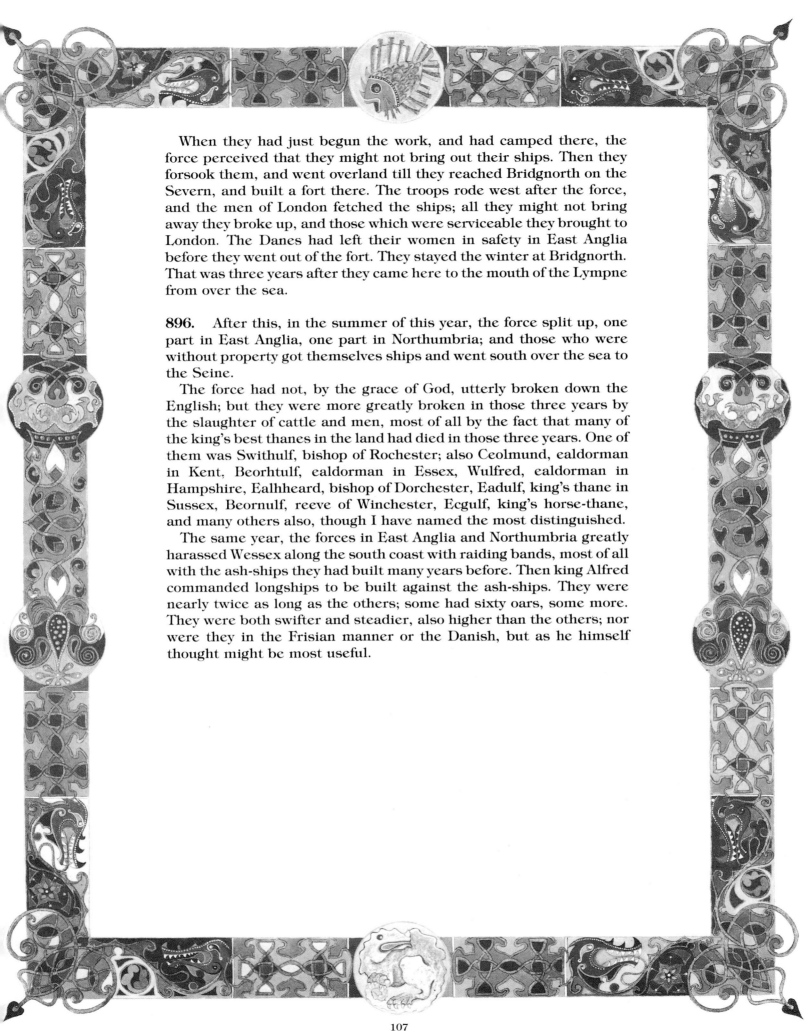

When they had just begun the work, and had camped there, the force perceived that they might not bring out their ships. Then they forsook them, and went overland till they reached Bridgnorth on the Severn, and built a fort there. The troops rode west after the force, and the men of London fetched the ships; all they might not bring away they broke up, and those which were serviceable they brought to London. The Danes had left their women in safety in East Anglia before they went out of the fort. They stayed the winter at Bridgnorth. That was three years after they came here to the mouth of the Lympne from over the sea.

896.   After this, in the summer of this year, the force split up, one part in East Anglia, one part in Northumbria; and those who were without property got themselves ships and went south over the sea to the Seine.

The force had not, by the grace of God, utterly broken down the English; but they were more greatly broken in those three years by the slaughter of cattle and men, most of all by the fact that many of the king's best thanes in the land had died in those three years. One of them was Swithulf, bishop of Rochester; also Ceolmund, ealdorman in Kent, Beorhtulf, ealdorman in Essex, Wulfred, ealdorman in Hampshire, Ealhheard, bishop of Dorchester, Eadulf, king's thane in Sussex, Beornulf, reeve of Winchester, Ecgulf, king's horse-thane, and many others also, though I have named the most distinguished.

The same year, the forces in East Anglia and Northumbria greatly harassed Wessex along the south coast with raiding bands, most of all with the ash-ships they had built many years before. Then king Alfred commanded longships to be built against the ash-ships. They were nearly twice as long as the others; some had sixty oars, some more. They were both swifter and steadier, also higher than the others; nor were they in the Frisian manner or the Danish, but as he himself thought might be most useful.

The Viking raids, which began as isolated attacks in the late 8th century and developed into a colonization movement from the mid-860s onwards, were not confined to the north and east of England. There were also Norse settlements in Scotland, the Isle of Man, and Ireland where a community grew up based on Dublin. By the early 10th century, the Irish-Norse themselves were expanding, invading Mercia and threatening the Danelaw. York was taken in 919, and Norse kings ruled there, on and off, until Eiric Bloodaxe was expelled and killed in 954.

Excavations in Norway and Sweden have produced a number of reminders of the Norse presence in England and Ireland. Some valuables were looted from their original homes and often melted down. Others may have been purchases or the gains of quite peaceful trading.

Above: Head of an 8th-century bishop's crozier from Ireland, found on the Swedish island of Helgo.

Left: 8th-century Irish casket or reliquary. Its new Viking owner scratched the name Rannveig on it in runes.

Opposite, top left: Ezra's study from the Codex Amiatinus, written at Jarrow on the orders of the first abbot, Ceolfrith (d. 716). He is using a book mount similar to the one on page 110, found in Norway. The manuscript, which influenced the illuminators of the Lindisfarne Gospels, is copied from an Italian original.

Below: Bucket, of either Irish or English origin, found in a Norwegian excavation.

Above: Figure of a man, probably from a reliquary, found in a Norwegian excavation.

Right: *Bronzework of Northumbrian origin found in a Norwegian grave. Originally a decorative book cover, it may have been seized by a Viking warrior, who took it home, punched a hole in it and made it into a pendant.*

Below: *Irish incense burner, discovered in a woman's grave in Norway.*

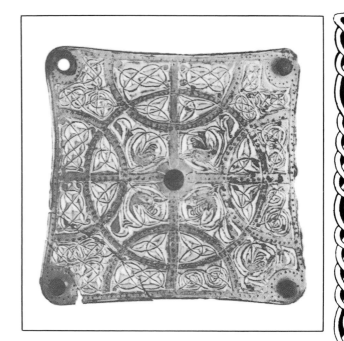

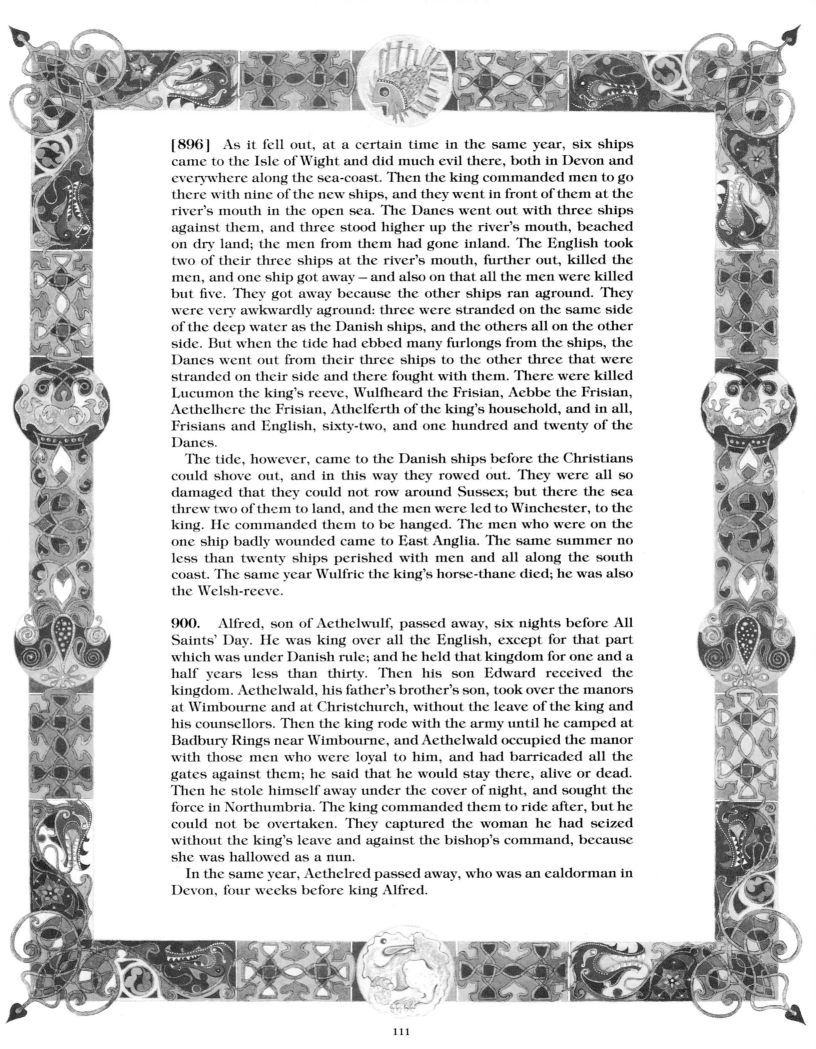

[896] As it fell out, at a certain time in the same year, six ships came to the Isle of Wight and did much evil there, both in Devon and everywhere along the sea-coast. Then the king commanded men to go there with nine of the new ships, and they went in front of them at the river's mouth in the open sea. The Danes went out with three ships against them, and three stood higher up the river's mouth, beached on dry land; the men from them had gone inland. The English took two of their three ships at the river's mouth, further out, killed the men, and one ship got away – and also on that all the men were killed but five. They got away because the other ships ran aground. They were very awkwardly aground: three were stranded on the same side of the deep water as the Danish ships, and the others all on the other side. But when the tide had ebbed many furlongs from the ships, the Danes went out from their three ships to the other three that were stranded on their side and there fought with them. There were killed Lucumon the king's reeve, Wulfheard the Frisian, Aebbe the Frisian, Aethelhere the Frisian, Athelferth of the king's household, and in all, Frisians and English, sixty-two, and one hundred and twenty of the Danes.

The tide, however, came to the Danish ships before the Christians could shove out, and in this way they rowed out. They were all so damaged that they could not row around Sussex; but there the sea threw two of them to land, and the men were led to Winchester, to the king. He commanded them to be hanged. The men who were on the one ship badly wounded came to East Anglia. The same summer no less than twenty ships perished with men and all along the south coast. The same year Wulfric the king's horse-thane died; he was also the Welsh-reeve.

900.   Alfred, son of Aethelwulf, passed away, six nights before All Saints' Day. He was king over all the English, except for that part which was under Danish rule; and he held that kingdom for one and a half years less than thirty. Then his son Edward received the kingdom. Aethelwald, his father's brother's son, took over the manors at Wimbourne and at Christchurch, without the leave of the king and his counsellors. Then the king rode with the army until he camped at Badbury Rings near Wimbourne, and Aethelwald occupied the manor with those men who were loyal to him, and had barricaded all the gates against them; he said that he would stay there, alive or dead. Then he stole himself away under the cover of night, and sought the force in Northumbria. The king commanded them to ride after, but he could not be overtaken. They captured the woman he had seized without the king's leave and against the bishop's command, because she was hallowed as a nun.

In the same year, Aethelred passed away, who was an ealdorman in Devon, four weeks before king Alfred.

902. Athelwald came here over the sea with all the ships he could get, and in Essex they submitted to him.

903. Aethelwald lured the East Anglian force into breaking the peace, so that they ravaged over the land of Mercia, until they came to Cricklade, went over the Thames there, seized all they could carry off both in and around Braydon and then went home-ward again. Then king Edward went after them, as quickly as he could gather his army, and ravaged all their land between Devil's Dyke and Fleam Dyke and the Ouse, and everything up to the northern fens. When he meant to leave there, he had it announced to the army that they would all leave together. The Kentish stayed on there against his command and seven messages he had sent to them. The force came upon them there, and they fought; ealdorman Sigulf was killed there, ealdorman Sigelm, Eadwold the king's thane, abbot Cenulf, Sigebriht son of Sigulf, Eadwald son of Acca, and many besides them although I have named the most distinguished. On the Danish side were killed Eohric their king, atheling Aethelwald, who had lured them into peace-breaking, Byrhtsige son of the atheling Beornoth, hold Ysopa, hold Oscytel, and very many besides them we might not now name. On either hand much slaughter was made, and of the Danes there were more killed, though they had the battlefield. Ealhswith passed away. That same year was the fight at The Holme between the Kentish and the Danes. Ealdorman Aethelwulf died, brother of Ealhswith, king Alfred's mother; and abbot Virgilus of the Scots, and the mass-priest Grimbold. In the same year a new church in Chester was hallowed, and the relics of St. Judoc brought there.

904. The moon darkened.

905. A comet appeared on October 20th.

906. Alfred died, who was town-reeve at Bath; and in the same year the peace was fastened at Tiddingford, just as king Edward advised, both with the East Anglians and the Northumbrians.

907. Chester was restored.

908. Denewulf died, who was bishop of Winchester.

909. St. Oswald's body was taken from Bardney into Mercia. Frithstan received the bishopric in Winchester; Asser died after that, who was bishop of Sherbourne. The same year, king Edward sent the army from both Wessex and Mercia, and it ravaged greatly among the northern force, both men and cattle, and killed many of the Danes; and they were in there for five weeks. St. Dunstan was born.

The descendants of Alfred who ruled Wessex from 900 to 955 gradually reconquered the Danelaw. For the first time there was not only an English king but also a unified kingdom of England. While none of these rulers had Alfred's diverse talents, they did carry out the policies he had begun: economic security, monastic reform and a revival of learning. None the less, they remain shadowy if powerful figures. The Chronicle entries for the years of Edward the Elder's reign (900–24) and after lack the vivid language of the accounts of Alfred's time, when the recording of history was encouraged by the court and inspired by a newly awakened patriotism. The Chronicles continued to be circulated in monastic communities; items of local interest were often added, and entries, both true and false, were copied from one version to another. For a short time a separate Chronicle was produced in Mercia, recounting the successes of Edward's sister Aethelflaed, 'lady of the Mercians', in Edward's campaigns against the Danes.

By the end of his reign, Edward had pushed the Danes north and was moving beyond the Humber and Mersey to Northumbria. His final achievement was the submission of all the smaller northern kings, who in 920 chose him as their 'father and lord'. Edward's authority in the far north was nominal, and the increasing seriousness of the Norse invasion, which the Chronicles ignore, probably lay behind the submission.

Edward as a military strategist is clearly admired by the Chroniclers. The army itself was strong and well organized, while its Danish opponents had lost the momentum and skill of the Viking army of the 860s. Although he was less compassionate than his father, Edward showed great determination and assurance as a military leader and as king.

Previous page: The Cuerdale hoard, found in 1849 in a lead chest in Lancashire, consisted of 1000 ounces of silver ingots, scrap metal and silver coins from English, Northumbrian, European and Oriental mints. It was probably buried hastily by Northumbrian Danes retreating after their defeat at the battle of Tettenhall in 910.

Below left: The Gosforth cross, Cumbria, the largest surviving sculpture from 10th-century England. The decoration is Borre style, developed by Norwegians in Ireland.

Below: Badbury Rings, Dorset. In 900, the first year of his reign, Edward attacked his cousin Aethelwald, who had rebelled against him, from this pre-Roman earthwork. Aethelwald fled to Northumbria and two years later persuaded the East Anglian Danes to join him in another attack on Wessex and Mercia, in which he was killed.

910. The English and the Danes fought at Tettenhall, on August 6th, and the English took the victory. A great force in ships came here from the south, from Brittany, and ravaged greatly by the Severn; but most of them died afterwards. The same year, Aethelflaed built the borough of *Bremesbyrig*.

The force in Northumbria broke the peace, and scorned every right that king Edward and his counsellors had offered them, and ravaged over the land of the Mercians. The king had gathered some hundred ships, and was then in Kent; the ships were going by the south coast, along the coast towards him. The force believed then that the greatest part of his support was in those ships, and that they might, unfought, fare where they would. When the king found out that they had gone harrying, he sent his troops from both Wessex and Mercia. They came upon the force from behind, when it was on its way home, and fought with them. They put the force to flight and killed many of them. King Eowils was killed, king Healfden, eorl Ohter, eorl Scurfa, hold Athulf, hold Benesing, Anlaf the Swart, and many more.

911. Aethelred, lord of the Mercians, died; and king Edward received the boroughs of London and Oxford, with all the lands which belonged to them.

912. Aethelflaed, lady of the Mercians, on the holy eve of the Invention of the Cross, came to *Scergeat* and built the borough there, and in the same year, that at Bridgnorth.

After Martinmas, king Edward commanded the northern borough at Hertford to be built, between the Maran and the Beane and the Lea. After that in summer, between Rogation and midsummer, king Edward went with some of his supporters to Maldon in Essex, and camped there for the time the borough was worked on and built at Witham. To him submitted a good part of the folk who had been under the Danish rule. Some of his supporters during that time, worked on the borough at Hertford on the south side of the Lea.

913. By the grace of God, Aethelflaed, lady of the Mercians, went with all the Mercians to Tamworth, and built the borough there in early summer and after, before Lammas, built that at Stafford. The year after that, the other was built at Eddisbury in early summer, and the same year, late in autumn, that at Warwick.

The force rode out after Easter, from Northampton and Leicester, broke the truce and killed many men at Hook Norton and thereabouts. Very soon after that, as the other force came home, they met a second band riding, that rode out against Luton. Then the people of those parts were aware of them, and fought against them; they put them to full flight, rescued all whom they had captured, also their horses and a great part of their weapons.

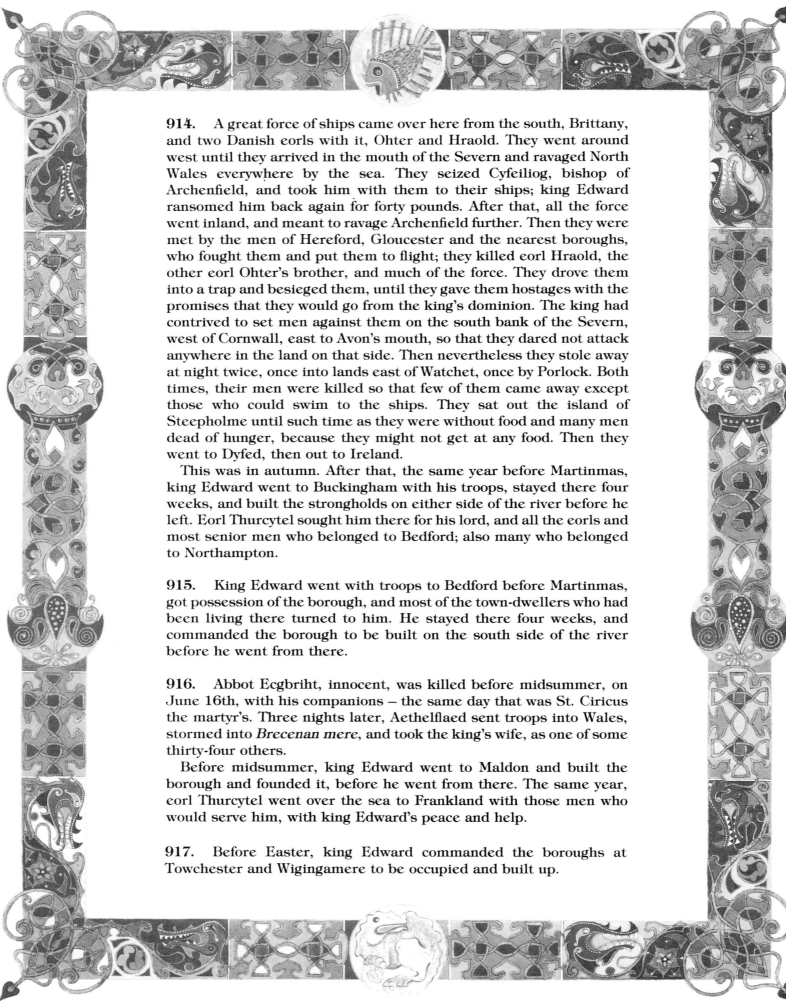

914. A great force of ships came over here from the south, Brittany, and two Danish eorls with it, Ohter and Hraold. They went around west until they arrived in the mouth of the Severn and ravaged North Wales everywhere by the sea. They seized Cyfeiliog, bishop of Archenfield, and took him with them to their ships; king Edward ransomed him back again for forty pounds. After that, all the force went inland, and meant to ravage Archenfield further. Then they were met by the men of Hereford, Gloucester and the nearest boroughs, who fought them and put them to flight; they killed eorl Hraold, the other eorl Ohter's brother, and much of the force. They drove them into a trap and besieged them, until they gave them hostages with the promises that they would go from the king's dominion. The king had contrived to set men against them on the south bank of the Severn, west of Cornwall, east to Avon's mouth, so that they dared not attack anywhere in the land on that side. Then nevertheless they stole away at night twice, once into lands east of Watchet, once by Porlock. Both times, their men were killed so that few of them came away except those who could swim to the ships. They sat out the island of Steepholme until such time as they were without food and many men dead of hunger, because they might not get at any food. Then they went to Dyfed, then out to Ireland.

This was in autumn. After that, the same year before Martinmas, king Edward went to Buckingham with his troops, stayed there four weeks, and built the strongholds on either side of the river before he left. Eorl Thurcytel sought him there for his lord, and all the eorls and most senior men who belonged to Bedford; also many who belonged to Northampton.

915. King Edward went with troops to Bedford before Martinmas, got possession of the borough, and most of the town-dwellers who had been living there turned to him. He stayed there four weeks, and commanded the borough to be built on the south side of the river before he went from there.

916. Abbot Ecgbriht, innocent, was killed before midsummer, on June 16th, with his companions – the same day that was St. Ciricus the martyr's. Three nights later, Aethelflaed sent troops into Wales, stormed into *Brecenan mere*, and took the king's wife, as one of some thirty-four others.

Before midsummer, king Edward went to Maldon and built the borough and founded it, before he went from there. The same year, eorl Thurcytel went over the sea to Frankland with those men who would serve him, with king Edward's peace and help.

917. Before Easter, king Edward commanded the boroughs at Towchester and Wigingamere to be occupied and built up.

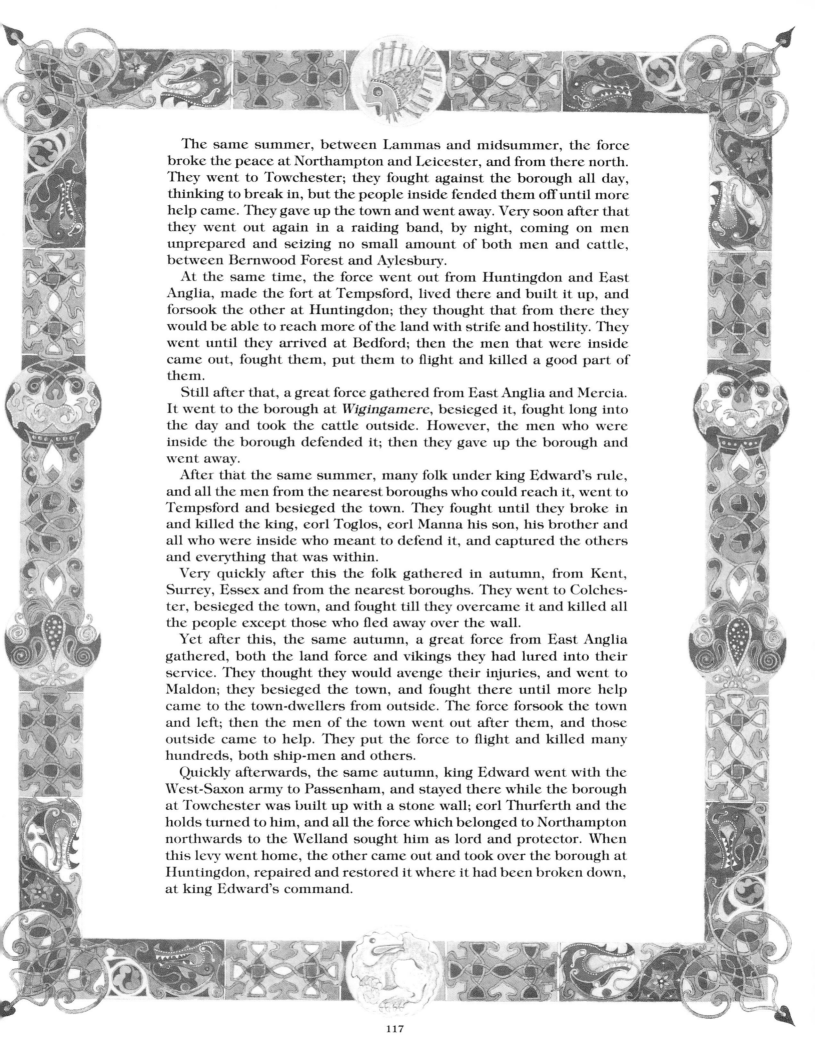

The same summer, between Lammas and midsummer, the force broke the peace at Northampton and Leicester, and from there north. They went to Towchester; they fought against the borough all day, thinking to break in, but the people inside fended them off until more help came. They gave up the town and went away. Very soon after that they went out again in a raiding band, by night, coming on men unprepared and seizing no small amount of both men and cattle, between Bernwood Forest and Aylesbury.

At the same time, the force went out from Huntingdon and East Anglia, made the fort at Tempsford, lived there and built it up, and forsook the other at Huntingdon; they thought that from there they would be able to reach more of the land with strife and hostility. They went until they arrived at Bedford; then the men that were inside came out, fought them, put them to flight and killed a good part of them.

Still after that, a great force gathered from East Anglia and Mercia. It went to the borough at *Wigingamere*, besieged it, fought long into the day and took the cattle outside. However, the men who were inside the borough defended it; then they gave up the borough and went away.

After that the same summer, many folk under king Edward's rule, and all the men from the nearest boroughs who could reach it, went to Tempsford and besieged the town. They fought until they broke in and killed the king, eorl Toglos, eorl Manna his son, his brother and all who were inside who meant to defend it, and captured the others and everything that was within.

Very quickly after this the folk gathered in autumn, from Kent, Surrey, Essex and from the nearest boroughs. They went to Colchester, besieged the town, and fought till they overcame it and killed all the people except those who fled away over the wall.

Yet after this, the same autumn, a great force from East Anglia gathered, both the land force and vikings they had lured into their service. They thought they would avenge their injuries, and went to Maldon; they besieged the town, and fought there until more help came to the town-dwellers from outside. The force forsook the town and left; then the men of the town went out after them, and those outside came to help. They put the force to flight and killed many hundreds, both ship-men and others.

Quickly afterwards, the same autumn, king Edward went with the West-Saxon army to Passenham, and stayed there while the borough at Towchester was built up with a stone wall; eorl Thurferth and the holds turned to him, and all the force which belonged to Northampton northwards to the Welland sought him as lord and protector. When this levy went home, the other came out and took over the borough at Huntingdon, repaired and restored it where it had been broken down, at king Edward's command.

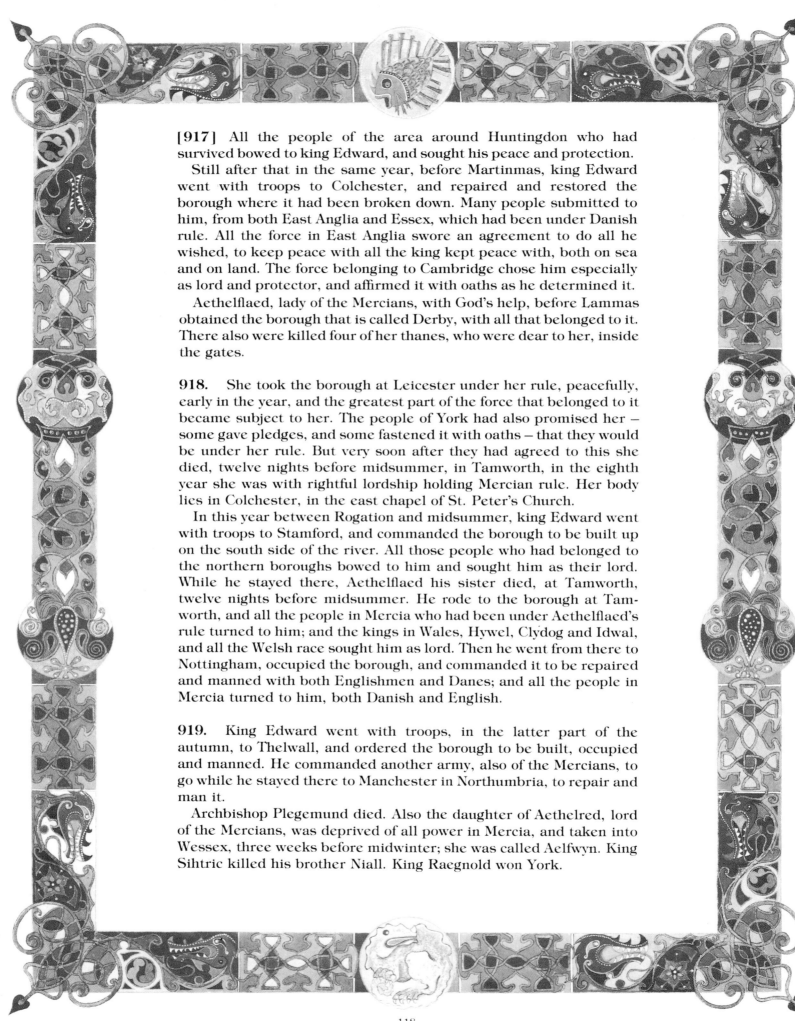

[917] All the people of the area around Huntingdon who had survived bowed to king Edward, and sought his peace and protection.

Still after that in the same year, before Martinmas, king Edward went with troops to Colchester, and repaired and restored the borough where it had been broken down. Many people submitted to him, from both East Anglia and Essex, which had been under Danish rule. All the force in East Anglia swore an agreement to do all he wished, to keep peace with all the king kept peace with, both on sea and on land. The force belonging to Cambridge chose him especially as lord and protector, and affirmed it with oaths as he determined it.

Aethelflaed, lady of the Mercians, with God's help, before Lammas obtained the borough that is called Derby, with all that belonged to it. There also were killed four of her thanes, who were dear to her, inside the gates.

918.   She took the borough at Leicester under her rule, peacefully, early in the year, and the greatest part of the force that belonged to it became subject to her. The people of York had also promised her — some gave pledges, and some fastened it with oaths — that they would be under her rule. But very soon after they had agreed to this she died, twelve nights before midsummer, in Tamworth, in the eighth year she was with rightful lordship holding Mercian rule. Her body lies in Colchester, in the east chapel of St. Peter's Church.

In this year between Rogation and midsummer, king Edward went with troops to Stamford, and commanded the borough to be built up on the south side of the river. All those people who had belonged to the northern boroughs bowed to him and sought him as their lord. While he stayed there, Aethelflaed his sister died, at Tamworth, twelve nights before midsummer. He rode to the borough at Tamworth, and all the people in Mercia who had been under Aethelflaed's rule turned to him; and the kings in Wales, Hywel, Clydog and Idwal, and all the Welsh race sought him as lord. Then he went from there to Nottingham, occupied the borough, and commanded it to be repaired and manned with both Englishmen and Danes; and all the people in Mercia turned to him, both Danish and English.

919.   King Edward went with troops, in the latter part of the autumn, to Thelwall, and ordered the borough to be built, occupied and manned. He commanded another army, also of the Mercians, to go while he stayed there to Manchester in Northumbria, to repair and man it.

Archbishop Plegemund died. Also the daughter of Aethelred, lord of the Mercians, was deprived of all power in Mercia, and taken into Wessex, three weeks before midwinter; she was called Aelfwyn. King Sihtric killed his brother Niall. King Raegnold won York.

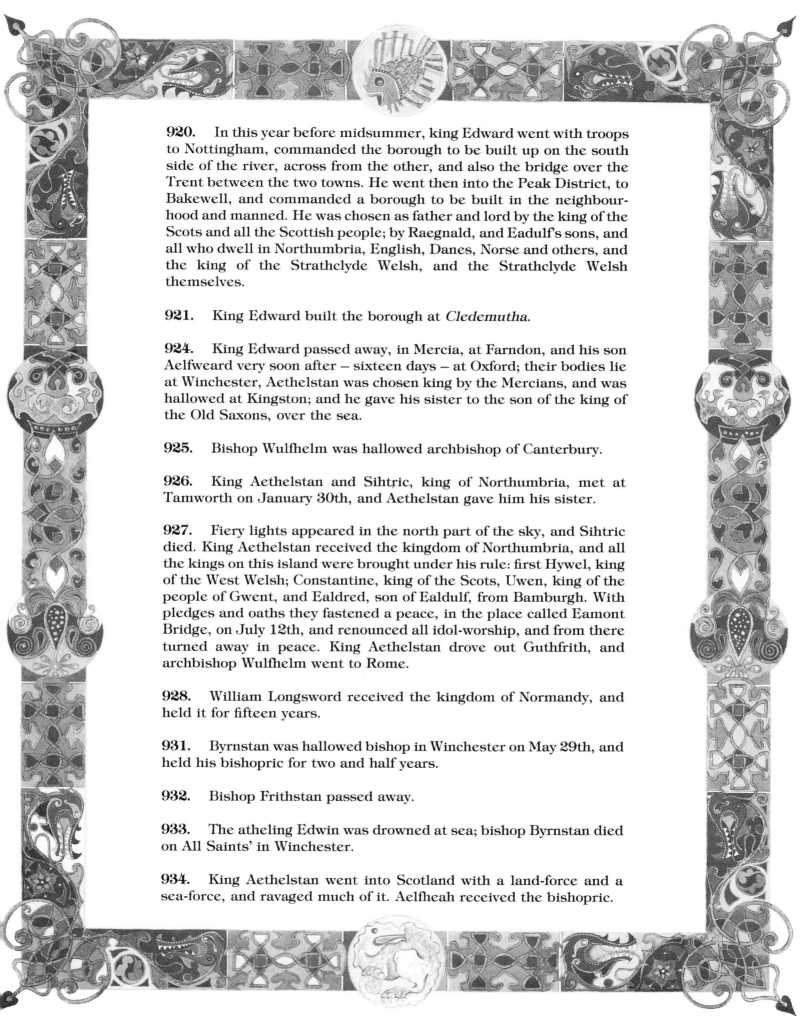

920. In this year before midsummer, king Edward went with troops to Nottingham, commanded the borough to be built up on the south side of the river, across from the other, and also the bridge over the Trent between the two towns. He went then into the Peak District, to Bakewell, and commanded a borough to be built in the neighbourhood and manned. He was chosen as father and lord by the king of the Scots and all the Scottish people; by Raegnald, and Eadulf's sons, and all who dwell in Northumbria, English, Danes, Norse and others, and the king of the Strathclyde Welsh, and the Strathclyde Welsh themselves.

921. King Edward built the borough at *Cledemutha*.

924. King Edward passed away, in Mercia, at Farndon, and his son Aelfweard very soon after – sixteen days – at Oxford; their bodies lie at Winchester, Aethelstan was chosen king by the Mercians, and was hallowed at Kingston; and he gave his sister to the son of the king of the Old Saxons, over the sea.

925. Bishop Wulfhelm was hallowed archbishop of Canterbury.

926. King Aethelstan and Sihtric, king of Northumbria, met at Tamworth on January 30th, and Aethelstan gave him his sister.

927. Fiery lights appeared in the north part of the sky, and Sihtric died. King Aethelstan received the kingdom of Northumbria, and all the kings on this island were brought under his rule: first Hywel, king of the West Welsh; Constantine, king of the Scots, Uwen, king of the people of Gwent, and Ealdred, son of Ealdulf, from Bamburgh. With pledges and oaths they fastened a peace, in the place called Eamont Bridge, on July 12th, and renounced all idol-worship, and from there turned away in peace. King Aethelstan drove out Guthfrith, and archbishop Wulfhelm went to Rome.

928. William Longsword received the kingdom of Normandy, and held it for fifteen years.

931. Byrnstan was hallowed bishop in Winchester on May 29th, and held his bishopric for two and half years.

932. Bishop Frithstan passed away.

933. The atheling Edwin was drowned at sea; bishop Byrnstan died on All Saints' in Winchester.

934. King Aethelstan went into Scotland with a land-force and a sea-force, and ravaged much of it. Aelfheah received the bishopric.

Frontispiece of a copy of Bede's Life of St Cuthbert, probably executed at Winchester, showing Aethelstan delivering the book when he visited the saint's shrine at Chester-le-Street, *County Durham, in 937. This was one of many gifts Aethelstan made to religious foundations during his northern campaigns.*

ethelstan succeeded in 924 and within a few years had conquered Northumbria and become overlord of Cornwall. He won a major victory at Brunnanburh in an alliance of West Saxons, Mercians and Danes. This victory preserved the confidence and culture of the English, and of the royal house of Wessex now bidding for political sovereignty in Britain. He was an able lawgiver and administrator, fostering unity by encouraging governors of the remoter areas to attend court.

Aethelstan was intellectually curious, with a strong character; he sent agents to buy objects throughout Europe, especially relics, and gave and received rich gifts.

Below: The 9th-century Rheims reliquary, traditionally held to have contained a fragment of the True Cross; Aethelstan also received a fragment of the Cross.

Above right: Aethelstan; 14th-century manuscript.

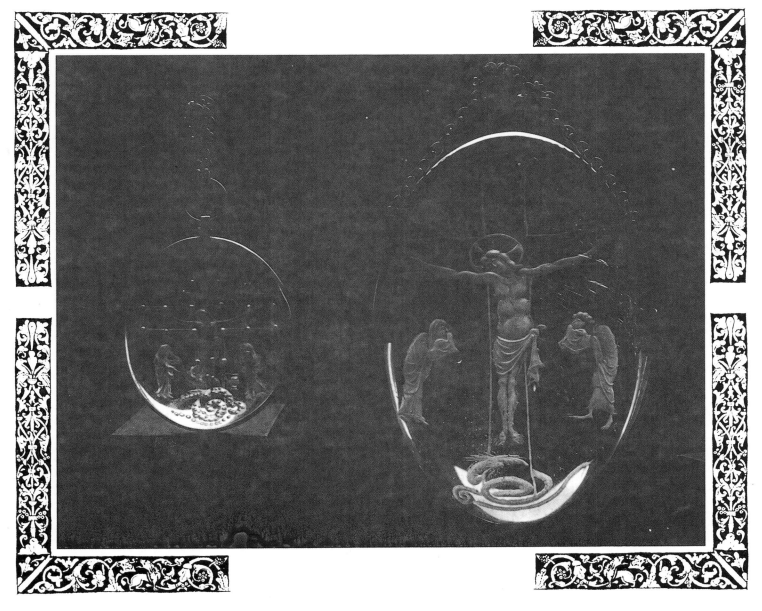

937. Aethelstan, king, lord of eorls, ring-giver to men, and his brother also, the atheling Edmund, lifelong glory struck in battle with sword's edge at Brunnanburh, broke the shield-wall, hewed linden-wood with hammer's leaving. Edward's sons, as they were noble-born, accustomed to battle, often on campaign had defended their land from each foe, hoard and home; the hated ones were crushed, people of the Scots, men of the ships, fated fell. The field was slick with men's blood, from when the burning sun in morning-time, mighty star, glided up overground, God's bright candle, the eternal Lord's till the noble work sank to its setting, many a man lay wrecked by spears, northern warrior shot over shield. So Scots also were sated with war; West-Saxons went forth all the day long on the enemy's tracks, hewing the fleeing forces from behind with blades new-sharpened. No stroke did the Mercians refuse to pay in the hard hand-play to any who with Olaf over sea's swell in the ship's lap sought land, fated to fall: five lay dead on the field, young kings put to sleep with the sword; so also seven of Olaf's eorls, and numberless slain among shipmen and Scots. The Northmen's lord was put to flight, forced by need to his ship with small company. Keep pressed sea, the king went out on fallow flood, saved his life. So also the old one fled away to his northern country, Constantine, hoary battle-man; he need not boast of the meeting of swords. He was severed from kin, deprived of friends on that field, slain at war, and left his son on the death-ground, destroyed by his wounds, young at war; he need have no proud words, the white-haired warrior, the wily one, about striking edges, nor Olaf either, With the remnants of an army they need not laugh that their battle-work was better where standards crossed and spears clashed in the meeting of men, when on the death-field they played with the sons of Edward. The Northmen went off in nailed ships, sad survivors of spears, on Ding's mere, over deep water seeking Dublin, Ireland again, ashamed in their hearts, So the brothers both together king and atheling sought their country, the land of Wessex, exulting in war. They left behind them sharing the dead the dusk-dressed one, the black raven, with hard beak of horn, and hoary-coated eagle, white-tailed, eating the carrion, greedy war-hawk, and that grey beast, the wolf of the wood. Nor was more slaughter on this island ever yet, so many folk felled, before this fight with sword's edge, as say the books, the old wise men, since from the east Angle and Saxon came up together over broad sea seeking Britain, who overcame the Welsh, eager for glory, and gained a land.

The victory of Eadred, King of Wessex (ruled 946–55), over Eric Bloodaxe at York in 954 brought the end of Scandinavian domination in Northumbria. A quarter century of peace followed, bringing a major religious and cultural revival.

The man behind this renaissance was Dunstan (c.909–88), abbot of Glastonbury, later archbishop of Canterbury, and the most powerful religious leader of the period. Dunstan had been a close friend and advisor of Eadred, but relations with Eadred's successor Eadwig (ruled 955–59) started on a bad footing. The 15-year-old king left the lengthy banquet staged after his coronation to dally with Aelfgyfu, whom he later married, and her mother. Dunstan was sent to bring him back; the king refused to come and force had to be used. The upshot was exile for Dunstan: the Chronicle entry for 956 records that he 'was driven over the sea'. Three years later, Eadwig was succeeded by his brother Edgar (ruled 959–75), who recalled Dunstan, appointing him to Canterbury in 961.

In the mid-10th century, the English Church was in a poor state, a feeble shadow of its former splendour. Monastic buildings had been destroyed, manuscripts plundered. Above all, laymen and clerks had displaced monks in the religious communities, and discipline had become uneven. Dunstan had used his years in exile well, observing and gaining inspiration from the life and ideals of the newly reformed monastic movement in France. On his return, and with Edgar's wholehearted support, he embarked on a rigorous programme of ecclesiastical reform and expansion. The cornerstone was the enforcement of the Benedictine rule, by which trained monks lived an ordered communal life of prayer, worship and labour. Monks were sent throughout the country to replace the lay clergy. Monasteries were rebuilt and new houses established. And in 970 the *Regularis Concordia*, a new set of regulations for monastic life in England based on Benedictine practice, was drawn up by Aethelwold, bishop of Winchester, with advice from representatives of continental foundations. The reforms were so successful, and the monks so well trained, that English monastic life survived unharmed through the Danish invasions until the Norman conquest.

Dunstan spent much time at court, advising Edgar on secular as well as religious matters. His influence was especially marked on the king's coronation. The ceremony was delayed for 14 years, until 973, when the king had reached 30, the age at which priests could be ordained. Dunstan revised the ceremony, making it an intensely religious occasion.

Edgar died suddenly in 975 and was buried by Dunstan at Glastonbury. As a patron of the new monasticism, he inevitably received high praise and approval from the Chroniclers, who were themselves monks. The concept of kingship also changed during his reign. As strong and forceful a political leader as many of his predecessors, Edgar was in addition held to be Christ's appointed, the source of divine judgement and authority over his people.

Above: Edgar, Dunstan and Aethelwold at work on the Regularis Concordia *in an illustration from the manuscript. A monk's day started at 1.30 am in summer, 2.30 in winter, finishing long hours later at 8.15 pm in summer, 6.30 in winter. There was one meal a day in winter, two in summer. The monks spent most of the time at prayer and worship, although there were two hours each morning for creative or manual labour. Below the three compilers is a monk, representing those for whom the work was intended.*

Previous page: Monks at their labours, preparing illuminated manuscripts. (Detail from a late 10th-century German ivory carving.)

Left and below left: The major 10th-century monastic centres have all vanished, even their foundations. Their building materials have been plundered, or they have been reconstructed or deliberately destroyed. Deerhurst, Gloucestershire, is one of the few surviving 10th-century monastic buildings. Even here the original apse has been destroyed and Norman side aisles have been added.

Below: St Dunstan writing. (Illustration from a 12th-century manuscript.)

940.   King Aethelstan passed away on October 27th, forty years less one night since king Alfred passed away; the atheling Edmund received the kingdom, and was then eighteen years old. The Northumbrians falsified their pledges, and chose Olaf of Ireland as their king. Wulfhelm was then archbishop of Canterbury.

942.   Edmund king   lord of the English,
his kinsmen's protector,   overcame Mercia,
praised for his deeds   as far as Dore,
Whitwell Gap,   the river Humber,
broad sea-stream.   He won five boroughs,
Leicester and Lincoln,   likewise Nottingham,
Stamford and Derby.   The Danes had been long
under the Norseman's rule   forced at need,
held in chains   of heathen slavery,
suffering long   until released again
to the glory of   the friend of warriors,
the son of Edward,   Edmund king.

943.   Olaf stormed Tamworth, and many dead fell on either hand; the Danes had the victory. They took much booty away with them, and Wulfrun was taken captive in that raid.

King Edmund besieged king Olaf and archbishop Wulfstan in Leicester, and might have overcome them had they not escaped out of the town that night. After this, Olaf obtained king Edmund's friendship, and king Edmund received him at baptism, and gave him kingly gifts. The same year, after a long space of time, he received king Raegnald at the bishop's hands.

944.   King Edmund overcame all Northumbrian lands in his power, and drove out the two kings, Olaf son of Sihtric and Raegnald son of Guthferth.

945.   King Edmund ravaged all Cumberland, and gave it all to Malcolm, king of the Scots, on the condition that he be his ally, both at sea and on land.

946.   King Edmund passed away on St. Augustine's Day; he had reigned six and a half years. It was widely known how he ended his days, that Liofa stabbed him at Pucklechurch. Aethelflaed of Damerham, ealdorman Aelfgar's daughter was then his queen. Then after him atheling Eadred his brother received the kingdom, and he brought all the land of Northumbria under his rule. The Scots then gave him oaths that they would do all he willed.

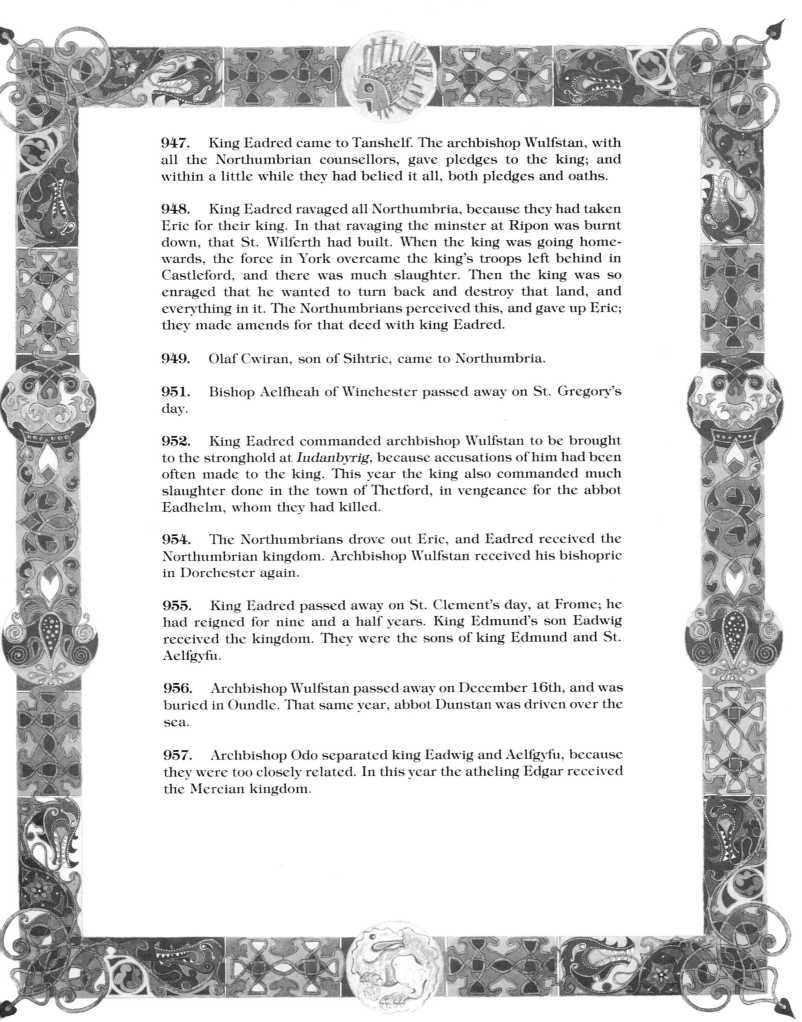

947. King Eadred came to Tanshelf. The archbishop Wulfstan, with all the Northumbrian counsellors, gave pledges to the king; and within a little while they had belied it all, both pledges and oaths.

948. King Eadred ravaged all Northumbria, because they had taken Eric for their king. In that ravaging the minster at Ripon was burnt down, that St. Wilferth had built. When the king was going homewards, the force in York overcame the king's troops left behind in Castleford, and there was much slaughter. Then the king was so enraged that he wanted to turn back and destroy that land, and everything in it. The Northumbrians perceived this, and gave up Eric; they made amends for that deed with king Eadred.

949. Olaf Cwiran, son of Sihtric, came to Northumbria.

951. Bishop Aelfheah of Winchester passed away on St. Gregory's day.

952. King Eadred commanded archbishop Wulfstan to be brought to the stronghold at *Iudanbyrig*, because accusations of him had been often made to the king. This year the king also commanded much slaughter done in the town of Thetford, in vengeance for the abbot Eadhelm, whom they had killed.

954. The Northumbrians drove out Eric, and Eadred received the Northumbrian kingdom. Archbishop Wulfstan received his bishopric in Dorchester again.

955. King Eadred passed away on St. Clement's day, at Frome; he had reigned for nine and a half years. King Edmund's son Eadwig received the kingdom. They were the sons of king Edmund and St. Aelfgyfu.

956. Archbishop Wulfstan passed away on December 16th, and was buried in Oundle. That same year, abbot Dunstan was driven over the sea.

957. Archbishop Odo separated king Eadwig and Aelfgyfu, because they were too closely related. In this year the atheling Edgar received the Mercian kingdom.

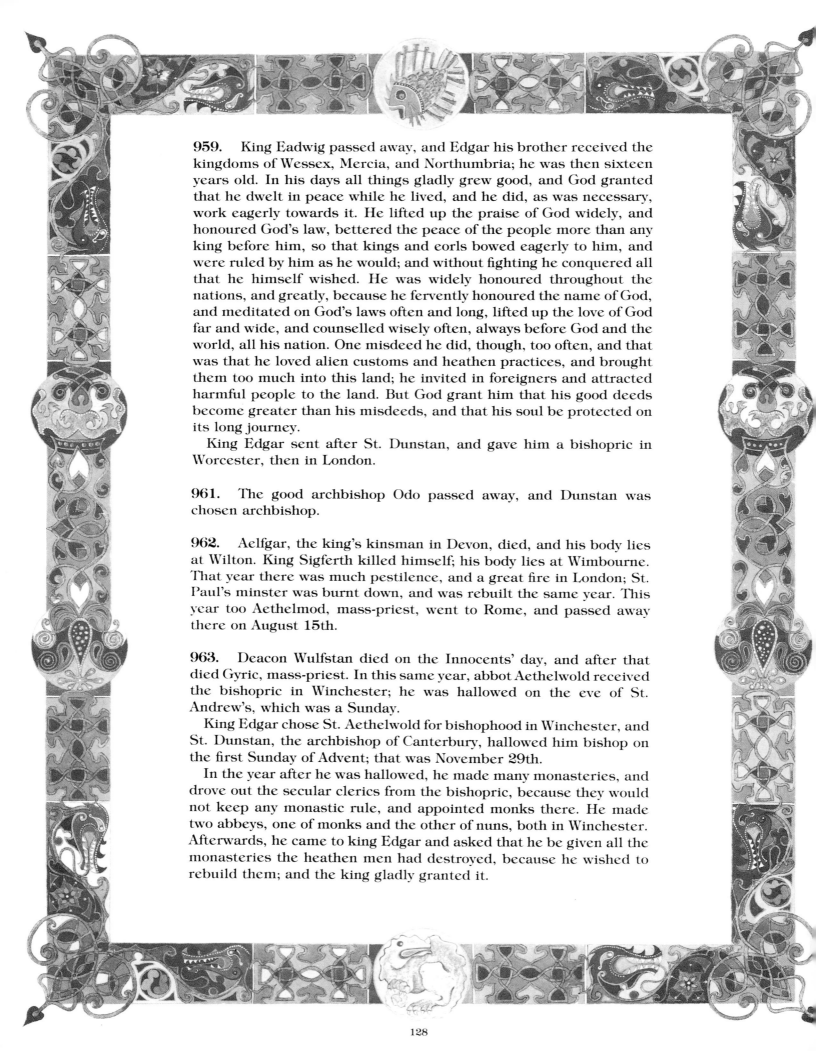

959. King Eadwig passed away, and Edgar his brother received the kingdoms of Wessex, Mercia, and Northumbria; he was then sixteen years old. In his days all things gladly grew good, and God granted that he dwelt in peace while he lived, and he did, as was necessary, work eagerly towards it. He lifted up the praise of God widely, and honoured God's law, bettered the peace of the people more than any king before him, so that kings and eorls bowed eagerly to him, and were ruled by him as he would; and without fighting he conquered all that he himself wished. He was widely honoured throughout the nations, and greatly, because he fervently honoured the name of God, and meditated on God's laws often and long, lifted up the love of God far and wide, and counselled wisely often, always before God and the world, all his nation. One misdeed he did, though, too often, and that was that he loved alien customs and heathen practices, and brought them too much into this land; he invited in foreigners and attracted harmful people to the land. But God grant him that his good deeds become greater than his misdeeds, and that his soul be protected on its long journey.

King Edgar sent after St. Dunstan, and gave him a bishopric in Worcester, then in London.

961. The good archbishop Odo passed away, and Dunstan was chosen archbishop.

962. Aelfgar, the king's kinsman in Devon, died, and his body lies at Wilton. King Sigferth killed himself; his body lies at Wimbourne. That year there was much pestilence, and a great fire in London; St. Paul's minster was burnt down, and was rebuilt the same year. This year too Aethelmod, mass-priest, went to Rome, and passed away there on August 15th.

963. Deacon Wulfstan died on the Innocents' day, and after that died Gyric, mass-priest. In this same year, abbot Aethelwold received the bishopric in Winchester; he was hallowed on the eve of St. Andrew's, which was a Sunday.

King Edgar chose St. Aethelwold for bishophood in Winchester, and St. Dunstan, the archbishop of Canterbury, hallowed him bishop on the first Sunday of Advent; that was November 29th.

In the year after he was hallowed, he made many monasteries, and drove out the secular clerics from the bishopric, because they would not keep any monastic rule, and appointed monks there. He made two abbeys, one of monks and the other of nuns, both in Winchester. Afterwards, he came to king Edgar and asked that he be given all the monasteries the heathen men had destroyed, because he wished to rebuild them; and the king gladly granted it.

Bishop Aethelwold came at that time to Ely, where St. Aethelthryth lies, and had the monastery made. He gave it to one of his monks, who was called Brihtnoth, hallowed him abbot, and set the monks there to serve God; formerly there had been nuns there. He bought many villages from the king, and made it very rich.

After, bishop Aethelwold came to the monastery of Peterborough, that had in the meantime been destroyed by the heathen folk, and he found there nothing but old walls and wild woods. He found hidden in the old wall documents that abbot Hedde had written, how king Wulfhere and Aethelred his brother had built it, how they had freed it from king, bishop and all worldly service; and how pope Agatho had affirmed it with his deed, and archbishop Deusdedit. He had the monastery built, set the abbot there, whose name was Aldulf, and placed monks there, where there had been nothing. He came to the king, and let him look on the writings that had been found. The king answered, and said, "I, Edgar, grant and give today before God, and before archbishop Dunstan, freedom to St. Peter's minster from king and bishop, and all the villages that belong thereto, that is Eastfield, Dogsthorpe, Eye, and Paston, I free it so no bishop has any command, only the abbot of the monastery. And I give the town that is called Oundle with all that belongs to it, that is the Eight Hundreds, with market and toll, freely, so that no king, bishop, eorl nor shire-reeve have any authority there; nor any one but the abbot alone, and those he appoints. I give Christ and St. Peter, at the bidding of bishop Aethelwold, the lands of Barrow, Warmington, Ashton, Kettering, Castor, Ailsworth, Walton, Werrington, Eye, Longthorpe and a minter in Stamford. Of this land and all else that belongs to the monastery, I say that it is free concerning criminal and civil jurisdiction, in matters of warranty and the judging of thieves. These privileges and all others I have said I grant to Christ and St. Peter; and I give two parts of Whittlesey Mere with waters, weirs and fens, through *Merelad* to the water called Nene, and so eastward to King's Delph. I will that the market be in that same town, and that no other be between Stamford and Huntingdon, and I will that the toll be given over this area: first, from Whittlesey Mere all the way to the king's toll of Norman Cross Hundreds, back again from Whittlesey Mere through *Merelad* on to the Nene, and as the water runs to Crowland, from Crowland to the Muscat, and from the Muscat to King's Delph and to Whittlesey Mere. And I will that all the freedom and all the forgiveness which my foregoers gave, that it stand. And I write and fasten it with the sign of Christ's cross +."

The Winchester style, predominant in the 10th and 11th centuries, represents the high point of Anglo-Saxon art. Its practitioners – members of monastic communities not just at Winchester but throughout southern England – drew heavily on continental influences. The school's chief innovations – the depiction of dignified, solid, naturalistic figures and a lively, delicate line used to express emotion and movement – ultimately derived from the 'late antique' art of Greece and Rome. But the immediate debt of English artists was to the 9th-century Frankish interpretations of classical ideas and to the fine Frankish style of drawing. The English artists added brilliant colours, ornamentation and patterns. Traditional English exuberance also attracted English artists to use line drawing to suggest drama, emotion and activity.

The West Saxon kings, especially Alfred and Aethelstan, encouraged a return to classical art and learning as part of the tradition of continental Christian civilization. And in the 10th century, the monastic revival and renewed contact with continental courts and culture gave particular impetus to the new art.

Opposite: The earliest true Winchester manuscript, produced in 966. The text is in gold throughout, and this page is painted on purple vellum, following continental custom. The figures are skilfully drawn and full of movement. The frame is part of the picture itself, a distinctive feature of the Winchester style. (King Edgar offering his charter to the New Minster at Winchester.)

Below left: This Benedictional (service book) of bishop Aethelwold, bishop of Winchester from 975 to 980, is the most sumptuous surviving production of the Winchester school and was painted there between 971 and 984 under Aethelwold's supervision. The glory of the manuscript is its colour and ornamentation. Huge, brilliantly coloured acanthus leaves spill out of the frame and every inch of the page is packed with decoration.

Below: The first glimmer of the Winchester style appears in this drawing of Dunstan at the feet of Christ. It may have been done by Dunstan himself during his continental exile in the late 950s.

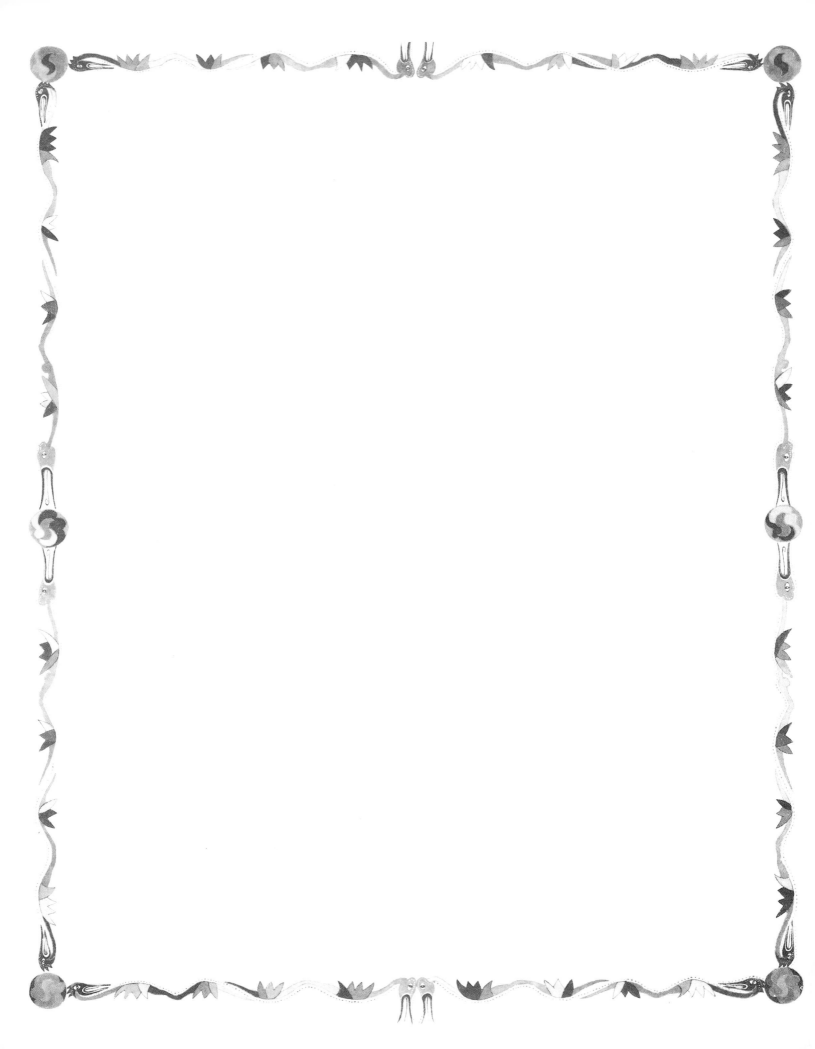

Part Three

964~1066

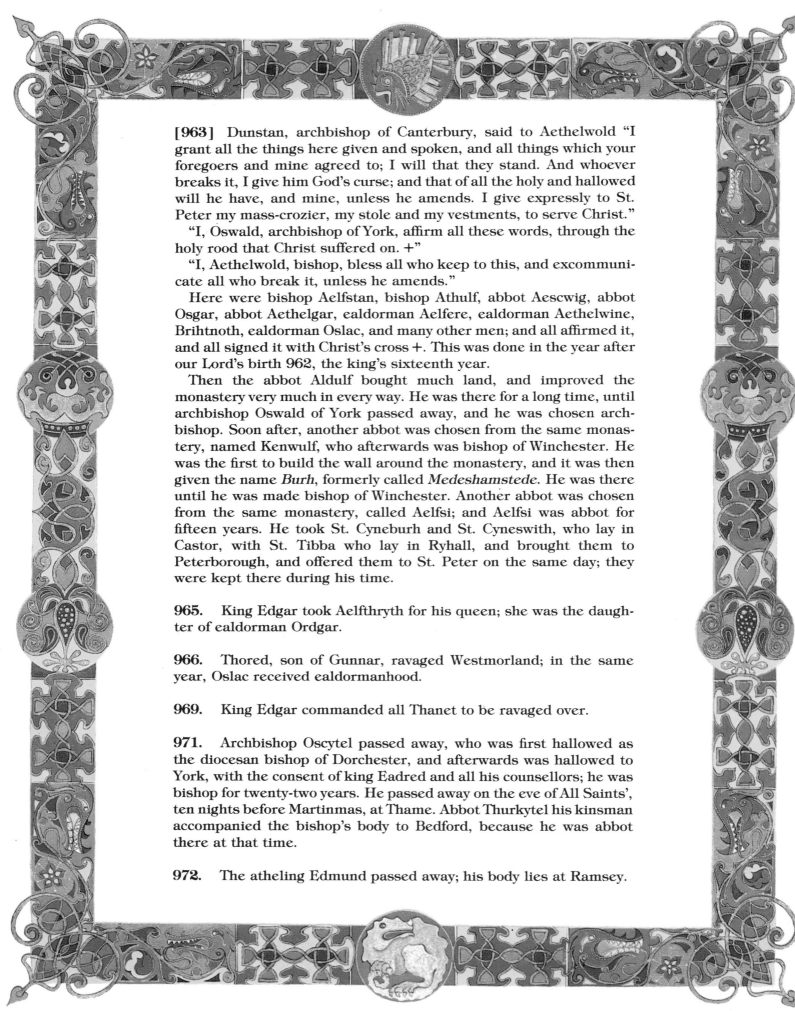

[963] Dunstan, archbishop of Canterbury, said to Aethelwold "I grant all the things here given and spoken, and all things which your foregoers and mine agreed to; I will that they stand. And whoever breaks it, I give him God's curse; and that of all the holy and hallowed will he have, and mine, unless he amends. I give expressly to St. Peter my mass-crozier, my stole and my vestments, to serve Christ."

"I, Oswald, archbishop of York, affirm all these words, through the holy rood that Christ suffered on. +"

"I, Aethelwold, bishop, bless all who keep to this, and excommunicate all who break it, unless he amends."

Here were bishop Aelfstan, bishop Athulf, abbot Aescwig, abbot Osgar, abbot Aethelgar, ealdorman Aelfere, ealdorman Aethelwine, Brihtnoth, ealdorman Oslac, and many other men; and all affirmed it, and all signed it with Christ's cross +. This was done in the year after our Lord's birth 962, the king's sixteenth year.

Then the abbot Aldulf bought much land, and improved the monastery very much in every way. He was there for a long time, until archbishop Oswald of York passed away, and he was chosen archbishop. Soon after, another abbot was chosen from the same monastery, named Kenwulf, who afterwards was bishop of Winchester. He was the first to build the wall around the monastery, and it was then given the name *Burh*, formerly called *Medeshamstede*. He was there until he was made bishop of Winchester. Another abbot was chosen from the same monastery, called Aelfsi; and Aelfsi was abbot for fifteen years. He took St. Cyneburh and St. Cyneswith, who lay in Castor, with St. Tibba who lay in Ryhall, and brought them to Peterborough, and offered them to St. Peter on the same day; they were kept there during his time.

965. King Edgar took Aelfthryth for his queen; she was the daughter of ealdorman Ordgar.

966. Thored, son of Gunnar, ravaged Westmorland; in the same year, Oslac received ealdormanhood.

969. King Edgar commanded all Thanet to be ravaged over.

971. Archbishop Oscytel passed away, who was first hallowed as the diocesan bishop of Dorchester, and afterwards was hallowed to York, with the consent of king Eadred and all his counsellors; he was bishop for twenty-two years. He passed away on the eve of All Saints', ten nights before Martinmas, at Thame. Abbot Thurkytel his kinsman accompanied the bishop's body to Bedford, because he was abbot there at that time.

972. The atheling Edmund passed away; his body lies at Ramsey.

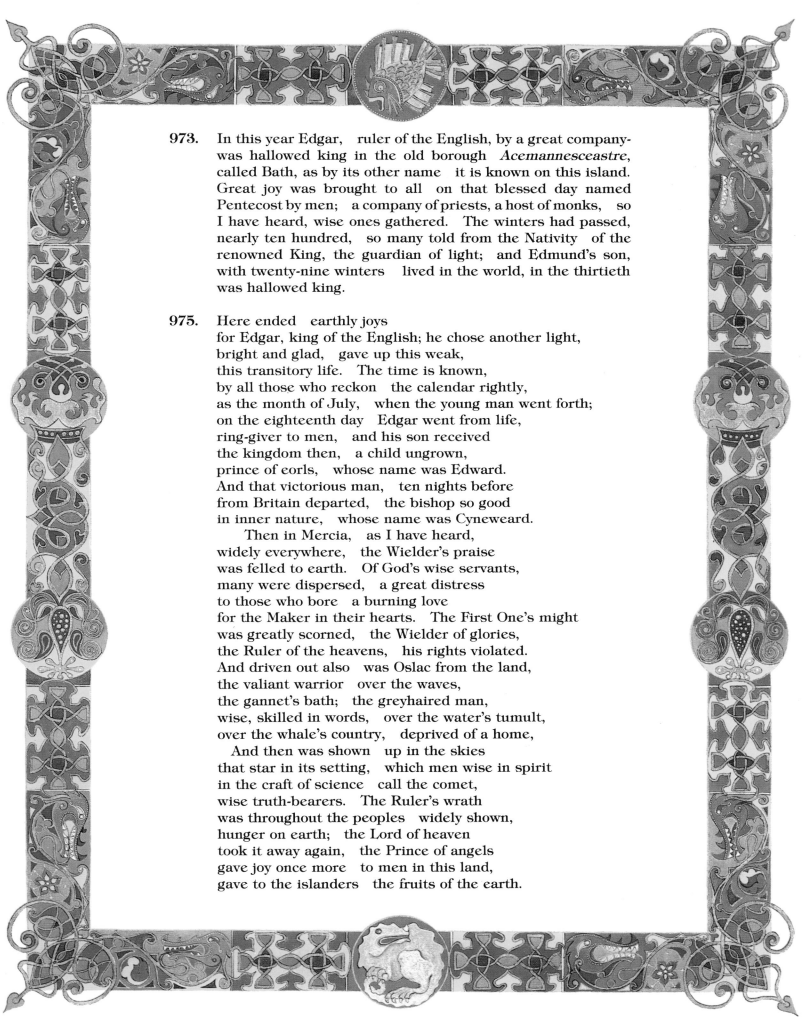

973. In this year Edgar,   ruler of the English, by a great company- was hallowed king in the old borough   *Acemannesceastre*, called Bath, as by its other name   it is known on this island. Great joy was brought to all   on that blessed day named Pentecost by men;   a company of priests, a host of monks,   so I have heard, wise ones gathered.   The winters had passed, nearly ten hundred,   so many told from the Nativity   of the renowned King, the guardian of light;   and Edmund's son, with twenty-nine winters   lived in the world, in the thirtieth was hallowed king.

975. Here ended   earthly joys
for Edgar, king of the English;   he chose another light,
bright and glad,   gave up this weak,
this transitory life.   The time is known,
by all those who reckon   the calendar rightly,
as the month of July,   when the young man went forth;
on the eighteenth day   Edgar went from life,
ring-giver to men,   and his son received
the kingdom then,   a child ungrown,
prince of eorls,   whose name was Edward.
And that victorious man,   ten nights before
from Britain departed,   the bishop so good
in inner nature,   whose name was Cyneweard.
    Then in Mercia,   as I have heard,
widely everywhere,   the Wielder's praise
was felled to earth.   Of God's wise servants,
many were dispersed,   a great distress
to those who bore   a burning love
for the Maker in their hearts.   The First One's might
was greatly scorned,   the Wielder of glories,
the Ruler of the heavens,   his rights violated.
And driven out also   was Oslac from the land,
the valiant warrior   over the waves,
the gannet's bath;   the greyhaired man,
wise, skilled in words,   over the water's tumult,
over the whale's country,   deprived of a home,
   And then was shown   up in the skies
that star in its setting,   which men wise in spirit
in the craft of science   call the comet,
wise truth-bearers.   The Ruler's wrath
was throughout the peoples   widely shown,
hunger on earth;   the Lord of heaven
took it away again,   the Prince of angels
gave joy once more   to men in this land,
gave to the islanders   the fruits of the earth.

Aethelred came to the throne in 978 in an atmosphere of suspicion and mistrust. Implicated in the murder of his half-brother Edward, who had succeeded Edgar three years before, he could neither win the loyalty of his nobles nor inspire patriotism and devotion in the people. Even discounting the prejudices of the Chroniclers, who clearly did not approve of him at all, he must have been weak and indecisive, given to sudden acts of violence. His nickname, the Unready, is a modern version of Unraed, first mentioned in the 13th century but based on earlier usage; Unraed means 'poor counsel', 'evil counsel' or 'unwise'.

Although Aethelred was very unlucky, and had poor advisers and military commanders, any king of England would have been hard pressed at this time. Across the North Sea, a strong Scandinavian state was emerging under the leadership of the autocratic king Harald of Denmark (nicknamed Bluetooth), who united Norway and Denmark and forcibly imposed Christianity on his subjects. The Viking armies Aethelred faced were fearsome and well organized, far more so than the relatively small bands that had raided from 835 onwards. Harald's shock troops did not intend to settle in England; their main interest was in obtaining ever increasing amounts of tribute money, Danegeld. Once Aethelred had been forced to pay for peace, they regularly returned to extract further payments. In 1006 they demanded 36,000 pounds of silver, and in 1012 they received 48,000.

The raids began on a small scale in 980, when Southampton, Thanet, Cornwall, Devon and London were sacked. More ominously, eleven years later a large, well-organized army led by Olaf Tryggvason, later king of Norway, landed at Folkestone and defeated the English at Maldon. Despite payments of Danegeld and a peace treaty, they invaded again in 992, in 994 and almost every year

Below: The Viking armies were trained in camps such as this at Trelleborg, primarily for internal conflicts, although their skills came in useful in foreign raids.

between 997 and 1014. National morale gradually crumbled. Leaders changed sides, and cities were betrayed. In 1011 Canterbury was besieged and taken 'by deceit': 'There man might see misery where he had seen bliss, in the wretched town from which Christianity first came to us, and joy before God and the world'.

In the 1010s, Aethelred's hold over his kingdom gradually became weaker. King Swein of Denmark landed in 1013 and was immediately accepted as king by Northumbria and eastern England. He took Oxford, Winchester and London and received Wessex's allegiance. By the end of the year, 'all the nation had accepted him as full king', and Aethelred had fled to Normandy. But after Swein's sudden death the next February, Aethelred drove Swein's son Cnut out and returned home on a wave of popular enthusiasm; 'full friendship was fastened with word and pledge' between monarch and people. Not for long: treachery soon reappeared at court, and heavy taxes were levied. Cnut returned and a year of inconclusive campaigning followed. Aethelred died in April 1016, and his son Edmund was immediately proclaimed king in London, while a larger and more representative group of nobles meeting at Southampton gave the crown to Cnut. After a summer of warfare, the two kings met in November. Edmund kept the lands south of the Thames, while Cnut was declared ruler of the rest of England. But by the end of the month Edmund had died, and 'Cnut received all the kingdom of England'.

The Chroniclers' account of Aethelred's reign makes much of the king's poor judgement and incompetence. It is almost completely concerned with the Danish wars, and the Chroniclers frequently inserted their own opinions and interpretations. The narrative was probably written retrospectively during Cnut's reign, when it would have been politic to place Aethelred's rule, however genuinely inadequate, in an even more unfavourable light.

Right: Seal of Godwine, one of Aethelred's ministers, dating from about 1000.

Right: Silver penny of Aethelred.

Left: Throughout his long reign, Aethelred never succeeded in winning the constant allegiance of the nobility. One of the most prominent turncoats was Aelfric, who was commander of the king's fleet at London in 992 when he warned the Danes of an attack. Even so, Aelfric remained in office, only to betray his king again in 1003. Seal of Aelfric.

Below: 10th-century Viking axe from Mammen, Jutland, the highly decorated weapon of an elite class of warriors. The Mammen style of Viking art, named from this axe, is characterized by the use of writhing animal ornament as an overall decoration.

Swein of Denmark and his army arrive in England where they established their headquarters in the old Danelaw. The king's campaign was successful, but he only ruled the English for two months before his sudden death. Illustration from a 15th-century manuscript.

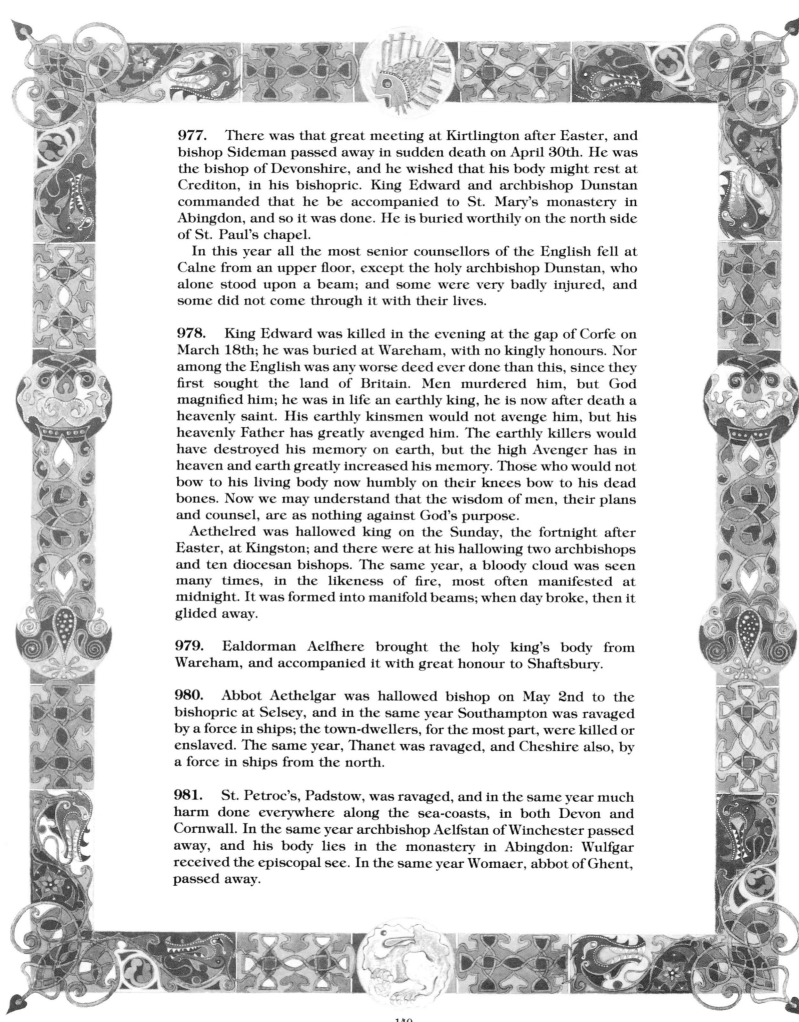

977. There was that great meeting at Kirtlington after Easter, and bishop Sideman passed away in sudden death on April 30th. He was the bishop of Devonshire, and he wished that his body might rest at Crediton, in his bishopric. King Edward and archbishop Dunstan commanded that he be accompanied to St. Mary's monastery in Abingdon, and so it was done. He is buried worthily on the north side of St. Paul's chapel.

In this year all the most senior counsellors of the English fell at Calne from an upper floor, except the holy archbishop Dunstan, who alone stood upon a beam; and some were very badly injured, and some did not come through it with their lives.

978. King Edward was killed in the evening at the gap of Corfe on March 18th; he was buried at Wareham, with no kingly honours. Nor among the English was any worse deed ever done than this, since they first sought the land of Britain. Men murdered him, but God magnified him; he was in life an earthly king, he is now after death a heavenly saint. His earthly kinsmen would not avenge him, but his heavenly Father has greatly avenged him. The earthly killers would have destroyed his memory on earth, but the high Avenger has in heaven and earth greatly increased his memory. Those who would not bow to his living body now humbly on their knees bow to his dead bones. Now we may understand that the wisdom of men, their plans and counsel, are as nothing against God's purpose.

Aethelred was hallowed king on the Sunday, the fortnight after Easter, at Kingston; and there were at his hallowing two archbishops and ten diocesan bishops. The same year, a bloody cloud was seen many times, in the likeness of fire, most often manifested at midnight. It was formed into manifold beams; when day broke, then it glided away.

979. Ealdorman Aelfhere brought the holy king's body from Wareham, and accompanied it with great honour to Shaftsbury.

980. Abbot Aethelgar was hallowed bishop on May 2nd to the bishopric at Selsey, and in the same year Southampton was ravaged by a force in ships; the town-dwellers, for the most part, were killed or enslaved. The same year, Thanet was ravaged, and Cheshire also, by a force in ships from the north.

981. St. Petroc's, Padstow, was ravaged, and in the same year much harm done everywhere along the sea-coasts, in both Devon and Cornwall. In the same year archbishop Aelfstan of Winchester passed away, and his body lies in the monastery in Abingdon: Wulfgar received the episcopal see. In the same year Womaer, abbot of Ghent, passed away.

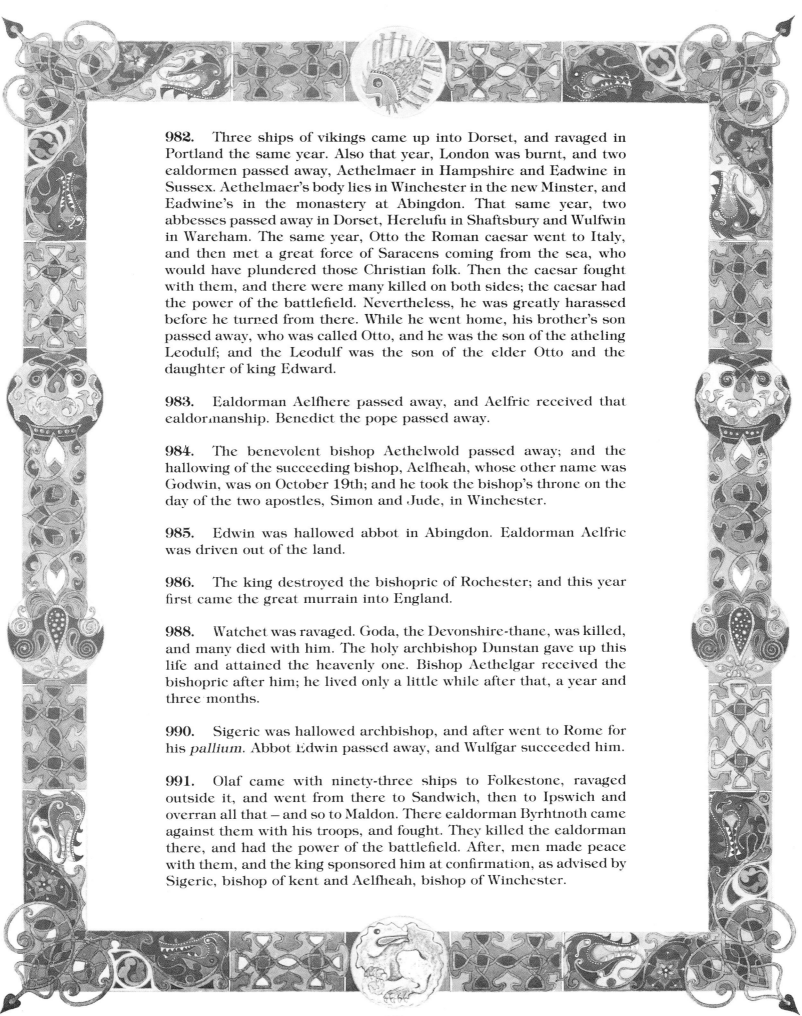

982. Three ships of vikings came up into Dorset, and ravaged in Portland the same year. Also that year, London was burnt, and two ealdormen passed away, Aethelmaer in Hampshire and Eadwine in Sussex. Aethelmaer's body lies in Winchester in the new Minster, and Eadwine's in the monastery at Abingdon. That same year, two abbesses passed away in Dorset, Herelufu in Shaftsbury and Wulfwin in Wareham. The same year, Otto the Roman caesar went to Italy, and then met a great force of Saracens coming from the sea, who would have plundered those Christian folk. Then the caesar fought with them, and there were many killed on both sides; the caesar had the power of the battlefield. Nevertheless, he was greatly harassed before he turned from there. While he went home, his brother's son passed away, who was called Otto, and he was the son of the atheling Leodulf; and the Leodulf was the son of the elder Otto and the daughter of king Edward.

983. Ealdorman Aelfhere passed away, and Aelfric received that ealdormanship. Benedict the pope passed away.

984. The benevolent bishop Aethelwold passed away; and the hallowing of the succeeding bishop, Aelfheah, whose other name was Godwin, was on October 19th; and he took the bishop's throne on the day of the two apostles, Simon and Jude, in Winchester.

985. Edwin was hallowed abbot in Abingdon. Ealdorman Aelfric was driven out of the land.

986. The king destroyed the bishopric of Rochester; and this year first came the great murrain into England.

988. Watchet was ravaged. Goda, the Devonshire-thane, was killed, and many died with him. The holy archbishop Dunstan gave up this life and attained the heavenly one. Bishop Aethelgar received the bishopric after him; he lived only a little while after that, a year and three months.

990. Sigeric was hallowed archbishop, and after went to Rome for his *pallium*. Abbot Edwin passed away, and Wulfgar succeeded him.

991. Olaf came with ninety-three ships to Folkestone, ravaged outside it, and went from there to Sandwich, then to Ipswich and overran all that — and so to Maldon. There ealdorman Byrhtnoth came against them with his troops, and fought. They killed the ealdorman there, and had the power of the battlefield. After, men made peace with them, and the king sponsored him at confirmation, as advised by Sigeric, bishop of kent and Aelfheah, bishop of Winchester.

Opposite page: Contemporary styles in Germany and northern France were more dignified and stately, with softer colours and less movement. (Page from the Registrum Gregorii, c.985, depicting the Holy Roman Emperor with symbols of the four parts of his Empire.)

Below: There is a marvellous feeling of lightness about the angels in this ivory panel done in Winchester in about 1000.

Below right: 10th- or 11th-century bronze censer cover from Canterbury, shaped like a house.

Right: Ivory relief depicting the baptism of Christ, dating from about 1000.

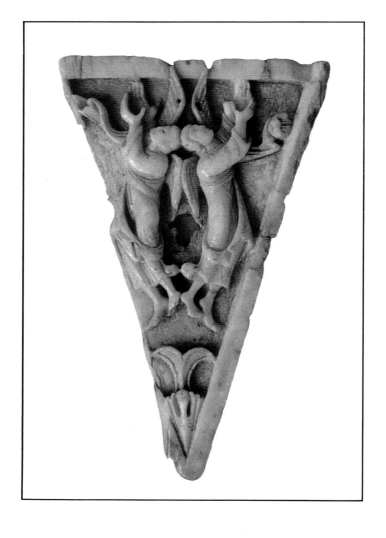

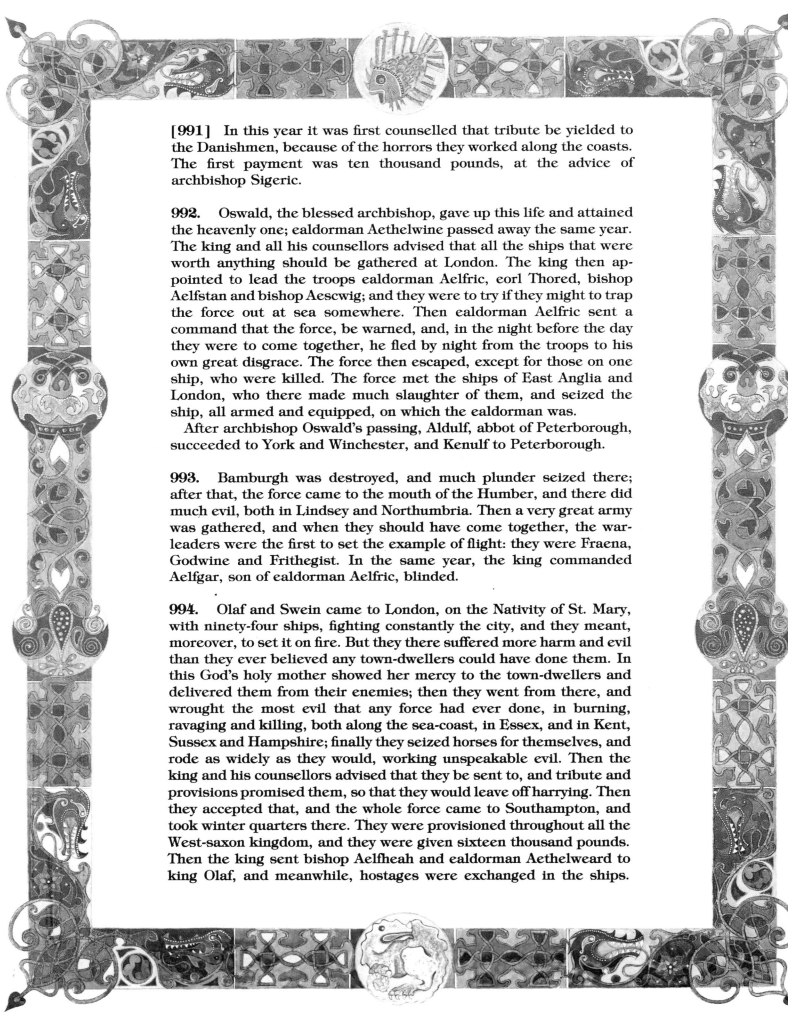

[991] In this year it was first counselled that tribute be yielded to the Danishmen, because of the horrors they worked along the coasts. The first payment was ten thousand pounds, at the advice of archbishop Sigeric.

992. Oswald, the blessed archbishop, gave up this life and attained the heavenly one; ealdorman Aethelwine passed away the same year. The king and all his counsellors advised that all the ships that were worth anything should be gathered at London. The king then appointed to lead the troops ealdorman Aelfric, eorl Thored, bishop Aelfstan and bishop Aescwig; and they were to try if they might to trap the force out at sea somewhere. Then ealdorman Aelfric sent a command that the force, be warned, and, in the night before the day they were to come together, he fled by night from the troops to his own great disgrace. The force then escaped, except for those on one ship, who were killed. The force met the ships of East Anglia and London, who there made much slaughter of them, and seized the ship, all armed and equipped, on which the ealdorman was.

After archbishop Oswald's passing, Aldulf, abbot of Peterborough, succeeded to York and Winchester, and Kenulf to Peterborough.

993. Bamburgh was destroyed, and much plunder seized there; after that, the force came to the mouth of the Humber, and there did much evil, both in Lindsey and Northumbria. Then a very great army was gathered, and when they should have come together, the war-leaders were the first to set the example of flight: they were Fraena, Godwine and Frithegist. In the same year, the king commanded Aelfgar, son of ealdorman Aelfric, blinded.

994. Olaf and Swein came to London, on the Nativity of St. Mary, with ninety-four ships, fighting constantly the city, and they meant, moreover, to set it on fire. But they there suffered more harm and evil than they ever believed any town-dwellers could have done them. In this God's holy mother showed her mercy to the town-dwellers and delivered them from their enemies; then they went from there, and wrought the most evil that any force had ever done, in burning, ravaging and killing, both along the sea-coast, in Essex, and in Kent, Sussex and Hampshire; finally they seized horses for themselves, and rode as widely as they would, working unspeakable evil. Then the king and his counsellors advised that they be sent to, and tribute and provisions promised them, so that they would leave off harrying. Then they accepted that, and the whole force came to Southampton, and took winter quarters there. They were provisioned throughout all the West-saxon kingdom, and they were given sixteen thousand pounds. Then the king sent bishop Aelfheah and ealdorman Aethelweard to king Olaf, and meanwhile, hostages were exchanged in the ships.

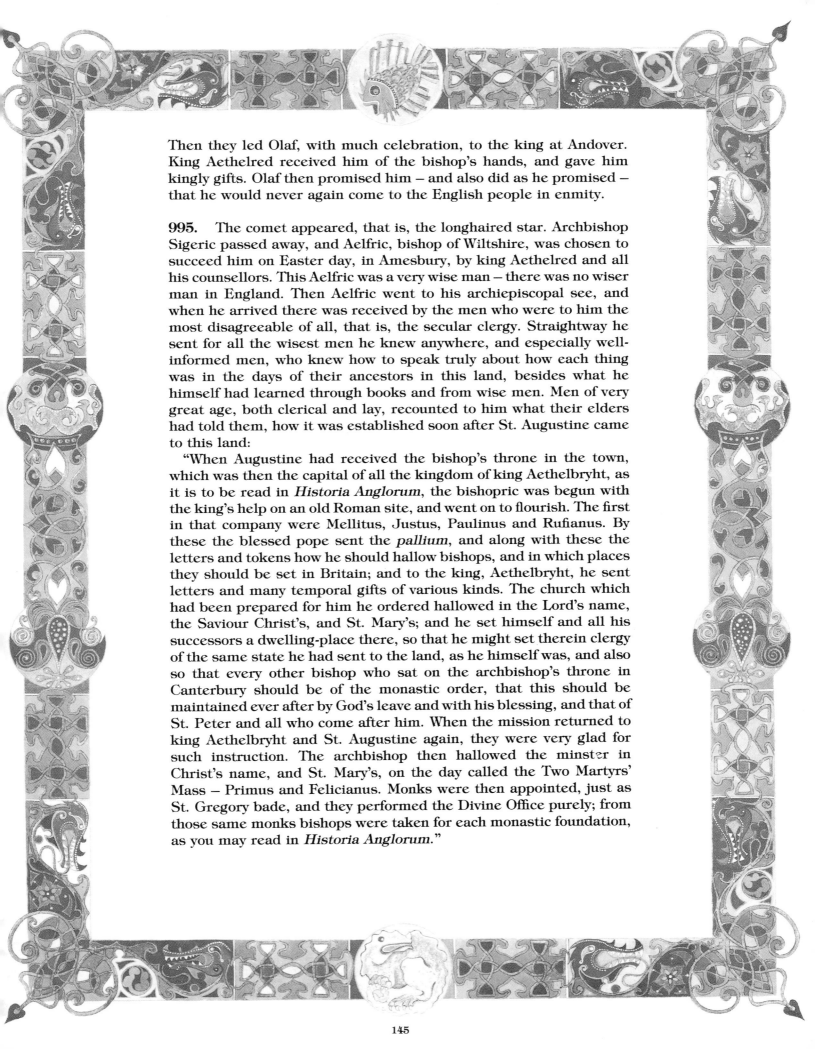

Then they led Olaf, with much celebration, to the king at Andover. King Aethelred received him of the bishop's hands, and gave him kingly gifts. Olaf then promised him – and also did as he promised – that he would never again come to the English people in enmity.

995.   The comet appeared, that is, the longhaired star. Archbishop Sigeric passed away, and Aelfric, bishop of Wiltshire, was chosen to succeed him on Easter day, in Amesbury, by king Aethelred and all his counsellors. This Aelfric was a very wise man – there was no wiser man in England. Then Aelfric went to his archiepiscopal see, and when he arrived there was received by the men who were to him the most disagreeable of all, that is, the secular clergy. Straightway he sent for all the wisest men he knew anywhere, and especially well-informed men, who knew how to speak truly about how each thing was in the days of their ancestors in this land, besides what he himself had learned through books and from wise men. Men of very great age, both clerical and lay, recounted to him what their elders had told them, how it was established soon after St. Augustine came to this land:

"When Augustine had received the bishop's throne in the town, which was then the capital of all the kingdom of king Aethelbryht, as it is to be read in *Historia Anglorum*, the bishopric was begun with the king's help on an old Roman site, and went on to flourish. The first in that company were Mellitus, Justus, Paulinus and Rufianus. By these the blessed pope sent the *pallium*, and along with these the letters and tokens how he should hallow bishops, and in which places they should be set in Britain; and to the king, Aethelbryht, he sent letters and many temporal gifts of various kinds. The church which had been prepared for him he ordered hallowed in the Lord's name, the Saviour Christ's, and St. Mary's; and he set himself and all his successors a dwelling-place there, so that he might set therein clergy of the same state he had sent to the land, as he himself was, and also so that every other bishop who sat on the archbishop's throne in Canterbury should be of the monastic order, that this should be maintained ever after by God's leave and with his blessing, and that of St. Peter and all who come after him. When the mission returned to king Aethelbryht and St. Augustine again, they were very glad for such instruction. The archbishop then hallowed the minster in Christ's name, and St. Mary's, on the day called the Two Martyrs' Mass – Primus and Felicianus. Monks were then appointed, just as St. Gregory bade, and they performed the Divine Office purely; from those same monks bishops were taken for each monastic foundation, as you may read in *Historia Anglorum*."

[995] Archbishop Aelfric was very glad that he had so many witnesses who were, in those times, very influential with the king. Furthermore, the same counsellors who were with the archbishop said:

"Thus, as we have related, monks always dwelt in Christ Church in Augustine's day, and those of Laurentius, Mellitus, Justus, Honorius, Deusdedit, Theodorus, Brithtwold, Tatwine, Nothelm, Cuthbert, Bregewine, Janberht, Aethelheard, Wulfred, and Feologild. But the same year Ceolnoth came to the archbishopric, there was so much pestilence that there was no one left in Christ Church but five monks. And also in his time there was strife and sorrow in this land, so that a person could think of nothing else. Now, thank God, it is in the power of the king, and yours, whether they might be therein any longer, for they might never better be brought out than they may now, if it is the king's will and yours." The archbishop then without delay went with all the counsellors straight to the king, and made known to him all that we have told here before; the king was very glad at these tidings, and said to the archbishop and the others, "It seems advisable to me that first of all you go to Rome for your *pallium*, that you make all this known to the pope, and that you go by his advice afterwards."

This seemed the best counsel. When the secular priests heard of this, they advised choosing two of their number to send to the pope, to offer him much treasure and silver on the condition that he give the *pallium* to them. But when they came to Rome, the pope would not do that, because they brought no letter from the king or any of the people, and he ordered them to go where they would. As soon as the priest turned back from there, archbishop Aelfric came to Rome; the pope received him with much honour, and bid him to say morning mass at St. Peter's altar. The pope himself put on him his own *pallium* and greatly honoured him. When this was done, the archbishop began telling the pope all about the secular priests, how it happened that they were in the monastery in his archbishopric; and the pope told him in turn how the priests had come to him, and offered much treasure so that he would give them the *pallium*. But the pope said, "Go now to England again, with God's blessing, St. Peter's and mine, and when you come home, put into your minster the same order of men as the blessed Gregory bade Augustine to set therein, by God's command, St. Peter's and mine." With this the archbishop returned to England. As soon as he came home, he occupied his see, and after, went to the king. The king and all his people thanked God for his return, that he had succeeded in his errand in a way that was entirely pleasing to them. He then turned to Canterbury, drove the clerics out of the monastery, and set monks therein, just as the pope had bidden him.

996.   Wulfstan was instated as bishop of London.

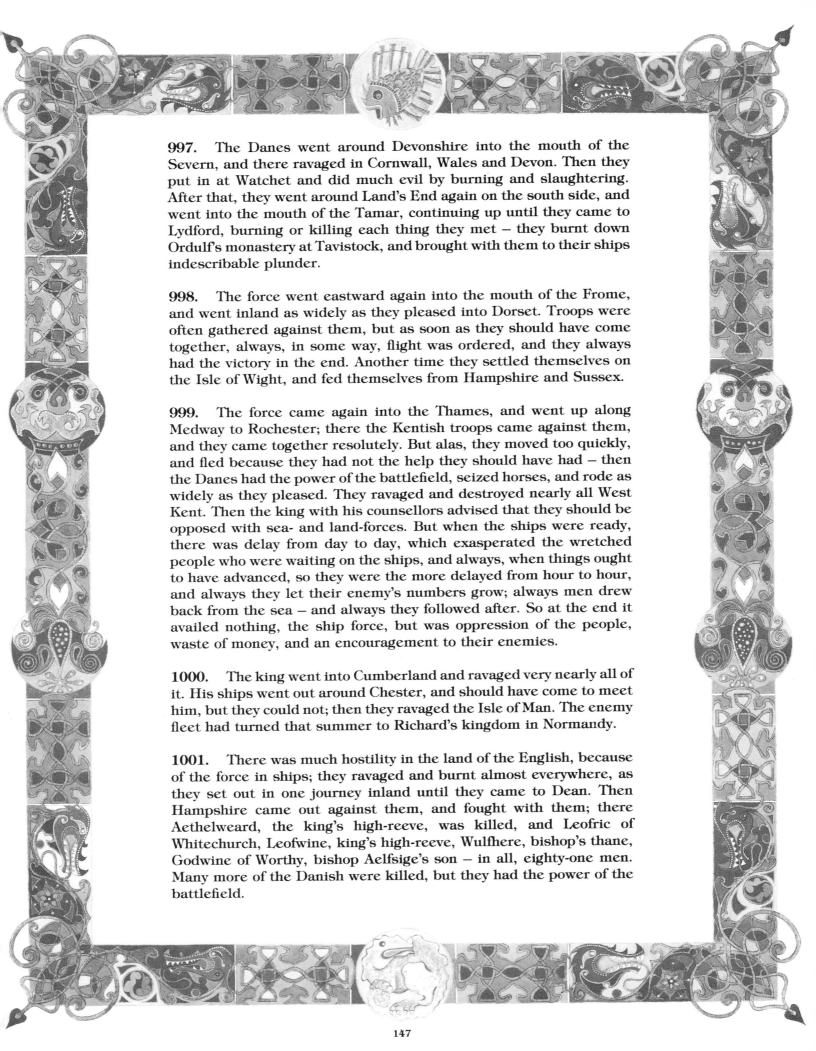

997. The Danes went around Devonshire into the mouth of the Severn, and there ravaged in Cornwall, Wales and Devon. Then they put in at Watchet and did much evil by burning and slaughtering. After that, they went around Land's End again on the south side, and went into the mouth of the Tamar, continuing up until they came to Lydford, burning or killing each thing they met – they burnt down Ordulf's monastery at Tavistock, and brought with them to their ships indescribable plunder.

998. The force went eastward again into the mouth of the Frome, and went inland as widely as they pleased into Dorset. Troops were often gathered against them, but as soon as they should have come together, always, in some way, flight was ordered, and they always had the victory in the end. Another time they settled themselves on the Isle of Wight, and fed themselves from Hampshire and Sussex.

999. The force came again into the Thames, and went up along Medway to Rochester; there the Kentish troops came against them, and they came together resolutely. But alas, they moved too quickly, and fled because they had not the help they should have had – then the Danes had the power of the battlefield, seized horses, and rode as widely as they pleased. They ravaged and destroyed nearly all West Kent. Then the king with his counsellors advised that they should be opposed with sea- and land-forces. But when the ships were ready, there was delay from day to day, which exasperated the wretched people who were waiting on the ships, and always, when things ought to have advanced, so they were the more delayed from hour to hour, and always they let their enemy's numbers grow; always men drew back from the sea – and always they followed after. So at the end it availed nothing, the ship force, but was oppression of the people, waste of money, and an encouragement to their enemies.

1000. The king went into Cumberland and ravaged very nearly all of it. His ships went out around Chester, and should have come to meet him, but they could not; then they ravaged the Isle of Man. The enemy fleet had turned that summer to Richard's kingdom in Normandy.

1001. There was much hostility in the land of the English, because of the force in ships; they ravaged and burnt almost everywhere, as they set out in one journey inland until they came to Dean. Then Hampshire came out against them, and fought with them; there Aethelweard, the king's high-reeve, was killed, and Leofric of Whitechurch, Leofwine, king's high-reeve, Wulfhere, bishop's thane, Godwine of Worthy, bishop Aelfsige's son – in all, eighty-one men. Many more of the Danish were killed, but they had the power of the battlefield.

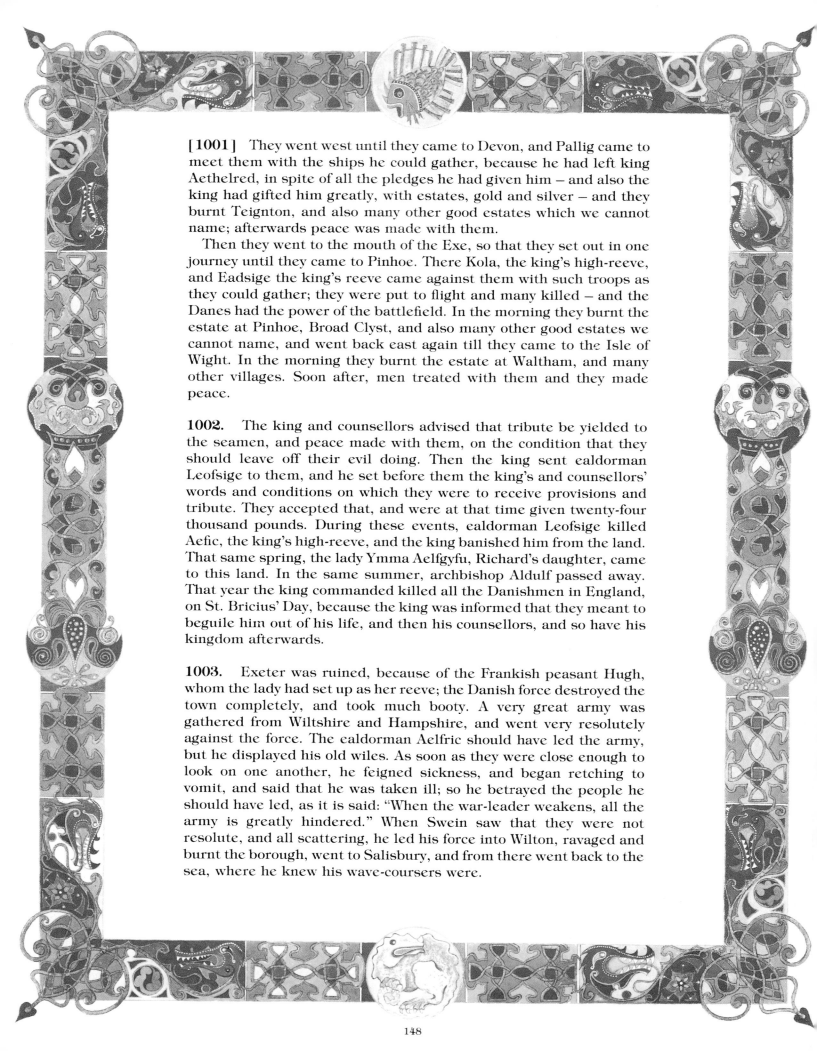

[1001] They went west until they came to Devon, and Pallig came to meet them with the ships he could gather, because he had left king Aethelred, in spite of all the pledges he had given him – and also the king had gifted him greatly, with estates, gold and silver – and they burnt Teignton, and also many other good estates which we cannot name; afterwards peace was made with them.

Then they went to the mouth of the Exe, so that they set out in one journey until they came to Pinhoe. There Kola, the king's high-reeve, and Eadsige the king's reeve came against them with such troops as they could gather; they were put to flight and many killed – and the Danes had the power of the battlefield. In the morning they burnt the estate at Pinhoe, Broad Clyst, and also many other good estates we cannot name, and went back east again till they came to the Isle of Wight. In the morning they burnt the estate at Waltham, and many other villages. Soon after, men treated with them and they made peace.

1002. The king and counsellors advised that tribute be yielded to the seamen, and peace made with them, on the condition that they should leave off their evil doing. Then the king sent ealdorman Leofsige to them, and he set before them the king's and counsellors' words and conditions on which they were to receive provisions and tribute. They accepted that, and were at that time given twenty-four thousand pounds. During these events, ealdorman Leofsige killed Aefic, the king's high-reeve, and the king banished him from the land. That same spring, the lady Ymma Aelfgyfu, Richard's daughter, came to this land. In the same summer, archbishop Aldulf passed away. That year the king commanded killed all the Danishmen in England, on St. Bricius' Day, because the king was informed that they meant to beguile him out of his life, and then his counsellors, and so have his kingdom afterwards.

1003. Exeter was ruined, because of the Frankish peasant Hugh, whom the lady had set up as her reeve; the Danish force destroyed the town completely, and took much booty. A very great army was gathered from Wiltshire and Hampshire, and went very resolutely against the force. The ealdorman Aelfric should have led the army, but he displayed his old wiles. As soon as they were close enough to look on one another, he feigned sickness, and began retching to vomit, and said that he was taken ill; so he betrayed the people he should have led, as it is said: "When the war-leader weakens, all the army is greatly hindered." When Swein saw that they were not resolute, and all scattering, he led his force into Wilton, ravaged and burnt the borough, went to Salisbury, and from there went back to the sea, where he knew his wave-coursers were.

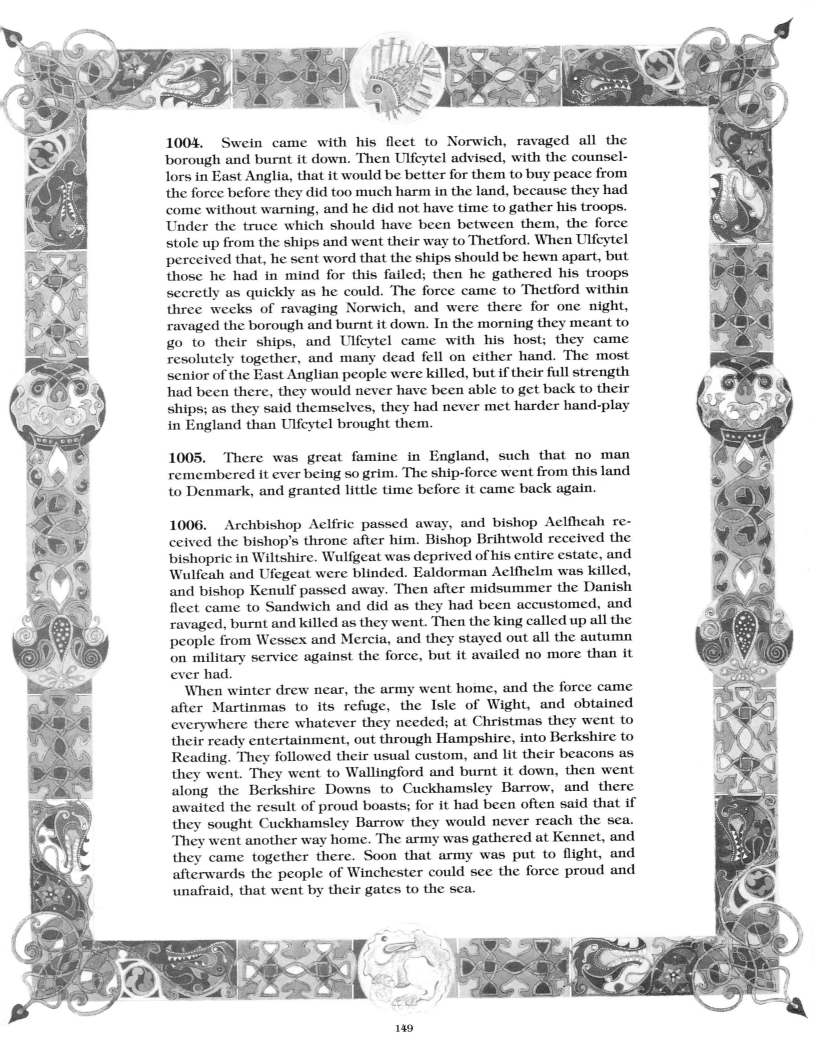

1004. Swein came with his fleet to Norwich, ravaged all the borough and burnt it down. Then Ulfcytel advised, with the counsellors in East Anglia, that it would be better for them to buy peace from the force before they did too much harm in the land, because they had come without warning, and he did not have time to gather his troops. Under the truce which should have been between them, the force stole up from the ships and went their way to Thetford. When Ulfcytel perceived that, he sent word that the ships should be hewn apart, but those he had in mind for this failed; then he gathered his troops secretly as quickly as he could. The force came to Thetford within three weeks of ravaging Norwich, and were there for one night, ravaged the borough and burnt it down. In the morning they meant to go to their ships, and Ulfcytel came with his host; they came resolutely together, and many dead fell on either hand. The most senior of the East Anglian people were killed, but if their full strength had been there, they would never have been able to get back to their ships; as they said themselves, they had never met harder hand-play in England than Ulfcytel brought them.

1005. There was great famine in England, such that no man remembered it ever being so grim. The ship-force went from this land to Denmark, and granted little time before it came back again.

1006. Archbishop Aelfric passed away, and bishop Aelfheah received the bishop's throne after him. Bishop Brihtwold received the bishopric in Wiltshire. Wulfgeat was deprived of his entire estate, and Wulfeah and Ufegeat were blinded. Ealdorman Aelfhelm was killed, and bishop Kenulf passed away. Then after midsummer the Danish fleet came to Sandwich and did as they had been accustomed, and ravaged, burnt and killed as they went. Then the king called up all the people from Wessex and Mercia, and they stayed out all the autumn on military service against the force, but it availed no more than it ever had.

When winter drew near, the army went home, and the force came after Martinmas to its refuge, the Isle of Wight, and obtained everywhere there whatever they needed; at Christmas they went to their ready entertainment, out through Hampshire, into Berkshire to Reading. They followed their usual custom, and lit their beacons as they went. They went to Wallingford and burnt it down, then went along the Berkshire Downs to Cuckhamsley Barrow, and there awaited the result of proud boasts; for it had been often said that if they sought Cuckhamsley Barrow they would never reach the sea. They went another way home. The army was gathered at Kennet, and they came together there. Soon that army was put to flight, and afterwards the people of Winchester could see the force proud and unafraid, that went by their gates to the sea.

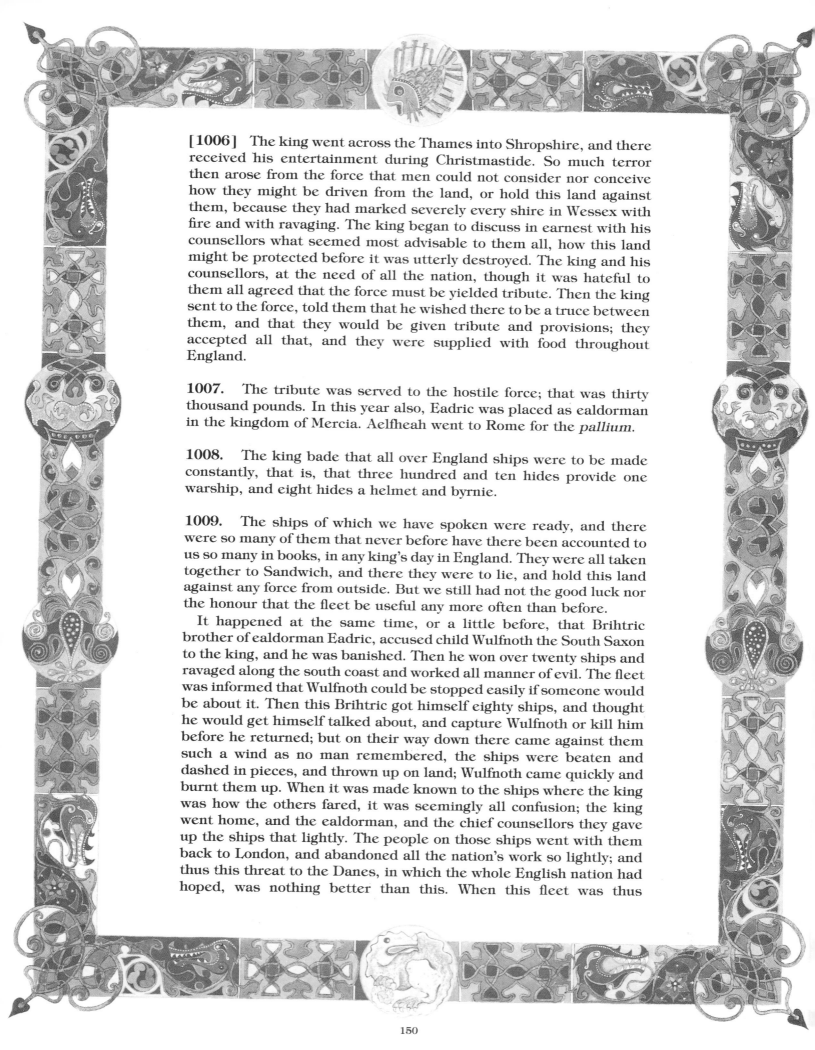

[1006] The king went across the Thames into Shropshire, and there received his entertainment during Christmastide. So much terror then arose from the force that men could not consider nor conceive how they might be driven from the land, or hold this land against them, because they had marked severely every shire in Wessex with fire and with ravaging. The king began to discuss in earnest with his counsellors what seemed most advisable to them all, how this land might be protected before it was utterly destroyed. The king and his counsellors, at the need of all the nation, though it was hateful to them all agreed that the force must be yielded tribute. Then the king sent to the force, told them that he wished there to be a truce between them, and that they would be given tribute and provisions; they accepted all that, and they were supplied with food throughout England.

1007. The tribute was served to the hostile force; that was thirty thousand pounds. In this year also, Eadric was placed as ealdorman in the kingdom of Mercia. Aelfheah went to Rome for the *pallium*.

1008. The king bade that all over England ships were to be made constantly, that is, that three hundred and ten hides provide one warship, and eight hides a helmet and byrnie.

1009. The ships of which we have spoken were ready, and there were so many of them that never before have there been accounted to us so many in books, in any king's day in England. They were all taken together to Sandwich, and there they were to lie, and hold this land against any force from outside. But we still had not the good luck nor the honour that the fleet be useful any more often than before.

It happened at the same time, or a little before, that Brihtric brother of ealdorman Eadric, accused child Wulfnoth the South Saxon to the king, and he was banished. Then he won over twenty ships and ravaged along the south coast and worked all manner of evil. The fleet was informed that Wulfnoth could be stopped easily if someone would be about it. Then this Brihtric got himself eighty ships, and thought he would get himself talked about, and capture Wulfnoth or kill him before he returned; but on their way down there came against them such a wind as no man remembered, the ships were beaten and dashed in pieces, and thrown up on land; Wulfnoth came quickly and burnt them up. When it was made known to the ships where the king was how the others fared, it was seemingly all confusion; the king went home, and the ealdorman, and the chief counsellors they gave up the ships that lightly. The people on those ships went with them back to London, and abandoned all the nation's work so lightly; and thus this threat to the Danes, in which the whole English nation had hoped, was nothing better than this. When this fleet was thus finished, soon after Lammas there came that immense enemy force, which we call Thurkil's force, to Sandwich; they went soon to Canterbury, and would have quickly overrun the town if they had not more quickly asked for peace with them; and all the East Kentish made peace with the force, and gave them three thousand pounds. The force, soon after that, went about until they came to the Isle of Wight; there and in Sussex, Hampshire and Berkshire they ravaged and burned as was their custom. The king commanded that all the nation be called out, that men hold against them on every side; but nevertheless they went where they would.

Then on a certain occasion when they went out, the king had surrounded them with the whole army, as they wanted to go to their ships; all the people were ready to attack them, but it was hindered through ealdorman Eadric as it always was. Then after Martinmas, they fared again to Kent, took winter quarters on the Thames and lived off Essex and the next shires on both sides of the Thames. They often attacked the town of London; but thanks be to God it yet stands sound, and they ever fared evilly there. After midwinter, they took a pass in the Chilterns, went to Oxford and burnt down the town; then they went on both sides of the Thames towards their ships. When they were warned that there was an army at London set against them they crossed over at Staines; thus they behaved all winter. In spring they were in Kent, repairing their ships.

1010. The aforesaid force came after Easter to East Anglia, landed at Ipswich, and went straight on to where they had heard that Ulfcytel was with his troops; this was on the first day of Ascension. The East Anglians soon fled; Cambridgeshire stood firmly against them. There was killed Aethelstan, the king's son-in-law, Oswi, his son, Eadwig, Aefic's brother, Wulfric, Leofwine's son, and many other good thanes, countless folk; the flight was first started by Thurcytel Mare's Head, and then the Danes had the power of the battlefield. There they were horsed, and after had control of East Anglia. For three months in that land they ravaged and burnt further into the wild fens they went, killed men and cattle, and burnt throughout the fens. They burnt down Thetford and Cambridge, and afterwards went southward into the Thames valley. The mounted men rode to meet the ships, and after went quickly westward in Oxfordshire, from there to Buckinghamshire along the Ouse until they came to Bedford, and so on to Tempsford, ever burning where they went. They returned to their ships with much plunder; and when they scattered to the ships, the troops should have come out again in case they intended to go inland. Then the troops went home; when the force was in the east, the troops were kept west, and when they were in the south, then our troops were in the north.

With the uneasy peace after the campaigns against the Danish invaders, there were good reasons for building new stone churches or replacing earlier wooden ones with stone structures. The monastic revival had increased the wealth of religious foundations, and the new monastic rule had brought new practices, such as bell-ringing, that in turn required new features, such as strong towers. In general, later Anglo-Saxon churches were more elaborate than the earlier ones; continental influences are apparent in the towers and, more rarely, in the construction of transepts. Surface decoration also became more accomplished: blind arcading and stripwork broke up the large surfaces. Alternating horizontal and vertical stones (long and short work) made corners more interesting. Windows were splayed on the inside and outside to let in light and keep rain out. Often there were galleries, now vanished, around part of the church interior, which account for the high doorways and windows of many naves.

The second, and far more overwhelming, wave of Danish invasions in the early 11th century brought building to a virtual halt. Economic chaos meant little new building during Cnut's reign (1016–35).

Continental Romanesque architecture reached England with Edward the Confessor (1042–66), who modelled Westminster Abbey on Saint-Jumièges in France where he had spent some time in exile, and after 1066 the Normans imposed their own version of Romanesque on all major cathedrals and monastic centres. Nevertheless, native styles continued: smaller local churches in the Anglo-Saxon style were built, and English workmen occasionally added ornamentation to a capital in the impressive but severe Norman buildings.

Left: St Peter, Barton-upon-Humber, Humberside, one of the most complete surviving Anglo-Saxon churches. The lower two levels of the tower, which are decorated with characteristic pilaster and stripwork, and the small west window date from the 10th century. The top of the tower is Norman.

Below left and right: Two characteristic Anglo-Saxon towers, at Sompting, Sussex (right) and Earls Barton, Northamptonshire. The tower at Sompting is the only one whose original roof survives; the main body of the church was rebuilt in the 12th century by the Knights Templar.

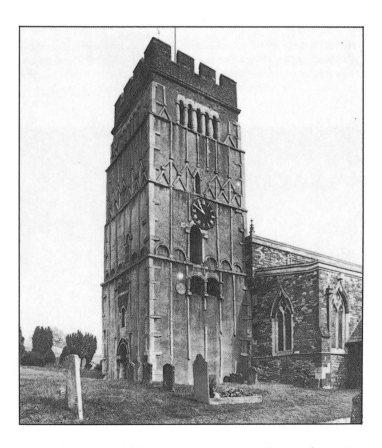

Opposite: Late 11th-century iron door hinge from the church at Stillingfleet, Yorkshire, showing the outline of a

Viking ship. Scandinavian motifs persist in Northumbrian art, recalling many generations of Viking raids.

Until about the mid-10th century, the art of the Scandinavian invaders was ignored in England as the product of a pagan enemy set on destroying civilized life and culture. Only gradually, as the Scandinavian settlers were slowly assimilated into the English population, did their art begin to appear alongside and merge with native styles and techniques. Anglo-Saxon artists and craftsmen took much of their inspiration from the Christian tradition – from biblical stories and from the lives of Christ, his disciples and the saints. Scandinavian art had as its subject matter the victorious armies of the Viking expansion and the heroes of legend; there was also much pagan religious symbolism. But Scandinavian techniques were more familiar – interlaced and stylized animals knotted and looped to cover every inch of surface space – and found a parallel in the old Saxon and Irish interlace of the Celtic Christian *Book of Kells* and *Book of Durrow*.

The Jellinge style was the first Scandinavian idiom to reach England, although it never spread further than the Danelaw and the areas of the north-west settled by the Norwegians. The introduction of its somewhat undisciplined interlace designs in the mid-10th century seems to have stimulated a successful combination of Anglo-Saxon and Norwegian subjects, especially in the north. In the south, the trend continued towards art forms influenced by Roman and French models brought in by travellers and church dignitaries.

The Ringerike style was a Viking interpretation of the Winchester art forms, with which it seems to have co-existed in the early 11th century. Ringerike forms are lighter and the animal decoration is combined with foliage itself derived from the Winchester models. Ringerike was too imitative to have much influence on contemporary English art, and even Cnut preferred and encouraged the Winchester artists.

Reconstruction of a Jellinge harness-bow from Mammen, Jutland, dating from the second quarter of the 10th century. The gilt bronze mounts are original, but the wooden shaft is modern. The reins went through the hole on the top.

The bound devil, a common image in both pagan and Saxon-Christian tradition, appears in 10th- and 11th-century English manuscripts. (10th-century cross, Kirkby Stephen, Cumbria.)

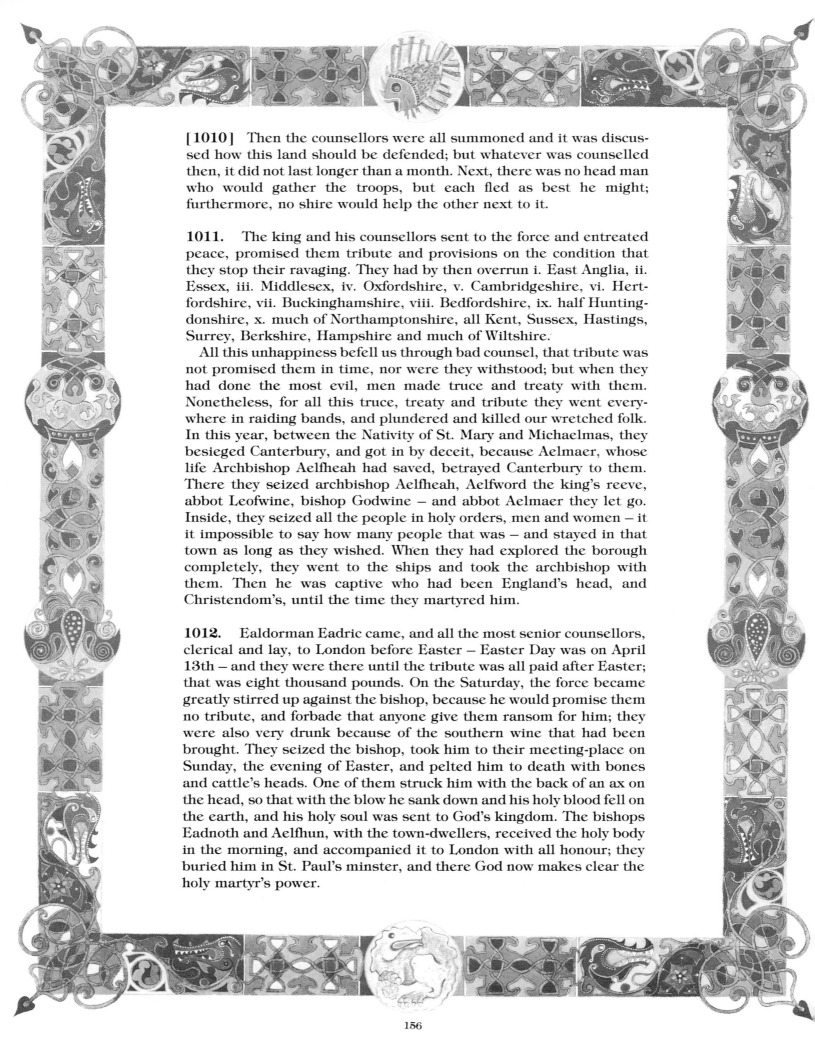

[1010] Then the counsellors were all summoned and it was discussed how this land should be defended; but whatever was counselled then, it did not last longer than a month. Next, there was no head man who would gather the troops, but each fled as best he might; furthermore, no shire would help the other next to it.

1011. The king and his counsellors sent to the force and entreated peace, promised them tribute and provisions on the condition that they stop their ravaging. They had by then overrun i. East Anglia, ii. Essex, iii. Middlesex, iv. Oxfordshire, v. Cambridgeshire, vi. Hertfordshire, vii. Buckinghamshire, viii. Bedfordshire, ix. half Huntingdonshire, x. much of Northamptonshire, all Kent, Sussex, Hastings, Surrey, Berkshire, Hampshire and much of Wiltshire.

All this unhappiness befell us through bad counsel, that tribute was not promised them in time, nor were they withstood; but when they had done the most evil, men made truce and treaty with them. Nonetheless, for all this truce, treaty and tribute they went everywhere in raiding bands, and plundered and killed our wretched folk. In this year, between the Nativity of St. Mary and Michaelmas, they besieged Canterbury, and got in by deceit, because Aelmaer, whose life Archbishop Aelfheah had saved, betrayed Canterbury to them. There they seized archbishop Aelfheah, Aelfword the king's reeve, abbot Leofwine, bishop Godwine – and abbot Aelmaer they let go. Inside, they seized all the people in holy orders, men and women – it it impossible to say how many people that was – and stayed in that town as long as they wished. When they had explored the borough completely, they went to the ships and took the archbishop with them. Then he was captive who had been England's head, and Christendom's, until the time they martyred him.

1012. Ealdorman Eadric came, and all the most senior counsellors, clerical and lay, to London before Easter – Easter Day was on April 13th – and they were there until the tribute was all paid after Easter; that was eight thousand pounds. On the Saturday, the force became greatly stirred up against the bishop, because he would promise them no tribute, and forbade that anyone give them ransom for him; they were also very drunk because of the southern wine that had been brought. They seized the bishop, took him to their meeting-place on Sunday, the evening of Easter, and pelted him to death with bones and cattle's heads. One of them struck him with the back of an ax on the head, so that with the blow he sank down and his holy blood fell on the earth, and his holy soul was sent to God's kingdom. The bishops Eadnoth and Aelfhun, with the town-dwellers, received the holy body in the morning, and accompanied it to London with all honour; they buried him in St. Paul's minster, and there God now makes clear the holy martyr's power.

1013. The year after the archbishop was martyred, the king appointed bishop Lifing to the archbishop's throne in Canterbury; and in the same year, before the month of August, came king Swein with his fleet to Sandwich, he went very quickly about East Anglia into the Humber's mouth, and so upward along the Trent till he came to Gainsborough. Eorl Uhtred and all Northumbria quickly bowed to him, all the folk of Lindsey, then the folk of the Five Boroughs, and soon all the force north of Watling Street; he was given hostages from each shire. When he understood that all the people had submitted to him, he bade that his force should be provisioned and horsed; he went south in full force, and entrusted his ships and the hostages to his son Cnut. After he came over Watling Street, they worked the most evil that a force might do. They went to Oxford, and the town-dwellers soon bowed to him, and gave hostages. From there they went to Winchester, and did the same, then eastward to London. Many of his people drowned in the Thames, because they did not look for a bridge. When he came to the town, the inhabitants would not submit, but held aganst him with all their force, because king Aethelred was inside, and Thurkil with him. Then king Swein went from there to Wallingford, over the Thames to Bath, and stayed there with his troops; ealdorman Aethelmaer came, and the western thanes with him. They all bowed to Swein and gave hostages. When he had thus fared, he went northward to his ships, and all the nation had accepted him as full king. The people of London afterwards submitted and gave hostages, because they feared that he would destroy them. Swein demanded full tribute and provisions for his force that winter. Thurkil demanded the same for the force that lay in Greenwich, and even so, they ravaged as often as they would. Then nothing went right for this nation, south or north. The king was for some time with the fleet that was on the Thames, and his lady went over the sea to her brother Richard, and Aelfsig, abbot of Peterborough, with her; the king sent bishop Aelfun with the athelings Edward and Alfred over the sea, that he might take charge of them. The king went from the fleet at Christmas to the Isle of Wight, and was there for the festival; and after the festival he went over the sea to Richard, and was there with him until the favourable time of Swein's death.

Above: Early 11th-century churchyard stone from St Paul's, London, ornamented in the Ringerike style with recognizable animals entangled in vegetation. Originally the surface of the stone was painted.

Left: 10th-century silver, niello and gold brooch from Gotland.

Opposite page, top: 11th-century elaborately decorated weather vane from a Viking ship. The style is Ringerike, with identifiable animals and plants.

Opposite page, bottom: 10th- or 11th-century hog-back tombstone from Cumbria showing a Viking army on the march. The shape may represent the house of the dead.

[1013] The time that the lady was with her brother beyond the sea, Aelfsig, abbot of Peterborough, who was with her, went to the minster called Boneval, where St. Florentine's body lay; he found there a wretched site, and wretched abbots and monks, because they had been plundered. He bought there, from the abbot and monks, the body of St. Florentine – all except the head – for five hundred pounds; and when he came back, he offered it to Christ and St. Peter.

1014. Swein ended his days on Candlemas, February 3rd, and the fleet all chose Cnut as king. All the counsellors, clerical and lay, advised that king Aethelred be sent after; they said that no lord was more dear to them than their natural lord, if he would govern them more justly than he had done. The king then sent hither his son Edward, with his messengers, commanded that all his nation be greeted, and said that he would be to them a faithful lord, better each of the things they all hated, and that everything should be forgiven which had been done or said against him, on the condition that they all agreed, without treachery, to turn to him; full friendship was fastened with word and pledge on both sides, and they declared every Danish king outlawed from England forever.

Then in spring king Aethelred came home to his own people, and he was gladly received by all of them. After Swein was dead, Cnut sat with his force in Gainsborough until Easter, and arranged with the people in Lindsey that they give them horses; later they all went out together harrying. King Aethelred came there in full force to Lindsey before they were ready; they ravaged, burnt, and killed all of mankind they could reach. This Cnut went out with his fleet, and so the wretched people were betrayed by him. He went southward until he came to Sandwich, and put ashore the hostages given to his father, with their hands, ears and noses cut off; and even with all this evil the king commanded twenty-one thousand pounds yielded to the force. This year on Michaelmas Eve came the great sea-flood widely through this land, and it ran up farther than it ever had, flooded many towns, and drowned countless human beings.

1015. There was a great council in Oxford, and ealdorman Eadric betrayed Sigeferth and Morcaer, the most senior thanes in the Seven Boroughs. He deceived them into coming to his chamber, and they were basely killed; the king took all their goods, and commanded Sigeferth's widow be seized and brought to Malmesbury. After a short time, atheling Edmund went there, took the woman against the king's will, and married her. Before the Nativity of St. Mary, the atheling went from west to north into the Five Boroughs, and soon took over all Sigeferth's and Morcaer's property, so that all folk bowed to him. At the same time, king Cnut came to Sandwich, went quickly around Kent into Wessex, until he came to the mouth of the Frome, and ravaged then in Dorset, Wiltshire and Somerset. The king lay sick then at Cosham. Ealdorman Eadric gathered troops, and the atheling Edmund did so in the north. When they were to come together, the ealdorman meant to betray the atheling, and they turned away without a fight because of that, and left an opening for their enemies. Ealdorman Eadric won over forty ships from the king, and joined Cnut; the West-Saxons bowed and gave hostages, and they horsed the force. It was there until midwinter.

1016.   Cnut came with his force, and ealdorman Eadric with him, across the Thames into Mercia at Cricklade. They went into Warwickshire during the season of Christmas, and ravaged, burnt and killed all they came across. The atheling Edmund began to gather troops; when the army was gathered, nothing would please them except that the king be there, and that they have the London-dwellers' help. They gave up that expedition, and each man took himself home. After Christmastide, it was ordered that each man fit for service report on pain of full punishment, and the king was sent to in London; they bade him come to meet the troops with all the aid he could gather. When they all came together, it availed no more than it ever had. The king was told that he would be betrayed by those who should have helped him. He forsook the army and turned again to London. The atheling Edmund rode to Northumbria, to eorl Uhtred, and everyone believed that they would gather troops against king Cnut. They went on an expedition into Staffordshire, Shropshire and to Chester, and ravaged on their side, and Cnut on his. They turned out through Buckinghamshire into Bedfordshire, and from there to Huntingdonshire, along the fens to Stamford into Lincolnshire, from there to Nottinghamshire, and so to Northumbria towards York. When Uhtred found this out, he stopped his ravaging and hurried northward; he had to submit by necessity, and all Northumbria with him. He gave hostages, but was killed nevertheless, and Thurcytel son of Nafena, with him. King Cnut put Eric as eorl in Northumbria, just as Uhtred had been, and afterwards went southward another way, keeping to the west. All the force came at Easter to ship, and the atheling Edmund went to London, to his father. After Easter, king Cnut went with all his ships towards London.

Then it befell that king Aethelred passed away before the ships arrived; he ended his days on St. George's Day, after much trouble and wretchedness in his life. After his end, all the counsellors who were in London, and the town-dwellers chose Edmund as king; and he stoutly protected his kingdom during his time.

Cnut became king in 1016 at the age of 23 – the first Danish king of all England. Perhaps because military activity came to an end, the Chronicles offer a very inadequate account of the remarkable successes of his 19-year reign. Cnut's first task was to establish his ascendancy in his new kingdom. He created four powerful new earldoms, devolving power on some of his most trusted and loyal advisors. He killed several leading nobles of the old regime, and brought Ymma, Aethelred's widow, back from Normandy and married her.

In 1018, the king and his counsellors met at Oxford to draw up laws governing the conduct of Danishmen and Englishmen. Cnut promised to dispense justice according to Edgar's law, to protect his subjects' rights and to follow Christian teachings. His subjects, Danish and English, promised obedience. Cnut restored the confidence of his subjects in their country and their king.

Secure at home, Cnut was able to return four times to Scandinavia, to oversee his Danish kingdoms, inherited on the death of his brother Harold in 1018; he also established himself as overlord of Norway. In 1027, he went to Rome, visiting holy shrines and attending Conrad II's coronation as Holy Roman Emperor. An enthusiastic Christian and patron of the arts, Cnut gave splendid gifts and land to many religious foundations. The most distinguished memorial of this exceptionally able leader is a code of secular and ecclesiastical law, which later served William the Conqueror as his best source of traditional legislation in England.

The best-known story of Cnut (or Canute) also provides an illuminating example of popular mythology. Cnut had himself seated at the water's edge, not to prove that he could command the waves to roll back, but to demonstrate to flattering courtiers that he could not – that even a king must accept limits to his authority.

Above: The death of St Olaf at the Battle of Stiklestad in 1030. The autocratic Olaf had lost the throne of Norway to Cnut, but the latter's rule was yet more oppressive, and Olaf's memory was rapidly sanctified. Magnus, Olaf's son, became king without opposition in 1035. (Marginal illustration from the Flateyjarbók, a 14th-century collection of Icelandic sagas.)

Below: Ashingdon Church, Essex, built by Cnut on the battlefield where he defeated Edmund, as a Christian memorial to his adversary. The south wall at the east end is part of Cnut's building.

Right: Queen Ymma receiving the manuscript of the Encomium Emma Reginae. The Encomium, a tribute to the widowed queen emphasizing her goodness and piety was written during the reign of her son Harthacnut (1040–42) to establish his right to the throne over other contestants. Among these were Edward, Ymma's son by her first marriage to Aethelred, of which, pointedly, no mention is made. Watching the ceremony are Harthacnut and Edward, who succeeded his half-brother.

Below right: Runestone from Uppland, Sweden, erected by two sons in memory of their father Ulf, who had commanded a Swedish attack on Cnut's Danish lands in 1026. The runes explain that for his services in England Ulf collected three portions of Danegeld. One was paid by Tostig, one by Thurkil (whom Cnut put in charge of East Anglia) and the third by Cnut himself.

Below: Cnut and Ymma Aelfgyfu placing a cross on the altar of the New Minster, Winchester. An excellent example of the Winchester school which Cnut strongly supported, the illustration portrays the monarch as a champion of Christianity. (Frontispiece of the 11th-century Liber Vitae, the register and martyrology of New Minster and Hyde Abbey, Winchester.)

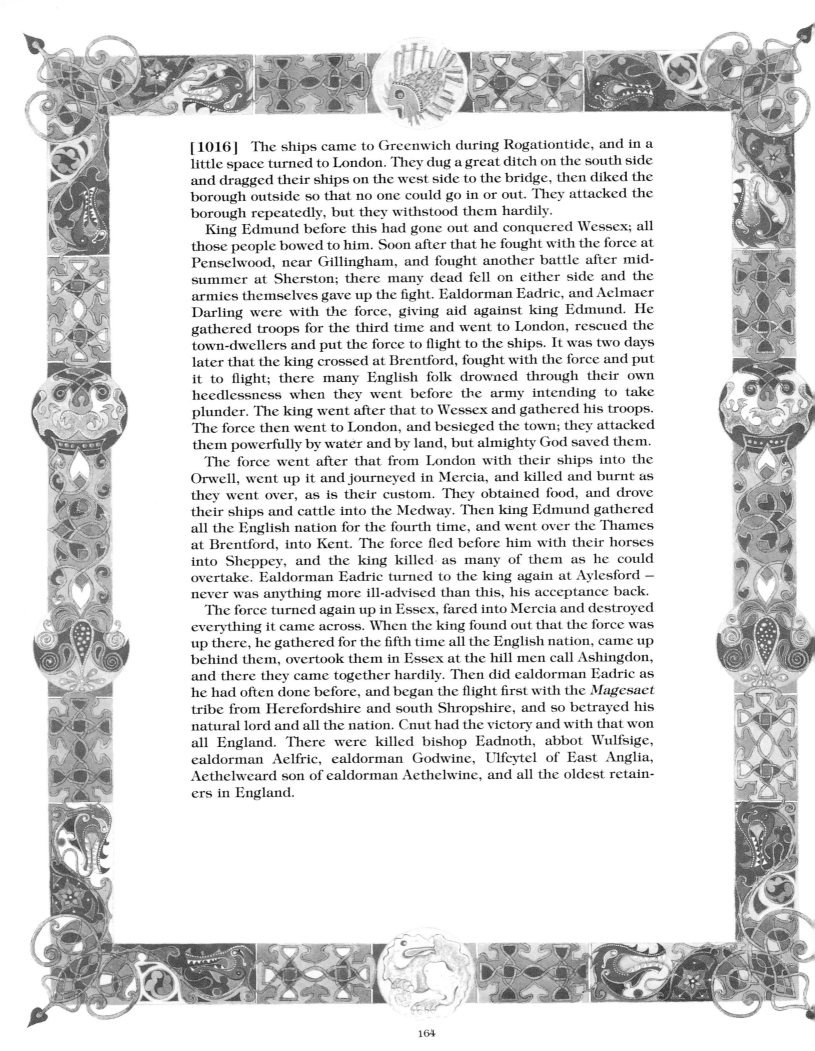

[1016] The ships came to Greenwich during Rogationtide, and in a little space turned to London. They dug a great ditch on the south side and dragged their ships on the west side to the bridge, then diked the borough outside so that no one could go in or out. They attacked the borough repeatedly, but they withstood them hardily.

King Edmund before this had gone out and conquered Wessex; all those people bowed to him. Soon after that he fought with the force at Penselwood, near Gillingham, and fought another battle after midsummer at Sherston; there many dead fell on either side and the armies themselves gave up the fight. Ealdorman Eadric, and Aelmaer Darling were with the force, giving aid against king Edmund. He gathered troops for the third time and went to London, rescued the town-dwellers and put the force to flight to the ships. It was two days later that the king crossed at Brentford, fought with the force and put it to flight; there many English folk drowned through their own heedlessness when they went before the army intending to take plunder. The king went after that to Wessex and gathered his troops. The force then went to London, and besieged the town; they attacked them powerfully by water and by land, but almighty God saved them.

The force went after that from London with their ships into the Orwell, went up it and journeyed in Mercia, and killed and burnt as they went over, as is their custom. They obtained food, and drove their ships and cattle into the Medway. Then king Edmund gathered all the English nation for the fourth time, and went over the Thames at Brentford, into Kent. The force fled before him with their horses into Sheppey, and the king killed as many of them as he could overtake. Ealdorman Eadric turned to the king again at Aylesford — never was anything more ill-advised than this, his acceptance back.

The force turned again up in Essex, fared into Mercia and destroyed everything it came across. When the king found out that the force was up there, he gathered for the fifth time all the English nation, came up behind them, overtook them in Essex at the hill men call Ashingdon, and there they came together hardily. Then did ealdorman Eadric as he had often done before, and began the flight first with the *Magesaet* tribe from Herefordshire and south Shropshire, and so betrayed his natural lord and all the nation. Cnut had the victory and with that won all England. There were killed bishop Eadnoth, abbot Wulfsige, ealdorman Aelfric, ealdorman Godwine, Ulfcytel of East Anglia, Aethelweard son of ealdorman Aethelwine, and all the oldest retainers in England.

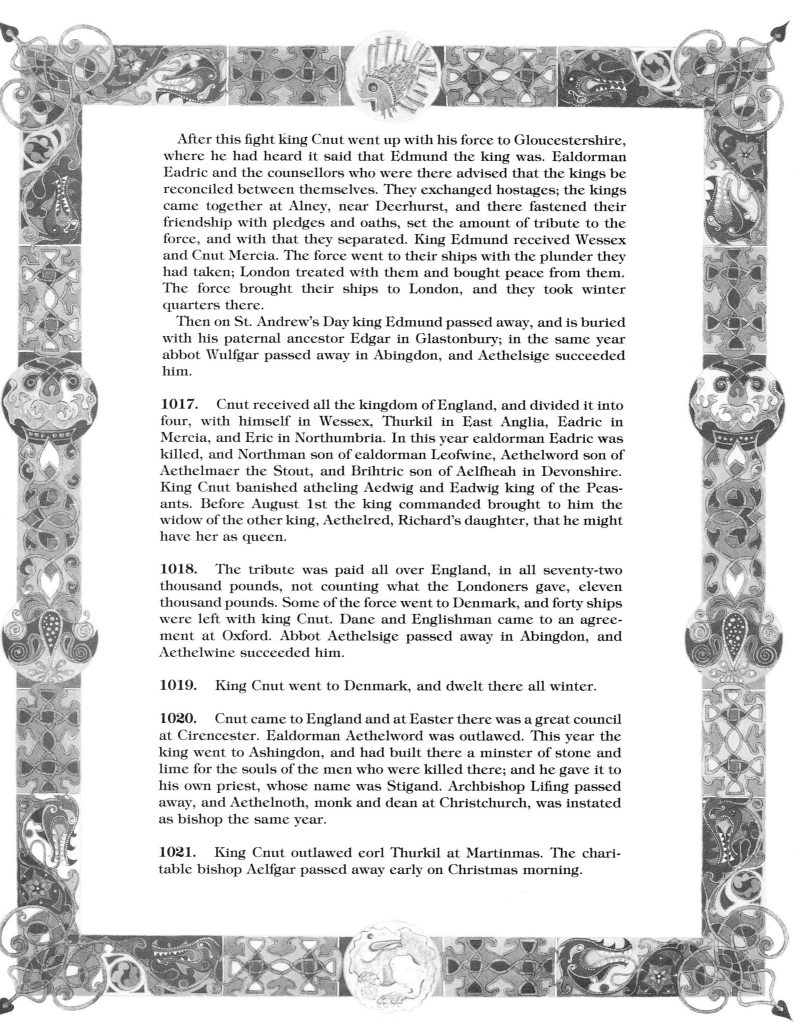

After this fight king Cnut went up with his force to Gloucestershire, where he had heard it said that Edmund the king was. Ealdorman Eadric and the counsellors who were there advised that the kings be reconciled between themselves. They exchanged hostages; the kings came together at Alney, near Deerhurst, and there fastened their friendship with pledges and oaths, set the amount of tribute to the force, and with that they separated. King Edmund received Wessex and Cnut Mercia. The force went to their ships with the plunder they had taken; London treated with them and bought peace from them. The force brought their ships to London, and they took winter quarters there.

Then on St. Andrew's Day king Edmund passed away, and is buried with his paternal ancestor Edgar in Glastonbury; in the same year abbot Wulfgar passed away in Abingdon, and Aethelsige succeeded him.

1017. Cnut received all the kingdom of England, and divided it into four, with himself in Wessex, Thurkil in East Anglia, Eadric in Mercia, and Eric in Northumbria. In this year ealdorman Eadric was killed, and Northman son of ealdorman Leofwine, Aethelword son of Aethelmaer the Stout, and Brihtric son of Aelfheah in Devonshire. King Cnut banished atheling Aedwig and Eadwig king of the Peasants. Before August 1st the king commanded brought to him the widow of the other king, Aethelred, Richard's daughter, that he might have her as queen.

1018. The tribute was paid all over England, in all seventy-two thousand pounds, not counting what the Londoners gave, eleven thousand pounds. Some of the force went to Denmark, and forty ships were left with king Cnut. Dane and Englishman came to an agreement at Oxford. Abbot Aethelsige passed away in Abingdon, and Aethelwine succeeded him.

1019. King Cnut went to Denmark, and dwelt there all winter.

1020. Cnut came to England and at Easter there was a great council at Cirencester. Ealdorman Aethelword was outlawed. This year the king went to Ashingdon, and had built there a minster of stone and lime for the souls of the men who were killed there; and he gave it to his own priest, whose name was Stigand. Archbishop Lifing passed away, and Aethelnoth, monk and dean at Christchurch, was instated as bishop the same year.

1021. King Cnut outlawed eorl Thurkil at Martinmas. The charitable bishop Aelfgar passed away early on Christmas morning.

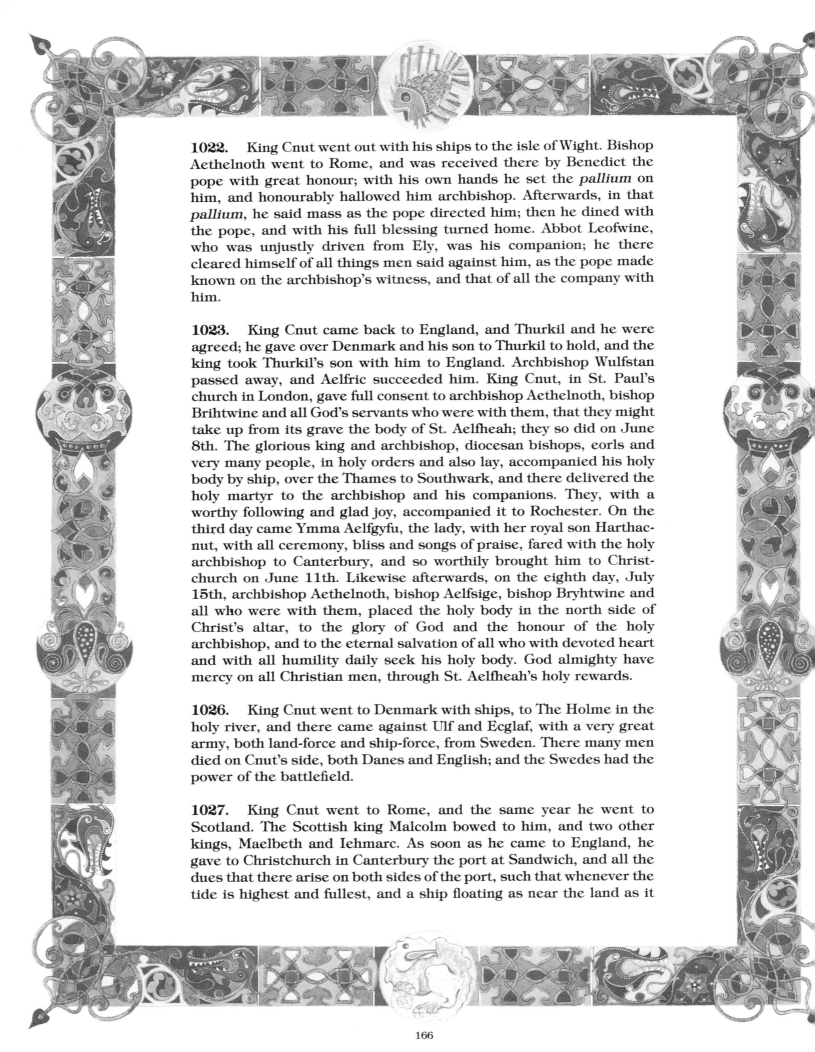

1022. King Cnut went out with his ships to the isle of Wight. Bishop Aethelnoth went to Rome, and was received there by Benedict the pope with great honour; with his own hands he set the *pallium* on him, and honourably hallowed him archbishop. Afterwards, in that *pallium*, he said mass as the pope directed him; then he dined with the pope, and with his full blessing turned home. Abbot Leofwine, who was unjustly driven from Ely, was his companion; he there cleared himself of all things men said against him, as the pope made known on the archbishop's witness, and that of all the company with him.

1023. King Cnut came back to England, and Thurkil and he were agreed; he gave over Denmark and his son to Thurkil to hold, and the king took Thurkil's son with him to England. Archbishop Wulfstan passed away, and Aelfric succeeded him. King Cnut, in St. Paul's church in London, gave full consent to archbishop Aethelnoth, bishop Brihtwine and all God's servants who were with them, that they might take up from its grave the body of St. Aelfheah; they so did on June 8th. The glorious king and archbishop, diocesan bishops, eorls and very many people, in holy orders and also lay, accompanied his holy body by ship, over the Thames to Southwark, and there delivered the holy martyr to the archbishop and his companions. They, with a worthy following and glad joy, accompanied it to Rochester. On the third day came Ymma Aelfgyfu, the lady, with her royal son Harthacnut, with all ceremony, bliss and songs of praise, fared with the holy archbishop to Canterbury, and so worthily brought him to Christchurch on June 11th. Likewise afterwards, on the eighth day, July 15th, archbishop Aethelnoth, bishop Aelfsige, bishop Bryhtwine and all who were with them, placed the holy body in the north side of Christ's altar, to the glory of God and the honour of the holy archbishop, and to the eternal salvation of all who with devoted heart and with all humility daily seek his holy body. God almighty have mercy on all Christian men, through St. Aelfheah's holy rewards.

1026. King Cnut went to Denmark with ships, to The Holme in the holy river, and there came against Ulf and Ecglaf, with a very great army, both land-force and ship-force, from Sweden. There many men died on Cnut's side, both Danes and English; and the Swedes had the power of the battlefield.

1027. King Cnut went to Rome, and the same year he went to Scotland. The Scottish king Malcolm bowed to him, and two other kings, Maelbeth and Iehmarc. As soon as he came to England, he gave to Christchurch in Canterbury the port at Sandwich, and all the dues that there arise on both sides of the port, such that whenever the tide is highest and fullest, and a ship floating as near the land as it

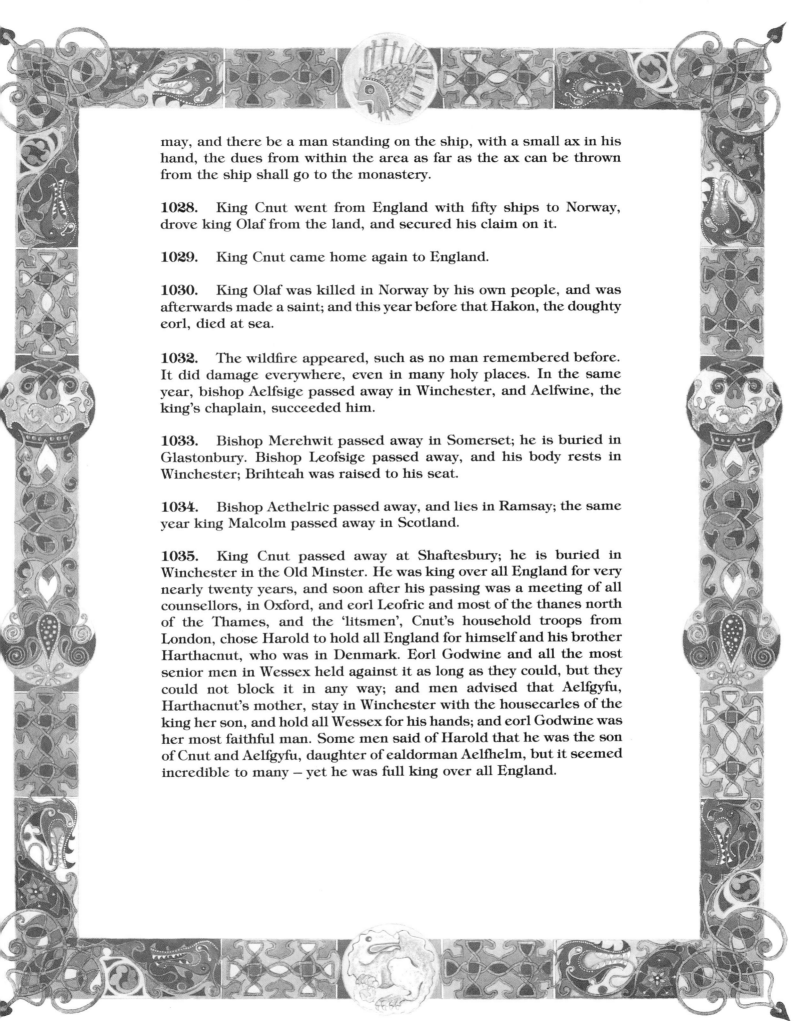

may, and there be a man standing on the ship, with a small ax in his hand, the dues from within the area as far as the ax can be thrown from the ship shall go to the monastery.

1028. King Cnut went from England with fifty ships to Norway, drove king Olaf from the land, and secured his claim on it.

1029. King Cnut came home again to England.

1030. King Olaf was killed in Norway by his own people, and was afterwards made a saint; and this year before that Hakon, the doughty eorl, died at sea.

1032. The wildfire appeared, such as no man remembered before. It did damage everywhere, even in many holy places. In the same year, bishop Aelfsige passed away in Winchester, and Aelfwine, the king's chaplain, succeeded him.

1033. Bishop Merehwit passed away in Somerset; he is buried in Glastonbury. Bishop Leofsige passed away, and his body rests in Winchester; Brihteah was raised to his seat.

1034. Bishop Aethelric passed away, and lies in Ramsay; the same year king Malcolm passed away in Scotland.

1035. King Cnut passed away at Shaftesbury; he is buried in Winchester in the Old Minster. He was king over all England for very nearly twenty years, and soon after his passing was a meeting of all counsellors, in Oxford, and eorl Leofric and most of the thanes north of the Thames, and the 'litsmen', Cnut's household troops from London, chose Harold to hold all England for himself and his brother Harthacnut, who was in Denmark. Eorl Godwine and all the most senior men in Wessex held against it as long as they could, but they could not block it in any way; and men advised that Aelfgyfu, Harthacnut's mother, stay in Winchester with the housecarles of the king her son, and hold all Wessex for his hands; and eorl Godwine was her most faithful man. Some men said of Harold that he was the son of Cnut and Aelfgyfu, daughter of ealdorman Aelfhelm, but it seemed incredible to many – yet he was full king over all England.

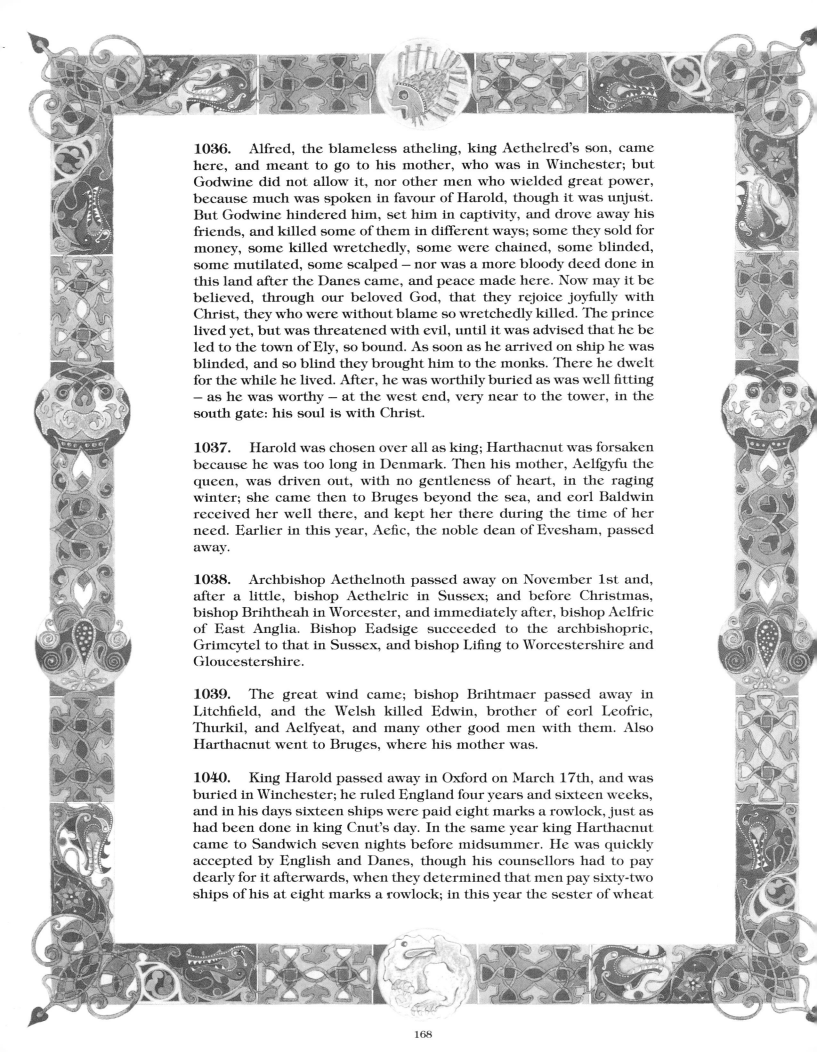

1036. Alfred, the blameless atheling, king Aethelred's son, came here, and meant to go to his mother, who was in Winchester; but Godwine did not allow it, nor other men who wielded great power, because much was spoken in favour of Harold, though it was unjust. But Godwine hindered him, set him in captivity, and drove away his friends, and killed some of them in different ways; some they sold for money, some killed wretchedly, some were chained, some blinded, some mutilated, some scalped – nor was a more bloody deed done in this land after the Danes came, and peace made here. Now may it be believed, through our beloved God, that they rejoice joyfully with Christ, they who were without blame so wretchedly killed. The prince lived yet, but was threatened with evil, until it was advised that he be led to the town of Ely, so bound. As soon as he arrived on ship he was blinded, and so blind they brought him to the monks. There he dwelt for the while he lived. After, he was worthily buried as was well fitting – as he was worthy – at the west end, very near to the tower, in the south gate: his soul is with Christ.

1037. Harold was chosen over all as king; Harthacnut was forsaken because he was too long in Denmark. Then his mother, Aelfgyfu the queen, was driven out, with no gentleness of heart, in the raging winter; she came then to Bruges beyond the sea, and eorl Baldwin received her well there, and kept her there during the time of her need. Earlier in this year, Aefic, the noble dean of Evesham, passed away.

1038. Archbishop Aethelnoth passed away on November 1st and, after a little, bishop Aethelric in Sussex; and before Christmas, bishop Brihtheah in Worcester, and immediately after, bishop Aelfric of East Anglia. Bishop Eadsige succeeded to the archbishopric, Grimcytel to that in Sussex, and bishop Lifing to Worcestershire and Gloucestershire.

1039. The great wind came; bishop Brihtmaer passed away in Litchfield, and the Welsh killed Edwin, brother of eorl Leofric, Thurkil, and Aelfyeat, and many other good men with them. Also Harthacnut went to Bruges, where his mother was.

1040. King Harold passed away in Oxford on March 17th, and was buried in Winchester; he ruled England four years and sixteen weeks, and in his days sixteen ships were paid eight marks a rowlock, just as had been done in king Cnut's day. In the same year king Harthacnut came to Sandwich seven nights before midsummer. He was quickly accepted by English and Danes, though his counsellors had to pay dearly for it afterwards, when they determined that men pay sixty-two ships of his at eight marks a rowlock; in this year the sester of wheat

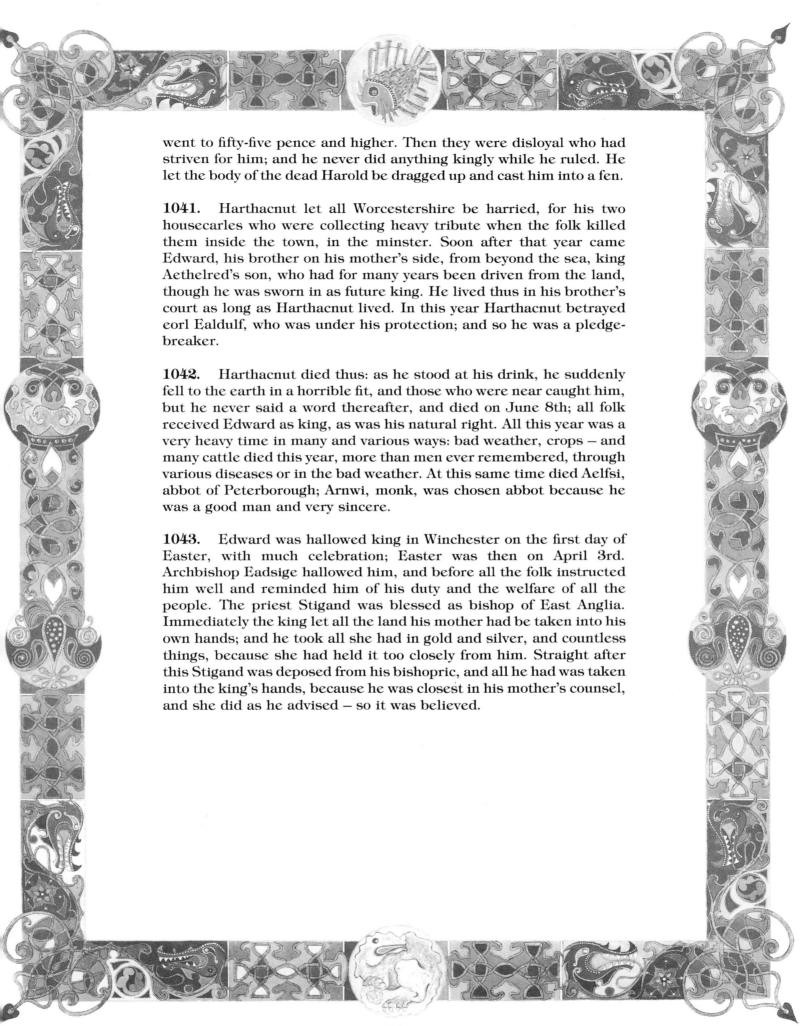

went to fifty-five pence and higher. Then they were disloyal who had striven for him; and he never did anything kingly while he ruled. He let the body of the dead Harold be dragged up and cast him into a fen.

1041.   Harthacnut let all Worcestershire be harried, for his two housecarles who were collecting heavy tribute when the folk killed them inside the town, in the minster. Soon after that year came Edward, his brother on his mother's side, from beyond the sea, king Aethelred's son, who had for many years been driven from the land, though he was sworn in as future king. He lived thus in his brother's court as long as Harthacnut lived. In this year Harthacnut betrayed eorl Ealdulf, who was under his protection; and so he was a pledge-breaker.

1042.   Harthacnut died thus: as he stood at his drink, he suddenly fell to the earth in a horrible fit, and those who were near caught him, but he never said a word thereafter, and died on June 8th; all folk received Edward as king, as was his natural right. All this year was a very heavy time in many and various ways: bad weather, crops – and many cattle died this year, more than men ever remembered, through various diseases or in the bad weather. At this same time died Aelfsi, abbot of Peterborough; Arnwi, monk, was chosen abbot because he was a good man and very sincere.

1043.   Edward was hallowed king in Winchester on the first day of Easter, with much celebration; Easter was then on April 3rd. Archbishop Eadsige hallowed him, and before all the folk instructed him well and reminded him of his duty and the welfare of all the people. The priest Stigand was blessed as bishop of East Anglia. Immediately the king let all the land his mother had be taken into his own hands; and he took all she had in gold and silver, and countless things, because she had held it too closely from him. Straight after this Stigand was deposed from his bishopric, and all he had was taken into the king's hands, because he was closest in his mother's counsel, and she did as he advised – so it was believed.

Above: Royal seal of Edward the Confessor, showing the monarch holding the dove of peace and the sword of war.

Below: Chapel erected by earl Odda in 1065 at Deerhurst, Gloucestershire. During the king's dispute with Godwine, Odda took over Godwine's earldom and commanded the fleet assembled to prevent his return. The chapel was subsequently incorporated in a house and remained undiscovered until the late 19th century.

Under Edward the Confessor (ruled 1042–65), England reverted to Anglo-Saxon rule, although only briefly. But Edward, Aethelred's son, had lived for 25 years in Normandy, throughout Cnut's reign and those of his two short-lived successors, Harold (1035–39) and Harthacnut (1039–42). Ties with Normandy grew increasingly close, especially towards the end of his reign, when the king spent less time on affairs of state and more on affairs of faith. Edward never produced an heir, and the succession problem cropped up throughout his reign. One obvious candidate was William of Normandy. In fact, according to Norman sources, he was promised the succession in 1051 or 1052, although the Chronicles do not mention this. But

Harold Hardrada, the king of Norway, considered himself the rightful heir as well, and within England earl Harold, a member of the powerful Godwine family, had a strong claim.

Threat of a Danish invasion dominated the early years of Edward's reign, although by 1051 he was confident enough to disband the standing fleet and dismiss his personal army of professional warriors.

Above: The anointing and crowning of Edward the Confessor. The ceremony was delayed until Easter 1043, ten months after he became king, perhaps because the religious festival would make the event more impressive. Among the notables attending were the kings of the Franks and the Danes and the Holy Roman Emperor. (Miniature from a 13th-century manuscript by Matthew Paris.)

The Chronicles devote a great deal of attention to a lengthy and complex quarrel between Edward and earl Godwine and his family in 1051 and 1052. It started with a minor incident in Dover, when one of Edward's French kinsmen was refused accommodation, and culminated in virtual civil war as two English armies faced each other on opposite sides of the Thames. The king's army refused to fight their compatriots, and Edward had to back down.

In the long term, however, the quarrel strengthened Edward's position. When Godwine died the following year, the main challenge to Edward's authority was removed. Although all Godwine's sons took over important earldoms, the balance of power became far more stable. A successful invasion of Scotland deposed Macbeth and replaced him with Malcolm, thus ensuring a peaceful neighbour to the north. With no threats from abroad (although there was a series of campaigns against the Welsh) and with trusted and powerful men running both Church and state, Edward retreated ever more from daily business, devoting himself to a simple life of hunting and private devotions.

Left: King Edward and his queen Edith partaking of a royal banquet. (Illustration from a 14th-century manuscript.)

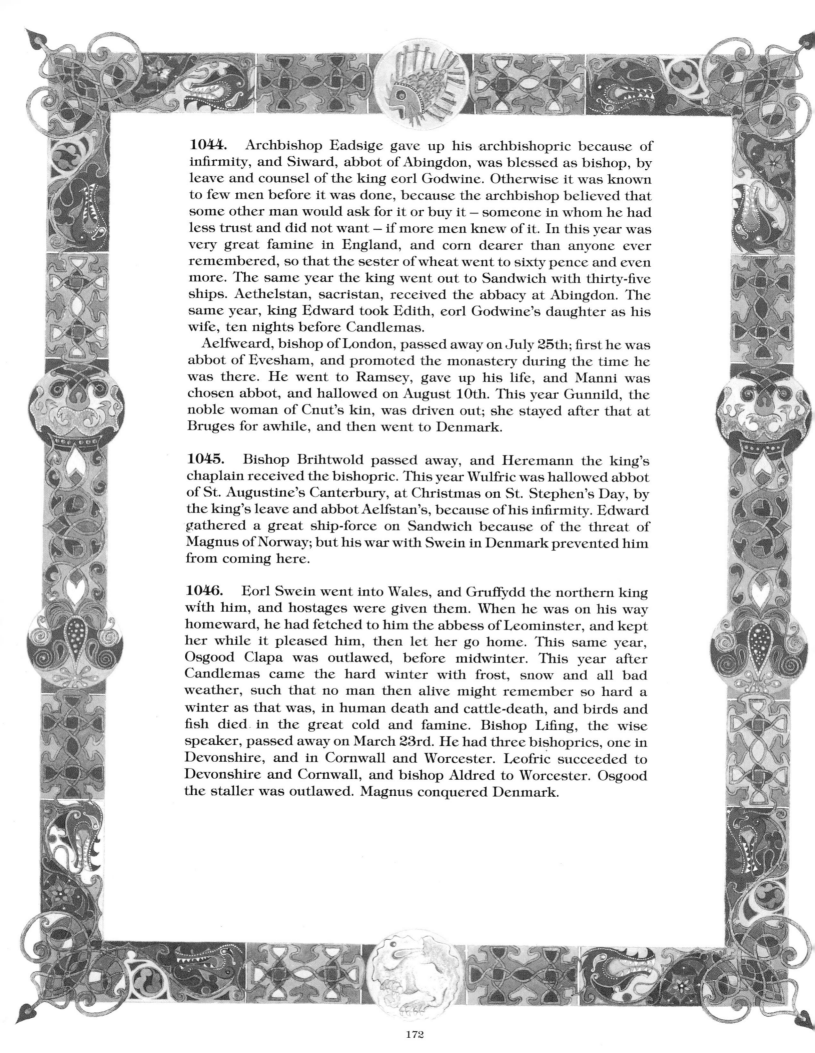

1044. Archbishop Eadsige gave up his archbishopric because of infirmity, and Siward, abbot of Abingdon, was blessed as bishop, by leave and counsel of the king eorl Godwine. Otherwise it was known to few men before it was done, because the archbishop believed that some other man would ask for it or buy it – someone in whom he had less trust and did not want – if more men knew of it. In this year was very great famine in England, and corn dearer than anyone ever remembered, so that the sester of wheat went to sixty pence and even more. The same year the king went out to Sandwich with thirty-five ships. Aethelstan, sacristan, received the abbacy at Abingdon. The same year, king Edward took Edith, eorl Godwine's daughter as his wife, ten nights before Candlemas.

Aelfweard, bishop of London, passed away on July 25th; first he was abbot of Evesham, and promoted the monastery during the time he was there. He went to Ramsey, gave up his life, and Manni was chosen abbot, and hallowed on August 10th. This year Gunnild, the noble woman of Cnut's kin, was driven out; she stayed after that at Bruges for awhile, and then went to Denmark.

1045. Bishop Brihtwold passed away, and Heremann the king's chaplain received the bishopric. This year Wulfric was hallowed abbot of St. Augustine's Canterbury, at Christmas on St. Stephen's Day, by the king's leave and abbot Aelfstan's, because of his infirmity. Edward gathered a great ship-force on Sandwich because of the threat of Magnus of Norway; but his war with Swein in Denmark prevented him from coming here.

1046. Eorl Swein went into Wales, and Gruffydd the northern king with him, and hostages were given them. When he was on his way homeward, he had fetched to him the abbess of Leominster, and kept her while it pleased him, then let her go home. This same year, Osgood Clapa was outlawed, before midwinter. This year after Candlemas came the hard winter with frost, snow and all bad weather, such that no man then alive might remember so hard a winter as that was, in human death and cattle-death, and birds and fish died in the great cold and famine. Bishop Lifing, the wise speaker, passed away on March 23rd. He had three bishoprics, one in Devonshire, and in Cornwall and Worcester. Leofric succeeded to Devonshire and Cornwall, and bishop Aldred to Worcester. Osgood the staller was outlawed. Magnus conquered Denmark.

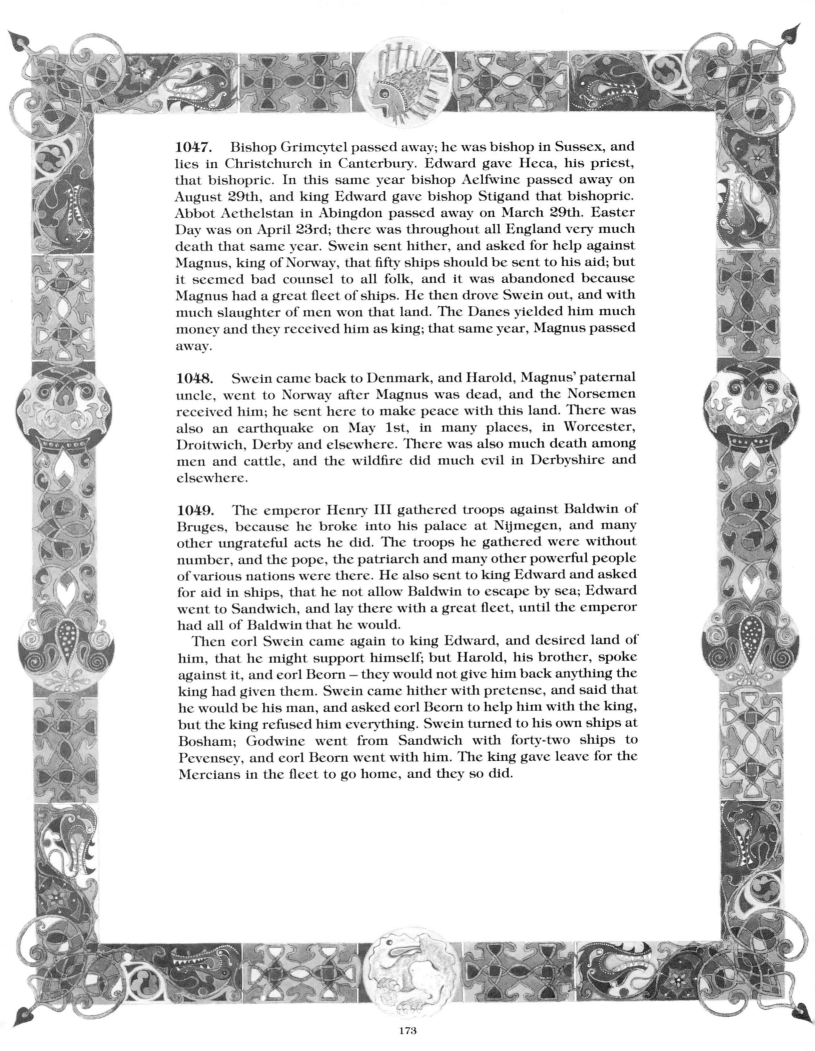

1047. Bishop Grimcytel passed away; he was bishop in Sussex, and lies in Christchurch in Canterbury. Edward gave Heca, his priest, that bishopric. In this same year bishop Aelfwine passed away on August 29th, and king Edward gave bishop Stigand that bishopric. Abbot Aethelstan in Abingdon passed away on March 29th. Easter Day was on April 23rd; there was throughout all England very much death that same year. Swein sent hither, and asked for help against Magnus, king of Norway, that fifty ships should be sent to his aid; but it seemed bad counsel to all folk, and it was abandoned because Magnus had a great fleet of ships. He then drove Swein out, and with much slaughter of men won that land. The Danes yielded him much money and they received him as king; that same year, Magnus passed away.

1048. Swein came back to Denmark, and Harold, Magnus' paternal uncle, went to Norway after Magnus was dead, and the Norsemen received him; he sent here to make peace with this land. There was also an earthquake on May 1st, in many places, in Worcester, Droitwich, Derby and elsewhere. There was also much death among men and cattle, and the wildfire did much evil in Derbyshire and elsewhere.

1049. The emperor Henry III gathered troops against Baldwin of Bruges, because he broke into his palace at Nijmegen, and many other ungrateful acts he did. The troops he gathered were without number, and the pope, the patriarch and many other powerful people of various nations were there. He also sent to king Edward and asked for aid in ships, that he not allow Baldwin to escape by sea; Edward went to Sandwich, and lay there with a great fleet, until the emperor had all of Baldwin that he would.

Then eorl Swein came again to king Edward, and desired land of him, that he might support himself; but Harold, his brother, spoke against it, and eorl Beorn – they would not give him back anything the king had given them. Swein came hither with pretense, and said that he would be his man, and asked eorl Beorn to help him with the king, but the king refused him everything. Swein turned to his own ships at Bosham; Godwine went from Sandwich with forty-two ships to Pevensey, and eorl Beorn went with him. The king gave leave for the Mercians in the fleet to go home, and they so did.

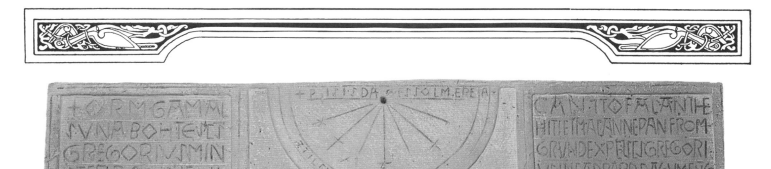

Above: Sundial from St Gregory's Minster, Kirkdale, North Yorkshire, which survives in what is believed to be its original position. The inscription reads: 'Orm, Gamal's son, bought St Gregory's Minster when it was all broken down and fallen and he let it be made anew from the ground to Christ and to S Gregory in the days of Edward the King and Tostig the Earl. This is the day's sun marking at each hour. And Haward me wrought and Brand Priest.' The earlier church had probably been destroyed by the Danes. Tostig became earl of Northumberland in 1055 and was killed at Stamford Bridge in 1066; the sundial and much of the church date from this time.

Below left: Stone angel at St Michael's and All Angels', Winterbourne Steepleton, Dorset, carved during the 10th century.

Opposite right and above: After 1066, England's new rulers imposed their own styles on major ecclesiastical buildings. Away from the main centres of Norman influence, however, older traditions persisted. At the late 12th-century church of St Mary and St David, Kilpeck, Herefordshire, a provincial Anglo-Norman style was followed, combining contemporary Scandinavian, Romanesque and Winchester influences. The ornamentation is lavish, tumbling from doorways, capitals, arches in rich profusion.

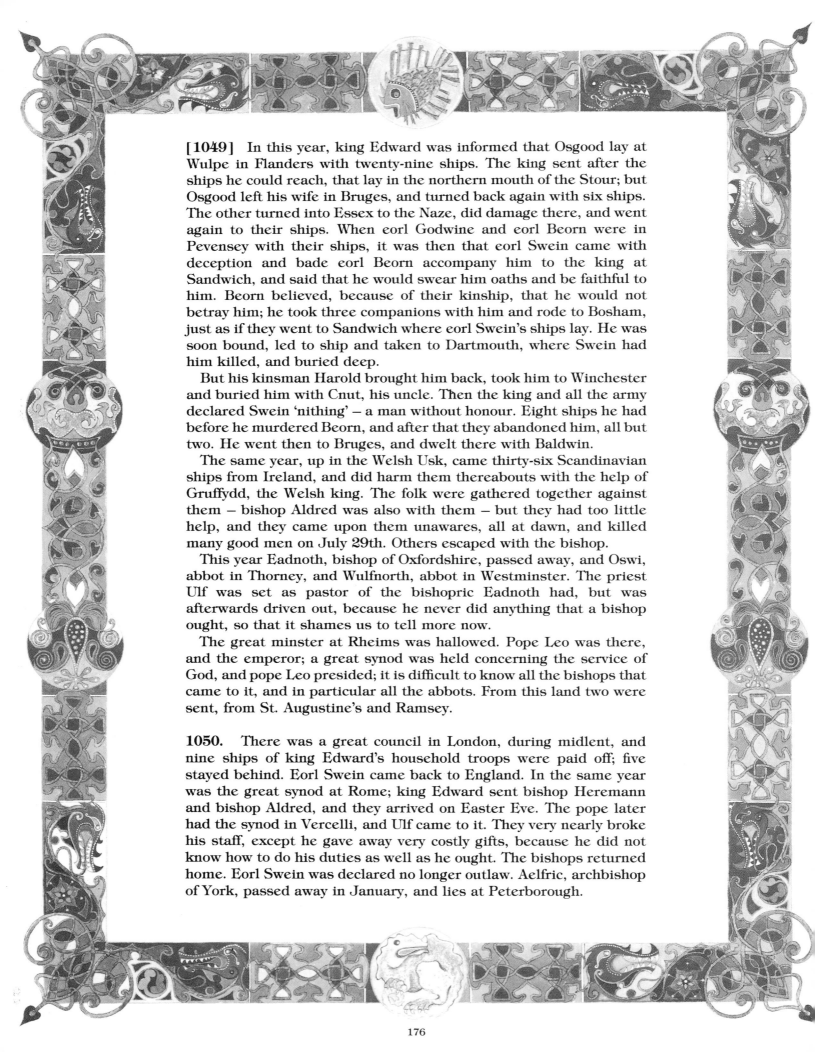

[1049] In this year, king Edward was informed that Osgood lay at Wulpe in Flanders with twenty-nine ships. The king sent after the ships he could reach, that lay in the northern mouth of the Stour; but Osgood left his wife in Bruges, and turned back again with six ships. The other turned into Essex to the Naze, did damage there, and went again to their ships. When eorl Godwine and eorl Beorn were in Pevensey with their ships, it was then that eorl Swein came with deception and bade eorl Beorn accompany him to the king at Sandwich, and said that he would swear him oaths and be faithful to him. Beorn believed, because of their kinship, that he would not betray him; he took three companions with him and rode to Bosham, just as if they went to Sandwich where eorl Swein's ships lay. He was soon bound, led to ship and taken to Dartmouth, where Swein had him killed, and buried deep.

But his kinsman Harold brought him back, took him to Winchester and buried him with Cnut, his uncle. Then the king and all the army declared Swein 'nithing' – a man without honour. Eight ships he had before he murdered Beorn, and after that they abandoned him, all but two. He went then to Bruges, and dwelt there with Baldwin.

The same year, up in the Welsh Usk, came thirty-six Scandinavian ships from Ireland, and did harm them thereabouts with the help of Gruffydd, the Welsh king. The folk were gathered together against them – bishop Aldred was also with them – but they had too little help, and they came upon them unawares, all at dawn, and killed many good men on July 29th. Others escaped with the bishop.

This year Eadnoth, bishop of Oxfordshire, passed away, and Oswi, abbot in Thorney, and Wulfnorth, abbot in Westminster. The priest Ulf was set as pastor of the bishopric Eadnoth had, but was afterwards driven out, because he never did anything that a bishop ought, so that it shames us to tell more now.

The great minster at Rheims was hallowed. Pope Leo was there, and the emperor; a great synod was held concerning the service of God, and pope Leo presided; it is difficult to know all the bishops that came to it, and in particular all the abbots. From this land two were sent, from St. Augustine's and Ramsey.

1050. There was a great council in London, during midlent, and nine ships of king Edward's household troops were paid off; five stayed behind. Eorl Swein came back to England. In the same year was the great synod at Rome; king Edward sent bishop Heremann and bishop Aldred, and they arrived on Easter Eve. The pope later had the synod in Vercelli, and Ulf came to it. They very nearly broke his staff, except he gave away very costly gifts, because he did not know how to do his duties as well as he ought. The bishops returned home. Eorl Swein was declared no longer outlaw. Aelfric, archbishop of York, passed away in January, and lies at Peterborough.

1051. King Edward gave Robert, bishop of London, the archbishopric of Canterbury. During spring; the same spring he went to Rome for his *pallium*, and the king gave the bishopric of London to Spearhafoc, abbot of Abingdon – that abbacy the king gave to his kinsman, bishop Rothulf. Then the archbishop came from Rome one day before the eve of St. Peter's Day, and he took the archbishop's throne at Christchurch on St. Peter's Day, and soon after went to the king. Spearhafoc met him on the way with the king's letter and seal, to the effect that he should instate him as bishop of London; the archbishop spoke against it, and said that the pope had forbidden that it be given him. Then the abbot went back again to the archbishop about it, and there asked for bishophood; the archbishop resolutely refused him, and said that the pope had forbidden it him. Then the abbot turned to London, and stayed in the bishopric the king had granted him, with his consent, all the summer and autumn.

Eustace came from beyond the sea, soon after the bishop, went to the king and spoke to him of what he would, then turned homeward. When he came to Canterbury, he ate there with his men, and went to Dover. When he was some miles from the sea, behind Dover, he put on his byrnie, and so did his companions; they fared to Dover. When they arrived, they meant to lodge where it pleased them; one of his men came, wishing to lodge at a householder's without his consent, wounded the householder, and the householder killed him. Eustace got on his horse, and his companions on theirs, went to the householder and killed him on own hearth, then went up to the town and killed, inside and out, more than twenty men. The townsmen killed nineteen on the other side, and wounded they knew not how many. Eustace escaped with a few men, went back to the king, and told him a part of what had happened. The king became very angry with the townsmen; he sent for eorl Godwine and bade him go into Kent in hostility, to Dover, because Eustace had told the king that it was more the fault of the townsmen than his – but it was not so. The eorl would not agree to go in, because it was hateful to him to injure his own following.

Then the king sent after all his counsellors, and bade them come to Gloucester near the second St. Mary's Day. The foreigners had built a castle in Herefordshire among eorl Swein's followers; they did much harm and insulted the king's men thereabouts where they might.

[1051] Eorl Godwine, eorl Swein and eorl Harold came together at Beverstone, and many men with them, to the end that they go to their natural lord and all the counsellors who were gathered there, to have the king's advice and aid, with that of all the counsellors, about how they might avenge the insult to the king and all the nation. Then the foreigners got to the king first, and accused the eorls, so that they might not come in his sight, because they said that they would come in treachery to the king. Eorl Siward, eorl Leofric and many folk had come north with them to the king; eorl Godwine and his sons were told that the king and the men with him meant to act against them, and they strengthened themselves resolutely against them, though it was hateful to them that they should stand against their natural lord. Then the counsellors on both sides advised that they stop all the damage, and the king gave God's peace and his full friendship to both sides.

Then the king and his counsellors advised another full council-meeting be held in London, at the autumn equinox. The king commanded the troops called up, both south of the Thames and north – that was the best force of all. Eorl Swein was declared outlaw, and eorl Godwine and eorl Harold were called to the meeting as quickly as they could travel to it – when they arrived out there, they were called in to the meeting. Godwine wanted protection and hostages, that he might unhindered come into the meeting and go out. Then the king wanted the allegiance of all the thanes that had been the eorls, and they all gave themselves into his hands; then the king sent again to them, and bade them come with twelve men into the king's council. The eorl asked again for protection and hostages, that he might clear himself of each charge that had been laid on him. The hostages were then refused him, and he was granted five nights' protection to leave the land. Then eorl Godwine and eorl Swein turned to Bosham, pushed off with their ships, went beyond the sea and sought Baldwin's protection; they dwelt there all winter. Eorl Harold went west to Ireland, and as soon as this happened, the king forsook the lady who was hallowed to him as queen, and had seized all that she had in land, gold, silver – in everything – and committed her to his sister at Wherwell.

Abbot Spearhafoc was driven out of the bishopric of London, and Willelm the king's priest instated thereto. Odda was set as eorl over Devonshire, Somerset, Dorset and Cornwall; and Aelfgar, son of eorl Leofric, was given the eorldom Harold had before.

1052. Ymma Aelfgyfu, king Edward's and Harthacnut's mother, passed away. In the same year, the king and counsellors advised that ships should be sent out to Sandwich, and eorl Ralph and eorl Odda were set to head them. Eorl Godwine then turned from Bruges with his ships to the Yser, and put out to sea one day before midsummer

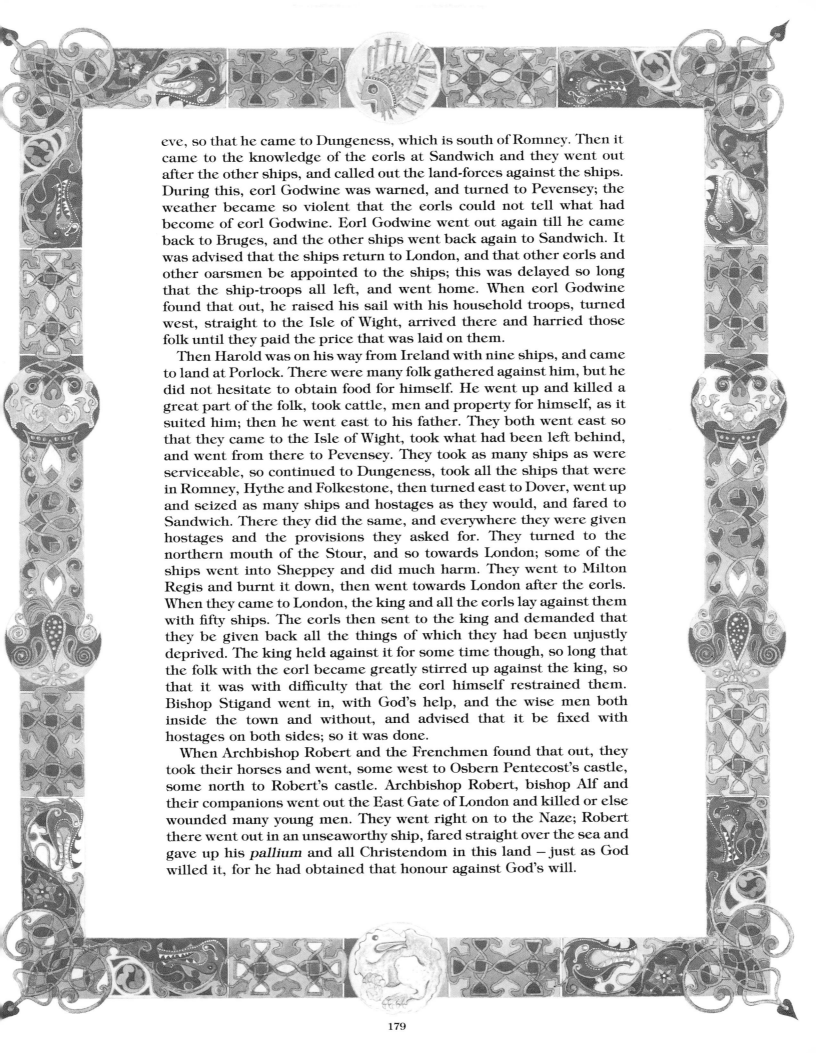

eve, so that he came to Dungeness, which is south of Romney. Then it came to the knowledge of the eorls at Sandwich and they went out after the other ships, and called out the land-forces against the ships. During this, eorl Godwine was warned, and turned to Pevensey; the weather became so violent that the eorls could not tell what had become of eorl Godwine. Eorl Godwine went out again till he came back to Bruges, and the other ships went back again to Sandwich. It was advised that the ships return to London, and that other eorls and other oarsmen be appointed to the ships; this was delayed so long that the ship-troops all left, and went home. When eorl Godwine found that out, he raised his sail with his household troops, turned west, straight to the Isle of Wight, arrived there and harried those folk until they paid the price that was laid on them.

Then Harold was on his way from Ireland with nine ships, and came to land at Porlock. There were many folk gathered against him, but he did not hesitate to obtain food for himself. He went up and killed a great part of the folk, took cattle, men and property for himself, as it suited him; then he went east to his father. They both went east so that they came to the Isle of Wight, took what had been left behind, and went from there to Pevensey. They took as many ships as were serviceable, so continued to Dungeness, took all the ships that were in Romney, Hythe and Folkestone, then turned east to Dover, went up and seized as many ships and hostages as they would, and fared to Sandwich. There they did the same, and everywhere they were given hostages and the provisions they asked for. They turned to the northern mouth of the Stour, and so towards London; some of the ships went into Sheppey and did much harm. They went to Milton Regis and burnt it down, then went towards London after the eorls. When they came to London, the king and all the eorls lay against them with fifty ships. The eorls then sent to the king and demanded that they be given back all the things of which they had been unjustly deprived. The king held against it for some time though, so long that the folk with the eorl became greatly stirred up against the king, so that it was with difficulty that the eorl himself restrained them. Bishop Stigand went in, with God's help, and the wise men both inside the town and without, and advised that it be fixed with hostages on both sides; so it was done.

When Archbishop Robert and the Frenchmen found that out, they took their horses and went, some west to Osbern Pentecost's castle, some north to Robert's castle. Archbishop Robert, bishop Alf and their companions went out the East Gate of London and killed or else wounded many young men. They went right on to the Naze; Robert there went out in an unseaworthy ship, fared straight over the sea and gave up his *pallium* and all Christendom in this land – just as God willed it, for he had obtained that honour against God's will.

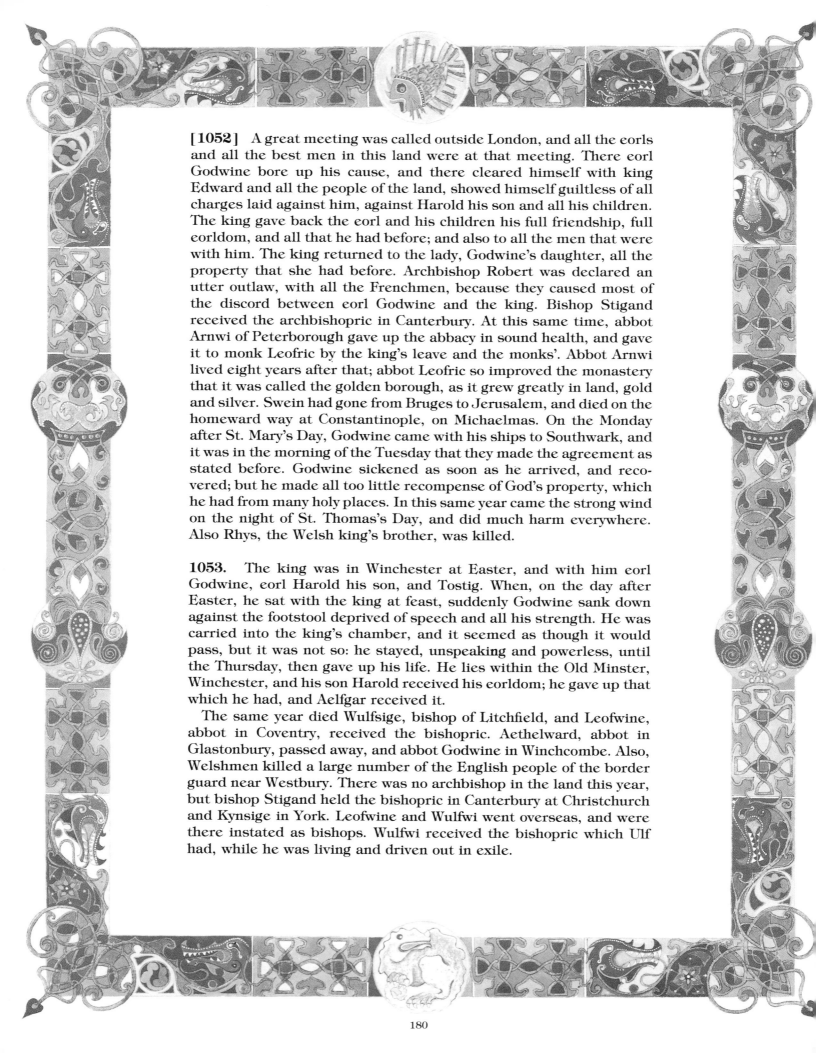

[1052] A great meeting was called outside London, and all the eorls and all the best men in this land were at that meeting. There eorl Godwine bore up his cause, and there cleared himself with king Edward and all the people of the land, showed himself guiltless of all charges laid against him, against Harold his son and all his children. The king gave back the eorl and his children his full friendship, full eorldom, and all that he had before; and also to all the men that were with him. The king returned to the lady, Godwine's daughter, all the property that she had before. Archbishop Robert was declared an utter outlaw, with all the Frenchmen, because they caused most of the discord between eorl Godwine and the king. Bishop Stigand received the archbishopric in Canterbury. At this same time, abbot Arnwi of Peterborough gave up the abbacy in sound health, and gave it to monk Leofric by the king's leave and the monks'. Abbot Arnwi lived eight years after that; abbot Leofric so improved the monastery that it was called the golden borough, as it grew greatly in land, gold and silver. Swein had gone from Bruges to Jerusalem, and died on the homeward way at Constantinople, on Michaelmas. On the Monday after St. Mary's Day, Godwine came with his ships to Southwark, and it was in the morning of the Tuesday that they made the agreement as stated before. Godwine sickened as soon as he arrived, and recovered; but he made all too little recompense of God's property, which he had from many holy places. In this same year came the strong wind on the night of St. Thomas's Day, and did much harm everywhere. Also Rhys, the Welsh king's brother, was killed.

1053.   The king was in Winchester at Easter, and with him eorl Godwine, eorl Harold his son, and Tostig. When, on the day after Easter, he sat with the king at feast, suddenly Godwine sank down against the footstool deprived of speech and all his strength. He was carried into the king's chamber, and it seemed as though it would pass, but it was not so: he stayed, unspeaking and powerless, until the Thursday, then gave up his life. He lies within the Old Minster, Winchester, and his son Harold received his eorldom; he gave up that which he had, and Aelfgar received it.

The same year died Wulfsige, bishop of Litchfield, and Leofwine, abbot in Coventry, received the bishopric. Aethelward, abbot in Glastonbury, passed away, and abbot Godwine in Winchcombe. Also, Welshmen killed a large number of the English people of the border guard near Westbury. There was no archbishop in the land this year, but bishop Stigand held the bishopric in Canterbury at Christchurch and Kynsige in York. Leofwine and Wulfwi went overseas, and were there instated as bishops. Wulfwi received the bishopric which Ulf had, while he was living and driven out in exile.

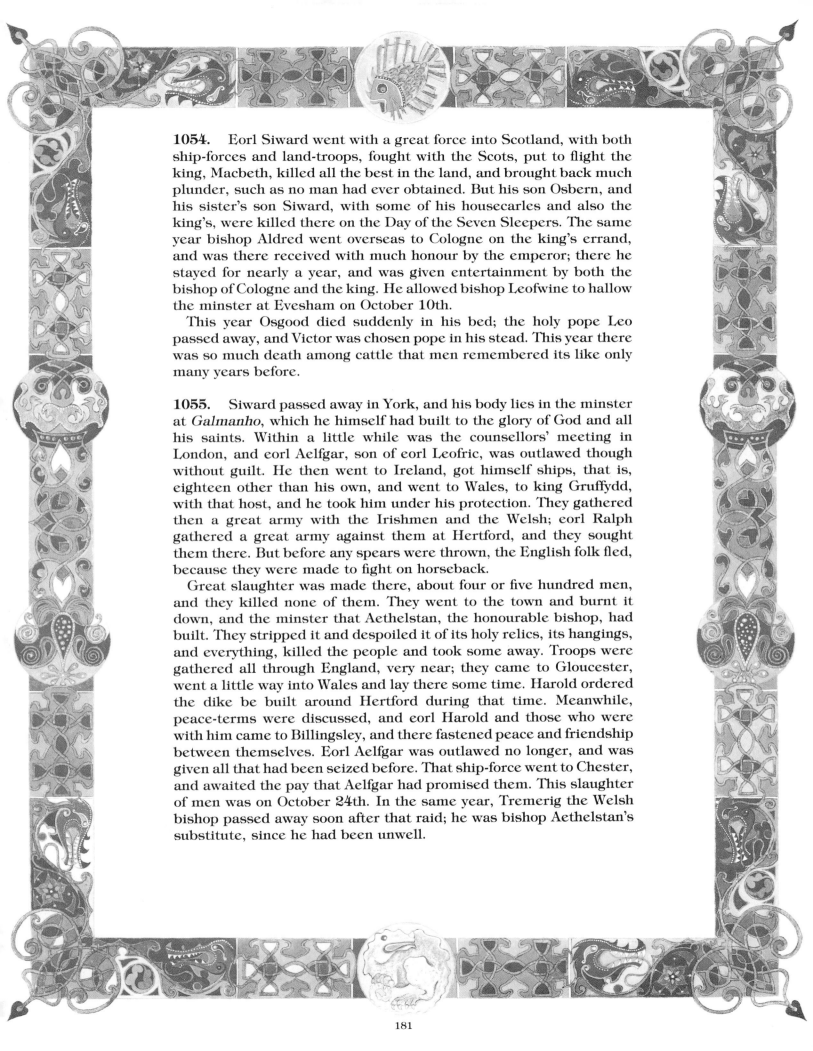

1054. Eorl Siward went with a great force into Scotland, with both ship-forces and land-troops, fought with the Scots, put to flight the king, Macbeth, killed all the best in the land, and brought back much plunder, such as no man had ever obtained. But his son Osbern, and his sister's son Siward, with some of his housecarles and also the king's, were killed there on the Day of the Seven Sleepers. The same year bishop Aldred went overseas to Cologne on the king's errand, and was there received with much honour by the emperor; there he stayed for nearly a year, and was given entertainment by both the bishop of Cologne and the king. He allowed bishop Leofwine to hallow the minster at Evesham on October 10th.

This year Osgood died suddenly in his bed; the holy pope Leo passed away, and Victor was chosen pope in his stead. This year there was so much death among cattle that men remembered its like only many years before.

1055. Siward passed away in York, and his body lies in the minster at *Galmanho*, which he himself had built to the glory of God and all his saints. Within a little while was the counsellors' meeting in London, and eorl Aelfgar, son of eorl Leofric, was outlawed though without guilt. He then went to Ireland, got himself ships, that is, eighteen other than his own, and went to Wales, to king Gruffydd, with that host, and he took him under his protection. They gathered then a great army with the Irishmen and the Welsh; eorl Ralph gathered a great army against them at Hertford, and they sought them there. But before any spears were thrown, the English folk fled, because they were made to fight on horseback.

Great slaughter was made there, about four or five hundred men, and they killed none of them. They went to the town and burnt it down, and the minster that Aethelstan, the honourable bishop, had built. They stripped it and despoiled it of its holy relics, its hangings, and everything, killed the people and took some away. Troops were gathered all through England, very near; they came to Gloucester, went a little way into Wales and lay there some time. Harold ordered the dike be built around Hertford during that time. Meanwhile, peace-terms were discussed, and eorl Harold and those who were with him came to Billingsley, and there fastened peace and friendship between themselves. Eorl Aelfgar was outlawed no longer, and was given all that had been seized before. That ship-force went to Chester, and awaited the pay that Aelfgar had promised them. This slaughter of men was on October 24th. In the same year, Tremerig the Welsh bishop passed away soon after that raid; he was bishop Aethelstan's substitute, since he had been unwell.

During the last years of Edward's reign, the succession dominated court politics. In 1057, the king's nephew, also called Edward, arrived in England from the Hungarian court, only to die before he even met the king. His family stayed on in the royal household; Edward treated the three young children as his own and may well have regarded the boy Edgar as a possible heir. However, there were other claimants. In Scandinavia, Norway and Denmark finally made peace, which left both Harold Hardrada, another contender, and Swein free to invade England. In Normandy, duke William was helped by the death of Henry I of France, which removed the threat of a French invasion of Normandy. His position was strengthened still more in 1064 by the visit of earl Harold (Godwine's son). This curious episode is ignored by the Chroniclers, but, not surprisingly, the Bayeux Tapestry makes much of it. The implication is that Edward sent earl Harold to confirm that he was making William his heir and that Harold pledged his own support for William at the same time. What Harold's intentions were is unclear, but his own chances were greatly improved when his extremely powerful brother Tostig, the earl of Northumbria, was overthrown in a rebellion and banished to Flanders.

King Edward was taken ill on Christmas Eve 1065 and was unable to attend the consecration of Westminster Abbey, which he had begun to rebuild in 1050. He died on Twelfth Night surrounded by his wife, earl Harold, the archbishop of Canterbury and numerous other dignitaries and was buried under a plain gravestone in the Abbey. Whether he did bequeath the kingdom to Harold remains uncertain. But later writers describe a death-bed speech in which he left his kingdom in Harold's care, and the Chroniclers recorded that he 'committed the kingdom' to Harold.

Edward was not especially wise, forceful or brave. Content to make decisions on a day-to-day basis rather than pursue a long-term policy, he could on occasion show determination and manipulate court factions. All too often, though, he was overwhelmed by the aggressive Godwine family. He was a mild man, and it was this mildness that was interpreted as religious fervour and later earned him his sainthood.

Like the Anglo-Saxon Chronicles, the Bayeux Tapestry is one of the best contemporary sources for the history of the Conquest and its immediate aftermath – although compiled from the Norman point of view. It was commissioned by Odo, William's half-brother who was bishop of Bayeux and earl of Kent, and was executed in England, although its designer may have been Norman or English. The tapestry records the invasion, from Harold's mission to William in 1064 to William's victory at Hastings. Further panels now lost probably took the story up to William's coronation.

Above: The death and burial of Edward. In the upper section, queen Edith is shown standing at the foot of Edward's death bed; also present are earl Harold and archbishop Stigand of Canterbury. The lower register shows the king's body being made ready for burial.

Opposite, far left: Edward briefs Harold on his mission to confirm to William that William has been chosen as Edward's heir.

Opposite left: Harold reports to Edward on his return.

Above: The newly erected Westminster Abbey, planned by Edward as his mausoleum. Modelled on the abbey church at Saint-Jumièges, it was built between 1050 and 1065 by English and Norman workmen and was larger than any known contemporary Norman church. It has a long nave with six bays, aisles and a wooden roof, a lantern tower and a presbytery with two bays.

Left: The funeral procession to Westminster Abbey: Edward's body is wrapped in a woollen shroud, and the bier is covered with an embroidered pall. Acolytes with bells accompany the bearers.

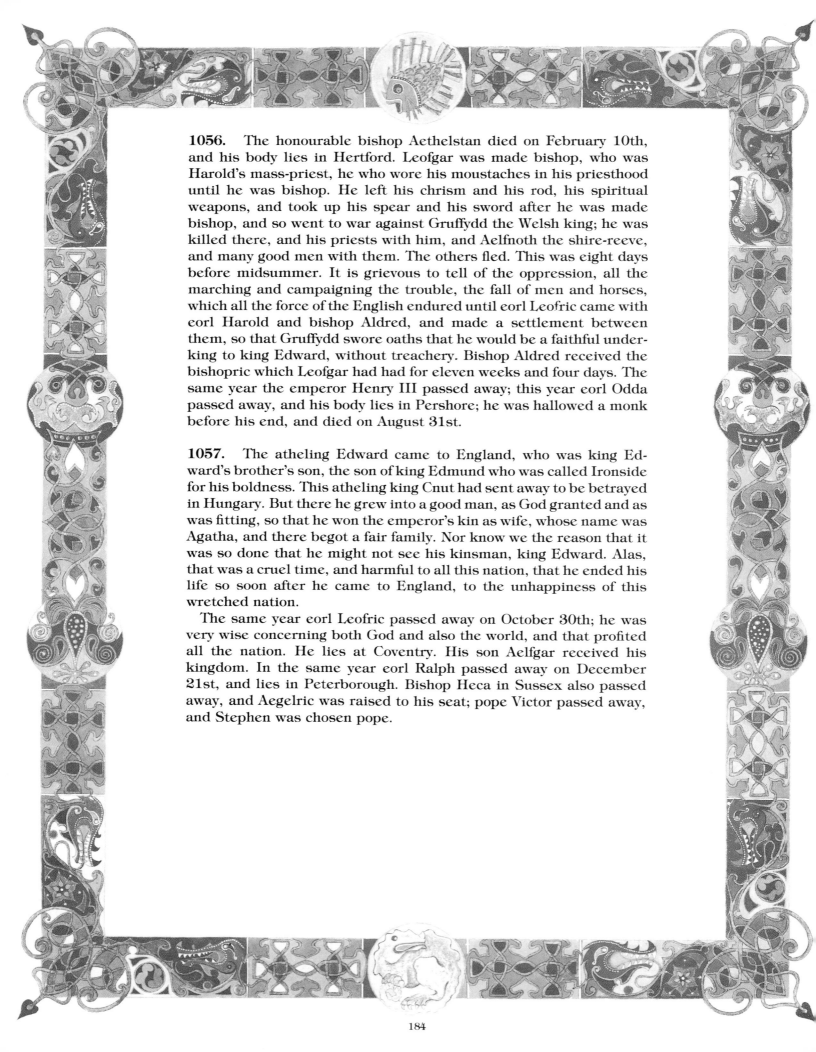

1056. The honourable bishop Aethelstan died on February 10th, and his body lies in Hertford. Leofgar was made bishop, who was Harold's mass-priest, he who wore his moustaches in his priesthood until he was bishop. He left his chrism and his rod, his spiritual weapons, and took up his spear and his sword after he was made bishop, and so went to war against Gruffydd the Welsh king; he was killed there, and his priests with him, and Aelfnoth the shire-reeve, and many good men with them. The others fled. This was eight days before midsummer. It is grievous to tell of the oppression, all the marching and campaigning the trouble, the fall of men and horses, which all the force of the English endured until eorl Leofric came with eorl Harold and bishop Aldred, and made a settlement between them, so that Gruffydd swore oaths that he would be a faithful under-king to king Edward, without treachery. Bishop Aldred received the bishopric which Leofgar had had for eleven weeks and four days. The same year the emperor Henry III passed away; this year eorl Odda passed away, and his body lies in Pershore; he was hallowed a monk before his end, and died on August 31st.

1057. The atheling Edward came to England, who was king Edward's brother's son, the son of king Edmund who was called Ironside for his boldness. This atheling king Cnut had sent away to be betrayed in Hungary. But there he grew into a good man, as God granted and as was fitting, so that he won the emperor's kin as wife, whose name was Agatha, and there begot a fair family. Nor know we the reason that it was so done that he might not see his kinsman, king Edward. Alas, that was a cruel time, and harmful to all this nation, that he ended his life so soon after he came to England, to the unhappiness of this wretched nation.

The same year eorl Leofric passed away on October 30th; he was very wise concerning both God and also the world, and that profited all the nation. He lies at Coventry. His son Aelfgar received his kingdom. In the same year eorl Ralph passed away on December 21st, and lies in Peterborough. Bishop Heca in Sussex also passed away, and Aegelric was raised to his seat; pope Victor passed away, and Stephen was chosen pope.

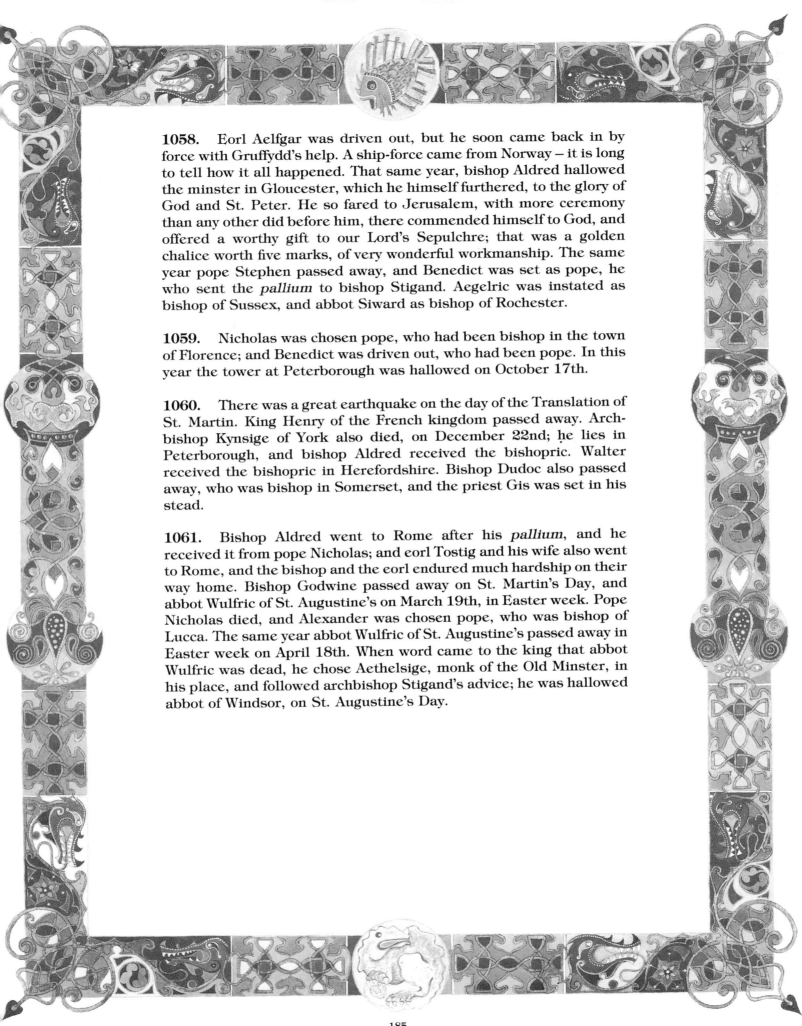

1058. Eorl Aelfgar was driven out, but he soon came back in by force with Gruffydd's help. A ship-force came from Norway – it is long to tell how it all happened. That same year, bishop Aldred hallowed the minster in Gloucester, which he himself furthered, to the glory of God and St. Peter. He so fared to Jerusalem, with more ceremony than any other did before him, there commended himself to God, and offered a worthy gift to our Lord's Sepulchre; that was a golden chalice worth five marks, of very wonderful workmanship. The same year pope Stephen passed away, and Benedict was set as pope, he who sent the *pallium* to bishop Stigand. Aegelric was instated as bishop of Sussex, and abbot Siward as bishop of Rochester.

1059. Nicholas was chosen pope, who had been bishop in the town of Florence; and Benedict was driven out, who had been pope. In this year the tower at Peterborough was hallowed on October 17th.

1060. There was a great earthquake on the day of the Translation of St. Martin. King Henry of the French kingdom passed away. Archbishop Kynsige of York also died, on December 22nd; he lies in Peterborough, and bishop Aldred received the bishopric. Walter received the bishopric in Herefordshire. Bishop Dudoc also passed away, who was bishop in Somerset, and the priest Gis was set in his stead.

1061. Bishop Aldred went to Rome after his *pallium*, and he received it from pope Nicholas; and eorl Tostig and his wife also went to Rome, and the bishop and the eorl endured much hardship on their way home. Bishop Godwine passed away on St. Martin's Day, and abbot Wulfric of St. Augustine's on March 19th, in Easter week. Pope Nicholas died, and Alexander was chosen pope, who was bishop of Lucca. The same year abbot Wulfric of St. Augustine's passed away in Easter week on April 18th. When word came to the king that abbot Wulfric was dead, he chose Aethelsige, monk of the Old Minster, in his place, and followed archbishop Stigand's advice; he was hallowed abbot of Windsor, on St. Augustine's Day.

Right: Remains of the abbey church at Jumièges, one of the leading religious centres of Normandy. Built between 1040 and 1067, it was the model for Westminster Abbey.

Below right: Lanfranc (c.1005–89), William's Italian archbishop of Canterbury from 1070, had previously been prior of Bec, the leading Benedictine foundation in Normandy. Under Lanfranc's leadership, the English Church was effectively Normanized. (Frontispiece of Lanfranc's treatise defending the doctrine of transubstantiation.)

Below: The abbey at Mont Saint-Michel, founded in 966 by Richard I of Normandy.

In 911 Charles the Simple, king of France, granted a part of northern France to the Norse Viking Rollo in the hope of establishing a buffer zone against raids by other Vikings. The settlers became the region's aristocracy, converted to Christianity and stoutly defended their land. By the end of the century their leader had assumed the title duke, the Norsemen had intermarried with the native French and had become French-speaking Normans and Christians, and the state itself was more powerful and secure than most of the other Frankish dukedoms. The dukes remained the increasingly nominal vassals of the French king and would usually fight for him when asked.

The Normans were successful warriors, and men came from the rest of France and from abroad to be trained as fighting men. They were not primarily interested in plunder, although they sacked and pillaged if opportunity arose; they fought for land, and by the mid-10th century they already controlled much of southern Italy, Sicily and Malta.

Under the two Williams, Normandy was controlled by deputies (usually relatives or close associates) responsible for order, good government and defence in specific districts. The country was small, and true organized feudalism had not yet evolved. The duties owed by the comtes, vicomtes and nobles were not rigidly laid down. None the less a vassal owed fealty to his overlord, that overlord to his, and so on. When in 1086 William was to ask all the English to swear loyalty to him above their own immediate lords, he reinforced a strong kingship above and beyond the feudal structure, and a system of control which neither the duke of Normandy nor even the king of France could claim. William expected – and got – obedience and service in return for gifts of land. Castles acted as strongpoints of the duke's authority. Non-ducal castles were strictly licensed, and as a result the nobles had no chance of building up strong empires.

The reformed ideas of Benedictine monasticism had considerable appeal since most Normans disliked the lax morals and the traffic in religious pardons which too many priests condoned. William encouraged reform from within, and, in exchange for ecclesiastical support for secular authority, built new monasteries, in the Romanesque style that reflected some of the eastern churches seen on campaigns abroad. The sacred arts flourished, and monastic schools attracted students from all over Europe.

By now Normandy was a prosperous land, although most wealth remained in the hands of the duke. Trade was encouraged, especially through Rouen, and towns grew around the major castles and monasteries. William ensured a steady supply of money by farming out the collection of rents and taxes; whatever surplus his agents collected was theirs to keep.

William was a strong duke and a formidable warrior. He threw off invasion by the king of France and the count of Anjou, conquered Maine and obtained Brittany's submission. Conquest of England, to whose throne he had in any case some claim, was the natural next step.

Below: Norman soldiers shown on a fragment of a pyx found at the Temple church, London.

1063. This year eorl Harold went after Christmas, from Gloucester to Rhuddlan, that was Gruffydd's, and burnt the estate, his ships and the sails they carried, and put him to flight. Then towards Rogation Harold went with ships from Bristol around Wales, and made peace with the people and exchanged hostages. Tostig went against them with land-troops and overcame that land. But in this same year, in autumn king Gruffydd was killed on August 5th by his own men, through the strife he was engaged in with eorl Harold. He was king over all Wales, and his head was brought to eorl Harold, and eorl Harold brought it to the king, with his ship's figure-head and ornamentation. King Edward committed that land to Griffin's two brothers, Bleddyn and Rhiwallon, and they swore oaths and gave hostages to the king and the eorl, that they would be without treachery in all things, also ready at his command on land or sea, and such tribute paid as was done formerly to the other king.

1065. Before Lammas eorl Harold commanded building done in Wales at Portskewet, now that he had conquered it, and there brought many goods, and thought to have king Edward there for the matters of hunting. But when it was all ready, Caradoc son of Gryffydd went to it with all the force he could gather, killed almost all those who worked on the building, and seized the goods which had been prepared. We know not who it was who first suggested this foolish raid; this was done on St. Bartholemew's day.

Soon after this the thanes all gathered together in Yorkshire and Northumberland, outlawed their eorl Tostig, killed all his retainers they could find, both English and Danes, and seized all his weapons in York, with the gold, silver and money they could discover anywhere else. They sent after Morkere, eorl Aelfgar's son, and chose him as eorl, and he went south with all the shires, with Nottinghamshire, Derbyshire and Lincolnshire, until he came to Northampton, and his brother Edwin came to him with the men in his eorldom; also many Welsh came with him. Eorl Harold came there to meet them, and they laid on him an errand to king Edward, and also sent messengers with him, demanding that they have Morkere as their eorl. The king granted this, sent Harold to them at Northampton on the eve of St. Simon and St. Jude's Day, and informed them of the same: they renewed king Cnut's laws there. The northern men did much harm around Northampton, while they went on their errand, in that they killed men, burnt houses and corn, and took all the cattle they could find; that was many thousands, and many hundreds of men they took, and led them north with them. So that shire and the shires near it were the worse for many winters. Eorl Tostig and his wife, and all who were of the same mind as he, went south over the sea with him to eorl Baldwin; he received them all, and they were there the whole winter.

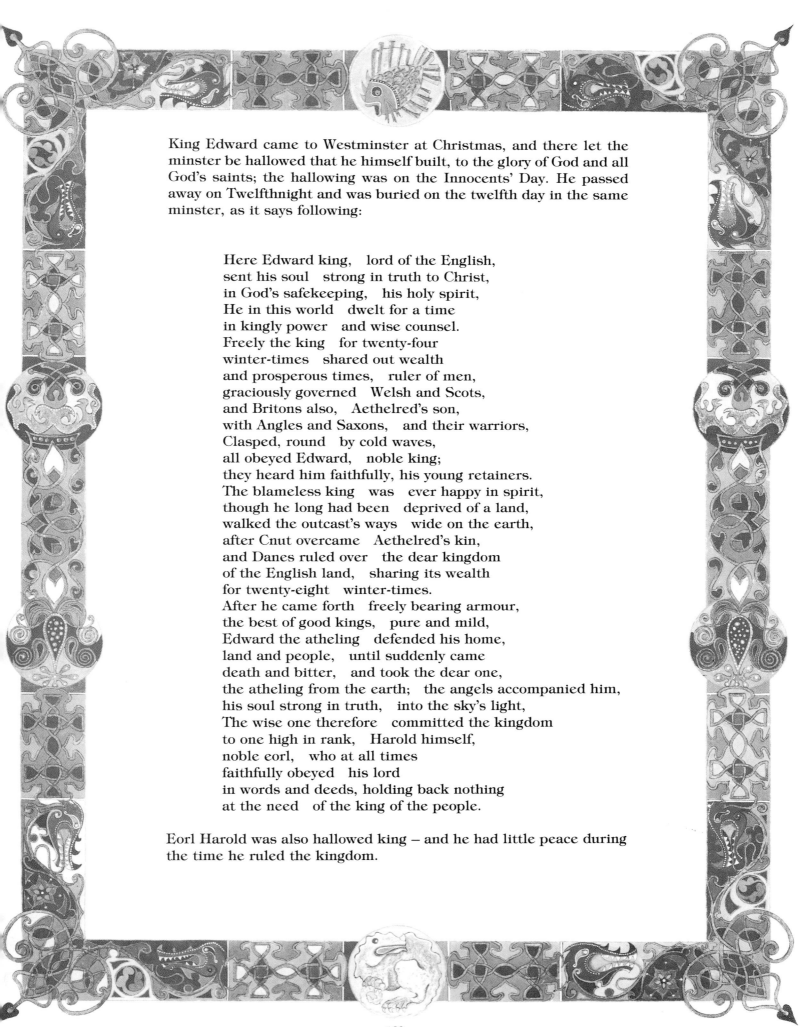

King Edward came to Westminster at Christmas, and there let the
minster be hallowed that he himself built, to the glory of God and all
God's saints; the hallowing was on the Innocents' Day. He passed
away on Twelfthnight and was buried on the twelfth day in the same
minster, as it says following:

Here Edward king,   lord of the English,
sent his soul   strong in truth to Christ,
in God's safekeeping,   his holy spirit,
He in this world   dwelt for a time
in kingly power   and wise counsel.
Freely the king   for twenty-four
winter-times   shared out wealth
and prosperous times,   ruler of men,
graciously governed   Welsh and Scots,
and Britons also,   Aethelred's son,
with Angles and Saxons,   and their warriors,
Clasped, round   by cold waves,
all obeyed Edward,   noble king;
they heard him faithfully, his young retainers.
The blameless king   was   ever happy in spirit,
though he long had been   deprived of a land,
walked the outcast's ways   wide on the earth,
after Cnut overcame   Aethelred's kin,
and Danes ruled over   the dear kingdom
of the English land,   sharing its wealth
for twenty-eight   winter-times.
After he came forth   freely bearing armour,
the best of good kings,   pure and mild,
Edward the atheling   defended his home,
land and people,   until suddenly came
death and bitter,   and took the dear one,
the atheling from the earth;   the angels accompanied him,
his soul strong in truth,   into the sky's light,
The wise one therefore   committed the kingdom
to one high in rank,   Harold himself,
noble eorl,   who at all times
faithfully obeyed   his lord
in words and deeds, holding back nothing
at the need   of the king of the people.

Eorl Harold was also hallowed king – and he had little peace during
the time he ruled the kingdom.

Above: The Normans felling trees, making boards, building ships and anchoring them in the water.

Left: The coronation of William in Westminster Abbey. The king is holding the sword and sceptre. Archbishop Stigand of Canterbury is shown on the Tapestry, but William was probably anointed by Ealdred, archbishop of York, as the pope had not yet recognized Stigand's appointment. Because William had won the crown in battle rather than by inheritance, the coronation ceremony was altered, and the people were asked in English and French whether they wished to have William as their king. The abbey guard outside misinterpreted the shout of approval as an attack on the king and set fire to several nearby buildings.

Below left: Halley's Comet was visible for several weeks during the spring of 1066 and was interpreted as an evil omen. Here an astrologer is shown explaining the comet's meaning to Harold.

All the illustrations on this page are from the Bayeux Tapestry.

Harold was crowned in Westminster Abbey on 6 January 1066, the day Edward was buried. In the circumstances, there could be no real dispute about the succession. Although he had no royal blood, Harold was the only proven leader available to protect England from invasion by William of Normandy or Harold Hardrada of Norway.

Almost immediately, William protested that Harold had broken his earlier pledge to support him as Edward's heir. When he got no answer, he began to prepare for invasion. He enlisted and trained a large army attracted by the promise of good wages and a share in the spoils of victory, collected supplies, built a fleet and obtained the support of the emperor Henry IV and the pope. On the other side of the Channel, however, things were not going so well. Harold was threatened with invasion on two fronts and marched north to York soon after his coronation. It was only with difficulty that he was able to assemble men and vessels along the Channel coast, ready to repel invaders.

Just when William was ready to sail, at the end of August, Harold's militia dispersed. This may have been for lack of supplies and money. But it is more likely that Harold changed his plans. Hardrada and Tostig, Harold's exiled brother, had invaded in the north. Leaving some of his army in the south, Harold marched hastily to meet them. Before he could reach York, Hardrada and Tostig took the city on 20 September, and the citizens agreed to join the invaders. Four days later, Harold surprised the resting Scandinavian army at Stamford Bridge and overwhelmed them; both Hardrada and Tostig were killed.

On 27 September the unfavourable winds that had penned William's fleet in the Somme estuary throughout September changed and the ships sailed for England. The English shore was unguarded, and early the next morning the Normans landed at Pevensey. (Only two ships were lost in the crossing, one of which held the expedition's soothsayer; William's comment was that he had failed to foresee his own death.) William quickly built a new fort within the remains of the Roman fort at Pevensey but soon transferred his base to Hastings. His men constructed a wooden castle surrounded by earthworks.

Harold heard of the invasion on 1 October in York. Thirteen days later, having returned to London, summoned new forces and marched on to Hastings, he faced William. William advanced to meet his enemy, forcing Harold to marshal his troops in a good but crowded position on a hill. The English fought bravely, beating back the Norman infantry and archers. The hill was held through the day but fighting ended when Harold was killed.

William now secured the ports of Romney and Dover, marched on Canterbury and received the submission of Winchester (where the treasury was kept) from Edith, Edward's widow. He then moved towards London. To isolate the city and compel its submission, he ravaged much of Surrey, north Hampshire, Berkshire and Oxfordshire. Edgar, the last of the line of Wessex kings, who had been appointed to succeed Harold, met William at Berkhamsted and acknowledged defeat. William was crowned in Westminster Abbey on Christmas Day. Anglo-Saxon England was no more.

Right: In this later depiction of the Battle of Hastings, William is seen killing Harold. In fact, Harold was probably killed by a random arrow shot by an unknown archer. (Illustration from a 14th-century manuscript.)

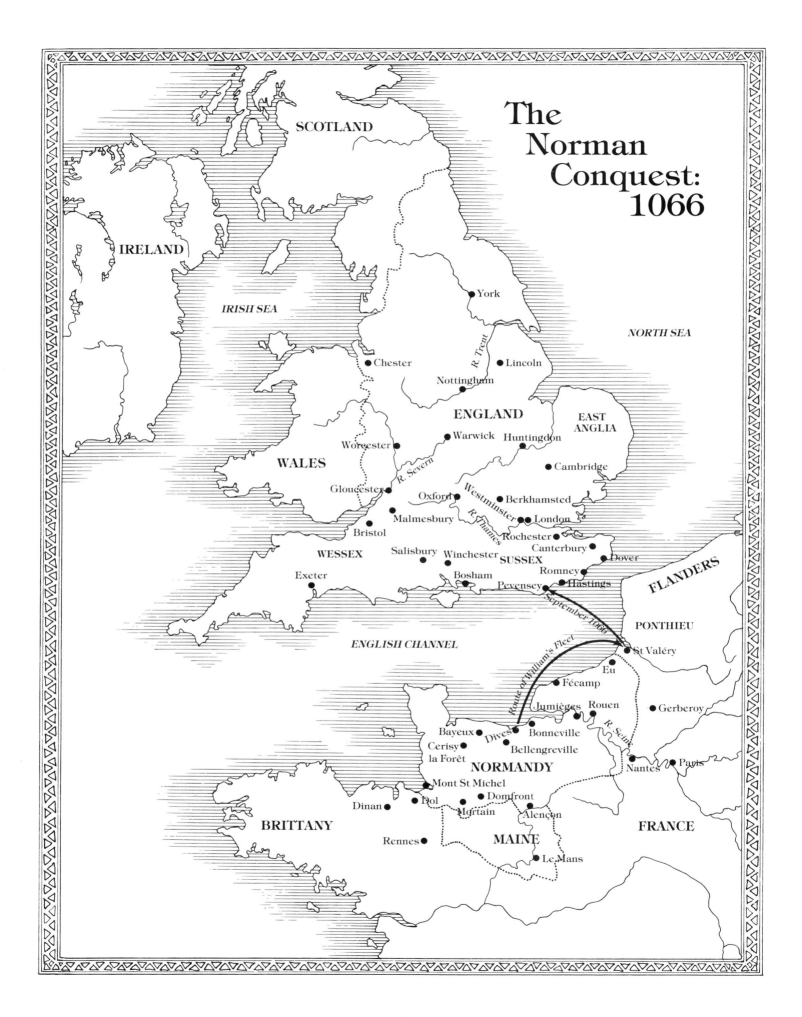

The Norman Conquest: 1066

SCOTLAND

IRELAND

IRISH SEA

NORTH SEA

York

Chester

Lincoln

Nottingham

ENGLAND

EAST ANGLIA

Warwick

Huntingdon

Worcester

Cambridge

WALES

R. Severn

Gloucester

Oxford

Westminster

Berkhamsted

Malmesbury

R. Thames

London

Bristol

Rochester

Canterbury

WESSEX

Salisbury

Winchester

SUSSEX

Dover

Exeter

Bosham

Romney

Pevensey

Hastings

FLANDERS

ENGLISH CHANNEL

September 1066

PONTHIEU

Route of William's Fleet

St Valéry

Eu

Fécamp

Jumièges

Rouen

Gerberoy

Bayeux

Dives

Bonneville

R. Seine

Cerisy la Forêt

Bellengreville

Nantes

Paris

NORMANDY

Mont St Michel

Dol

Domfront

Dinan

Mortain

Alençon

BRITTANY

Rennes

MAINE

FRANCE

Le Mans

192

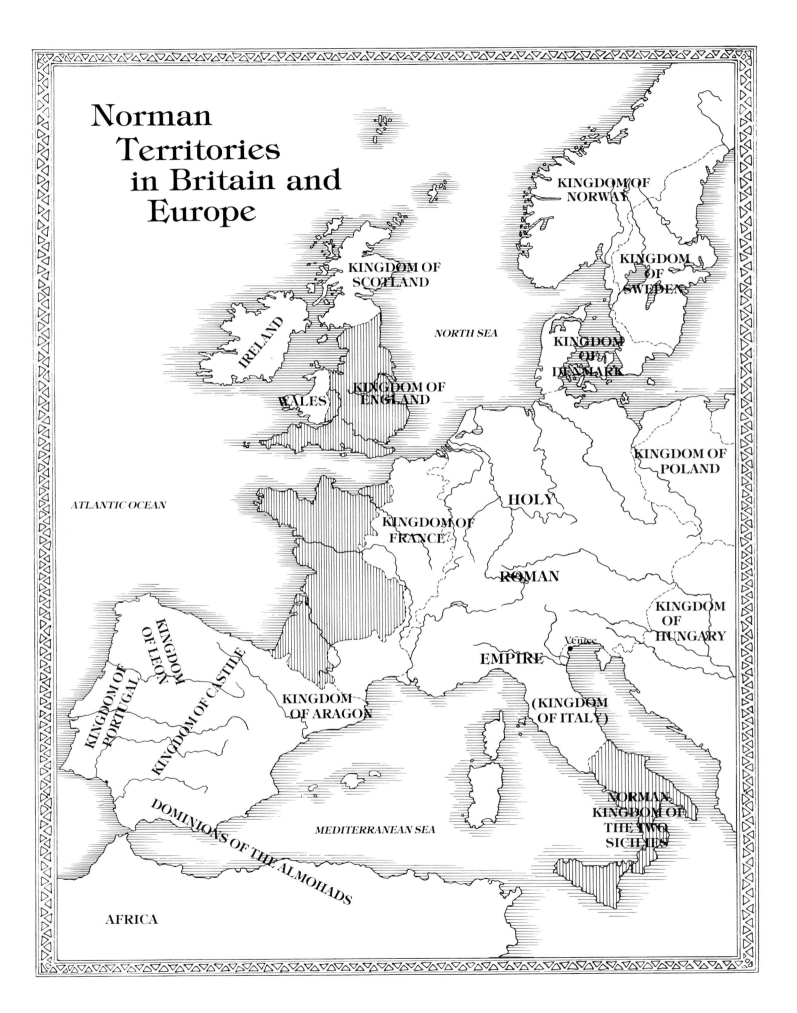

Norman
Territories
in Britain and
Europe

KINGDOM OF
NORWAY

KINGDOM
OF
SWEDEN

KINGDOM OF
SCOTLAND

IRELAND

NORTH SEA

KINGDOM
OF
DENMARK

KINGDOM OF
POLAND

WALES

KINGDOM OF
ENGLAND

ATLANTIC OCEAN

HOLY

KINGDOM OF
FRANCE

ROMAN

KINGDOM
OF
HUNGARY

KINGDOM
OF LEON

Venice

EMPIRE

KINGDOM OF
PORTUGAL

KINGDOM OF CASTILE

(KINGDOM
OF ITALY)

KINGDOM
OF ARAGON

NORMAN
KINGDOM OF
THE TWO
SICILIES

DOMINIONS OF THE ALMOHADS

MEDITERRANEAN SEA

AFRICA

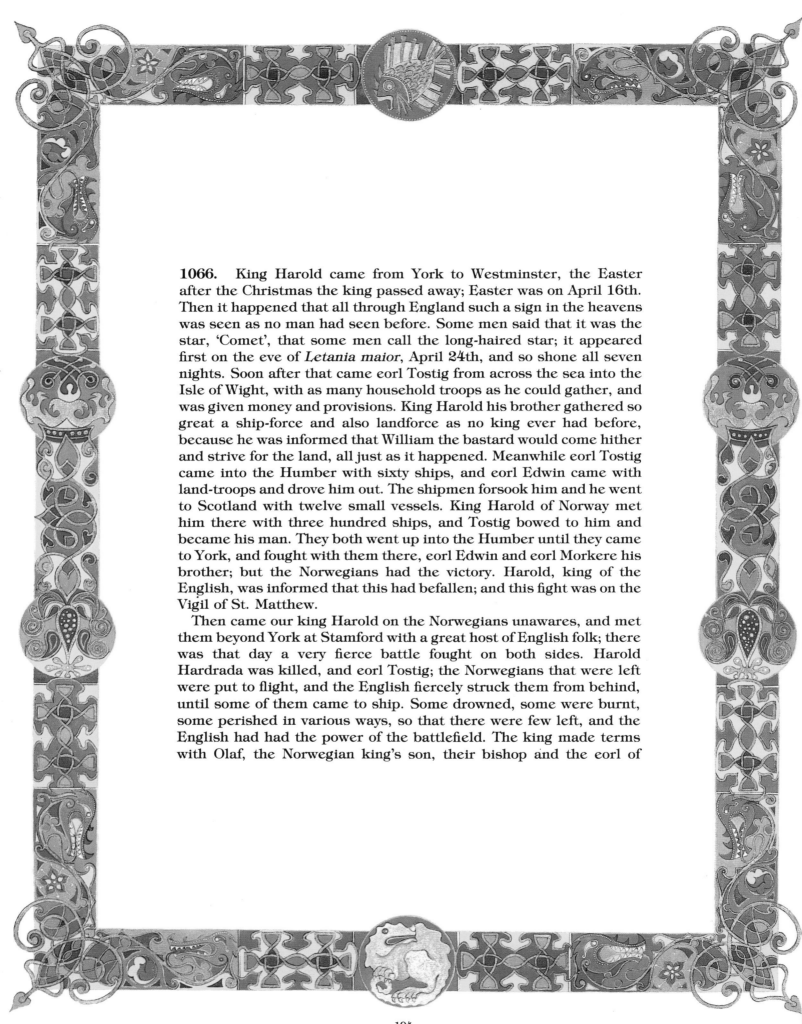

1066. King Harold came from York to Westminster, the Easter after the Christmas the king passed away; Easter was on April 16th. Then it happened that all through England such a sign in the heavens was seen as no man had seen before. Some men said that it was the star, 'Comet', that some men call the long-haired star; it appeared first on the eve of *Letania maior*, April 24th, and so shone all seven nights. Soon after that came eorl Tostig from across the sea into the Isle of Wight, with as many household troops as he could gather, and was given money and provisions. King Harold his brother gathered so great a ship-force and also landforce as no king ever had before, because he was informed that William the bastard would come hither and strive for the land, all just as it happened. Meanwhile eorl Tostig came into the Humber with sixty ships, and eorl Edwin came with land-troops and drove him out. The shipmen forsook him and he went to Scotland with twelve small vessels. King Harold of Norway met him there with three hundred ships, and Tostig bowed to him and became his man. They both went up into the Humber until they came to York, and fought with them there, eorl Edwin and eorl Morkere his brother; but the Norwegians had the victory. Harold, king of the English, was informed that this had befallen; and this fight was on the Vigil of St. Matthew.

Then came our king Harold on the Norwegians unawares, and met them beyond York at Stamford with a great host of English folk; there was that day a very fierce battle fought on both sides. Harold Hardrada was killed, and eorl Tostig; the Norwegians that were left were put to flight, and the English fiercely struck them from behind, until some of them came to ship. Some drowned, some were burnt, some perished in various ways, so that there were few left, and the English had had the power of the battlefield. The king made terms with Olaf, the Norwegian king's son, their bishop and the eorl of

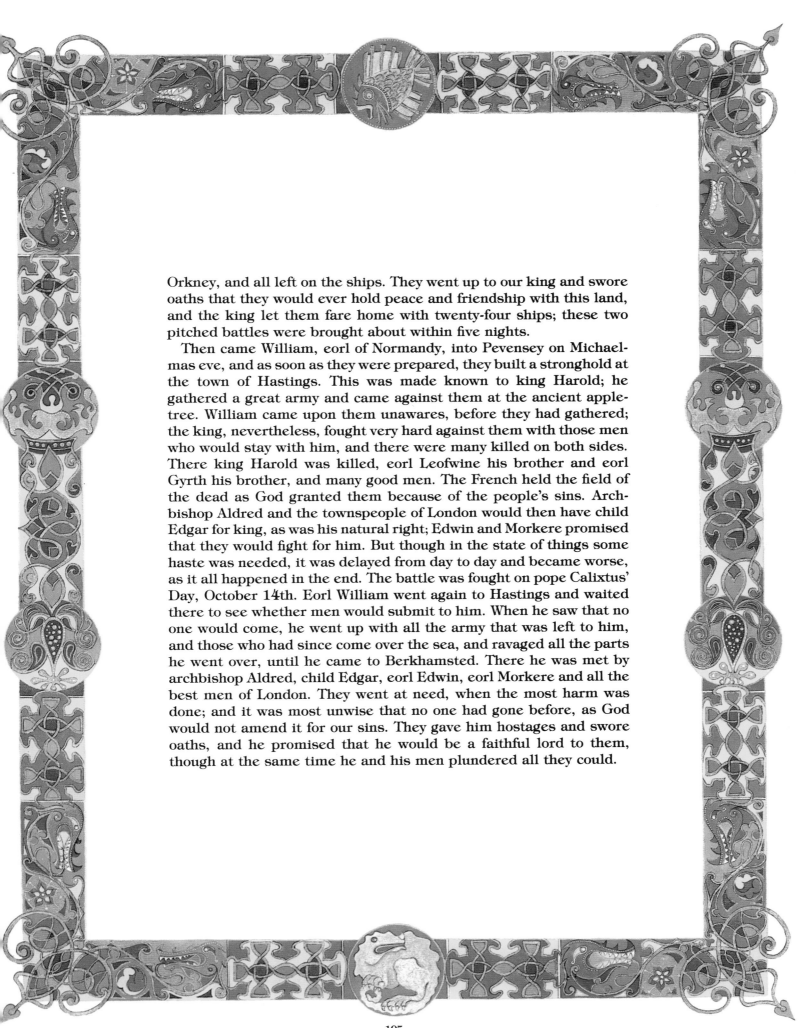

Orkney, and all left on the ships. They went up to our king and swore oaths that they would ever hold peace and friendship with this land, and the king let them fare home with twenty-four ships; these two pitched battles were brought about within five nights.

Then came William, eorl of Normandy, into Pevensey on Michaelmas eve, and as soon as they were prepared, they built a stronghold at the town of Hastings. This was made known to king Harold; he gathered a great army and came against them at the ancient appletree. William came upon them unawares, before they had gathered; the king, nevertheless, fought very hard against them with those men who would stay with him, and there were many killed on both sides. There king Harold was killed, eorl Leofwine his brother and eorl Gyrth his brother, and many good men. The French held the field of the dead as God granted them because of the people's sins. Archbishop Aldred and the townspeople of London would then have child Edgar for king, as was his natural right; Edwin and Morkere promised that they would fight for him. But though in the state of things some haste was needed, it was delayed from day to day and became worse, as it all happened in the end. The battle was fought on pope Calixtus' Day, October 14th. Eorl William went again to Hastings and waited there to see whether men would submit to him. When he saw that no one would come, he went up with all the army that was left to him, and those who had since come over the sea, and ravaged all the parts he went over, until he came to Berkhamsted. There he was met by archbishop Aldred, child Edgar, eorl Edwin, eorl Morkere and all the best men of London. They went at need, when the most harm was done; and it was most unwise that no one had gone before, as God would not amend it for our sins. They gave him hostages and swore oaths, and he promised that he would be a faithful lord to them, though at the same time he and his men plundered all they could.

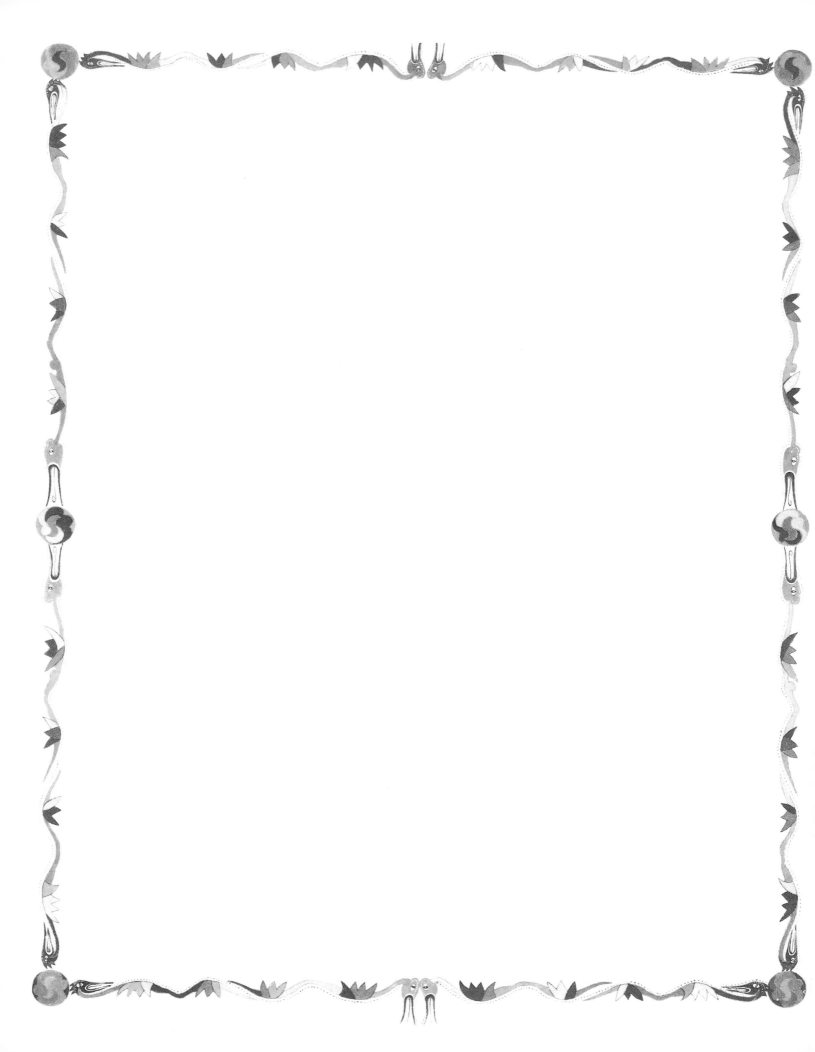

Part Four
1067~1085

1067. The king came back to England on St. Nicholas' Day, and the same day was burnt down Christchurch in Canterbury. Abbot Wulfwi passed away, and is buried in his bishopric at Dorchester. Eadric the Wild and the Welsh became unquiet and fought with the castle-men in Hereford, and did them much damage.

The king set a heavy tribute on poor folk, though nevertheless still let his men harry all that they went over. Then he went to Devonshire and besieged the town of Exeter for eighteen days; there many of his troops were killed. But he promised them good and did evil, and they gave him the town because the thanes had betrayed them.

That summer child Edgar went out with his mother Agatha, his two sisters Margaret and Christina, Maerleswegen, and many good men with them. They came to Scotland into king Malcolm's protection, and he took them all in. Then king Malcolm began to desire his sister Margaret for his wife, but he and all his men long spoke against it, and also her herself refused.

> She said she would not wed him, nor anyone,
> if God's high mercy   granted it,
> that she her maidenhead   for the mighty Lord
> might keep in her heart and body   in this brief life,
> in pure continence   to please him.

The king urged her brother until he said yes, but he could do nothing else, because they had come under his rule. It befell as God had foreseen it, as it might not be otherwise; just as he in his gospel said that even one sparrow cannot fall into a snare without his foreknowledge. The foreknowing Shaper knew beforehand what he would have of her, because she was to increase the praise of God in that land, and guide the king from the erring path, humble him to a better way, together with his people, to lay aside evil customs the nation had followed, just as she did later. The king received her then against her will; her customs were pleasing to him, and he thanked God, who had given him such a mate. He thought wisely on it, as he was a very prudent man, turned himself to God and scorned every impurity. As the apostle Paul, teacher of all nations, says: *Salvabitur vir infidelis per mulieriem fidelem sic et mulier infidelis per virum fidelem, et reliquia*, that is in our language, 'Very often the unbelieving husband is hallowed and healed through a righteous wife, and so likewise such a wife through a believing husband.' This aforesaid woman afterwards in that land did many useful deeds to the glory of God, and also to the royal estate, as was fitting to her ancestry. Of believing and noble kin she was sprung: her father was the atheling Edward, son of king Edmund, son of Aethelred, son of Edgar, son of Eadred, and so forth in the kingly line; and her mother's kin go back to the emperor Henry, who had dominion over Rome.

Harold's mother Gytha fared out, and many good wives of men with her into the isle of Flatholme, dwelt there for some time, and from there went over the sea to St. Omer.

This Easter the king came to Winchester; Easter was on March 23rd. Soon after that came the lady Mathild to this land. Archbishop Aldred hallowed her queen at Westminster on Whit-Sunday. It was then made known to the king that the folk to the north had gathered together, and would stand against him if he came. He then went to Nottingham and built a castle there, so from there to York, and there built two castles, in Lincoln and elsewhere in those parts. Eorl Gospatric and the best men went to Scotland.

During this, Harold's sons came from Ireland with a ship-force into the mouth of the Avon unexpectedly, and soon ravaged over all the area. They went to Bristol, and meant to break into the town, but the town-dwellers fought against them hardily; when they could win nothing from that town, they went to ship with what they had plundered, so fared to Somerset, and went inland there. The staller Eadnoth fought with them and was killed there, and many good men on each side; away from there sailed those who were left.

1068. King William gave eorl Robert eorldom over the land of Northumbria, but the men of that land overtook him in the town of Durham and killed him, and nine hundred men with him. Soon after, the atheling Edgar came with all the Northumbrians to York, and the townsmen came to terms with him. King William came south on him unawares with an overwhelming force and put them to flight. They killed those who could not flee – that was many hundreds of men – and ravaged the borough. On St. Peter's minster they wrought disgrace and all the others also ravaged and outraged. The atheling went again to Scotland.

1069. After this came Harold's sons from Ireland at midsummer with sixty-four ships into the mouth of the Taw, and went unexpectedly inland. Eorl Brian came upon them unawares with no small host, fought with them, and killed all the best men in that fleet; the other small host fled out to the ships, and Harold's sons went back to Ireland.

Archbishop Aldred passed away in York, and is buried there in his bishopric; he went forth on the day of saints Protus and Hyacinthus. He held the archbishopric with great honour for ten years less fifteen weeks. Soon after there came from Denmark three of king Swein's sons with two hundred and forty ships, and eorl Osbeorn and eorl Thurkil, into the mouth of the Humber. There they were met by child Edgar, eorl Waltheof, Maerleswegen and eorl Gospatric with the Northumbrians, and all the people of the land, riding and marching with an immense force greatly rejoicing – all of one mind they went to York, stormed the castle, threw it down, and won there countless treasures. There they killed many hundreds of Frenchmen and took many with them to ship. Before the shipmen came here the French had burnt the town, and also the holy minster of St. Peter they had all ravaged and burnt down. When the king found this out, he went northward with all the troops he could gather, and ravaged and laid waste the shire and all that was in it. That fleet lay all winter in the Humber, where the king could not reach it. The king was on Christmas Day in York, and so stayed all the winter in the land. He came to Winchester the same Easter, and bishop Aethelric of Peterborough was accused and led to Westminster; his brother, bishop Aethelwine, was outlawed.

1070. Eorl Waltheof came to terms with the king. That same spring the king allowed all the monasteries in England to be plundered. The same year came king Swein from Denmark into the Humber; the folk of that land came to meet him and made peace with him, believing that he would overcome the land. Then the Danish bishop, Christian, came into Ely, and eorl Osbeorn and the Danish housecarles with them. The English folk of the fenlands came to them, believing that they would win all the land.

The monks of Peterborough heard it said that their own men meant to plunder the monastery – that was Hereward and his band – because they heard it said that the king had given the abbacy to a French abbot called Turold, that he was a very hard man, and that he had come into Stamford with all his Frenchmen. There was a sacristan named Yware, who by night took all he could, gospels, chasubles, copes, robes and such little things as he could quickly. He went soon before dawn to the abbot Turold, said to him that he sought his protection, and told him how outlaws were to come to Peterborough; he did all that at the advice of the monks. Soon in the morning came all the outlaws with many ships and meant to enter the monastery; the monks withstood them so that they could not come in. Then they set fire to it, burnt all the monks' houses and all the town but one house. By means of fire they came in at the Bolhithe Gate, and the monks came to meet them and asked for peace; but they heeded nothing, went into the minster, climbed up the holy rood, took the king's-helm from our Lord's head, all of pure of gold, and took the footrest underneath his feet, that was all of red gold. They climbed up to the tower and brought down the altar-frontal that was hidden there. They took two golden shrines and nine silver there; and they took fifteen great roods, both gold and silver. They took so much gold and silver, so many treasures in money, cloth and books that no man could reckon it to another; and they said they did it in loyalty to the monastery.

After, they went to their ships, fared to Ely, and there gave over all the treasure; the Danes believed that they would overcome the Frenchmen. They then drove out all the monks, leaving no one there but one monk; he was called Leofwine the Tall, and he lay sick in the infirmary. Then came abbot Turold, and eight times twenty Frenchmen with him, all fully armed. When he came there he found it burnt inside and out, all but the church alone; by then the outlaws were afloat, as they knew he would come there. This was done on June 2nd. The two kings, William and Swein, were reconciled, the Danish men fared out of Ely with all the aforesaid treasure and took it away with them. When they reached mid-sea, a great storm came and drove apart all the ships the treasures were in. Some went to Norway, some to Ireland; and some to Denmark – all that came there were the altar-frontal, some shrines, some roods, and many of the other treasures. They brought it to a king's town and put it all into the church there; then later in their heedlessness and their drunkenness they burnt the church and all that was in it in one night. Thus was the minster of Peterborough burnt down and plundered – almighty God have mercy on it in his great gentleness of heart. And thus the abbot, Turold, came to Peterborough, and the monks came again and did Christ's service in the church, that had stood fully seven nights without any kind of service. When bishop Aethelric heard tell of this he excommunicated all the men who had done that evil deed.

There was much famine that year. That summer the fleet came from the north in the Humber into the Thames, lay there for two nights and headed for Denmark. Eorl Baldwin passed away and his son Arnulf received the kingdom. Eorl William should have been his protector, and the French king also; eorl Robert came and killed his kinsman Arnulf and the eorl put the king to flight and killed many thousands of his men.

Above: The Abbaye aux Hommes, Caen, established by William and his queen Mathild as penance for their unca-nonical marriage. It is not known for certain why the pope forbade the match, but Lanfranc was able to persuade the next pope to sanction the marriage on condition that the abbey, and its sister Abbaye aux Dames, were built.

Opposite top right: William armed for battle, accompanied by followers on horseback.

Opposite top left: William's great passion, remembered by English and Norman chroniclers alike, was for hunting. He demolished no less than 60 Hampshire villages to create the New Forest and expanded other forests. The penalty for poaching royal game was death.

Opposite bottom: A tall man (5 feet 10 inches), William was in fact more heavily built than this 15th-century artist has portrayed him.

The illegitimate son of Robert, Duke of Normandy, William (1027–87) succeeded his father when he was only seven. While still in his teens he had to defend his dukedom against both ambitious neighbours and internal challengers. His success in maintaining his position no doubt taught him to manage his men, his government and his resources. But, as with all strong leaders of this time, it was the compelling personality of the man himself – his forcefulness, his energy, and the confidence and determination he displayed at all times – that made him an almost legendary figure: a Conqueror.

A strong, charismatic military leader, William inspired his men, never hesitating to lead them into battle. But, despite his successes in the field, he never over-reached himself and resisted the temptation to expand into Wales, Scotland and Ireland in costly and debilitating campaigns.

William stands out as a forceful and able statesman in an age of petty wars, shifting loyalties and weak and confused governments. He quickly analysed those institutions (such as the judicial system) worth keeping in his new kingdom and those where change was necessary. Order was his watchword: he kept a strong hold over his potentially unruly barons, yet retained their loyalty, and taxed his subjects heavily, tying them to the land.

In an age of heavy eating and drinking and lax morality, William is remembered as abstemious and puritanical. Perhaps in reaction to his birth, he was absolutely faithful to his wife and had no tolerance for married clergy. He was either injured or overcome by exhaustion while leading his army through the burning town of Nantes in 1087 – as usual he had set fire to the fields around the town and surprised its defenders by his sudden appearance at the gates. Six weeks later he died at the abbey of Saint-Gervais, near Rouen.

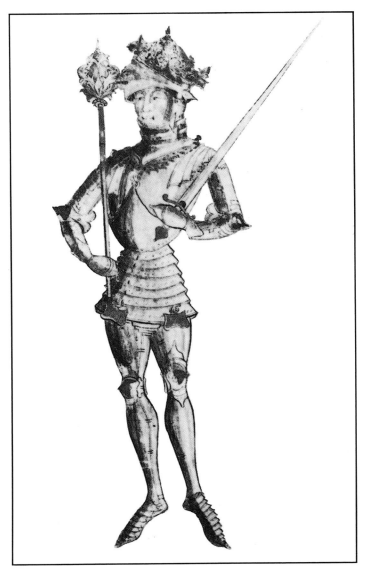

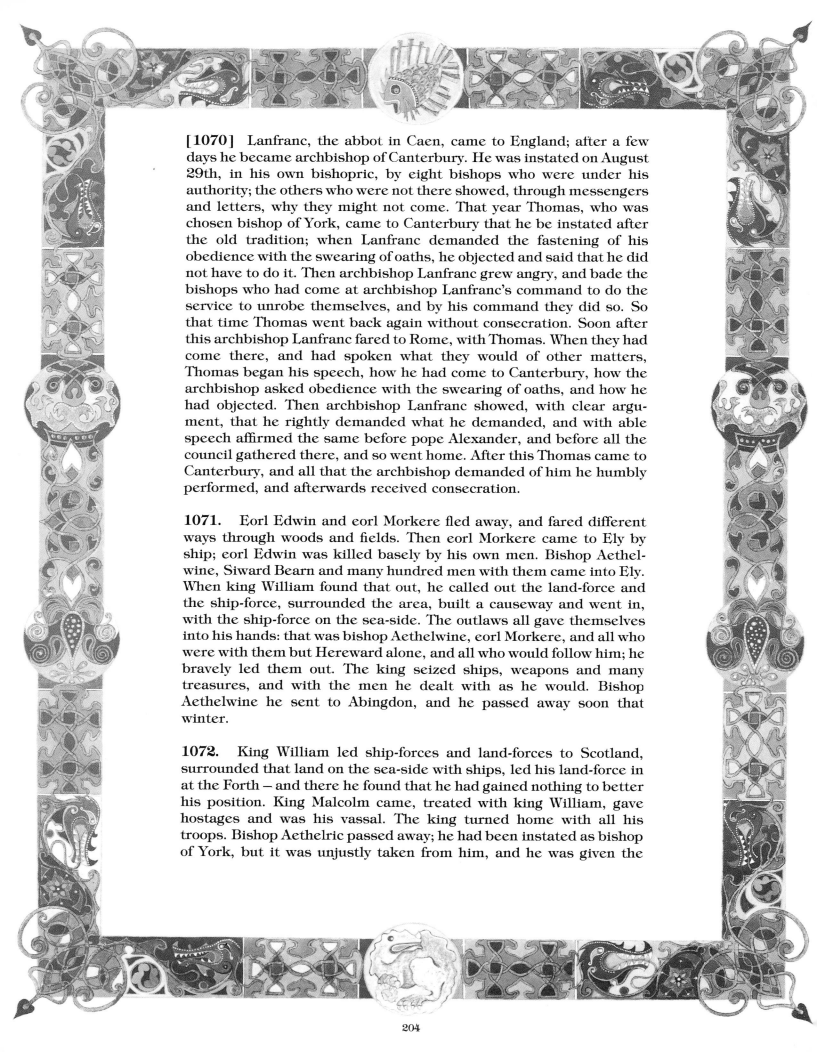

[1070] Lanfranc, the abbot in Caen, came to England; after a few days he became archbishop of Canterbury. He was instated on August 29th, in his own bishopric, by eight bishops who were under his authority; the others who were not there showed, through messengers and letters, why they might not come. That year Thomas, who was chosen bishop of York, came to Canterbury that he be instated after the old tradition; when Lanfranc demanded the fastening of his obedience with the swearing of oaths, he objected and said that he did not have to do it. Then archbishop Lanfranc grew angry, and bade the bishops who had come at archbishop Lanfranc's command to do the service to unrobe themselves, and by his command they did so. So that time Thomas went back again without consecration. Soon after this archbishop Lanfranc fared to Rome, with Thomas. When they had come there, and had spoken what they would of other matters, Thomas began his speech, how he had come to Canterbury, how the archbishop asked obedience with the swearing of oaths, and how he had objected. Then archbishop Lanfranc showed, with clear argument, that he rightly demanded what he demanded, and with able speech affirmed the same before pope Alexander, and before all the council gathered there, and so went home. After this Thomas came to Canterbury, and all that the archbishop demanded of him he humbly performed, and afterwards received consecration.

1071.   Eorl Edwin and eorl Morkere fled away, and fared different ways through woods and fields. Then eorl Morkere came to Ely by ship; eorl Edwin was killed basely by his own men. Bishop Aethelwine, Siward Bearn and many hundred men with them came into Ely. When king William found that out, he called out the land-force and the ship-force, surrounded the area, built a causeway and went in, with the ship-force on the sea-side. The outlaws all gave themselves into his hands: that was bishop Aethelwine, eorl Morkere, and all who were with them but Hereward alone, and all who would follow him; he bravely led them out. The king seized ships, weapons and many treasures, and with the men he dealt with as he would. Bishop Aethelwine he sent to Abingdon, and he passed away soon that winter.

1072.   King William led ship-forces and land-forces to Scotland, surrounded that land on the sea-side with ships, led his land-force in at the Forth – and there he found that he had gained nothing to better his position. King Malcolm came, treated with king William, gave hostages and was his vassal. The king turned home with all his troops. Bishop Aethelric passed away; he had been instated as bishop of York, but it was unjustly taken from him, and he was given the bishopric in Durham. He had it while he would; he afterwards gave it up, went to Peterborough, to St. Peter's monastery, and there lived as a religious for twelve years. After king William won England, he was taken from Peterborough and sent to Westminster. He passed away on October 15th, and he is buried in that minster, in St. Nicholas' Chapel.

1073. King William led the English and French forces over the sea, and won the land of Maine. The Englishmen greatly marred it; they destroyed the vineyards and burnt the towns. They greatly marred it and bent it all to William's hands, and afterwards they turned home to England.

1074. King William went over the sea to Normandy. Child Edgar came from Flanders into Scotland on St. Grimbald's Day, and king Malcolm and his sister Margaret received them with great honour. At the same time, king Philip of the French kingdom sent a letter to him, and bade that he come to him; he would give him the castle at Montreuil, so that he might thereafter daily do mischief to his enemies. Lo, then king Malcolm and his sister Margaret gave him and all his men great gifts, many treasures in skins faced with purple cloth, marten-skin robes, miniver and ermineskins, costly robes, vessels gold and silver, and he led him and all his shipmen with great honour from his dominion. But on the journey evil befell them when they were out at sea, in that very fierce weather came upon them; the raging sea and strong wind threw them on land and broke up all their ships. They themselves hardly came to land; nearly all their treasures were lost. Also, some of his men were caught by the Frenchmen, but he himself and his men most able to travel fared back again to Scotland, some going grievously on foot, some miserably riding. Then king Malcolm counselled him to send to king William over the sea, to ask his protection; and he so did. The king granted him that.

Again king Malcolm and his sister gave Edgar and all his men countless treasures, and very worthily sent him again from their dominion. The shire-reeve of York came to meet him at Durham, fared all the way with him, and found them meat and fodder at each castle they came to, until they came over the sea to the king. King William then received him with great honour. Then he was there in his court, and took such dues as he laid on him.

1075. King William gave eorl Ralph the daughter of William, the son of Osbeorn; this same Ralph was Breton on his mother's side, and Ralph his father was English, born in Norfolk. Because of this the king gave his son the eorldom there, and Suffolk also. He then led his wife to Norwich.

MVSEVM
BRITAN
NICVM

Ego Wilhelmus cognomine Bastardus Rex Anglie do concedo tibi Nepoti meo Alano Britannie comiti et heredibus tuis imperpetuum omnes villas et terras que nuper fuerunt Comitis Eadwini in Eboracscira cum feodis militum et ecclesiis et aliis libertatibus et consuetudinibus ita libere et honorifice sicut idem Eadwinus ea tenuit. Datum in obsidione coram civitate Eboraci.

Williams's first task was to consolidate his hold over London and to extend and strengthen his rule over the rest of the country. In London he made an immediate start on the White Tower and meanwhile toured the country, setting his troops to building and fortifying castles. He also imposed heavy taxation and began to distribute among his supporters land forfeited by the English nobles.

Castles were the main means by which William asserted his authority. The earliest constructions were motte and bailey, quickly thrown up to control a town or subdue an uprising. The motte, a mound usually about 100 feet in diameter and some 50 feet high, was built at one side of the circular bailey, which was surrounded by a ditch and a bank ringed with wooden barricades. A wooden tower on top housed the garrison and could be used as a final point of retreat.

In the early years of the Conquest, a castle's main function was attack. But increasing political unrest meant that castles later became defensive strongholds, often erected by individual nobles to guard their property. Stone replaced wood as the normal building material, and in some castles the wooden bailey stockade gave way to a stone curtain wall with battlements, often studded with towers to give extra strength. Elsewhere, a well-fortified square or rectangular stone keep became the castle's strongpoint.

(Continued on page 242)

Above: The castle at Dinan, Britanny, from the Bayeux Tapestry. A stepped timber flying bridge connects the bailey and the motte, which is surrounded by a crenellated timber palisade with a fighting platform.

Opposite: William the Conqueror receiving the allegiance of his nephew Alain le Roux, to whom he granted land that had formerly belonged to Edwin, earl of Mercia, a prominent English rebel against Norman rule. (Illustration from a 13th-century English history.)

Below: The earliest Norman castles consisted of a motte and bailey. The enclosed bailey contained buildings and was surrounded by a stockade and ditch. The motte, the strongest point, was topped by a wooden tower and ringed around its base by another ditch. Berkhamsted castle is typical of those raised immediately after the Conquest.

[1075] On Christmas Day archbishop Aldred hallowed William king at Westminster, and he pledged with his hand on Christ's book, and also swore before he would set the crown on his head that he would rule this nation as well as any king before him at his best, if they would be faithful to him. Nevertheless, he laid recompense-charges on men very heavily, and in spring went away over the sea to Normandy, and took with him archbishop Stigand, abbot Aethelnoth of Glastonbury, child Edgar, eorl Edwin, eorl Morkere, eorl Waltheof and many other good men of England. Bishop Odo and eorl William remained here, built castles widely throughout this nation, oppressed the people wretchedly, and it afterwards grew much more evil. May the end be good when God wills it.

Leofric, then abbot of Peterborough, was with that same campaign, fell sick there, came home and was dead soon after that on All Saints' Eve; God have mercy on his soul. In his day was all happiness and all good in Peterborough; he was dear to all folk, so that the king gave St. Peter and him the abbacy in Burton-on-Trent, that in Coventry which eorl Leofric his uncle had founded, that of Crowland, and that of Thorney. He brought such property into the monastery of Peterborough in gold, silver, cloth and land as no other ever did before or after him. Then golden borough turned to wretched borough. The monks chose the priest Brand as abbot, because he was a very good man and very wise. They sent him to the atheling Edgar, because the folk of that land believed that he should be king; the atheling agreed to it gladly. When king William heard that, he grew very angry and said that the abbot had slighted him. Then good men came between them and settled the matter, because the abbot was a good man. He gave the king forty marks in gold as a settlement, then lived a little while after that, for only three years. After that came all trouble and all evil to the monastery. God have mercy on it.

That was the bridal feast, alas,
Through which death to many came to pass.

There was eorl Roger, eorl Waltheof, bishops and abbots, and they plotted there that they would drive their natural lord from his kingdom; this was soon made known to the king in Normandy. Earl Ralph and eorl Roger were leaders in this plot. They lured in the Bretons, and sent also to Denmark after a ship-force. Roger went west to his eorldom, and gathered his people to the king's hurt, he thought; but it turned into great harm to himself. Ralph meant to go forth also with his eorldom, but the Norman castle-men in England and the folk of that land came against them, and hindered them all so that they did nothing — so that he was glad to flee to his ships, and left his wife behind in the castle. She held it until they made terms with

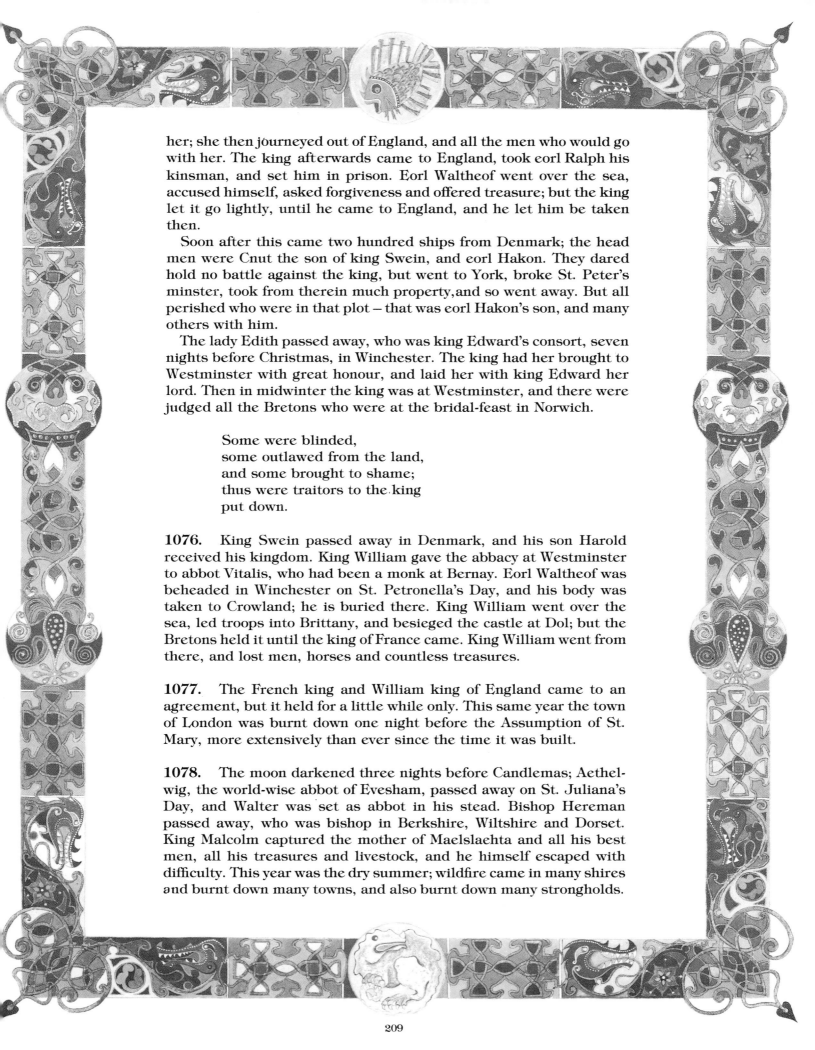

her; she then journeyed out of England, and all the men who would go with her. The king afterwards came to England, took eorl Ralph his kinsman, and set him in prison. Eorl Waltheof went over the sea, accused himself, asked forgiveness and offered treasure; but the king let it go lightly, until he came to England, and he let him be taken then.

Soon after this came two hundred ships from Denmark; the head men were Cnut the son of king Swein, and eorl Hakon. They dared hold no battle against the king, but went to York, broke St. Peter's minster, took from therein much property, and so went away. But all perished who were in that plot – that was eorl Hakon's son, and many others with him.

The lady Edith passed away, who was king Edward's consort, seven nights before Christmas, in Winchester. The king had her brought to Westminster with great honour, and laid her with king Edward her lord. Then in midwinter the king was at Westminster, and there were judged all the Bretons who were at the bridal-feast in Norwich.

> Some were blinded,
> some outlawed from the land,
> and some brought to shame;
> thus were traitors to the king
> put down.

1076. King Swein passed away in Denmark, and his son Harold received his kingdom. King William gave the abbacy at Westminster to abbot Vitalis, who had been a monk at Bernay. Eorl Waltheof was beheaded in Winchester on St. Petronella's Day, and his body was taken to Crowland; he is buried there. King William went over the sea, led troops into Brittany, and besieged the castle at Dol; but the Bretons held it until the king of France came. King William went from there, and lost men, horses and countless treasures.

1077. The French king and William king of England came to an agreement, but it held for a little while only. This same year the town of London was burnt down one night before the Assumption of St. Mary, more extensively than ever since the time it was built.

1078. The moon darkened three nights before Candlemas; Aethelwig, the world-wise abbot of Evesham, passed away on St. Juliana's Day, and Walter was set as abbot in his stead. Bishop Hereman passed away, who was bishop in Berkshire, Wiltshire and Dorset. King Malcolm captured the mother of Maelslaehta and all his best men, all his treasures and livestock, and he himself escaped with difficulty. This year was the dry summer; wildfire came in many shires and burnt down many towns, and also burnt down many strongholds.

Above and opposite: Hay-making and ploughing.
(Illustration from an early 11th-century calendar.)

Left: William probably never saw the finished Domesday Book, although he may have examined some of the information gathered before he sailed for Normandy in the summer of 1086. It was later written out in its final form by one scribe, and provided William's successors with a detailed description of the property and wealth of much of their kingdom. This is the first page of the entry on Wiltshire.

Below: At Appleton-le-Moors, North Yorkshire, the modern main street preserves the 11th-century plan of the village. Houses lined the single street, the small plots at the back leading directly into the fields.

In 1085, William 'sent his men over all England into each shire' to investigate his subjects and their property. The Domesday Book thus enabled the king to check that none of his barons had seized land unlawfully and also to calculate the rents and fees due from each landholder. (The Book takes its name from the Old English word *dom*, meaning 'assessment', because it assessed the worth of the king's realm.)

At the time of the Conquest most people worked on the land. Life was hard, barely above subsistence level. The main crops were grain, grown as food for both men and animals and to make ale, the national drink. The Domesday Book frequently refers to 'plough lands' and 'ploughs', which were the essential agricultural tool. They were often shared, although some estates and some working men owned their own ploughs and teams. Partly because every available field was cultivated, there were very few herds of animals, although pigs were numerous, as they could forage in woodland. Much of the country was covered by forest, marsh and fen, which were gradually being cleared.

Most people lived in villages in the centre of arable land. Some men were free and owned their own land, but even they had to pay their lord a nominal rent and help bring in the harvest. Most people were in the next class down: they had their own plough land – perhaps 20 or 30 acres – allocated in strips within the communal open fields, but had to work two or three days a week on the lord's land, pay him rent and supply him with produce. Shepherds, carpenters, stonemasons and other craftsmen had smaller plots and worked shorter hours on the lord's land. The bottom rank was landless serfs, compelled to spend all their time tilling the lord's estates and forbidden to leave their village. All the villagers' land was parcelled out by an overseer called a reeve, who also organized ploughing and dealt with payments, duties and disputes.

By the end of William's reign the villager had lost many of his privileges and was securely tied to his lord. He also suffered because land was sub-let to ruthless landlords; even the king was guilty of this practice, and those at the bottom of the social scale suffered higher taxation and rents. William's devastation of the land to subdue opposition at the start of his reign left a legacy of chaos and starvation in many areas, especially the north. The spate of castle-building also forced people off the land. Against all these changes the villager had little or no protection.

Below: Seal of William I showing the king holding a sword.

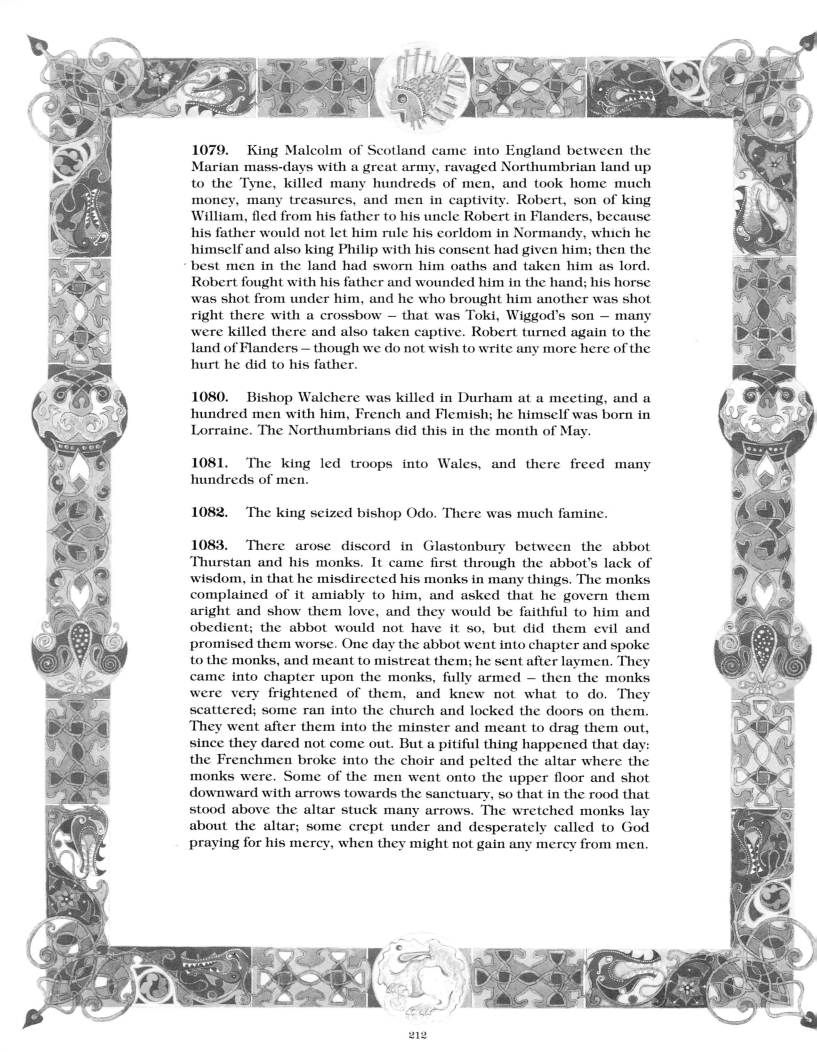

1079. King Malcolm of Scotland came into England between the Marian mass-days with a great army, ravaged Northumbrian land up to the Tyne, killed many hundreds of men, and took home much money, many treasures, and men in captivity. Robert, son of king William, fled from his father to his uncle Robert in Flanders, because his father would not let him rule his eorldom in Normandy, which he himself and also king Philip with his consent had given him; then the best men in the land had sworn him oaths and taken him as lord. Robert fought with his father and wounded him in the hand; his horse was shot from under him, and he who brought him another was shot right there with a crossbow – that was Toki, Wiggod's son – many were killed there and also taken captive. Robert turned again to the land of Flanders – though we do not wish to write any more here of the hurt he did to his father.

1080. Bishop Walchere was killed in Durham at a meeting, and a hundred men with him, French and Flemish; he himself was born in Lorraine. The Northumbrians did this in the month of May.

1081. The king led troops into Wales, and there freed many hundreds of men.

1082. The king seized bishop Odo. There was much famine.

1083. There arose discord in Glastonbury between the abbot Thurstan and his monks. It came first through the abbot's lack of wisdom, in that he misdirected his monks in many things. The monks complained of it amiably to him, and asked that he govern them aright and show them love, and they would be faithful to him and obedient; the abbot would not have it so, but did them evil and promised them worse. One day the abbot went into chapter and spoke to the monks, and meant to mistreat them; he sent after laymen. They came into chapter upon the monks, fully armed – then the monks were very frightened of them, and knew not what to do. They scattered; some ran into the church and locked the doors on them. They went after them into the minster and meant to drag them out, since they dared not come out. But a pitiful thing happened that day: the Frenchmen broke into the choir and pelted the altar where the monks were. Some of the men went onto the upper floor and shot downward with arrows towards the sanctuary, so that in the rood that stood above the altar stuck many arrows. The wretched monks lay about the altar; some crept under and desperately called to God praying for his mercy, when they might not gain any mercy from men.

What can we say, but that they shot fiercely? The others broke the door down and went in, struck some of the monks dead, and wounded many therein, so that blood came from the altar onto the steps, and from the steps onto the floor. There were three struck dead there and eighteen wounded.

The same year passed away Mathild, king William's queen, on the day after All Saints'; and the same year after midwinter the king had a severe and heavy tax announced over all England, that was seventy-two pence for each hide of land.

1085. Men declared, and said it truly, that Cnut, king of Denmark, Swein's son, was directed hither, and meant to win this land with the help of eorl Robert of Flanders, because Cnut had married Robert's daughter. When William, king of England – who was then staying in Normandy because he had both England and Normandy – found this out, he fared into England with as great a force of riding and marching men of France and Brittany as ever before sought this land, so that men wondered how this land could feed all the force. But the king let the force disperse throughout all the land to his vassals, and they fed the force, each according to the produce of his land. Men had much affliction that year; the king let the land by the sea be laid waste, so that if his enemies came up they would have nothing that could be taken quickly. But when the king found out the truth, that his enemies had been hindered and could not begin their journey, he let some of the force fare to their own land, and some he held in this land over the winter.

Then in midwinter the king was in Gloucester with his counsellors and held his court there for five days, and after the archbishop and clergy held a synod for three days. There Mauricius was chosen bishop of London, William as bishop of Norfolk and Robert as bishop of Cheshire; they were all the king's chaplains. After this the king had great deliberations and very deep speech with his counsellors about this land, how it was occupied and by what men. He then sent his men over all England into each shire, and had it made out how many hides of land were in the shire; what the king himself had in land, and in livestock on the land; what dues he had from property each twelve months from the shire; also he let it be written down how much land his archbishops had, his diocesan bishops, his abbots and his eorls – though I tell it lengthily – what and how much each man who was holding land in England, in land, in livestock, and how much money it was worth. So very closely did he let it be searched out that there was not a single hide nor rod of land – nor, further, it is shameful to tell, though it seemed to him no shame to do it – not an ox, a cow, a pig was left out, that was not set in his document; and all the documents were brought to him afterwards.

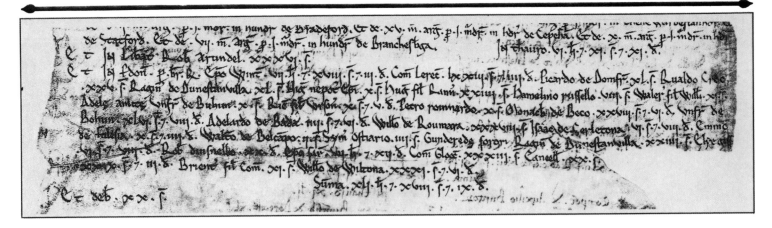

William and his successors swore in their coronation oath to preserve the 'good and ancient laws' of the Anglo-Saxon kings. Apart from the new forest laws, all the old English customs and written laws which varied considerably from place to place, were maintained. There was no attempt to codify the law or bring in a new system. The four Norman kings were mainly interested in making sure that some kind of justice was done and peace maintained – and especially that the subsequent financial rewards were controlled by the monarch.

The courts of the shire (or county courts) and the hundred court (a general assembly) were responsible for collecting taxes and enforcing military service as well as dispensing justice. William did increase the power of the sheriffs, who controlled these courts and had to produce set sums of money from the fines levied. As taxmen as well as overseers of justice, the sheriffs were free to extort what they could so long as they sent on the required money to the royal treasury. Often they 'farmed out' some of their sources of revenue, so that demands on people at the bottom of the social scale became even more severe – a problem that William ignored.

William also despatched trusted men to resolve especially important cases, which were often disputes about land tenure between a baron and either the Church or the Crown. If a baron wished to take his case to a royal court, he followed the practice developed by the Anglo Saxon monarchs of purchasing, at considerable cost, a royal writ, to which the royal circuit judge at the assizes would eventually respond. Bribery was rife, and decisions of lower courts were often over-ridden in return for money paid.

The judges operating this traditional procedure were Norman. They also followed the Anglo-Saxon tradition of calling a number of men to swear an oath endorsing a litigant's claim. By taking this procedure over in the royal courts William became credited with the invention of the jury system.

William I and his successors met their ministers and an inner circle of advisers frequently, and always at Christmas, Easter and Whitsun, in an

Top: From at least the reign of Henry I, possibly earlier, a sheriff's credits, or his failure to produce the required revenue, were recorded each year on the Pipe Rolls. The sheriffs were summoned to London to appear before a newly constituted financial court responsible for royal revenues. This evolved into the Court of the Exchequer, so called because accounting was done on a check tablecloth. The nation's chief minister of finance is still known as the Chancellor of the Exchequer.

Left: 12th-century matrix of walrus found at York. The inscription suggests that it belonged to a toll-collector called Snarrus.

assembly much like the Anglo-Saxon Witan. Judicial questions and government business were discussed, and some special cases were heard. Most of the inner circle were either relatives of the monarch or completely trustworthy servants, who were consulted, but had no veto or vote.

The barons retained their 'manorial courts', which dealt only with cases arising on their lands. Although William I kept these small courts under control, under his successors increasing baronial power brought them greater prominence. Eventually Henry I stopped the barons hearing civil cases, so returning this lucrative business to the shire and hundred courts. Henry also increased the power of the royal judges, giving them a regular circuit and founding a permanent court of supreme appeal known as the Curia Regis – the highest judicial body presided over by a royal judge and still consisting of a lay jury. These permanent royal courts began to lay down and develop laws that superseded local customs. This was the start of the law code formulated by Henry II, the first post-Conquest king to make a real attempt to straighten out English law and establish a sound judicial system.

A continual annoyance was the growing papal insistence on maintaining separate courts for the clergy, out of the king's jurisdiction. Henry II finally gave in after the murder of Becket.

Above: An Anglo-Saxon monarch presiding over his Witan, or court of justice. The Norman monarchs too held such courts, at which decisions about major cases were made. (Illustration from 11th-century paraphrase of the bible, partly translated by Aelfric, a major writer of the 10th-century monastic revival.)

Below: Writ issued by William II making grants of land to Battle Abbey. The King's seal appears at the foot of the document.

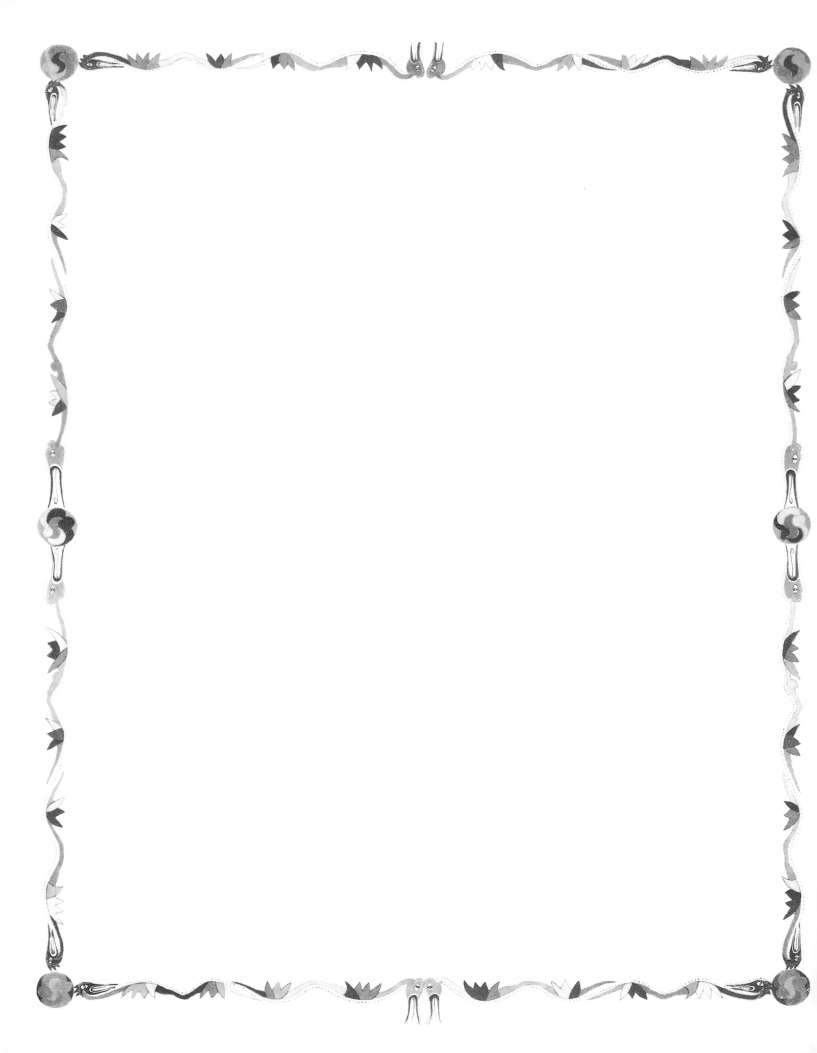

Part Five
1086~1154

1086. The king bore his crown and held his court in Winchester at Easter; he went so that he was by Pentecost at Westminster, and dubbed his son Henry knight there. After, he went about so that he came at Lammas to Salisbury; there his counsellors came to him, and all men who were holding land that were of worth from all over England, whosoever's vassals they were. They all bowed to him and were his vassals, and swore him oaths of loyalty that they would, against all other men, be loyal to him. Then he fared to the Isle of Wight, because he meant to go to Normandy, and so afterwards did – though first he did as he was wont, and obtained very heavy taxes from his vassals where he might have any pretext, justly or otherwise. Then after, he fared to Normandy, and the atheling Edgar, the kinsman of king Edward, turned away from him because he had no great honour from him; but almighty God give him honour in the life to come. Christina, the atheling's sister, moved into the nunnery at Romsey and received holy rest as a religious.

That same year was a very heavy one, a very oppressive and sorrowful year in England in the death of livestock; corn and crops were stopped in their growth, and such great misfortune in the weather that man cannot easily imagine it. Such violent thunder and lightning there was that it killed many men; and ever it worsened with men, more and more. Almighty God amend it when it be his will.

1087. One thousand and eighty-seven years after our Saviour Christ's nativity, in the twenty-first year that William reigned and ruled over England as God granted him, fell a very heavy and very pestilential year in this land. Such disease came among men that full night every other man was in the worst way, that is, with fever, and that so severely that many men died in this evil. After, through the severe bad weather, as we told before, came very great famine all over England, so that many hundreds of people died a wretched death through hunger. Alas, how miserable and how pitiful a time was that, when wretched men lay fevered full near to death, and after came sharp hunger and undid them withal.

Who cannot pity such a time? Or who is so hard-hearted that he cannot weep for such misfortune? But such things come to pass for the sins of the people, that they will not love God and righteousness. So it was in those days, that little righteousness was in this land with any people, except with the monks alone where they lived properly. The king and the head men loved much, and overmuch, the greed for gold and silver, and cared not how sinfully it was obtained so long as it came to them. The king granted his land on hard terms, as dearly as he might. When some other came, and bid more than the first had given, the king let it to the man who offered more. When there came a third, and bid yet more, the king let it into the hands of the men who bid most of all, nor cared how very sinfully the reeves got it from poor

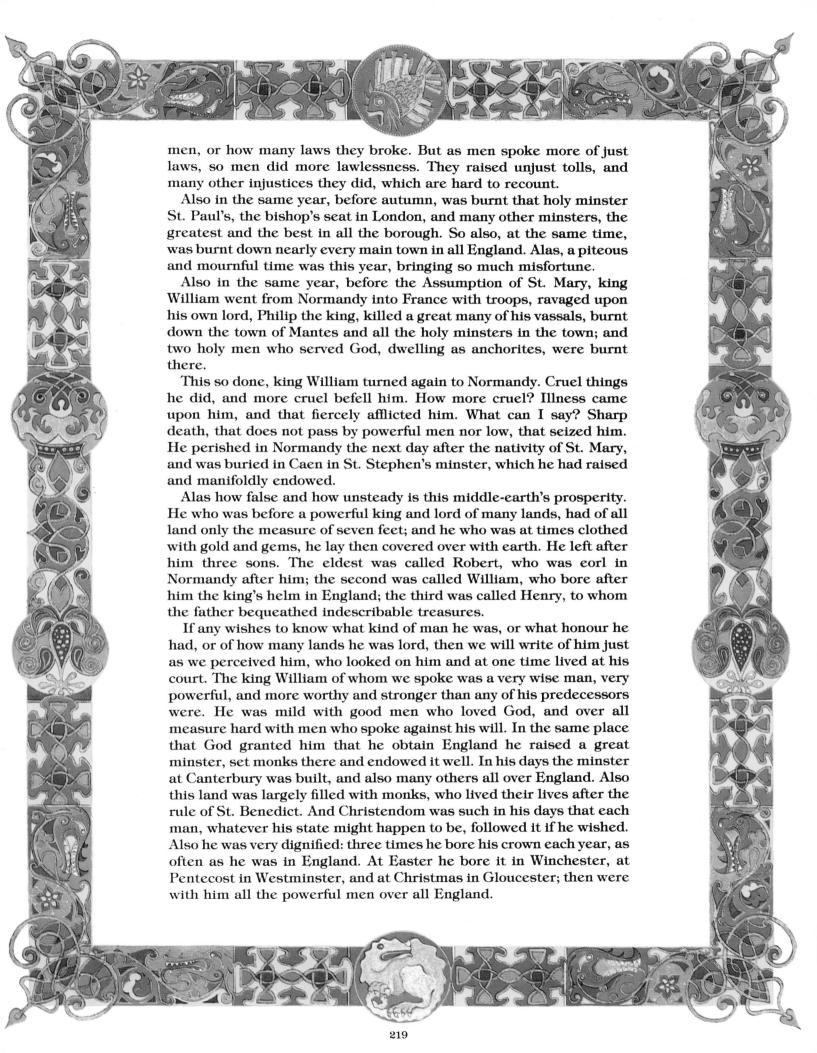

men, or how many laws they broke. But as men spoke more of just laws, so men did more lawlessness. They raised unjust tolls, and many other injustices they did, which are hard to recount.

Also in the same year, before autumn, was burnt that holy minster St. Paul's, the bishop's seat in London, and many other minsters, the greatest and the best in all the borough. So also, at the same time, was burnt down nearly every main town in all England. Alas, a piteous and mournful time was this year, bringing so much misfortune.

Also in the same year, before the Assumption of St. Mary, king William went from Normandy into France with troops, ravaged upon his own lord, Philip the king, killed a great many of his vassals, burnt down the town of Mantes and all the holy minsters in the town; and two holy men who served God, dwelling as anchorites, were burnt there.

This so done, king William turned again to Normandy. Cruel things he did, and more cruel befell him. How more cruel? Illness came upon him, and that fiercely afflicted him. What can I say? Sharp death, that does not pass by powerful men nor low, that seized him. He perished in Normandy the next day after the nativity of St. Mary, and was buried in Caen in St. Stephen's minster, which he had raised and manifoldly endowed.

Alas how false and how unsteady is this middle-earth's prosperity. He who was before a powerful king and lord of many lands, had of all land only the measure of seven feet; and he who was at times clothed with gold and gems, he lay then covered over with earth. He left after him three sons. The eldest was called Robert, who was eorl in Normandy after him; the second was called William, who bore after him the king's helm in England; the third was called Henry, to whom the father bequeathed indescribable treasures.

If any wishes to know what kind of man he was, or what honour he had, or of how many lands he was lord, then we will write of him just as we perceived him, who looked on him and at one time lived at his court. The king William of whom we spoke was a very wise man, very powerful, and more worthy and stronger than any of his predecessors were. He was mild with good men who loved God, and over all measure hard with men who spoke against his will. In the same place that God granted him that he obtain England he raised a great minster, set monks there and endowed it well. In his days the minster at Canterbury was built, and also many others all over England. Also this land was largely filled with monks, who lived their lives after the rule of St. Benedict. And Christendom was such in his days that each man, whatever his state might happen to be, followed it if he wished. Also he was very dignified: three times he bore his crown each year, as often as he was in England. At Easter he bore it in Winchester, at Pentecost in Westminster, and at Christmas in Gloucester; then were with him all the powerful men over all England.

[1087] A hard man he was, and fierce; no man dared against his will. He had eorls in chains, who went against his will; bishops he deposed from their bishoprics and thanes he set in prison. Next, he did not spare his own brother, called Odo; he was a very powerful bishop in Normandy – Bayeux was his bishopric – and was the foremost man next to the king. He had an eorldom in England, and when the king was in Normandy he was the master of this land; and him he set in prison. Among other things it is not to be forgotten, that good peace he made in this land, so that a man of any account might fare over the kingdom with a bosom full of gold unmolested; and no man dared kill another man, even if he had done much evil to him; and if any man lay with a woman against her will, he soon lost those limbs he played with.

He reigned over England, and so searched it through with his craft that there was not a hide of land in England that he knew not what he had from it and what its worth was, and after had it set down in his document. Wales was in his power; he built castles therein, and ruled all the people there. So also Scotland he subjected by his great strength. Normandy was his natural land, and over the eorldom called Maine he reigned. If he had lived two years yet he would have won Ireland with his cunning, and without any weapons. Truly, in his time men had much oppression and many injuries.

> He had castles made and oppressed poor men;
> the king was very hard
> and took of his underlings many marks of gold,
> and many more hundred pounds of silver,
> that he took by weight, unjustly,
> from his people for little need.
> Into avarice was he fallen
> and greediness he loved overall.
> He set many deer free, and laid a law upon it, that whoever
> slew hart or hind should be blinded.
> As he forbade the killing of harts
> he forbade the killing of boars,
> and he loved the stags as if he were their father.
> He decreed also that hares must go free.
> The rich complained, the poor lamented;
> but he was so hard he set their hate at naught,
> but they must in all the king's will follow
> if they would live or have land –
> land, or goods, or have his good will.
> Welaway! That any man should grow so proud,
> to think himself lifted up over all men;
> almighty God show his soul mildheartedness,
> and forgive him for his sins.

These things we have written of king William, both good and evil, so that good men take after the goodness and eschew all the evil, and go on the way that takes us to the heavenly kingdom.

Many things can we write which came to pass in that year. So it was in Denmark that the Danes, who had been reckoned of all folk the most loyal, were turned to the greatest disloyalty. They chose and bowed to king Cnut, swore him oaths, and after killed him basely in a church. Also it happened in Spain that the heathen men went and ravaged the Christian men, and brought many into their power. But the Christian king, who was called Alfonso, sent everywhere into each land and entreated help; and help came to him from each land that was Christian. They went and killed or drove away all the heathen folk, and won their land again through God's help.

Also in this same land, here, passed away many powerful men: Stigand, bishop of Chichester; the abbot of St. Augustine's; the abbot of Bath and that of Pershore; then the lord of all of them, William, king of England, about whom we have spoken.

After his death his son, called William just as his father was, received the kingdom and was blessed by archbishop Lanfranc at Westminster, three days before Michaelmas, and all men in England bowed to him and swore him oaths. This done, the king fared to Winchester and looked on the mathom-house, and the treasures which his father had gathered – it was impossible for any man to say how much was gathered there in gold, silver, vessels, pelts, gems and many other precious things, which it would be tedious to recount. The king did as his father bade him before he was dead, and shared out the treasure for his father's soul, to each monastery that was in England; to one monastery ten gold marks, to another six, and to each country church sixty pence; and into each shire was sent a hundred pounds in money to share out to poor men for his soul; and before he passed away he bade that all men in captivity under his rule should be released. The king was in London at Christmas.

William I was a genuinely religious and practical man who believed that the Anglo-Saxon Church and monastic system required thorough reform. He deposed Stigand, Edward the Confessor's archbishop of Canterbury, in favour of the learned and efficient Lanfranc, who in turn replaced the English abbots and bishops with Normans, many of whom were in debt to the king or related to him. Twenty years after the Conquest there was only one English abbot, Wulfstan of Worcester, and English saints had been removed from the calendars of the Church.

The Normans found Anglo-Saxon church buildings inadequate and unimpressive. A vast rebuilding programme got under way, and in a single generation a new style of ecclesiastical architecture was imposed throughout the country. The size of the major cathedrals begun after the Conquest surpassed anything already built in Normandy. The money came from the new bishops, who were also substantial landowners, while lesser nobles financed the reconstruction of smaller churches, in order to ensure their personal salvation, and to impress one another and the king.

Master masons were in charge of building operations. The massive new churches had wide doors and windows, their weight carried on great semicircular arches. The weight of the top of the building was absorbed by huge columns in the nave. The Normans also built large central towers, although these often collapsed later. Experiment was encouraged, and the greatest problem – how to construct a stone roof – was eventually solved at Durham, where the choir aisles and nave were vaulted with slightly pointed ribbed arches.

The large blocks of stone used for the walls were fitted neatly together, in contrast with the rather haphazard masonry of the Anglo-Saxons. Since there was no decoration or sculpture, interiors were at first very austere, although the walls were painted. Later, columns, doors and windows were ornamented, especially with multiple strings of geometric designs; tympani with scenes and figures appeared over doorways and blind arcading was used again to break the monotony.

By 1175 the dominance of the Norman style was finished. When Canterbury was ruined by fire in 1174, it was rebuilt in a different and distinctive style: English architecture had found an individual identity.

Left: The nave arcade of Norwich cathedral, built between 1094 and 1145.

Below: The austere west front of Southwell minster, Nottinghamshire, started in 1108.

Above: Elaborate carving above the west door of Lincoln cathedral, c.1145.

Right: St Mary the Virgin, Iffley, near Oxford, built between 1175 and 1185, is one of the last Norman churches erected in England – and a glorious example of that style. Thereafter the Early English style predominated.

Below: The nave of Rochester cathedral, built by Gundulf in 1080.

Left: The prior's door of Ely cathedral.

Below: Durham cathedral, most impressive of all the early Norman constructions, took only 40 years to build. This was the first stone-roofed building in Europe.

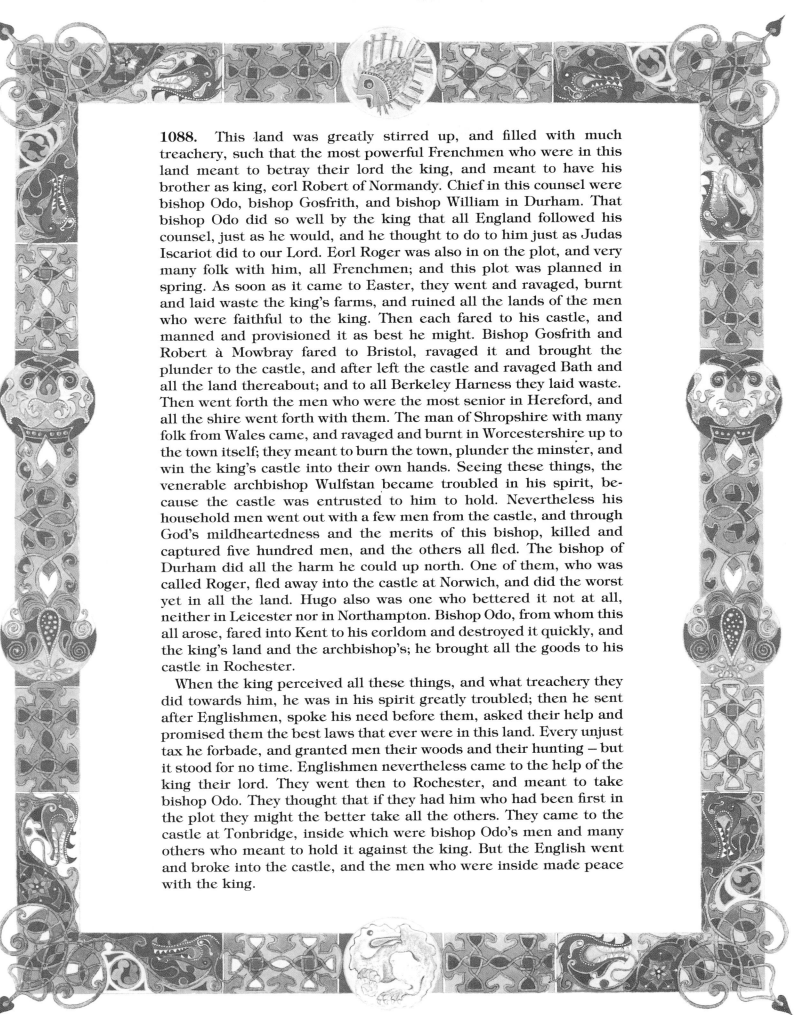

1088. This land was greatly stirred up, and filled with much treachery, such that the most powerful Frenchmen who were in this land meant to betray their lord the king, and meant to have his brother as king, eorl Robert of Normandy. Chief in this counsel were bishop Odo, bishop Gosfrith, and bishop William in Durham. That bishop Odo did so well by the king that all England followed his counsel, just as he would, and he thought to do to him just as Judas Iscariot did to our Lord. Eorl Roger was also in on the plot, and very many folk with him, all Frenchmen; and this plot was planned in spring. As soon as it came to Easter, they went and ravaged, burnt and laid waste the king's farms, and ruined all the lands of the men who were faithful to the king. Then each fared to his castle, and manned and provisioned it as best he might. Bishop Gosfrith and Robert à Mowbray fared to Bristol, ravaged it and brought the plunder to the castle, and after left the castle and ravaged Bath and all the land thereabout; and to all Berkeley Harness they laid waste. Then went forth the men who were the most senior in Hereford, and all the shire went forth with them. The man of Shropshire with many folk from Wales came, and ravaged and burnt in Worcestershire up to the town itself; they meant to burn the town, plunder the minster, and win the king's castle into their own hands. Seeing these things, the venerable archbishop Wulfstan became troubled in his spirit, because the castle was entrusted to him to hold. Nevertheless his household men went out with a few men from the castle, and through God's mildheartedness and the merits of this bishop, killed and captured five hundred men, and the others all fled. The bishop of Durham did all the harm he could up north. One of them, who was called Roger, fled away into the castle at Norwich, and did the worst yet in all the land. Hugo also was one who bettered it not at all, neither in Leicester nor in Northampton. Bishop Odo, from whom this all arose, fared into Kent to his eorldom and destroyed it quickly, and the king's land and the archbishop's; he brought all the goods to his castle in Rochester.

When the king perceived all these things, and what treachery they did towards him, he was in his spirit greatly troubled; then he sent after Englishmen, spoke his need before them, asked their help and promised them the best laws that ever were in this land. Every unjust tax he forbade, and granted men their woods and their hunting – but it stood for no time. Englishmen nevertheless came to the help of the king their lord. They went then to Rochester, and meant to take bishop Odo. They thought that if they had him who had been first in the plot they might the better take all the others. They came to the castle at Tonbridge, inside which were bishop Odo's men and many others who meant to hold it against the king. But the English went and broke into the castle, and the men who were inside made peace with the king.

225

Above: Carisbrooke Castle, Isle of Wight, where bishop Odo was arrested in 1088. Odo, the king's uncle, supported the claim of duke Robert of Normandy to the English throne and led the rebellion against William Rufus in the first year of the new king's reign. Odo was banished from England and died on crusade with duke Robert at Palermo in 1097. The wooden castle buildings of Odo's time were soon replaced by more durable constructions of stone.

Opposite: After Lanfranc's death in 1089, the archbishopric of Canterbury remained vacant for four years until the king fell ill. Believing he was close to death, he offered it to Anselm, abbot of Bec, who, it is said, accepted it so reluctantly that the ring had to be pushed onto his finger. Anselm's disagreements with the king were so great that he fled the country in 1097. (Portrait of Anselm from a late 12th-century manuscript.)

As soon as he heard of his father's death, William Rufus sailed from Normandy to claim his English kingdom. His first act as king was to distribute part of the royal treasure to monasteries, churches and the poor 'for his father's soul'. Almost immediately, in 1088, he was faced with a series of uprisings led by bishop Odo, which he swiftly overwhelmed. The king, who thanked his people for their support and made promises of good government, was never to be so popular again. As soon as the danger of rebellion had passed, he increased taxation and enforced royal privileges more strictly. Popular resentment grew. Only Lanfranc, archbishop of Canterbury, could control some of the king's excesses, and after the archbishop died in 1089 William's violence and disagreeable qualities became yet more evident.

The attempt to wrest Normandy from his brother Robert's control was a persistent obsession. He invaded in 1090, made peace a year later, invaded again in 1093 and finally acquired the duchy in 1096 in exchange for 100,000 silver marks which Robert needed to join the First Crusade. The taxes William imposed to raise this sum were so severe that the treasures of churches and monasteries

Above: William Rufus, from a 15th-century manuscript.

were melted down, and many men were made homeless: the Chroniclers, perhaps not entirely without prejudice, describe it as a year of famine and wretchedness.

Throughout his reign William tried in vain to subdue the Welsh, until eventually he gave up and built a line of castles along the Welsh marches. The burden of yet more taxes, to pay for these campaigns, together with poor weather and meagre harvests, caused much suffering.

William Rufus was killed while hunting in the New Forest on 2 August 1100, in circumstances that have never been clarified. Although it was accepted as an accident, his death was also interpreted as an act of God against a dangerously irreligious king. So too was the collapse of the tower of Winchester cathedral, where the king was buried. The Chroniclers assess the king severely: 'He was very harsh and fierce with his men, his land and all his neighbours, and very much feared ...'

[1088] The king went towards Rochester, and believed that bishop Odo was there; but it became known that the bishop had gone to the castle at Pevensey. The king went and besieged the castle with a great force for six weeks.

Meanwhile the eorl of Normandy, Robert the king's brother, gathered very many folk, and thought to win England with the help of the men who were in this land against the king; he sent his men to this land, and meant to come himself later. But the Englishmen who watched the sea seized some of those men, and killed and drowned more than any man knows to tell.

After their provisions failed them in the castle, they entreated a truce, gave it back to the king, and the bishop swore that he would leave England and no more come into this land unless the king sent after him, and that he would give back the castle in Rochester. Just as the bishop went, and was to give over the castle – and the king sent his men with him – the men who were in the castle rose up and took the bishop and the king's men, and put them in captivity. In the castle were some very good knights, Eustace the young, and eorl Roger's sons, and all the best-born men in this land or Normandy.

When the king perceived these things, he went after with the force he had there, and sent all over England, and bade that each man who was not a 'nithing', a scoundrel, should come to him, French and English, from town or from country. Then many folk came to him; he went to Rochester and besieged the castle until those who were inside came to terms and gave up the castle. Bishop Odo, with the men in the castle, fared over the sea; the bishop thus gave up the honour he had in this land. The king afterwards sent forces to Durham and let the castle be surrounded; the bishop came to terms, gave over the castle, lost his bishopric and went over the sea; the king gave their land to the men who were loyal to him.

1089. The venerable father and solace of monks, archbishop Lanfranc, went from this life, but we have hope that he went to the heavenly kingdom. So also happened all over England a great earthquake on August 11th, and it was a very late year in corn and each kind of crop, so that many men reaped their corn only at Martinmas and yet later.

1090. The king was considering how he might take vengeance on his brother Robert, betray him and win Normandy from him. By craft or treasure he obtained the castle at St. Valéry, and the harbour; and the castle at Aumale, and therein set his knights. They did harm to the land in ravaging and burning. After this he obtained more castles and set his knights therein.

The eorl, Robert, who saw that his sworn vassals betrayed him, and gave their castles away to his harm, sent to his lord Philip, king of

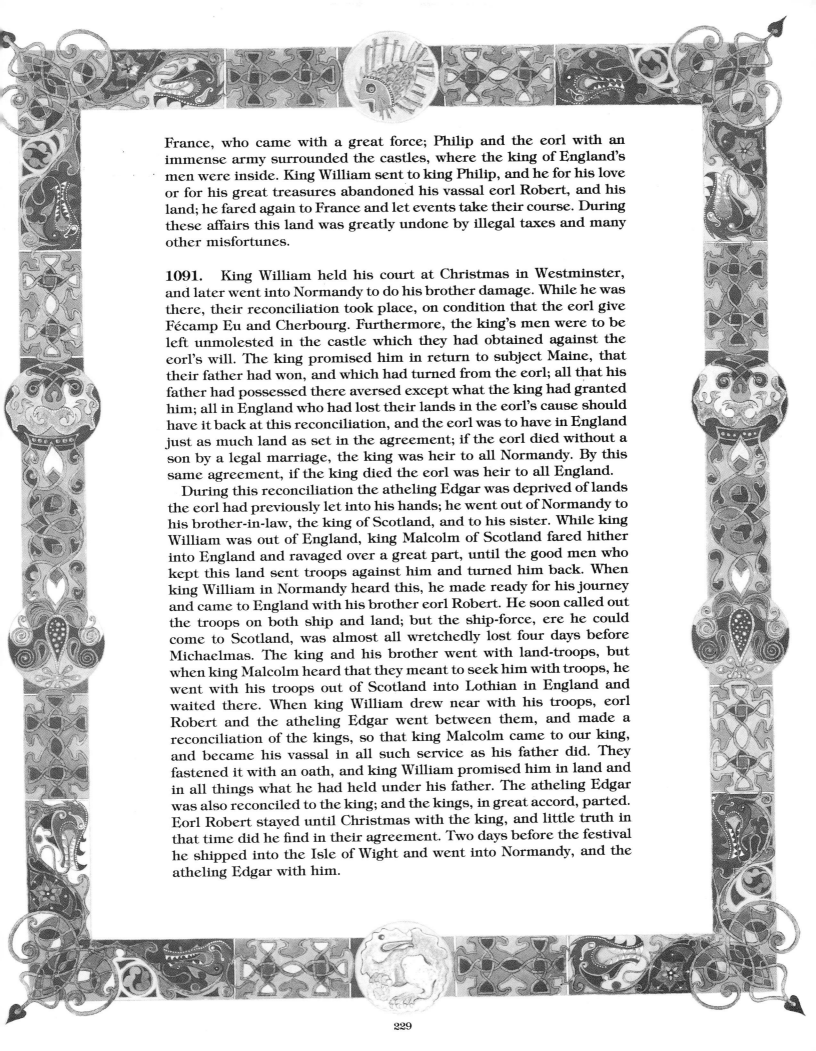

France, who came with a great force; Philip and the eorl with an immense army surrounded the castles, where the king of England's men were inside. King William sent to king Philip, and he for his love or for his great treasures abandoned his vassal eorl Robert, and his land; he fared again to France and let events take their course. During these affairs this land was greatly undone by illegal taxes and many other misfortunes.

1091. King William held his court at Christmas in Westminster, and later went into Normandy to do his brother damage. While he was there, their reconciliation took place, on condition that the eorl give Fécamp Eu and Cherbourg. Furthermore, the king's men were to be left unmolested in the castle which they had obtained against the eorl's will. The king promised him in return to subject Maine, that their father had won, and which had turned from the eorl; all that his father had possessed there aversed except what the king had granted him; all in England who had lost their lands in the eorl's cause should have it back at this reconciliation, and the eorl was to have in England just as much land as set in the agreement; if the eorl died without a son by a legal marriage, the king was heir to all Normandy. By this same agreement, if the king died the eorl was heir to all England.

During this reconciliation the atheling Edgar was deprived of lands the eorl had previously let into his hands; he went out of Normandy to his brother-in-law, the king of Scotland, and to his sister. While king William was out of England, king Malcolm of Scotland fared hither into England and ravaged over a great part, until the good men who kept this land sent troops against him and turned him back. When king William in Normandy heard this, he made ready for his journey and came to England with his brother eorl Robert. He soon called out the troops on both ship and land; but the ship-force, ere he could come to Scotland, was almost all wretchedly lost four days before Michaelmas. The king and his brother went with land-troops, but when king Malcolm heard that they meant to seek him with troops, he went with his troops out of Scotland into Lothian in England and waited there. When king William drew near with his troops, eorl Robert and the atheling Edgar went between them, and made a reconciliation of the kings, so that king Malcolm came to our king, and became his vassal in all such service as his father did. They fastened it with an oath, and king William promised him in land and in all things what he had held under his father. The atheling Edgar was also reconciled to the king; and the kings, in great accord, parted. Eorl Robert stayed until Christmas with the king, and little truth in that time did he find in their agreement. Two days before the festival he shipped into the Isle of Wight and went into Normandy, and the atheling Edgar with him.

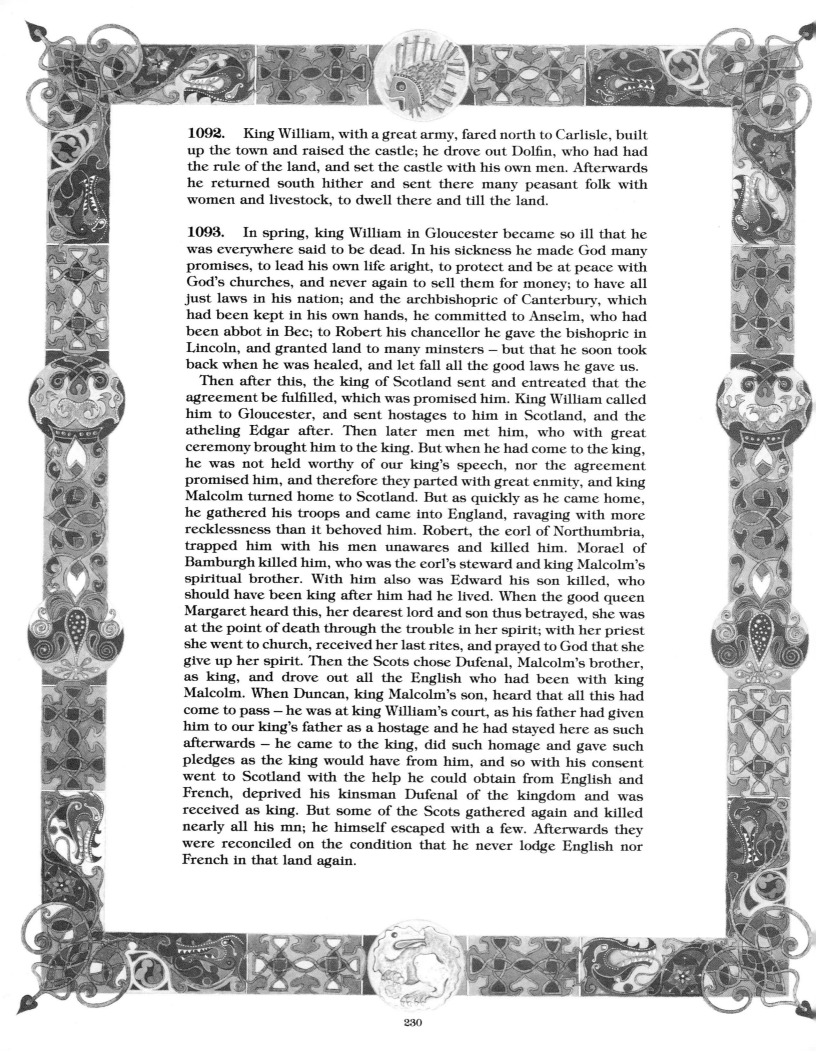

1092. King William, with a great army, fared north to Carlisle, built up the town and raised the castle; he drove out Dolfin, who had had the rule of the land, and set the castle with his own men. Afterwards he returned south hither and sent there many peasant folk with women and livestock, to dwell there and till the land.

1093. In spring, king William in Gloucester became so ill that he was everywhere said to be dead. In his sickness he made God many promises, to lead his own life aright, to protect and be at peace with God's churches, and never again to sell them for money; to have all just laws in his nation; and the archbishopric of Canterbury, which had been kept in his own hands, he committed to Anselm, who had been abbot in Bec; to Robert his chancellor he gave the bishopric in Lincoln, and granted land to many minsters – but that he soon took back when he was healed, and let fall all the good laws he gave us.

Then after this, the king of Scotland sent and entreated that the agreement be fulfilled, which was promised him. King William called him to Gloucester, and sent hostages to him in Scotland, and the atheling Edgar after. Then later men met him, who with great ceremony brought him to the king. But when he had come to the king, he was not held worthy of our king's speech, nor the agreement promised him, and therefore they parted with great enmity, and king Malcolm turned home to Scotland. But as quickly as he came home, he gathered his troops and came into England, ravaging with more recklessness than it behoved him. Robert, the eorl of Northumbria, trapped him with his men unawares and killed him. Morael of Bamburgh killed him, who was the eorl's steward and king Malcolm's spiritual brother. With him also was Edward his son killed, who should have been king after him had he lived. When the good queen Margaret heard this, her dearest lord and son thus betrayed, she was at the point of death through the trouble in her spirit; with her priest she went to church, received her last rites, and prayed to God that she give up her spirit. Then the Scots chose Dufenal, Malcolm's brother, as king, and drove out all the English who had been with king Malcolm. When Duncan, king Malcolm's son, heard that all this had come to pass – he was at king William's court, as his father had given him to our king's father as a hostage and he had stayed here as such afterwards – he came to the king, did such homage and gave such pledges as the king would have from him, and so with his consent went to Scotland with the help he could obtain from English and French, deprived his kinsman Dufenal of the kingdom and was received as king. But some of the Scots gathered again and killed nearly all his mn; he himself escaped with a few. Afterwards they were reconciled on the condition that he never lodge English nor French in that land again.

230

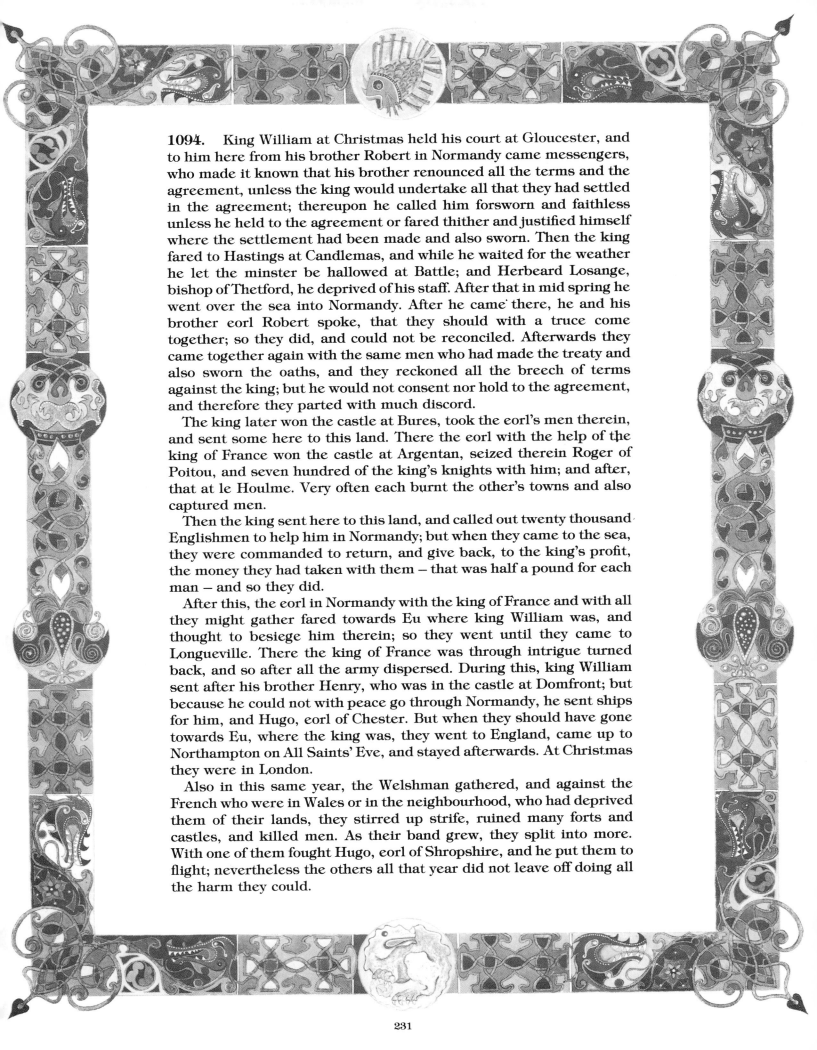

1094. King William at Christmas held his court at Gloucester, and to him here from his brother Robert in Normandy came messengers, who made it known that his brother renounced all the terms and the agreement, unless the king would undertake all that they had settled in the agreement; thereupon he called him forsworn and faithless unless he held to the agreement or fared thither and justified himself where the settlement had been made and also sworn. Then the king fared to Hastings at Candlemas, and while he waited for the weather he let the minster be hallowed at Battle; and Herbeard Losange, bishop of Thetford, he deprived of his staff. After that in mid spring he went over the sea into Normandy. After he came there, he and his brother eorl Robert spoke, that they should with a truce come together; so they did, and could not be reconciled. Afterwards they came together again with the same men who had made the treaty and also sworn the oaths, and they reckoned all the breech of terms against the king; but he would not consent nor hold to the agreement, and therefore they parted with much discord.

The king later won the castle at Bures, took the eorl's men therein, and sent some here to this land. There the eorl with the help of the king of France won the castle at Argentan, seized therein Roger of Poitou, and seven hundred of the king's knights with him; and after, that at le Houlme. Very often each burnt the other's towns and also captured men.

Then the king sent here to this land, and called out twenty thousand Englishmen to help him in Normandy; but when they came to the sea, they were commanded to return, and give back, to the king's profit, the money they had taken with them – that was half a pound for each man – and so they did.

After this, the eorl in Normandy with the king of France and with all they might gather fared towards Eu where king William was, and thought to besiege him therein; so they went until they came to Longueville. There the king of France was through intrigue turned back, and so after all the army dispersed. During this, king William sent after his brother Henry, who was in the castle at Domfront; but because he could not with peace go through Normandy, he sent ships for him, and Hugo, eorl of Chester. But when they should have gone towards Eu, where the king was, they went to England, came up to Northampton on All Saints' Eve, and stayed afterwards. At Christmas they were in London.

Also in this same year, the Welshman gathered, and against the French who were in Wales or in the neighbourhood, who had deprived them of their lands, they stirred up strife, ruined many forts and castles, and killed men. As their band grew, they split into more. With one of them fought Hugo, eorl of Shropshire, and he put them to flight; nevertheless the others all that year did not leave off doing all the harm they could.

[1094] The Scots trapped and killed their king, Duncan, and after him again for another time took his kinsman Dufenal as king, through whose counsel and instigation he was betrayed to death.

1095. King William was, in the four days before Christmas, at Wissant, and after the fourth day journeyed here to this land, and came up at Dover. Henry, the king's brother, dwelt in this land until spring, then journeyed over the sea to Normandy with much treasure as the king's supporter against their brother eorl Robert. He frequently made war on him, and did him great harm, in both land and men.

At Easter the king held his court in Winchester; eorl Robert of Northumbria would not come to court, and the king was therefore greatly stirred against him. He sent and sternly told him that if he were worthy of protection he would at Pentecost come to court. This year Easter was on March 25th, and after Easter on the eve of St. Ambrose's Day, that is April 4th, nearly all over this land were seen to fall many stars from heaven, not one or two, but so thickly they might not be counted. After this at Pentecost the king was in Windsor, and all his counsellors with him except the eorl from Northumbria, because the king would neither give him hostages nor grant terms of protection for him to come and go.

Therefore the king called out his army, and went to Northumbria against the eorl; as soon as he came there, he overcame nearly all the best of the eorl's court in a fort, and put them into captivity. He besieged the castle at Tynemouth until he won it, with the eorl's brother therein and all who were with him, and after went to Bamburgh, and besieged the eorl therein. But when he saw that he might not win it, he commanded a castle made in front of Bamburgh, and called it in his language Maluesin, that is in English, Evil Neighbour. He set it strongly with his men and later went south. Soon after the king had gone south, the eorl went one night out of Bamburgh towards Tynemouth, but those in the new castle were aware of him, went after him and fought. They wounded him, and later captured him; of those who were with him, some were killed and some taken alive.

Meanwhile it was made know to the king that the Welshmen had ruined a castle in Wales, called Montgomery, and killed eorl Hugo's men, who should have held it; therfore he quickly commanded the troops called out. After Michaelmas he went into Wales; his troops split up and went all through the land, so that the army came together on All Saints' at Snowdon. But the Welsh kept scattering into the mountains and moors so that they could not be got at, and the king turned homeward, because he saw that he could do no more there that winter.

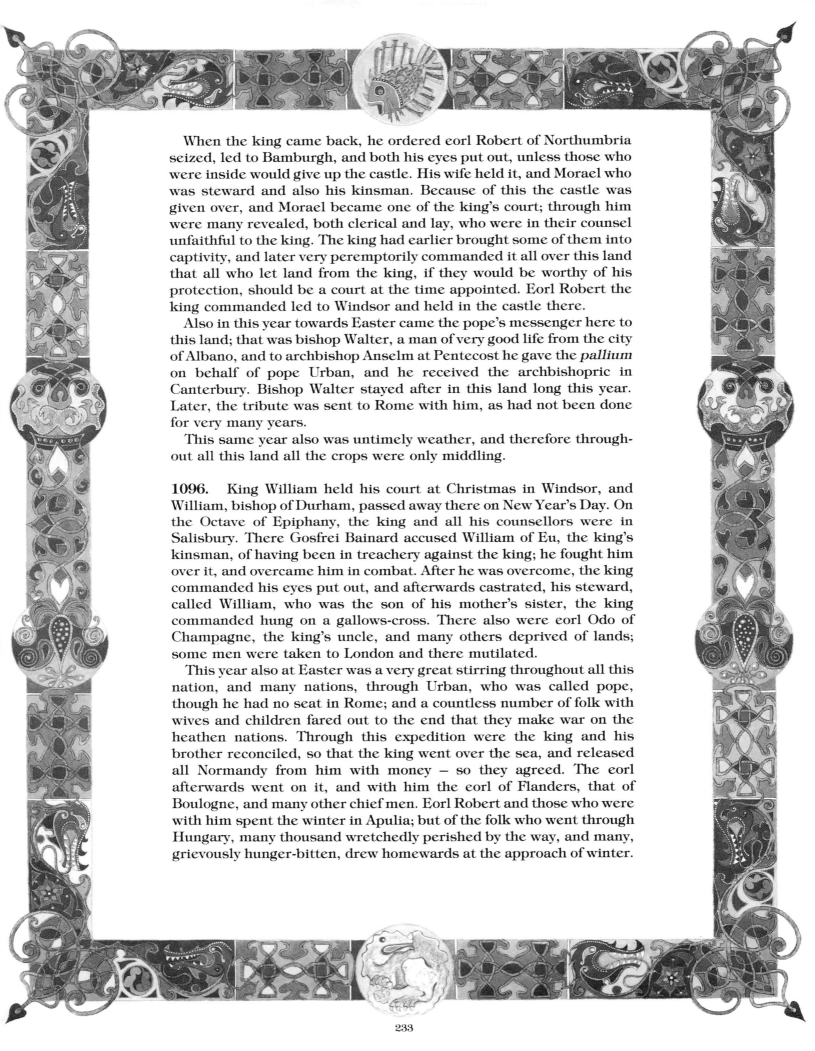

When the king came back, he ordered eorl Robert of Northumbria seized, led to Bamburgh, and both his eyes put out, unless those who were inside would give up the castle. His wife held it, and Morael who was steward and also his kinsman. Because of this the castle was given over, and Morael became one of the king's court; through him were many revealed, both clerical and lay, who were in their counsel unfaithful to the king. The king had earlier brought some of them into captivity, and later very peremptorily commanded it all over this land that all who let land from the king, if they would be worthy of his protection, should be a court at the time appointed. Eorl Robert the king commanded led to Windsor and held in the castle there.

Also in this year towards Easter came the pope's messenger here to this land; that was bishop Walter, a man of very good life from the city of Albano, and to archbishop Anselm at Pentecost he gave the *pallium* on behalf of pope Urban, and he received the archbishopric in Canterbury. Bishop Walter stayed after in this land long this year. Later, the tribute was sent to Rome with him, as had not been done for very many years.

This same year also was untimely weather, and therefore throughout all this land all the crops were only middling.

1096. King William held his court at Christmas in Windsor, and William, bishop of Durham, passed away there on New Year's Day. On the Octave of Epiphany, the king and all his counsellors were in Salisbury. There Gosfrei Bainard accused William of Eu, the king's kinsman, of having been in treachery against the king; he fought him over it, and overcame him in combat. After he was overcome, the king commanded his eyes put out, and afterwards castrated, his steward, called William, who was the son of his mother's sister, the king commanded hung on a gallows-cross. There also were eorl Odo of Champagne, the king's uncle, and many others deprived of lands; some men were taken to London and there mutilated.

This year also at Easter was a very great stirring throughout all this nation, and many nations, through Urban, who was called pope, though he had no seat in Rome; and a countless number of folk with wives and children fared out to the end that they make war on the heathen nations. Through this expedition were the king and his brother reconciled, so that the king went over the sea, and released all Normandy from him with money – so they agreed. The eorl afterwards went on it, and with him the eorl of Flanders, that of Boulogne, and many other chief men. Eorl Robert and those who were with him spent the winter in Apulia; but of the folk who went through Hungary, many thousand wretchedly perished by the way, and many, grievously hunger-bitten, drew homewards at the approach of winter.

The First Crusade was primarily launched to safeguard the pilgrim routes to Jerusalem and save the holy places of Christianity from the invasion of Seljuk Turks. But there were also political motives: it was in the interest of both pope and Normans to assist the weak Byzantine emperor in Constantinople in the eventual hope of uniting the eastern and western branches of the Christian Church.

Pope Urban II announced the Crusade at the Council of Clermont in November 1095. His word spread to all the countries of the Christian west, and thousands of men began to assemble. While many were genuinely inspired by religious motives and proved disciplined soldiers, others were adventurers, greedy for the reputed wealth of the eastern princes. Land-hunger was another spur: many had lost out on the spoils of earlier conquests and were anxious to colonize new territory. To younger sons and landless knights and their followers, the Crusades promised adventure, loot and a chance to fight for their religion.

In 1097 an enormous force gathered at Constantinople. The Normans were enthusiastic supporters of the 'holy war', and of the eight leaders of the Crusade five were Norman or had Norman connections, among them Robert, William I's son. The 'official' armies were made up of knights, nobles and churchmen from different countries. But there were also several 'unofficial' bands of Crusaders — peasants, zealots, thieves and outcasts who looted and killed indiscriminately.

The first was the most successful of all the Crusades. After a long and bitter fight, Antioch was taken. The city was not handed over to the emperor but was developed as a separate Norman state, surviving until the mid-12th century. In July 1099 Jerusalem fell after a long siege and a savage massacre of Jews and Muslims. Many Crusaders then went home. But some stayed to confront further attacks from the Turks and to fight in shifting alliances among themselves. The political situation disintegrated rapidly; Jerusalem was retaken by Islam in 1189, and by 1304 the whole of Palestine had returned to the Muslim faith.

Above: Tympanum from St George's Church, Fordington, Dorset, depicting St George helping Crusaders besieged at Antioch during the First Crusade.

Opposite below: Effigy of Robert, duke of Normandy, one of the leaders of the First Crusade; he pawned his duchy to his brother William Rufus for money to go on Crusade.

Right: A Crusader doing homage. (Illustration from the Westminster Psalter, late 12th century.)

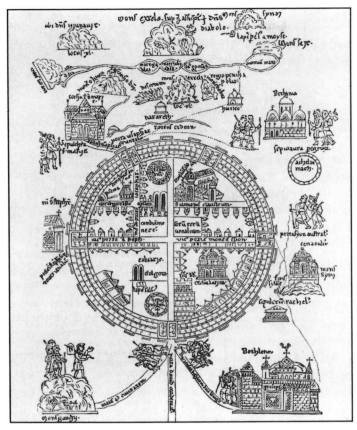

Above: 12th-century map of Crusader Jerusalem, produced for pilgrims visiting the Holy City.

Above: Church of the Holy Sepulchre, Cambridge, built by the Knights Templar – a monastic order founded in 1115 to protect pilgrims on the road to Jerusalem.

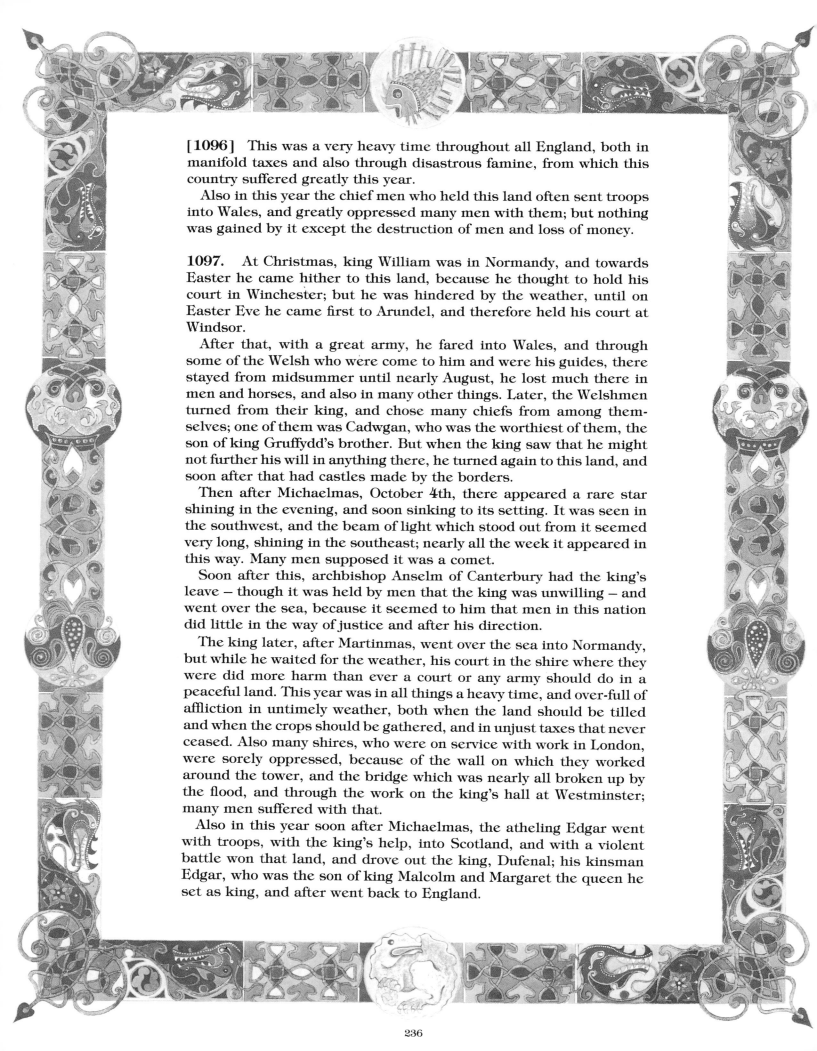

[1096] This was a very heavy time throughout all England, both in manifold taxes and also through disastrous famine, from which this country suffered greatly this year.

Also in this year the chief men who held this land often sent troops into Wales, and greatly oppressed many men with them; but nothing was gained by it except the destruction of men and loss of money.

1097. At Christmas, king William was in Normandy, and towards Easter he came hither to this land, because he thought to hold his court in Winchester; but he was hindered by the weather, until on Easter Eve he came first to Arundel, and therefore held his court at Windsor.

After that, with a great army, he fared into Wales, and through some of the Welsh who were come to him and were his guides, there stayed from midsummer until nearly August, he lost much there in men and horses, and also in many other things. Later, the Welshmen turned from their king, and chose many chiefs from among themselves; one of them was Cadwgan, who was the worthiest of them, the son of king Gruffydd's brother. But when the king saw that he might not further his will in anything there, he turned again to this land, and soon after that had castles made by the borders.

Then after Michaelmas, October 4th, there appeared a rare star shining in the evening, and soon sinking to its setting. It was seen in the southwest, and the beam of light which stood out from it seemed very long, shining in the southeast; nearly all the week it appeared in this way. Many men supposed it was a comet.

Soon after this, archbishop Anselm of Canterbury had the king's leave – though it was held by men that the king was unwilling – and went over the sea, because it seemed to him that men in this nation did little in the way of justice and after his direction.

The king later, after Martinmas, went over the sea into Normandy, but while he waited for the weather, his court in the shire where they were did more harm than ever a court or any army should do in a peaceful land. This year was in all things a heavy time, and over-full of affliction in untimely weather, both when the land should be tilled and when the crops should be gathered, and in unjust taxes that never ceased. Also many shires, who were on service with work in London, were sorely oppressed, because of the wall on which they worked around the tower, and the bridge which was nearly all broken up by the flood, and through the work on the king's hall at Westminster; many men suffered with that.

Also in this year soon after Michaelmas, the atheling Edgar went with troops, with the king's help, into Scotland, and with a violent battle won that land, and drove out the king, Dufenal; his kinsman Edgar, who was the son of king Malcolm and Margaret the queen he set as king, and after went back to England.

1098. At Christmas king William was in Normandy; bishop Walchelin in Winchester and abbot Baldwin in Bury St. Edmunds both passed away in this festival. In this year also during the summer, in Berkshire at Finchampstead, a pool of blood welled up, as many truthful men said who had seen it.

Eorl Hugo was killed in Anglesey by sea-rovers, and his brother Robert became his heir, as he had the king's consent.

Before Michaelmas the heavens appeared as though they were burning, nearly all night. This was a very grievous year through manifold taxes, and through the heavy rains which did not cease all year; nearly all the tilled land in low places was ruined.

1099. King William was at Christmas in Normandy, at Easter came here to this land, and at Pentecost, for the first time, held his court inside his new building at Westminster. There he gave Ranulf his chaplain the bishopric in Durham, he who had directed all his councils and conducted them all over England. Soon after he went over the sea, and drove the eorl, Helias de la Flèche, out of Maine, and later set it under his rule; so at Michaelmas King William came back to England.

This year also at Martinmas, the great sea-flood came up and did so much harm that no man remembered its like before, that was the same day as the first of the new moon.

1100. King William held his court at Christmas in Gloucester, at Easter in Winchester, and at Pentecost in Westminster.

At Pentecost was seen, in a village in Berkshire, blood welling from the earth, as many said who had seen it. Thereafter, on the morning after Lammas, king William at the hunt was shot dead with an arrow by one of his own men, and after brought to Winchester, and buried in that bishopric; that was the thirtieth year that he had the kingdom.

He was very harsh and fierce with his men, his land and all his neighbours, and very much feared. He was ever agreeable to evil men's advice, and through his own greed he was ever vexing this nation with force and with unjust taxes. Therefore in his days all justice declined; every injustice arose before God and the world. God's churches he oppressed, and when the heads of bishoprics and abbacies passed on, he either sold all for money or held it in his own hands and let it out for rent, because he meant to be the heir of every man, clerical or lay; so that the day he fell, he had in his own hands the archbishopric of Canterbury and that of Winchester, Salisbury and eleven abbacies, all let out for rent. And though I stretch it out long, all that was hateful to God and just men, all that was customary in his day. Therefore he was to nearly all his people hateful, and abominable to God. So his end revealed, because in the middle of his wrongs, without repentance or any amendment for his deeds, he died.

Above: Henry dreams that the clergy and common men protest against his government. He is then caught in a storm and prays for deliverance, promising to change his harsh government, withhold the collection of taxes and go on pilgrimage to Bury St Edmunds if his life is saved. (Illustrations from the Chronicle of John of Worcester, probably drawn by him.)

Although Henry was in the hunting party when William Rufus died, whether he took part in a conspiracy will never be known. But from his point of view his brother's death could not have come at a better time, nor in a better place. He rode straight to Winchester, claimed the royal treasury and three days later was crowned in Westminster Abbey.

Henry I followed the custom of his predecessors and immediately issued a charter announcing his intention of correcting the abuses of the previous reign: vacant sees were filled (though with men loyal to the king), and Anselm was recalled. But a few weeks later, duke Robert, the king's older brother, returned to Normandy from the First Crusade ready to claim the English throne. After mutual provocations, the two brothers renounced their claims on each other's lands. But Henry remained determined to take Normandy by force, and on 28 September 1106, 40 years to the day after William the Conqueror's decisive victory at Hastings, he defeated Robert near Avranches in a pitched battle that lasted less than an hour.

Henry was now king of England and Normandy. He quickly restored order, punishing rebel barons, razing castles and consolidating his father's system of government. His influence on continental politics increased. Alliances with a number of neighbouring states were formed, but his principal opponents – Louis VI of France and the counts of Flanders and Anjou, plus a number of Norman barons – were increasingly restive and there were continual wars and local battles. Finally, by 1120, peace and stability seemed to have arrived at last, and Henry returned to England. But on the crossing Henry's only son was lost, along with a number of prominent courtiers: the succession was put in jeopardy.

The cost to the English people of the continuing wars in Normandy was excessive. The Chroniclers also mention crop failures, severe weather and the tyrannical injustice of the courts: 'the man who had any property was deprived of it by severe taxes and severe courts; the man who had none died of hunger.' Although by and large successful, Henry's rule was punctuated by sudden bouts of savagery: in 1125, 'all the moneyers in England' were summoned to Winchester, and both innocent and guilty were mutilated as a punishment for circulating large quantities of false coins.

After the death of his son, Henry became increasingly concerned about the succession, and in 1127 made his barons and bishops swear their allegiance to his widowed daughter, Matilda, as his heir. She was then sent to be married to the count of Anjou. The last years of the king's reign were relatively trouble-free, and Henry died in 1135 on a hunting trip near Lyons, as a result of eating too many lampreys, a dish forbidden by his doctors.

Right: Seal of William of Corbeil, archbishop of Canterbury from 1123 to 1136. William had been a lay canon of St Osyth's, Essex, and was appointed in spite of objections from the monastic community. The pope sanctioned the appointment when Henry made a diplomatic contribution to the papal purse.

Below: Henry I mourning for his son, drowned when the White Ship sank in the Channel. Only a butcher from Rouen survived, and he reported that passengers and crew were all drunk before the ship put to sea.

[1100] On the Thursday William was killed, and on the next morning buried; and after he was buried, the counsellors who were near at hand chose his brother Henry as king. He gave the rights to the bishopric in Winchester to William Giffard, and afterwards went to London. On the Sunday thereafter, before the altar in Westminster, God and all the folk, he promised to put down all the injustices that were in his brother's time, and to hold to the best laws that stood in any king's day before him. After that the bishop of London, Mauricius, hallowed him king; all this land bowed to him, swore oaths and became his vassals.

Soon after that the king, at the advice of those around him, let Ranulf the bishop of Durham be taken, brought to the tower in London and held there. Then before Michaelmas, Anselm the arch-bishop of Canterbury came here to this land, as king Henry, by his counsellors' advice, had sent after him, for he had gone out of the land because of the injustice king William did him.

Later, soon after, the king took Mathilda for his wife, the daughter of king Malcolm of Scotland and Margaret the good queen, king Edward's kinswoman, of the rightful kingly line of England. On Martinmas she was with great honour given to him in Westminster.

This same year also in autumn came eorl Robert home into Normandy, and Robert of Flanders, and Eustace eorl of Boulogne, from Jerusalem. As soon as eorl Robert came into Normandy, he was gladly received by all folk, except in the castles that were set with king Henry's men, against whom he had many contests and battles.

1101. At Christmas king Henry held his court at Westminster, and at Easter at Winchester; and soon thereafter, the chief men in this land became hostile to the king, both because of their own great disloyalty and also through eorl Robert of Normandy, who was intent upon war with this land. The king sent ships out to sea then, to the hindering of his brother, but some of them later failed of need, turned from the king and bowed to eorl Robert. Then at midsummer the king fared out to Pevensey with all his army against his brother, and abided his coming there; but meanwhile eorl Robert came up at Portsmouth twelve nights before Lammas. The king with all his army went against them, but the chief men went between them, and reconciled the brothers on the condition that the king give up all that he held by force against the eorl in Normandy, and all who in England had been deprived of their land on account of the eorl were to have it again; also that eorl Eustace have all his father's land here in this land, and that eorl Robert should have each year three thousand marks of silver; and that whichever of the brothers outlasted the other be heir to all England and also Normandy, unless the dead one had an heir by a legal marriage. And this they fastened then with oaths, twelve of the highest on either side. The eorl stayed afterwards over

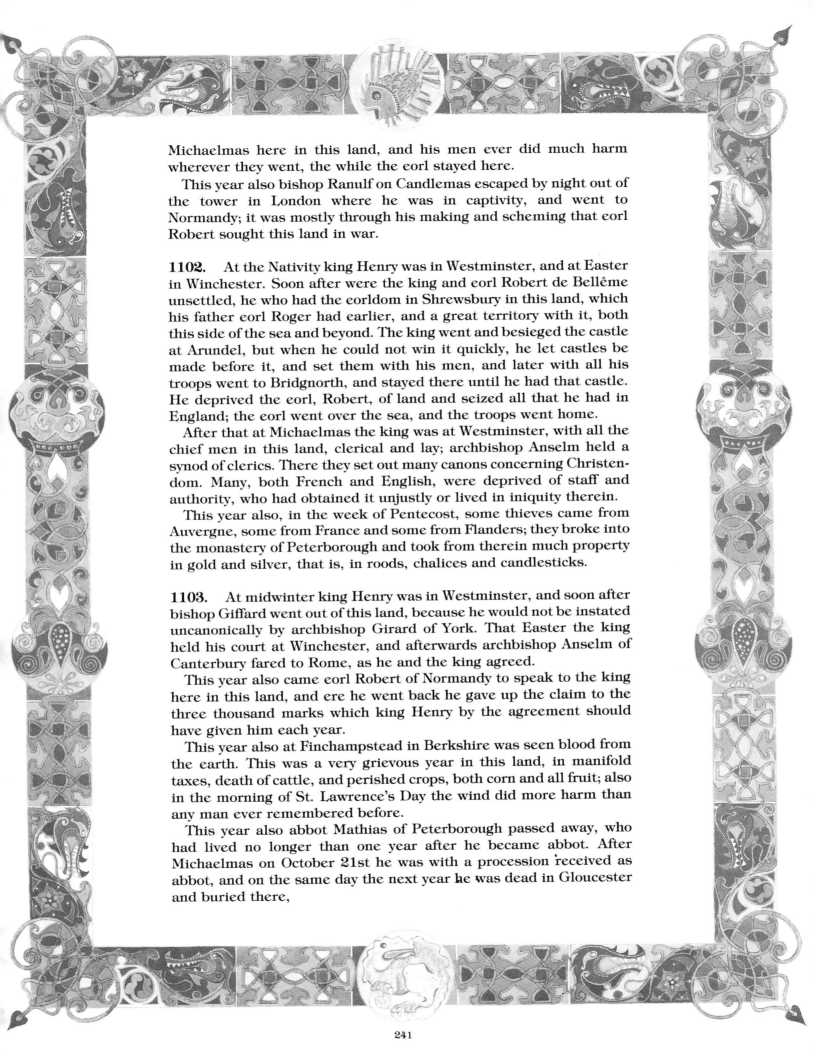

Michaelmas here in this land, and his men ever did much harm wherever they went, the while the eorl stayed here.

This year also bishop Ranulf on Candlemas escaped by night out of the tower in London where he was in captivity, and went to Normandy; it was mostly through his making and scheming that eorl Robert sought this land in war.

1102. At the Nativity king Henry was in Westminster, and at Easter in Winchester. Soon after were the king and eorl Robert de Bellême unsettled, he who had the eorldom in Shrewsbury in this land, which his father eorl Roger had earlier, and a great territory with it, both this side of the sea and beyond. The king went and besieged the castle at Arundel, but when he could not win it quickly, he let castles be made before it, and set them with his men, and later with all his troops went to Bridgnorth, and stayed there until he had that castle. He deprived the eorl, Robert, of land and seized all that he had in England; the eorl went over the sea, and the troops went home.

After that at Michaelmas the king was at Westminster, with all the chief men in this land, clerical and lay; archbishop Anselm held a synod of clerics. There they set out many canons concerning Christendom. Many, both French and English, were deprived of staff and authority, who had obtained it unjustly or lived in iniquity therein.

This year also, in the week of Pentecost, some thieves came from Auvergne, some from France and some from Flanders; they broke into the monastery of Peterborough and took from therein much property in gold and silver, that is, in roods, chalices and candlesticks.

1103. At midwinter king Henry was in Westminster, and soon after bishop Giffard went out of this land, because he would not be instated uncanonically by archbishop Girard of York. That Easter the king held his court at Winchester, and afterwards archbishop Anselm of Canterbury fared to Rome, as he and the king agreed.

This year also came eorl Robert of Normandy to speak to the king here in this land, and ere he went back he gave up the claim to the three thousand marks which king Henry by the agreement should have given him each year.

This year also at Finchampstead in Berkshire was seen blood from the earth. This was a very grievous year in this land, in manifold taxes, death of cattle, and perished crops, both corn and all fruit; also in the morning of St. Lawrence's Day the wind did more harm than any man ever remembered before.

This year also abbot Mathias of Peterborough passed away, who had lived no longer than one year after he became abbot. After Michaelmas on October 21st he was with a procession received as abbot, and on the same day the next year he was dead in Gloucester and buried there,

Even though they were strengthened by layering clay and gravel, mottes were not stable enough to take the weight of a stone tower. Between 1066 and 1100, only two stone keeps were built, the White Tower and Colchester. But their plans became models for later keeps.

By the late 12th century, ever more sophisticated weapons and military tactics were making the square or rectangular stone keeps obsolete. They were simple to undermine and were replaced by round or octagonal towers that also deflected projectiles more easily. Eventually towers were abandoned altogether.

Below: One of the last keeps built was at Pembroke, in about 1200. The round tower was difficult to undermine and gave a greater range of fire. Soon after, keeps were finally abandoned for a combination of thick outer walls with round towers and a formidable gatehouse.

Above: The keep at Dover castle was one of the largest built in the 12th century. Each of the four floors was divided by a wall, and small rooms were set into the thick outer walls.

During Stephen's reign the number of baronial castles increased considerably. Under Henry II — who devoted at least ten per cent of his income to castles — their construction once again became a royal activity. The larger royal castles, administered by sheriffs, functioned as occasional royal residences, local government offices, military barracks, prisons and centres for revenue collection, while the smaller castles, especially those on the borders, housed garrisons to keep the peace and deter Welsh or Scottish raiding parties.

Left: The first castle at Rochester was built soon after the Conquest and was replaced by the existing structure in 1089. This was built for William Rufus by Gundulf, bishop of Rochester, and was one of the first stone castles. The tower keep was added in 1127 by archbishop William of Corbeil.

Below left: Builders at work. (Illustration from an 11th-century English manuscript.)

Below: The White Tower was built by William the Conqueror on the banks of the Thames and made use of the solid Roman city walls. The rooms were stacked one on top of the other to increase security, with storage areas at the base and work and living quarters above. The entrance was well above ground level.

1104. At Christmas king Henry held his court in Westminster, at Easter in Winchester, and at Pentecost again in Westminster. This year the first day of Pentecost was on June 5th, and on the Tuesday after appeared four circles around the sun at mid-day, white in hue, each interwoven with the other, as though painted. All who saw it were filled with wonder, for they remembered nothing like it before.

Hereafter eorl Robert and Robert de Bellême, he who king Henry had deprived of lands and driven from England, were reconciled; and through their reconciliation the king of England and the eorl of Normandy became hostile. The king sent his people over the sea to Normandy, and the chief men in the land there received them. In treachery to their lord the eorl they lodged them in their castles; from there they wrought much affliction on the eorl in ravaging and burning. Also this year William eorl of Mortain went from this land into Normandy; but as soon as he was gone, he worked against the king, for which the king seized everything of his and his land here.

Nor is it easy to tell of the misery the land was enduring in these times, through various and manifold injustices and taxes, which never lessened or ceased; and always wherever the king went, he was through his court plundering his wretched folk thoroughly, very often along with burning and manslaughter.

> All this was God to provoke,
> and to oppress this wretched folk.

1105. At the Nativity king Henry held his court at Windsor, and after, in spring, he went over the sea into Normandy against his brother eorl Robert; during the time he stayed there he won from his brother Caen and Bayeux, and almost all the castles and chief men in the land there were subject to him. Later in the autumn he came home again, and what he had won in Normandy was afterwards friendly and obedient to him — except where near eorl William of Mortain, where he frequently harassed as much as he could, for the loss of his land in England. And before Christmas came Robert eorl of Bellême here to this land to the king.

This was a grievous year in this land in perishing crops, and through manifold taxes which never lessened before the king went over the sea, while he was there nor when he came back again.

1106. King Henry was on the Nativity at Westminster, and held his court there; during the festival, Robert de Bellême went without reconciliation from the king out of this land into Normandy. Thereafter, before the spring, the king was at Northampton, and his brother eorl Robert of Normandy came to him because the king would not give back that which he had seized from him. They parted without a reconciliation, and the eorl soon went back over the sea again.

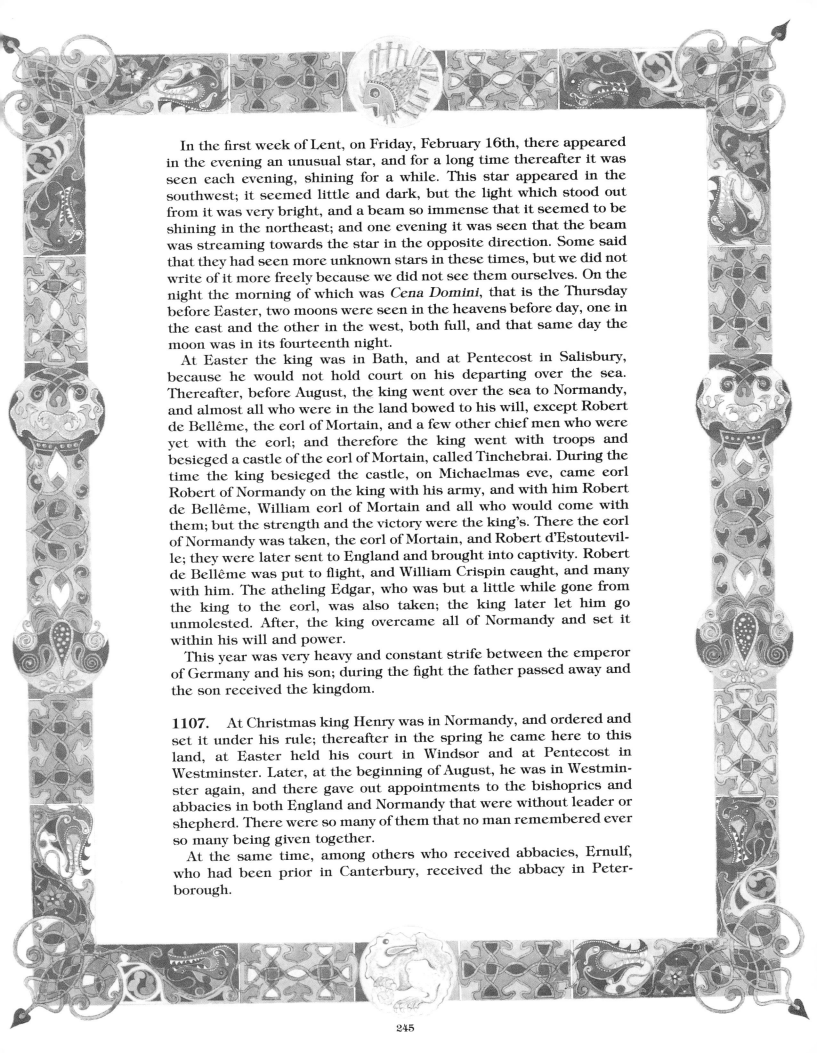

In the first week of Lent, on Friday, February 16th, there appeared in the evening an unusual star, and for a long time thereafter it was seen each evening, shining for a while. This star appeared in the southwest; it seemed little and dark, but the light which stood out from it was very bright, and a beam so immense that it seemed to be shining in the northeast; and one evening it was seen that the beam was streaming towards the star in the opposite direction. Some said that they had seen more unknown stars in these times, but we did not write of it more freely because we did not see them ourselves. On the night the morning of which was *Cena Domini*, that is the Thursday before Easter, two moons were seen in the heavens before day, one in the east and the other in the west, both full, and that same day the moon was in its fourteenth night.

At Easter the king was in Bath, and at Pentecost in Salisbury, because he would not hold court on his departing over the sea. Thereafter, before August, the king went over the sea to Normandy, and almost all who were in the land bowed to his will, except Robert de Bellême, the eorl of Mortain, and a few other chief men who were yet with the eorl; and therefore the king went with troops and besieged a castle of the eorl of Mortain, called Tinchebrai. During the time the king besieged the castle, on Michaelmas eve, came eorl Robert of Normandy on the king with his army, and with him Robert de Bellême, William eorl of Mortain and all who would come with them; but the strength and the victory were the king's. There the eorl of Normandy was taken, the eorl of Mortain, and Robert d'Estouteville; they were later sent to England and brought into captivity. Robert de Bellême was put to flight, and William Crispin caught, and many with him. The atheling Edgar, who was but a little while gone from the king to the eorl, was also taken; the king later let him go unmolested. After, the king overcame all of Normandy and set it within his will and power.

This year was very heavy and constant strife between the emperor of Germany and his son; during the fight the father passed away and the son received the kingdom.

1107. At Christmas king Henry was in Normandy, and ordered and set it under his rule; thereafter in the spring he came here to this land, at Easter held his court in Windsor and at Pentecost in Westminster. Later, at the beginning of August, he was in Westminster again, and there gave out appointments to the bishoprics and abbacies in both England and Normandy that were without leader or shepherd. There were so many of them that no man remembered ever so many being given together.

At the same time, among others who received abbacies, Ernulf, who had been prior in Canterbury, received the abbacy in Peterborough.

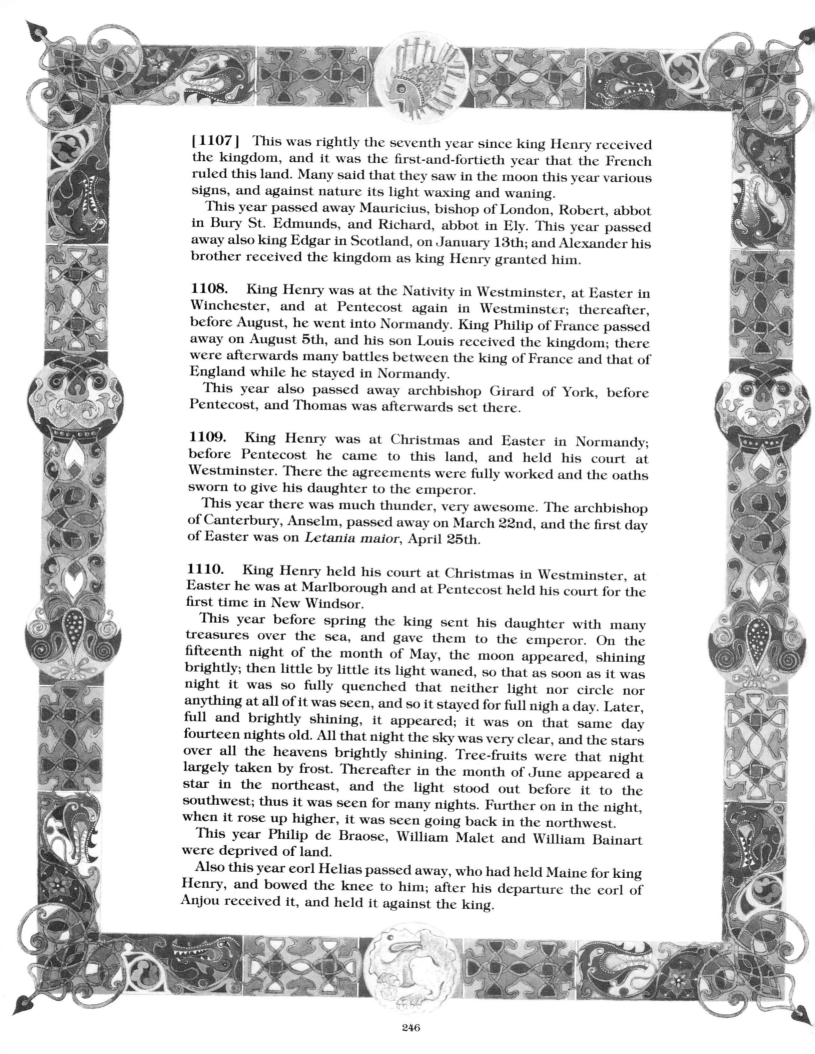

[1107] This was rightly the seventh year since king Henry received the kingdom, and it was the first-and-fortieth year that the French ruled this land. Many said that they saw in the moon this year various signs, and against nature its light waxing and waning.

This year passed away Mauricius, bishop of London, Robert, abbot in Bury St. Edmunds, and Richard, abbot in Ely. This year passed away also king Edgar in Scotland, on January 13th; and Alexander his brother received the kingdom as king Henry granted him.

1108. King Henry was at the Nativity in Westminster, at Easter in Winchester, and at Pentecost again in Westminster; thereafter, before August, he went into Normandy. King Philip of France passed away on August 5th, and his son Louis received the kingdom; there were afterwards many battles between the king of France and that of England while he stayed in Normandy.

This year also passed away archbishop Girard of York, before Pentecost, and Thomas was afterwards set there.

1109. King Henry was at Christmas and Easter in Normandy; before Pentecost he came to this land, and held his court at Westminster. There the agreements were fully worked and the oaths sworn to give his daughter to the emperor.

This year there was much thunder, very awesome. The archbishop of Canterbury, Anselm, passed away on March 22nd, and the first day of Easter was on *Letania maior*, April 25th.

1110. King Henry held his court at Christmas in Westminster, at Easter he was at Marlborough and at Pentecost held his court for the first time in New Windsor.

This year before spring the king sent his daughter with many treasures over the sea, and gave them to the emperor. On the fifteenth night of the month of May, the moon appeared, shining brightly; then little by little its light waned, so that as soon as it was night it was so fully quenched that neither light nor circle nor anything at all of it was seen, and so it stayed for full nigh a day. Later, full and brightly shining, it appeared; it was on that same day fourteen nights old. All that night the sky was very clear, and the stars over all the heavens brightly shining. Tree-fruits were that night largely taken by frost. Thereafter in the month of June appeared a star in the northeast, and the light stood out before it to the southwest; thus it was seen for many nights. Further on in the night, when it rose up higher, it was seen going back in the northwest.

This year Philip de Braose, William Malet and William Bainart were deprived of land.

Also this year eorl Helias passed away, who had held Maine for king Henry, and bowed the knee to him; after his departure the eorl of Anjou received it, and held it against the king.

This was a very grievous year in the land, through tribute the king took for his daughter's dowry, and through bad weather, by which all the earth-crops were greatly spoiled, and the tree-crops over all this land nearly all perished.

This year, work was begun on the new minster at Chertsey.

1111. King Henry did not bear his crown at Christmas, nor Easter, nor Pentecost, and in August he fared over the sea to Normandy because of hostility against him on some of the borders of France, and mostly because of the eorl of Anjou, who held Maine against him. After he came there, many fierce raids, burnings and ravagings they did between them.

This year passed away eorl Robert of Flanders, and his son Baldwin succeeded thereto.

This year there was a very long winter, a heavy time and severe; through that the earth-crops were greatly spoiled, and there was the most death among livestock that anyone could remember.

1112. All this year king Henry stayed in Normandy because of the hostilities with France, and with the eorl of Anjou, who held Maine against him. During the time he was there, he deprived of land the eorl of Evreux and William Crispin, and drove them out of the land; Philip de Braose he gave back his land, who had been deprived of it, and Robert de Bellême he let be taken and put into prison.

This was a very good year, fruitful in woods and fields, but it was a heavy and sorrowful time through raging pestilence.

1113. King Henry was on the Nativity, Easter and Pentecost in Normandy, and thereafter in summer he sent hither to the land Robert de Bellême into the castle at Wareham, and himself soon after came to the land.

1114. King Henry held his court at the Nativity in Windsor, and this year he held no other afterwards.

At midsummer he went with troops into Wales; the Welshmen came and made a truce with the king, and he let castles be worked there. Thereafter in September he went over the sea to Normandy.

This year towards the end of May was seen a rare star with a long beam of light shining for many nights. Also in this year was so great an ebb-tide everywhere that no one remembered the like before; it was such that men went riding and walking over the Thames east of London Bridge. This year were very great winds in the month of October; but it was immeasurably great on the night of the Octave of St. Martin, November 18th, and that was seen everywhere in the woods and villages afterwards.

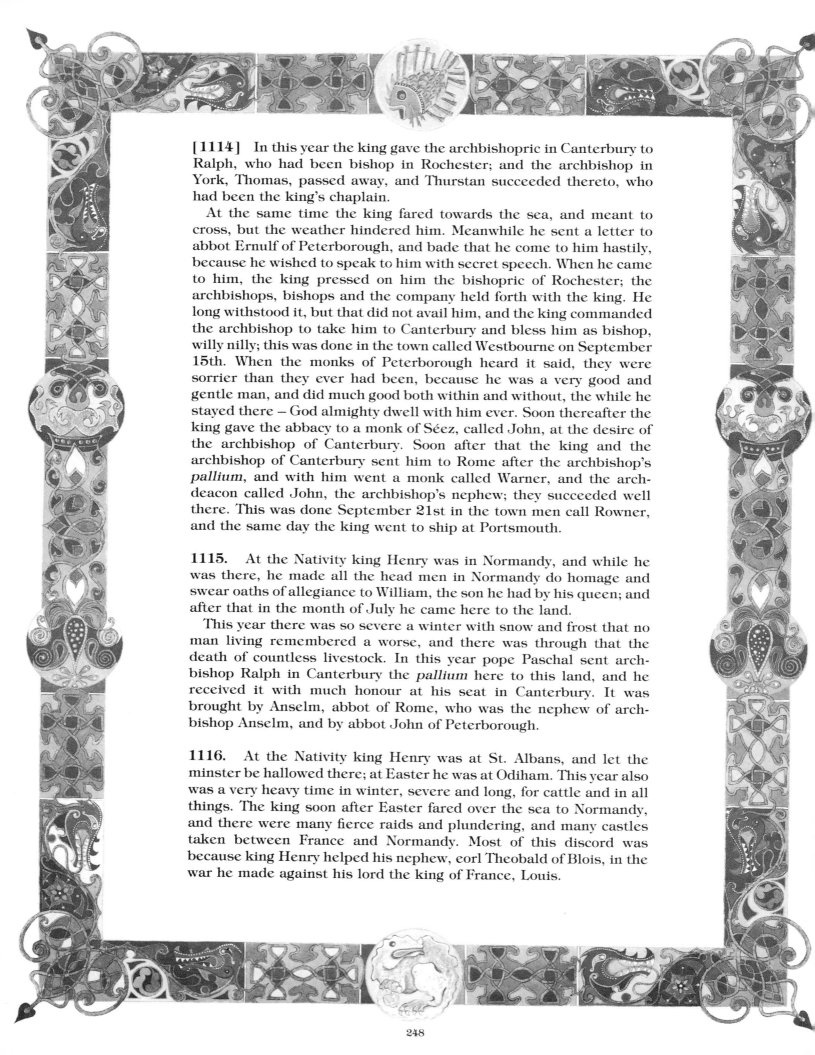

[1114] In this year the king gave the archbishopric in Canterbury to Ralph, who had been bishop in Rochester; and the archbishop in York, Thomas, passed away, and Thurstan succeeded thereto, who had been the king's chaplain.

At the same time the king fared towards the sea, and meant to cross, but the weather hindered him. Meanwhile he sent a letter to abbot Ernulf of Peterborough, and bade that he come to him hastily, because he wished to speak to him with secret speech. When he came to him, the king pressed on him the bishopric of Rochester; the archbishops, bishops and the company held forth with the king. He long withstood it, but that did not avail him, and the king commanded the archbishop to take him to Canterbury and bless him as bishop, willy nilly; this was done in the town called Westbourne on September 15th. When the monks of Peterborough heard it said, they were sorrier than they ever had been, because he was a very good and gentle man, and did much good both within and without, the while he stayed there – God almighty dwell with him ever. Soon thereafter the king gave the abbacy to a monk of Séez, called John, at the desire of the archbishop of Canterbury. Soon after that the king and the archbishop of Canterbury sent him to Rome after the archbishop's *pallium*, and with him went a monk called Warner, and the archdeacon called John, the archbishop's nephew; they succeeded well there. This was done September 21st in the town men call Rowner, and the same day the king went to ship at Portsmouth.

1115. At the Nativity king Henry was in Normandy, and while he was there, he made all the head men in Normandy do homage and swear oaths of allegiance to William, the son he had by his queen; and after that in the month of July he came here to the land.

This year there was so severe a winter with snow and frost that no man living remembered a worse, and there was through that the death of countless livestock. In this year pope Paschal sent archbishop Ralph in Canterbury the *pallium* here to this land, and he received it with much honour at his seat in Canterbury. It was brought by Anselm, abbot of Rome, who was the nephew of archbishop Anselm, and by abbot John of Peterborough.

1116. At the Nativity king Henry was at St. Albans, and let the minster be hallowed there; at Easter he was at Odiham. This year also was a very heavy time in winter, severe and long, for cattle and in all things. The king soon after Easter fared over the sea to Normandy, and there were many fierce raids and plundering, and many castles taken between France and Normandy. Most of this discord was because king Henry helped his nephew, eorl Theobald of Blois, in the war he made against his lord the king of France, Louis.

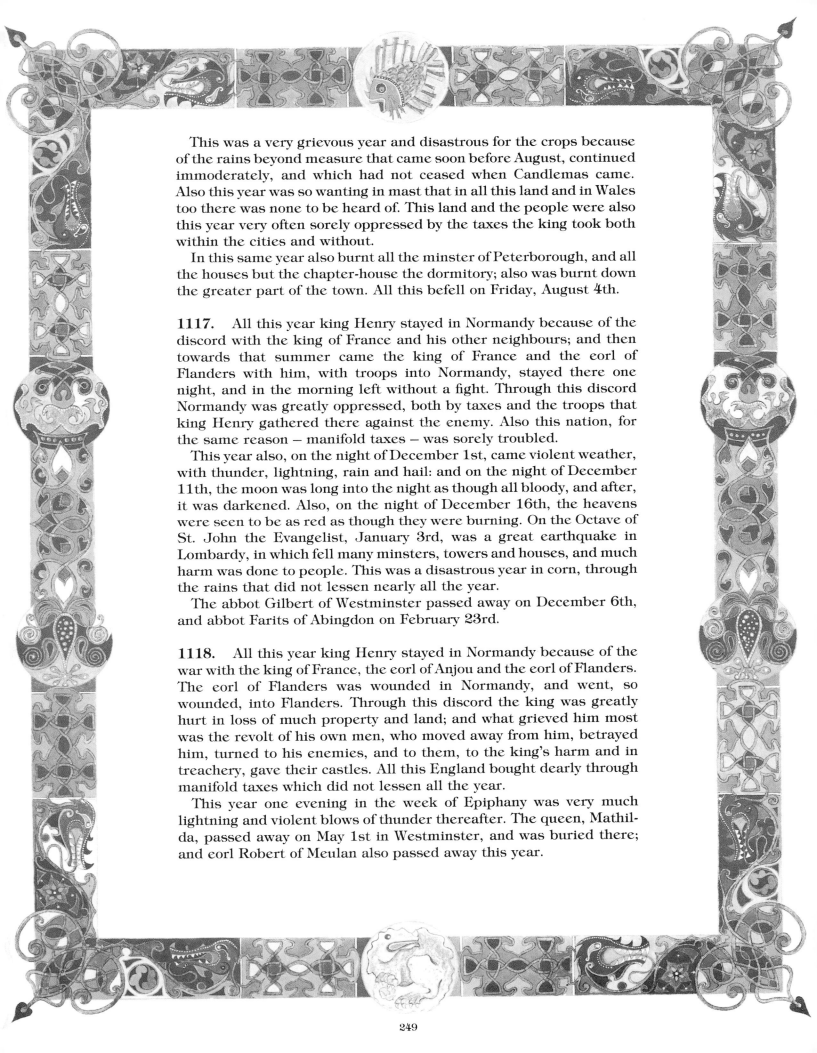

This was a very grievous year and disastrous for the crops because of the rains beyond measure that came soon before August, continued immoderately, and which had not ceased when Candlemas came. Also this year was so wanting in mast that in all this land and in Wales too there was none to be heard of. This land and the people were also this year very often sorely oppressed by the taxes the king took both within the cities and without.

In this same year also burnt all the minster of Peterborough, and all the houses but the chapter-house the dormitory; also was burnt down the greater part of the town. All this befell on Friday, August 4th.

1117. All this year king Henry stayed in Normandy because of the discord with the king of France and his other neighbours; and then towards that summer came the king of France and the eorl of Flanders with him, with troops into Normandy, stayed there one night, and in the morning left without a fight. Through this discord Normandy was greatly oppressed, both by taxes and the troops that king Henry gathered there against the enemy. Also this nation, for the same reason – manifold taxes – was sorely troubled.

This year also, on the night of December 1st, came violent weather, with thunder, lightning, rain and hail: and on the night of December 11th, the moon was long into the night as though all bloody, and after, it was darkened. Also, on the night of December 16th, the heavens were seen to be as red as though they were burning. On the Octave of St. John the Evangelist, January 3rd, was a great earthquake in Lombardy, in which fell many minsters, towers and houses, and much harm was done to people. This was a disastrous year in corn, through the rains that did not lessen nearly all the year.

The abbot Gilbert of Westminster passed away on December 6th, and abbot Farits of Abingdon on February 23rd.

1118. All this year king Henry stayed in Normandy because of the war with the king of France, the eorl of Anjou and the eorl of Flanders. The eorl of Flanders was wounded in Normandy, and went, so wounded, into Flanders. Through this discord the king was greatly hurt in loss of much property and land; and what grieved him most was the revolt of his own men, who moved away from him, betrayed him, turned to his enemies, and to them, to the king's harm and in treachery, gave their castles. All this England bought dearly through manifold taxes which did not lessen all the year.

This year one evening in the week of Epiphany was very much lightning and violent blows of thunder thereafter. The queen, Mathilda, passed away on May 1st in Westminster, and was buried there; and eorl Robert of Meulan also passed away this year.

[1118] Also, this year on St. Thomas's Day was a very great, immeasurable wind, such that no man living remembered a greater — and that was seen everywhere in both houses and trees. This year also passed away pope Paschal; John of Gaeta received the papacy, he whose other name was Gelasius.

1119.   All this year king Henry stayed in Normandy, and was, in the war with the king of France and also with his own men, who had with treachery left him, often greatly afflicted, until the two kings in Normandy with their folk came together in battle. There was the king of France put to flight and all his best men seized. Later, many of king Henry's men moved to him, and accorded with him against whom they had previously held their castles. Some of the castles he took by force.

This year fared William, the son of king Henry and queen Mathilda, into Normandy to his father, and there was given and wedded to him the daughter of the eorl of Anjou. On Michaelmas Eve was a great earthquake in some places here in this land, though greatest in Gloucestershire and Worcestershire.

In this same year passed away pope Gelasius, on this side of the mountains, and was buried in Cluny; after him the archbishop of Vienne was chosen pope, who was named Calixtus, and who later on the Day of St. Luke the Evangelist came into France, in Rheims, and there held a council. Archbishop Thurstan of York went there, and because he against law, against the seat of Canterbury and against the king's will received his state from the pope, the king denied him any return to England. He thus lost his archbishopric and went with the pope towards Rome.

Also in this year passed away eorl Baldwin of Flanders of the wound he received in Normandy; and after him his father's sister's son Carl received the kingdom; he was the son of Cnut, the holy king of Denmark.

1120.   This year were reconciled the kings of England and France; and after their reconciliation, all king Henry's own men against him in Normandy were accorded with him, and the eorls of Flanders and Ponthieu. Later on, king Henry settled his castles and his land in Normandy as he wished it, and so before Advent came here to the land. On that voyage were drowned the king's two sons, William and Richard, Richard eorl of Chester, Ottuel his brother, and very many of the king's court: stewards, chamberlains, cupbearers, various officers, and an untold number of the foremost people died with them. Their death was to their friends a two-fold pain: one, that they so suddenly lost life, and the other that few of their bodies were found afterwards.

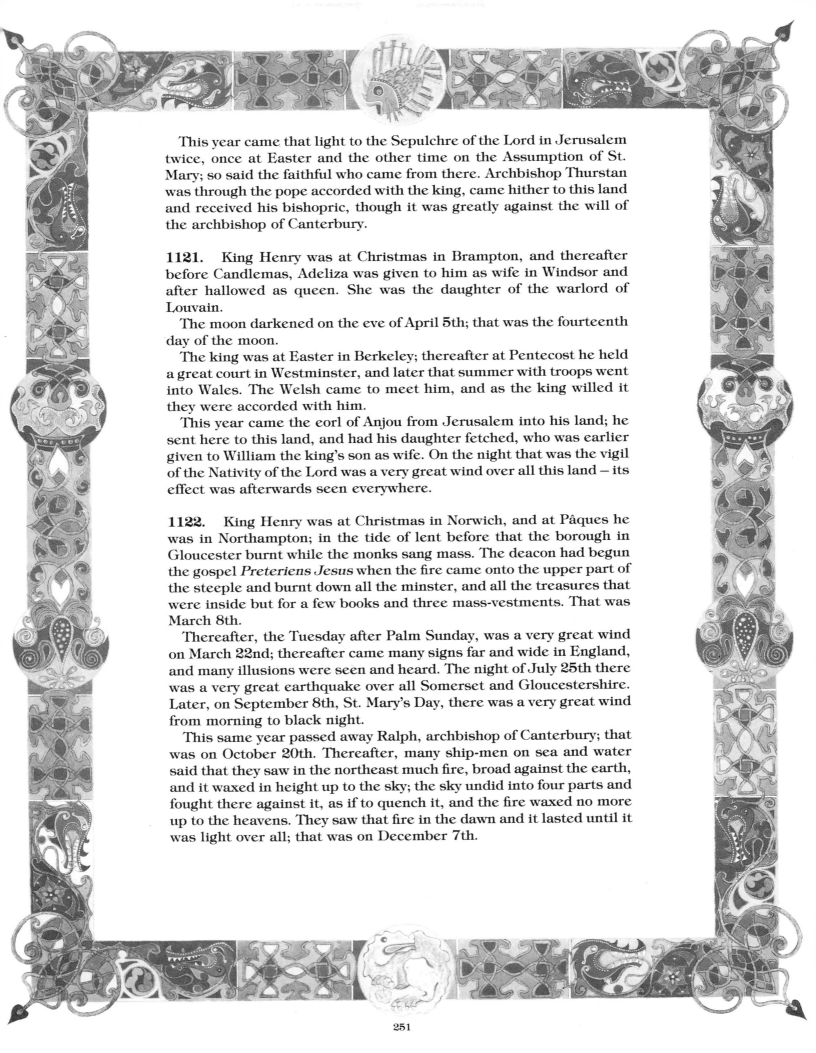

This year came that light to the Sepulchre of the Lord in Jerusalem twice, once at Easter and the other time on the Assumption of St. Mary; so said the faithful who came from there. Archbishop Thurstan was through the pope accorded with the king, came hither to this land and received his bishopric, though it was greatly against the will of the archbishop of Canterbury.

1121. King Henry was at Christmas in Brampton, and thereafter before Candlemas, Adeliza was given to him as wife in Windsor and after hallowed as queen. She was the daughter of the warlord of Louvain.

The moon darkened on the eve of April 5th; that was the fourteenth day of the moon.

The king was at Easter in Berkeley; thereafter at Pentecost he held a great court in Westminster, and later that summer with troops went into Wales. The Welsh came to meet him, and as the king willed it they were accorded with him.

This year came the eorl of Anjou from Jerusalem into his land; he sent here to this land, and had his daughter fetched, who was earlier given to William the king's son as wife. On the night that was the vigil of the Nativity of the Lord was a very great wind over all this land – its effect was afterwards seen everywhere.

1122. King Henry was at Christmas in Norwich, and at Pâques he was in Northampton; in the tide of lent before that the borough in Gloucester burnt while the monks sang mass. The deacon had begun the gospel *Preteriens Jesus* when the fire came onto the upper part of the steeple and burnt down all the minster, and all the treasures that were inside but for a few books and three mass-vestments. That was March 8th.

Thereafter, the Tuesday after Palm Sunday, was a very great wind on March 22nd; thereafter came many signs far and wide in England, and many illusions were seen and heard. The night of July 25th there was a very great earthquake over all Somerset and Gloucestershire. Later, on September 8th, St. Mary's Day, there was a very great wind from morning to black night.

This same year passed away Ralph, archbishop of Canterbury; that was on October 20th. Thereafter, many ship-men on sea and water said that they saw in the northeast much fire, broad against the earth, and it waxed in height up to the sky; the sky undid into four parts and fought there against it, as if to quench it, and the fire waxed no more up to the heavens. They saw that fire in the dawn and it lasted until it was light over all; that was on December 7th.

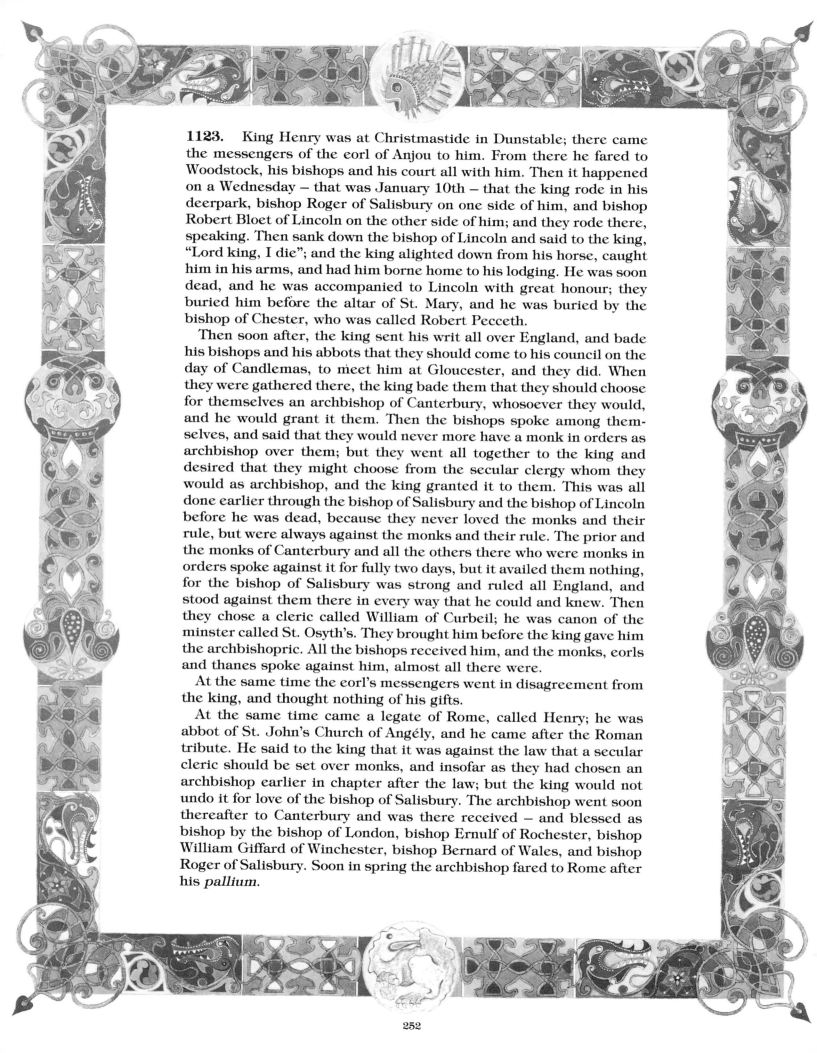

1123. King Henry was at Christmastide in Dunstable; there came the messengers of the eorl of Anjou to him. From there he fared to Woodstock, his bishops and his court all with him. Then it happened on a Wednesday – that was January 10th – that the king rode in his deerpark, bishop Roger of Salisbury on one side of him, and bishop Robert Bloet of Lincoln on the other side of him; and they rode there, speaking. Then sank down the bishop of Lincoln and said to the king, "Lord king, I die"; and the king alighted down from his horse, caught him in his arms, and had him borne home to his lodging. He was soon dead, and he was accompanied to Lincoln with great honour; they buried him before the altar of St. Mary, and he was buried by the bishop of Chester, who was called Robert Pecceth.

Then soon after, the king sent his writ all over England, and bade his bishops and his abbots that they should come to his council on the day of Candlemas, to meet him at Gloucester, and they did. When they were gathered there, the king bade them that they should choose for themselves an archbishop of Canterbury, whosoever they would, and he would grant it them. Then the bishops spoke among themselves, and said that they would never more have a monk in orders as archbishop over them; but they went all together to the king and desired that they might choose from the secular clergy whom they would as archbishop, and the king granted it to them. This was all done earlier through the bishop of Salisbury and the bishop of Lincoln before he was dead, because they never loved the monks and their rule, but were always against the monks and their rule. The prior and the monks of Canterbury and all the others there who were monks in orders spoke against it for fully two days, but it availed them nothing, for the bishop of Salisbury was strong and ruled all England, and stood against them there in every way that he could and knew. Then they chose a cleric called William of Curbeil; he was canon of the minster called St. Osyth's. They brought him before the king gave him the archbishopric. All the bishops received him, and the monks, eorls and thanes spoke against him, almost all there were.

At the same time the eorl's messengers went in disagreement from the king, and thought nothing of his gifts.

At the same time came a legate of Rome, called Henry; he was abbot of St. John's Church of Angély, and he came after the Roman tribute. He said to the king that it was against the law that a secular cleric should be set over monks, and insofar as they had chosen an archbishop earlier in chapter after the law; but the king would not undo it for love of the bishop of Salisbury. The archbishop went soon thereafter to Canterbury and was there received – and blessed as bishop by the bishop of London, bishop Ernulf of Rochester, bishop William Giffard of Winchester, bishop Bernard of Wales, and bishop Roger of Salisbury. Soon in spring the archbishop fared to Rome after his *pallium*.

Above: Inhabited initial from one of the earliest Norman manuscripts, brought to Christ Church, Canterbury, from the abbey of Bec in Normandy soon after the invasion. Anglo-Saxon art had already influenced the Norman artists, but they preferred greater solidity, and also used human figures in the decoration of initials.

Throughout Anglo-Saxon England, the tradition of manuscript illumination was the keystone of the visual arts. Illuminated books became the showcase for new ideas, foreign or native, and, carried from place to place, inspired craftsmen working in other media. Well before 1066, the Normans were familiar with the Winchester style, and English books were eagerly sought by continental courts, scholars and monasteries. English monastic artists were acknowledged as masters of manuscript illumination.

In contrast with architecture, where radical new styles followed the Conquest, changes in the visual arts came more slowly. Upheavals in the monastic system brought the production of illuminated manuscripts to a halt for a number of years. Its resumption heralded one of the greatest eras of English book-making. The new Norman monks and abbots introduced a simple, beautiful style of Carolingian script. Decoration took second place to a clear text and was usually limited to beautifully ornamented and coloured initial letters. Although the manuscripts were written by monks, the artists responsible for the letters seem to have been laymen who travelled from one abbey to another.

The most inventive illuminated initials were done between 1120 and 1150, when climbing human figures and flowers were introduced. These highly accomplished miniatures are reminiscent of the Anglo-Saxon Winchester style in their lightness of feeling, sureness of line and action portrayed in figures. Often entire biblical or domestic scenes occur within the confines of a single letter.

While the Anglo-Saxons had used sculpture as decoration or as a separate art form, the Normans used sculptural forms as part of the structure of a building. At first, Norman sculpture, inspired principally by illuminated manuscripts, consisted of geometric patterns and simple designs on capitals, which were themselves painted. During the early 12th century, capitals came to be sculpted and carved in low relief, and more elaborate compositions were placed around windows, over doors and on fonts. In many smaller churches Anglo-Saxon art styles continued, and Anglo-Saxon craftsmen working on Norman buildings gave a new and more

Below: Elaborately decorated letter in which human and animal figures riotously intermingle.

lively interpretation to the awkward, solid Norman designs. Human figures, animals playing musical instruments, zodiac figures and crowded scenes appear on capitals. More monumental sculpture was done, and all sculpture took on three-dimensional qualities.

Contact with the art of southern Italy and Byzantium through the men returning from the Crusades provided inspiration for design, but the old Anglo-Saxon tradition also remained a strong influence. English embroidery was already known for its sumptuous goldwork on church vestments combining many Anglo-Saxon and Norman motifs. By the mid-12th century, Anglo-Norman manuscript illumination and sculpture had grown into a distinctive style and was itself influencing art in Normandy and France.

Below and below right: Norman artists practising in England also excelled in many minor arts. Norman ivories, unlike earlier Anglo-Saxon examples, were formal and rigid, the flesh hard, the draperies stiff. (Adoration of the Magi, late 11th century; The Deposition from the Cross, 1150.)

Above: An unusual lion, moustachioed and with his tail ending in a leaf, decorates this capital in Canterbury cathedral.

Above: Anglo-Norman figure sculpture from the tympanum of the abbey church at Malmesbury, Wiltshire.

Below: Bronze knocker from the sanctuary door at Durham cathedral.

Below: Illuminator illuminated; an initial capital in which the artist has portrayed himself at work.

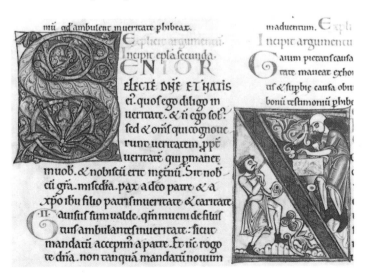

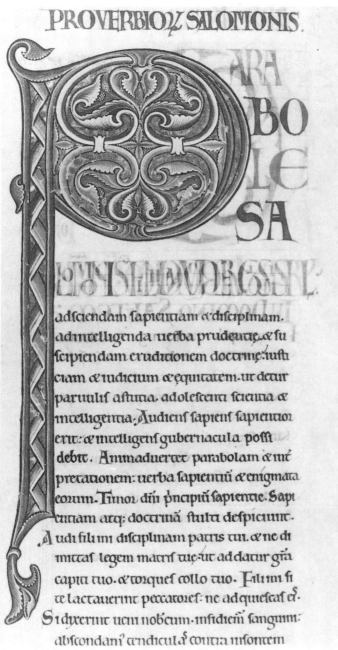

Above: Large-sized bibles and religious scripts were prepared in great numbers in the monastic scriptora using the Carolingian hand. Norman illuminated manuscripts, like their Anglo-Saxon predecessors, were written in Latin, which was the universal language of the Church and government. (The Vulgate Bible, written during the second half of the 12th century.)

Right: This candlestick from Gloucester cathedral, donated by the abbot Peter (1104–13), is a good example of native work. The Normans were not usually very interested in metalwork.

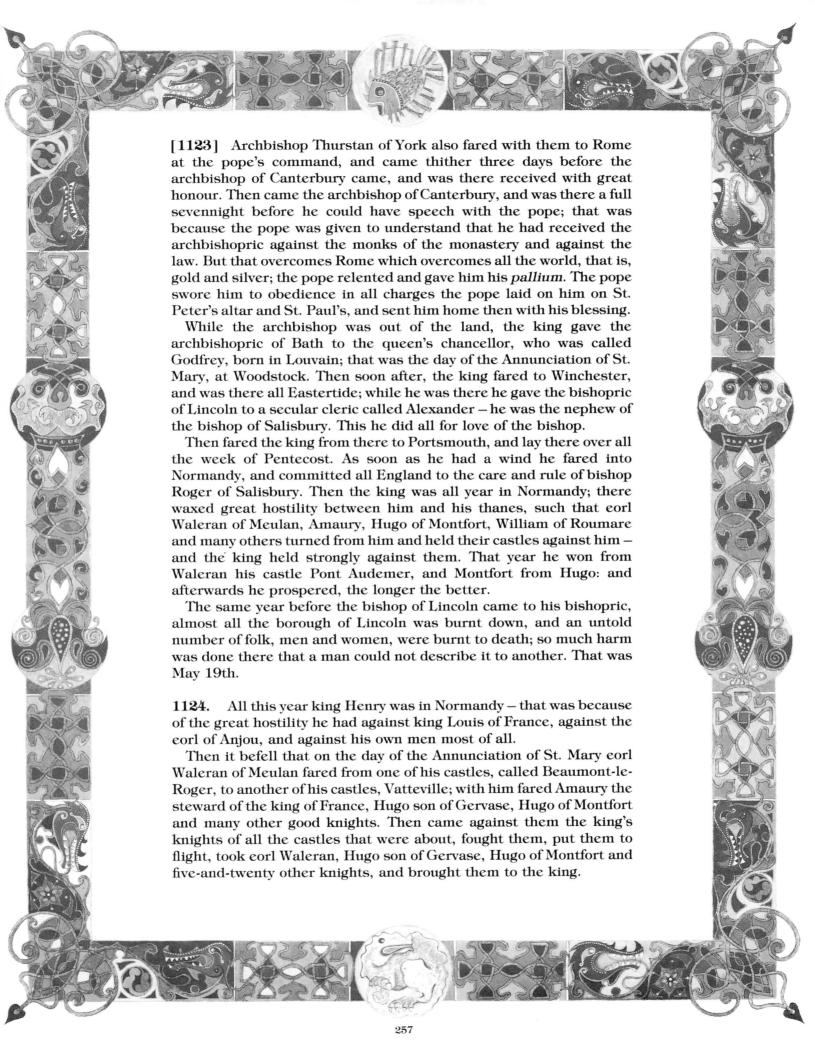

[1123] Archbishop Thurstan of York also fared with them to Rome at the pope's command, and came thither three days before the archbishop of Canterbury came, and was there received with great honour. Then came the archbishop of Canterbury, and was there a full sevennight before he could have speech with the pope; that was because the pope was given to understand that he had received the archbishopric against the monks of the monastery and against the law. But that overcomes Rome which overcomes all the world, that is, gold and silver; the pope relented and gave him his *pallium*. The pope swore him to obedience in all charges the pope laid on him on St. Peter's altar and St. Paul's, and sent him home then with his blessing.

While the archbishop was out of the land, the king gave the archbishopric of Bath to the queen's chancellor, who was called Godfrey, born in Louvain; that was the day of the Annunciation of St. Mary, at Woodstock. Then soon after, the king fared to Winchester, and was there all Eastertide; while he was there he gave the bishopric of Lincoln to a secular cleric called Alexander – he was the nephew of the bishop of Salisbury. This he did all for love of the bishop.

Then fared the king from there to Portsmouth, and lay there over all the week of Pentecost. As soon as he had a wind he fared into Normandy, and committed all England to the care and rule of bishop Roger of Salisbury. Then the king was all year in Normandy; there waxed great hostility between him and his thanes, such that eorl Waleran of Meulan, Amaury, Hugo of Montfort, William of Roumare and many others turned from him and held their castles against him – and the king held strongly against them. That year he won from Waleran his castle Pont Audemer, and Montfort from Hugo: and afterwards he prospered, the longer the better.

The same year before the bishop of Lincoln came to his bishopric, almost all the borough of Lincoln was burnt down, and an untold number of folk, men and women, were burnt to death; so much harm was done there that a man could not describe it to another. That was May 19th.

1124. All this year king Henry was in Normandy – that was because of the great hostility he had against king Louis of France, against the eorl of Anjou, and against his own men most of all.

Then it befell that on the day of the Annunciation of St. Mary eorl Waleran of Meulan fared from one of his castles, called Beaumont-le-Roger, to another of his castles, Vatteville; with him fared Amaury the steward of the king of France, Hugo son of Gervase, Hugo of Montfort and many other good knights. Then came against them the king's knights of all the castles that were about, fought them, put them to flight, took eorl Waleran, Hugo son of Gervase, Hugo of Montfort and five-and-twenty other knights, and brought them to the king.

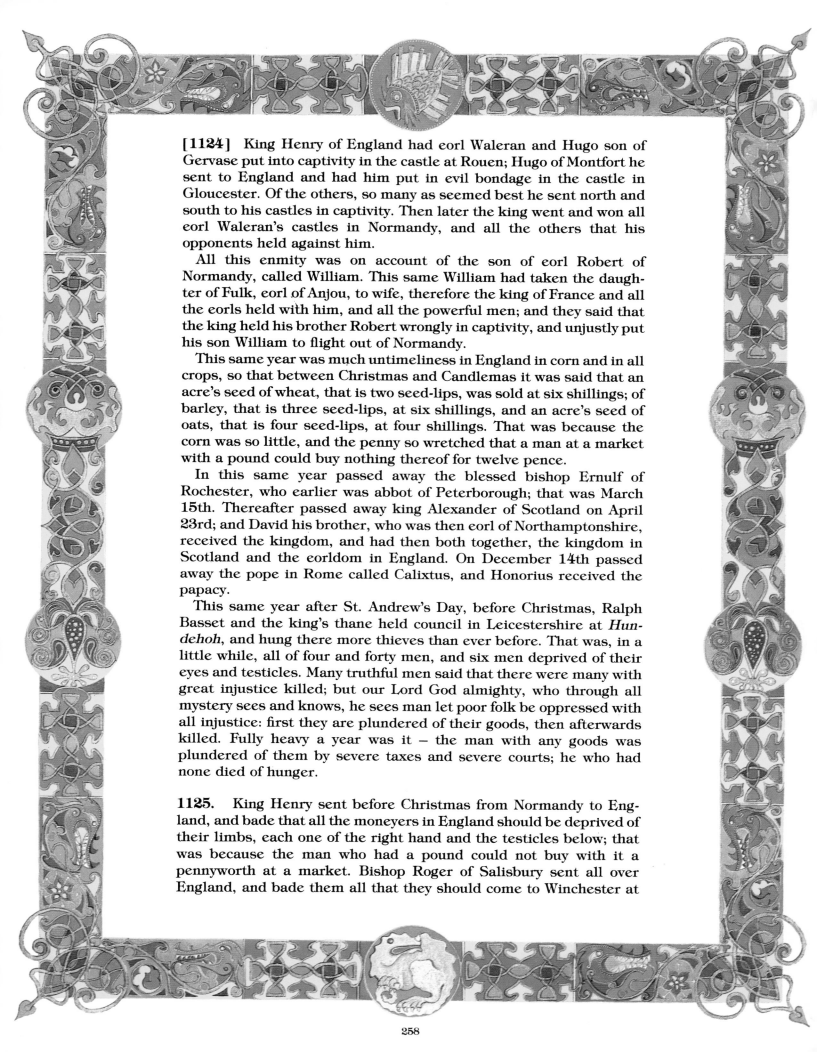

[1124] King Henry of England had eorl Waleran and Hugo son of Gervase put into captivity in the castle at Rouen; Hugo of Montfort he sent to England and had him put in evil bondage in the castle in Gloucester. Of the others, so many as seemed best he sent north and south to his castles in captivity. Then later the king went and won all eorl Waleran's castles in Normandy, and all the others that his opponents held against him.

All this enmity was on account of the son of eorl Robert of Normandy, called William. This same William had taken the daughter of Fulk, eorl of Anjou, to wife, therefore the king of France and all the eorls held with him, and all the powerful men; and they said that the king held his brother Robert wrongly in captivity, and unjustly put his son William to flight out of Normandy.

This same year was much untimeliness in England in corn and in all crops, so that between Christmas and Candlemas it was said that an acre's seed of wheat, that is two seed-lips, was sold at six shillings; of barley, that is three seed-lips, at six shillings, and an acre's seed of oats, that is four seed-lips, at four shillings. That was because the corn was so little, and the penny so wretched that a man at a market with a pound could buy nothing thereof for twelve pence.

In this same year passed away the blessed bishop Ernulf of Rochester, who earlier was abbot of Peterborough; that was March 15th. Thereafter passed away king Alexander of Scotland on April 23rd; and David his brother, who was then eorl of Northamptonshire, received the kingdom, and had then both together, the kingdom in Scotland and the eorldom in England. On December 14th passed away the pope in Rome called Calixtus, and Honorius received the papacy.

This same year after St. Andrew's Day, before Christmas, Ralph Basset and the king's thane held council in Leicestershire at *Hundehoh*, and hung there more thieves than ever before. That was, in a little while, all of four and forty men, and six men deprived of their eyes and testicles. Many truthful men said that there were many with great injustice killed; but our Lord God almighty, who through all mystery sees and knows, he sees man let poor folk be oppressed with all injustice: first they are plundered of their goods, then afterwards killed. Fully heavy a year was it – the man with any goods was plundered of them by severe taxes and severe courts; he who had none died of hunger.

1125.   King Henry sent before Christmas from Normandy to England, and bade that all the moneyers in England should be deprived of their limbs, each one of the right hand and the testicles below; that was because the man who had a pound could not buy with it a pennyworth at a market. Bishop Roger of Salisbury sent all over England, and bade them all that they should come to Winchester at

Christmas. When they came thither, they were seized one by one, and each deprived of the right hand and the testicles below. All this was done within the Twelvenight, and it was all with great justice, because they had ruined all the land with their great fraud; they bought all that dearly.

In this same year the pope sent from Rome to this land a cardinal who was named John of Crema. He came first to the king in Normandy; the king received him with much honour, and after commended him to archbishop William of Canterbury. He escorted him to Canterbury, and he was there received with much honour and a great procession, and he sang the high mass on Easter Day at Christ's altar. Afterwards he fared over all England to all bishoprics and abbacies that were in this land. Overall he was received with honour, and they all gave him great gifts and glorious. Later he held his council in London fully three days, on the Nativity of St. Mary in September, with archbishops, diocesan bishops, abbots, clerics and laymen; he proclaimed the same laws that archbishop Anselm had earlier proclaimed, and many more, though it availed little. From there he fared over the sea soon after Michaelmas, and so to Rome; the archbishop William of Canterbury, archbishop Thurstan of York, bishop Alexander of Lincoln, John the bishop of Glasgow, and Geoffrey the abbot of St. Albans, were there received by pope Honorius with great honour, and were there all winter.

In this same year was so great a flood on St. Lawrence's Day that many towns and many men were drowned, bridges broken up, corn and meadowland ruined withal; there was famine and disease among men and cattle, and more crop-failure than in many years before.

And in this same year passed away abbot John of Peterborough, on October 14th.

1126. All this year king Henry was in Normandy right until after autumn; then he came to this land between the Nativity of St. Mary and Michaelmas. With him came the queen, and his daughter that he had earlier given the emperor Henry of Lorraine as wife. He brought with him eorl Waleran and Hugo son of Gervase: the eorl he sent to Bridgnorth in captivity, and from there he sent him to Wallingford, later, and Hugo to Windsor, and had him put into hard bondage.

Then after Michaelmas came the Scottish king, David, from Scotland into this land; king Henry received him with much honour, and he stayed then all year in this land.

In this same year, the king had his brother Robert taken from bishop Roger of Salisbury and committed him to his son Robert, eorl of Gloucester, had him taken to Bristol and there put in the castle. That was all done through the advice of his daughter, and through that of the Scottish king David, her uncle.

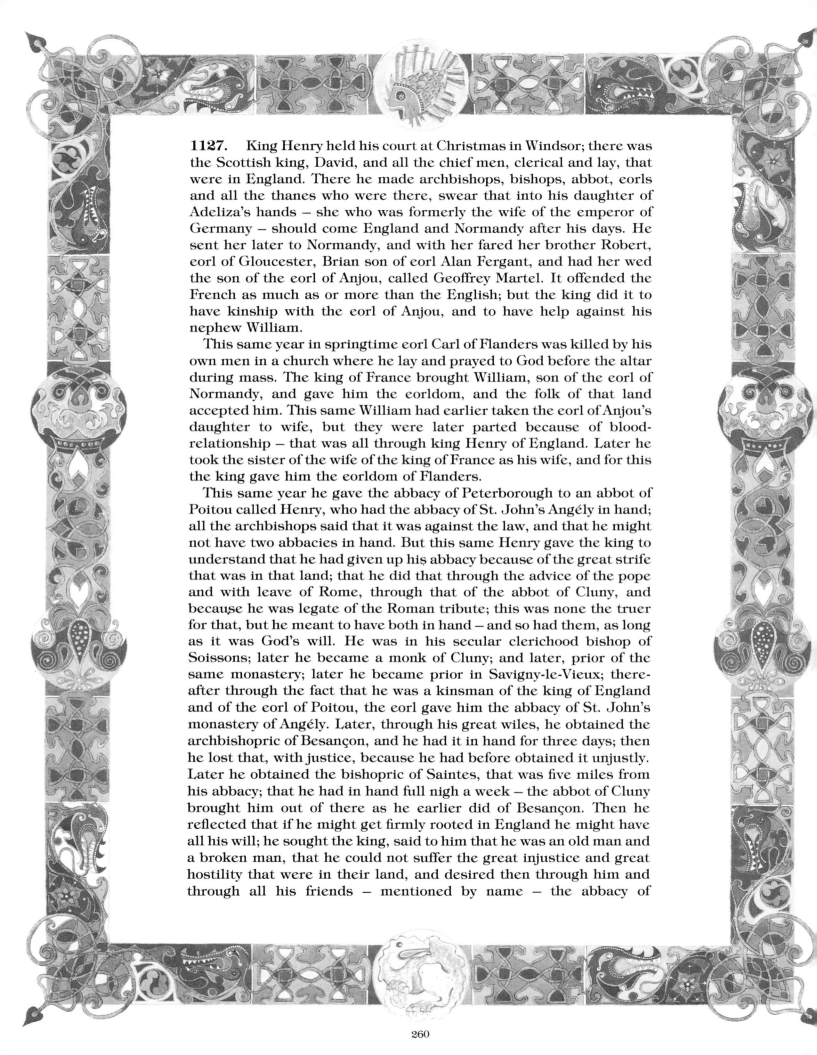

1127. King Henry held his court at Christmas in Windsor; there was the Scottish king, David, and all the chief men, clerical and lay, that were in England. There he made archbishops, bishops, abbot, eorls and all the thanes who were there, swear that into his daughter of Adeliza's hands – she who was formerly the wife of the emperor of Germany – should come England and Normandy after his days. He sent her later to Normandy, and with her fared her brother Robert, eorl of Gloucester, Brian son of eorl Alan Fergant, and had her wed the son of the eorl of Anjou, called Geoffrey Martel. It offended the French as much as or more than the English; but the king did it to have kinship with the eorl of Anjou, and to have help against his nephew William.

This same year in springtime eorl Carl of Flanders was killed by his own men in a church where he lay and prayed to God before the altar during mass. The king of France brought William, son of the eorl of Normandy, and gave him the eorldom, and the folk of that land accepted him. This same William had earlier taken the eorl of Anjou's daughter to wife, but they were later parted because of blood-relationship – that was all through king Henry of England. Later he took the sister of the wife of the king of France as his wife, and for this the king gave him the eorldom of Flanders.

This same year he gave the abbacy of Peterborough to an abbot of Poitou called Henry, who had the abbacy of St. John's Angély in hand; all the archbishops said that it was against the law, and that he might not have two abbacies in hand. But this same Henry gave the king to understand that he had given up his abbacy because of the great strife that was in that land; that he did that through the advice of the pope and with leave of Rome, through that of the abbot of Cluny, and because he was legate of the Roman tribute; this was none the truer for that, but he meant to have both in hand – and so had them, as long as it was God's will. He was in his secular clerichood bishop of Soissons; later he became a monk of Cluny; and later, prior of the same monastery; later he became prior in Savigny-le-Vieux; thereafter through the fact that he was a kinsman of the king of England and of the eorl of Poitou, the eorl gave him the abbacy of St. John's monastery of Angély. Later, through his great wiles, he obtained the archbishopric of Besançon, and he had it in hand for three days; then he lost that, with justice, because he had before obtained it unjustly. Later he obtained the bishopric of Saintes, that was five miles from his abbacy; that he had in hand full nigh a week – the abbot of Cluny brought him out of there as he earlier did of Besançon. Then he reflected that if he might get firmly rooted in England he might have all his will; he sought the king, said to him that he was an old man and a broken man, that he could not suffer the great injustice and great hostility that were in their land, and desired then through him and through all his friends – mentioned by name – the abbacy of

Peterborough. And the king gave it to him, because he was his kinsman, and because he was the chief man to swear oaths and bear witness when the son of the eorl of Normandy and the daughter of the eorl of Anjou were parted for blood-relationship. Thus was the abbacy basely given away between Christmas and Candlemas at London, and so he fared with the king to Winchester, and from there he came to Peterborough, and there he stayed just as does the drone in the hive. All that the bees draw in is eaten by the drone, and taken out — and so he did. All that he might take, within and without, from clerical and lay, he sent over the sea; no good he did there, not did he leave any goods there. Nor shall it be thought strange what we say as truth, for it was fully known over all the land, that as soon as he arrived there — that was the Sunday EXSURGE QAURE OBDORMIS DOMINE is sung — it was heard and seen by many men: many hunters hunting. The hunters were black, and great and loathly, and their hounds all black, and wide-eyed and loathly, and they rode on black horses and black he-goats. This was seen in the very deer-park in the town of Peterborough, and in all the woods from the same town to Stamford; and the monks heard the horns blowing that they blew at night. Truthful men who kept watch at night said that it seemed to them that there might well be about twenty or thirty horn-blowers. This was seen and heard from when he came, all through Lenten tide until Easter. This was his coming in; of his going out we cannot yet say. May God provide it.

1128. All this year king Henry was in Normandy because of the hostility that was between him and his nephew the eorl of Flanders; but the eorl was wounded in a fight with a young man, and so wounded he fared to St. Bertin's monastery at St. Omer; he as soon became a monk there, lived five days, died and was buried there. God have mercy on his soul. That was July 27th.

This same year passed away bishop Ranulf Passeflambard of Durham, and was buried there on September 5th.

This same year fared the aforesaid abbot Henry home to his own minster of Poitou by the king's leave. He gave it to the king to understand that he would give up all, the monastery and the land, and dwell with him there in England, in the monastery of Peterborough, but it was none the more true. He did it because he meant through his great wiles to be there twelve months or more, then come back again. God almighty show his mercy on that unhappy place.

[1128] Hugo of the Templars came from Jerusalem to the king in Normandy; the king received him with much honour, gave him much treasure in gold and silver, and afterwards sent him to England, where he was received by all good men; all gave him treasure, in Scotland, also, and sent by him much property all in gold and silver. He summoned folk out to Jerusalem, and then with him went so many folk as never before nor since the first journey in pope Urban's day, though it availed little. He said that a full war was set between the Christians and the heathen; when they came thither it was naught but lying, and thus wretchedly were all those folk afflicted.

1129.   The king sent to England after eorl Waleran, and after Hugo son of Gervase; they exchanged hostages and Hugo fared home to his own land, to France. Waleran remained with the king, and the king gave him all his land but his castle alone. Later, when the king came to England in autumn the eorl came with him, and they became just as good friends as they had been enemies before.

Soon, by the king's counsel and by his leave, archbishop William of Canterbury sent all over England, and bade bishops, abbots, archdeacons, all priors, monks and canons in all cells in England, and all who had Christendom to rule and look after, that they should all come to London at Michaelmas, and there should speak concerning all God's laws. When they came thither – the council began on Monday and was held till Friday – it all came out; it was all about archdeacons's wives, and priest's wives. They had to give them up by St. Andrew's Day, and he would would not do that would forgo his church, his house, and his home, and never more have any claim to them. This commanded archbishop William of Canterbury and all the diocesan bishops then in England, and the king gave them all leave to go home. So they fared home; nor availed anything all the decrees – they all kept their wives by the king's leave, just as they did before.

This same year passed away bishop William Giffard of Winchester, and was buried there on January 25th. King Henry gave the bishopric after Michaelmas to his nephew, abbot Henry of Glastonbury, and he was hallowed by archbishop William of Canterbury.

The same year pope Honorius passed away; before he was long dead, there were two popes chosen. The one was called Peter: he was a monk of Cluny, and was born of the most powerful people of Rome; with him held those of Rome and the duke of Sicily. The other was called Gregory: he was a cleric, and was driven out of Rome by the other pope and by his kinsmen; with him held the emperor of Germany, the king of France and king Henry of England, and all on this side of the mountains. Now there occurred more heresy in England than ever before. Christ give guidance to his wretched folk.

This year also on the eve of St. Nicholas's day, a little before day, was a great earthquake.

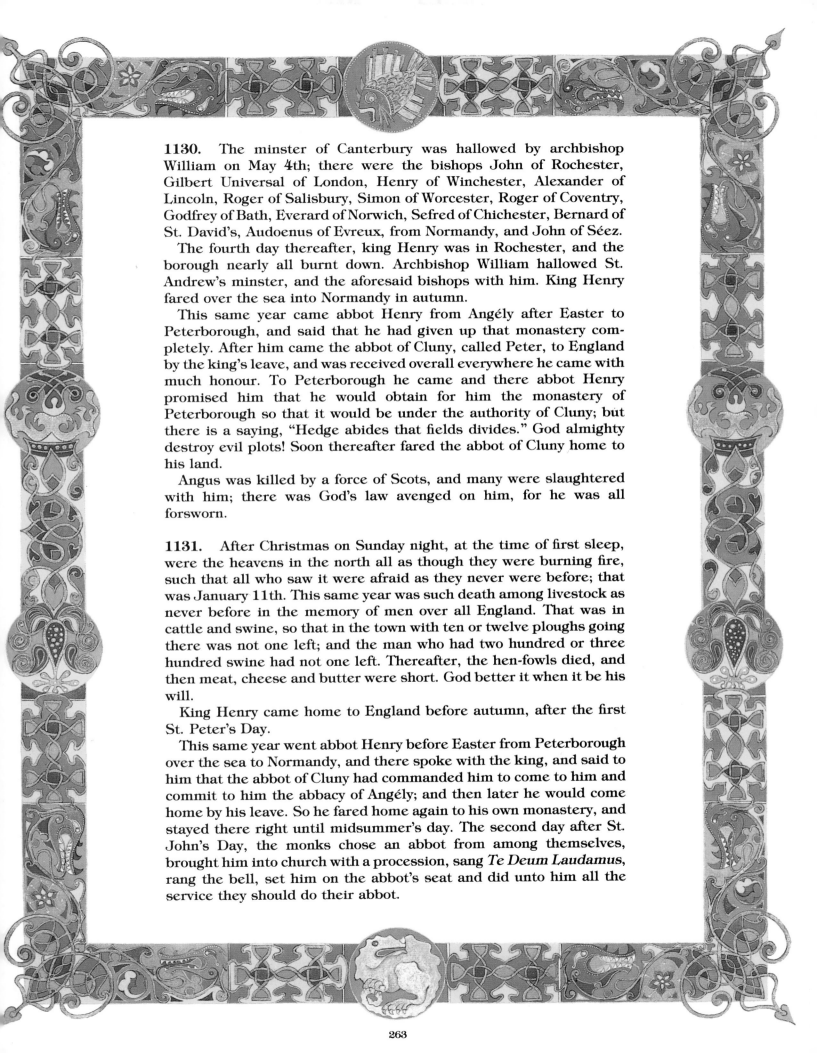

1130. The minster of Canterbury was hallowed by archbishop William on May 4th; there were the bishops John of Rochester, Gilbert Universal of London, Henry of Winchester, Alexander of Lincoln, Roger of Salisbury, Simon of Worcester, Roger of Coventry, Godfrey of Bath, Everard of Norwich, Sefred of Chichester, Bernard of St. David's, Audoenus of Evreux, from Normandy, and John of Séez.

The fourth day thereafter, king Henry was in Rochester, and the borough nearly all burnt down. Archbishop William hallowed St. Andrew's minster, and the aforesaid bishops with him. King Henry fared over the sea into Normandy in autumn.

This same year came abbot Henry from Angély after Easter to Peterborough, and said that he had given up that monastery completely. After him came the abbot of Cluny, called Peter, to England by the king's leave, and was received overall everywhere he came with much honour. To Peterborough he came and there abbot Henry promised him that he would obtain for him the monastery of Peterborough so that it would be under the authority of Cluny; but there is a saying, "Hedge abides that fields divides." God almighty destroy evil plots! Soon thereafter fared the abbot of Cluny home to his land.

Angus was killed by a force of Scots, and many were slaughtered with him; there was God's law avenged on him, for he was all forsworn.

1131. After Christmas on Sunday night, at the time of first sleep, were the heavens in the north all as though they were burning fire, such that all who saw it were afraid as they never were before; that was January 11th. This same year was such death among livestock as never before in the memory of men over all England. That was in cattle and swine, so that in the town with ten or twelve ploughs going there was not one left; and the man who had two hundred or three hundred swine had not one left. Thereafter, the hen-fowls died, and then meat, cheese and butter were short. God better it when it be his will.

King Henry came home to England before autumn, after the first St. Peter's Day.

This same year went abbot Henry before Easter from Peterborough over the sea to Normandy, and there spoke with the king, and said to him that the abbot of Cluny had commanded him to come to him and commit to him the abbacy of Angély; and then later he would come home by his leave. So he fared home again to his own monastery, and stayed there right until midsummer's day. The second day after St. John's Day, the monks chose an abbot from among themselves, brought him into church with a procession, sang *Te Deum Laudamus*, rang the bell, set him on the abbot's seat and did unto him all the service they should do their abbot.

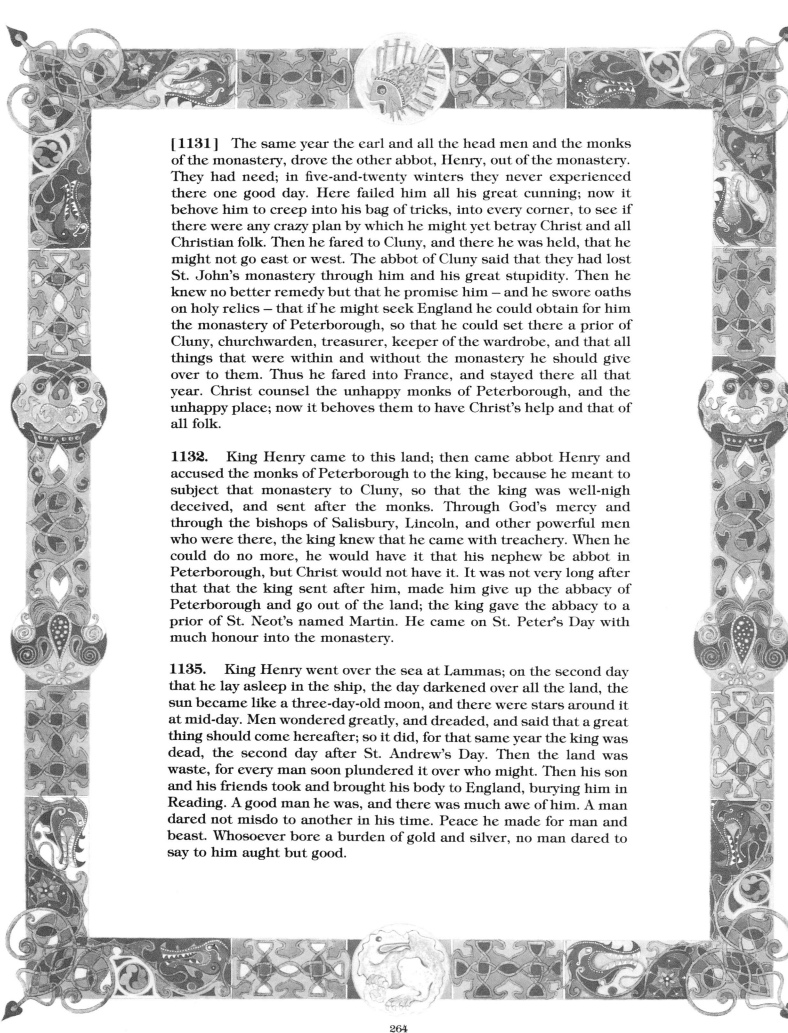

[1131] The same year the earl and all the head men and the monks of the monastery, drove the other abbot, Henry, out of the monastery. They had need; in five-and-twenty winters they never experienced there one good day. Here failed him all his great cunning; now it behove him to creep into his bag of tricks, into every corner, to see if there were any crazy plan by which he might yet betray Christ and all Christian folk. Then he fared to Cluny, and there he was held, that he might not go east or west. The abbot of Cluny said that they had lost St. John's monastery through him and his great stupidity. Then he knew no better remedy but that he promise him — and he swore oaths on holy relics — that if he might seek England he could obtain for him the monastery of Peterborough, so that he could set there a prior of Cluny, churchwarden, treasurer, keeper of the wardrobe, and that all things that were within and without the monastery he should give over to them. Thus he fared into France, and stayed there all that year. Christ counsel the unhappy monks of Peterborough, and the unhappy place; now it behoves them to have Christ's help and that of all folk.

1132.   King Henry came to this land; then came abbot Henry and accused the monks of Peterborough to the king, because he meant to subject that monastery to Cluny, so that the king was well-nigh deceived, and sent after the monks. Through God's mercy and through the bishops of Salisbury, Lincoln, and other powerful men who were there, the king knew that he came with treachery. When he could do no more, he would have it that his nephew be abbot in Peterborough, but Christ would not have it. It was not very long after that that the king sent after him, made him give up the abbacy of Peterborough and go out of the land; the king gave the abbacy to a prior of St. Neot's named Martin. He came on St. Peter's Day with much honour into the monastery.

1135.   King Henry went over the sea at Lammas; on the second day that he lay asleep in the ship, the day darkened over all the land, the sun became like a three-day-old moon, and there were stars around it at mid-day. Men wondered greatly, and dreaded, and said that a great thing should come hereafter; so it did, for that same year the king was dead, the second day after St. Andrew's Day. Then the land was waste, for every man soon plundered it over who might. Then his son and his friends took and brought his body to England, burying him in Reading. A good man he was, and there was much awe of him. A man dared not misdo to another in his time. Peace he made for man and beast. Whosoever bore a burden of gold and silver, no man dared to say to him aught but good.

During this was his nephew come into England, Stephen de Blois, and came to London; the folk of London received him, sent after archbishop William Curbeil, and hallowed him king on midwinter's day. In this king's time was all strife, evil and robbery, for against him soon rose the powerful men who were traitors. First of all Baldwin de Redvers held Exeter against him; the king besieged it, and later Baldwin accorded with him. Then others took to holding their castles against him, and David, king of Scotland, took to warring with him. Then, nevertheless, their messengers fared between them, they came together and were reconciled – though it little availed.

1137. King Stephen went over the sea to Normandy, and was there received, because they believed that he would be all that his uncle was, and because he had gotten his treasury; but he dealt it out and scattered it foolishly. Much had king Henry gathered, gold and silver, but no good was done with it to save his soul.

When King Stephen came to England, he held his council at Oxford, and there he seized bishop Roger of Salisbury, and his nephews, bishop Alexander of London, and chancellor Roger and put them all in prison until they gave up their castles. When the traitors perceived that he was a mild man, gentle and good, and did them no justice, they all wondered. They had done him homage and sworn him oaths, but they held no troth. They were all forsworn and their oaths abandoned, for every powerful man made his castles and then held them against him, and filled the land full of castles. They oppressed the wretched men of the land hard with work on the castles, and when the castles were made they filled them with devils and evil men. Then they took the people they believed had any goods, both by night and by day, men and women, and put them in prison; they were after gold and silver, and tortured them with unspeakable tortures, for never were martyrs tortured as they were. Men hung them by the feet and smoked them with foul smoke. Men hung them by the thumbs, others by the head, and hung byrnies on their feet. Men put knotted strings about their heads and twisted them so that they went to the brain. They put them in prisons with adders, snakes and toads therein, and killed them thus. Some they put into a *crucethus*, that is, a chest that is short, narrow and shallow, and put sharp stones therein, pressed the man therein and broke all his limbs. In many castles were *lof* and *grin*, that is, chains that two or three men had enough to do to bear one, so made that it is fastened to a beam and a sharp iron done on around a man's throat and his neck, that he might not move from there any way, neither sit nor lie not sleep, but bear all the iron. Many thousands they killed with hunger.

Above: Portrait of Stephen from a 14th-century manuscript on the laws of England.

Above: Portrait of the empress Matilda from a 15th-century English manuscript.

Below: Henry of Blois, a benefactor of the arts, landowner and financier, was bishop of Winchester and simultaneously abbot of Glastonbury in the early 1150s. There is an account of his stay in Rome in 1151, when the Romans were puzzled to see him buying ancient statues to send back to England. (15th-century English manuscript showing Henry with a ring he gave to St Alban's Abbey.)

Below: Castle Hedingham, Essex, where Stephen's wife died in 1152. The castle was one of many erected during the baronial wars of the 1140s and consists of a great tower set within a bailey.

Henry's daughter Matilda was disagreeable, proud and much disliked, and after Henry's death the barons and leading churchmen transferred their allegiance to Stephen, a grandson of William the Conqueror and brother of the count of Blois. Stephen quickly crossed to England, seized the treasury and was crowned in Westminster Abbey before Matilda could challenge him.

Stephen was a pleasant and good-natured king – qualities that must have come as a welcome change after the stern rule of William I and his sons. But forcefulness was a necessary quality for an English monarch in the 12th century. Stephen found too late that the land or offices he granted encouraged wealth and independence, not personal loyalty. On the battlefield he was a brave soldier but a poor tactician, unreliable and all too capable of making the wrong decision at critical moments.

At first the barons rallied to Stephen. But after he had failed to seize Normandy their loyalty began to waver. Then, in 1139, he committed a fateful blunder by arresting the powerful bishop of Salisbury and his family and taking his substantial wealth. The Church leaders were outraged.

Matilda arrived in England to press her claim to the throne. With the king's forces occupying Oxford and Matilda and her brother Robert of Gloucester established in the west, the time of anarchy began.

Although the ever more powerful barons claimed to be fighting for either Matilda or Stephen, their main concern was to protect and increase their own wealth and property. Many changed sides several times, often prompted by lavish gifts. Most of the military action consisted of raids for plunder, but after a battle at Lincoln in 1141 Stephen was captured and Matilda proclaimed queen. Nine months later Stephen was restored, and an uneasy peace with the Church was concluded. Matilda and Robert remained until Robert died in 1147 and Matilda returned to Normandy.

The torture and famine described in the Chronicles certainly happened in some areas, especially in the east. But in general the worst disorders were local – neighbouring barons used the prevailing anarchy to fight one another or raid nearby towns. The soldiers were mostly mercenaries; the ordinary people tried not to take part in the barons' wars – although they were often its victims. Many new ecclesiastical buildings were started (Stephen's reign saw the greatest period of Norman architecture), and the business of government continued.

Below: Geoffrey of Anjou, Matilda's second husband and Henry II's father. (Plaque above his tomb in Le Mans cathedral.)

[1137] I neither know how nor can tell all the horrors they did to the unhappy people in this land, that lasted nineteen years while Stephen was king; and ever it was worse and worse. They laid taxes on the towns all the while, and called it 'tenserie', protection money; when poor men had no more to give, they plundered and burnt all the towns, so that though you might well fare all day, never would you find a man staying in a town, nor land tilled. Then was corn dear, and meat, and cheese and butter, for there was none in the land. Poor men died of hunger, some went out for alms who were once powerful men, and some fled out of the land.

Never yet was more wretchedness in the land, nor ever did heathen men do worse than they did, for against all custom they spared neither church nor churchyard, but seized all the goods therein, and later burned the church and all together. Nor did they spare in the land either abbots or priests, but plundered monks and clerics – and every man robbed another if he could. If two or three men came riding to a town, all the township fled before them, believing they were robbers. Bishops and clergy cursed them ever, but it was nothing to them, for they were all utterly cursed, forsworn and lost.

Wherever the land was tilled, the earth bore no corn, for the land was all ruined with such deeds; and they said openly that Christ slept, and his saints. Such, and more than we know how to say, we suffered nineteen years for our sins.

In this evil time, abbot Martin held his abbey twenty years, half a year and eight days with great toil, found the monks and the guests all that was needed, and kept much cheer in the house. Notwithstanding this, he worked on the church, added thereto lands and rents, and improved it greatly; he had it roofed, and brought them into the new minster on St. Peter's Day with much ceremony. That was *anno ab incarnatione Domini Mcxl, a combustione loci xxiii*. He fared to Rome, and was there received by pope Eugenius; he got there privileges, one for all the lands in the abbacy, another of the land belonging to the office of sacrist; had he lived longer, he meant to do the same regarding the treasurer's office. He regained lands that powerful men held by force: from William Malduit, who held Rockingham castle, he won Cottingham and Easton Maudit; from Hugo of Waterville he won Irthlingborough and Stanwick, and sixty shillings a year from Aldwinkle. He made many monks, planted a vineyard, made many buildings, and changed the layout of the town to better than it was before. He was a good monk and a good man, therefore God and good men loved him.

Now we will say some part of what happened during Stephen's time. In his time, the Jews of Norwich bought a Christian child before Easter, and pained him all the same pains our Lord suffered. On Good Friday they hung him on a cross because of his love for our Lord, and afterwards buried him. They believed that it would be concealed, but our Lord revealed that he was a holy martyr; the monks took him, buried him solemnly in the minster, and he made there for our Lord wondrous and manifold miracles. He is called St. William.

1138 . . . 1153. King David of Scotland came with a vast army to this land, and meant to win this land. William, eorl of Aumale, to whom the king had committed York, came against him, with other trustworthy men and a few followers, fought with them and put the king to flight in the battle of the Standard, and killed many of his following.

This year king Stephen meant to take Robert, eorl of Gloucester, the son of king Henry; but he could not, for he was aware of it.

William, archbishop of Canterbury passed away, and the king made Theobald archbishop, who was abbot in Bec [1139].

In spring, the sun and the day darkened, about noon of the day, when people ate, and people lit candles to eat by; that was March 20th [1140], and people wondered greatly at it.

Great war grew between the king and Rannulf, eorl of Chester, not because he did not give him all he asked – as he did all others – but because ever the more he gave them the worse they were to him. The eorl held Lincoln against the king, and deprived him of all that he ought to have. The king went thither, and besieged him and his brother William de Roumare in the castle; the eorl stole out, went after Robert, eorl of Gloucester, and brought him thither with a great army. They fought hard on Candlemas against their lord, and seized him, for his men betrayed him and fled. They took him to Bristol and there put him in prison and fetters. Then was all England more troubled than it ever was, and all evil was in the land.

King Henry's daughter came, who had been empress in Germany, and now was countess in Anjou. She came to London, and the folk of London meant to take her; she fled, and lost much there.

The bishop of Winchester, Henry, brother of king Stephen, spoke with eorl Robert, and with the empress, and swore them oaths that he would never more hold with the king his brother, cursed all the men who held with him, said to them that he would give up Winchester to them, and had them come there. When they were therein, then came the king's queen with all her strength and besieged them so that there was much hunger inside. [1141] When they could not suffer it longer, they stole out and fled; they were aware of them outside, followed them, took Robert eorl of Gloucester, led him to Rochester and there put him in prison. The empress fled into a monastery.

Henry's quarrel with Thomas à Becket led to the arch-bishop's murder on 29 December 1170 in Canterbury cathedral by four impetuous knights, who thought they were fulfilling Henry's wishes. Probably they were not – but Henry had not anticipated the consequences of his angry remarks about Becket. The king accepted responsibility for the murder: even an elaborate penance at the martyr's tomb was not enough. (Page from a 14th-century illuminated manuscript, above; stained glass from Canterbury cathedral depicting the murder, opposite page, top.)

After Stephen's death, Henry returned to England to claim the crown. The first of the Plantagenet kings, his immediate goal was to establish order after the years of internal warfare and constant civil strife, and part of this peacemaking was the code of written laws that was to form the basis of the English legal system. To establish a sense of justice was a personal challenge to Henry, and he frequently sat in judgement in person; circuit judges representing royal justice travelled throughout the country and trial by local juries gave Englishmen a sense of immediate involvement with the king's justice.

Henry's main assets were energy and an ability to organize. Although he travelled throughout England, he spent most of his reign keeping his continental empire in order, and coping with the growing rivalry and ambitions of his four sons, Henry, Richard, Geoffrey and John. His queen, Eleanor, had been married first to Louis of France; her own possessions of Aquitaine, Auvergne and Poitou originally tipped the balance of power in Henry's favour. However, the young princes, often aided by Eleanor, were difficult and rebellious. Eleanor was eventually held captive for over 15 years. After Henry II's death, Richard became king of England but died overseas in 1199. John, who succeeded him, is best known for signing the Magna Carta.

King Henry was a competent warrior with a sharp temper, although he usually preferred diplomacy. He was a well-read man, knew several

Below: Tomb of Henry II at Fontevrault.

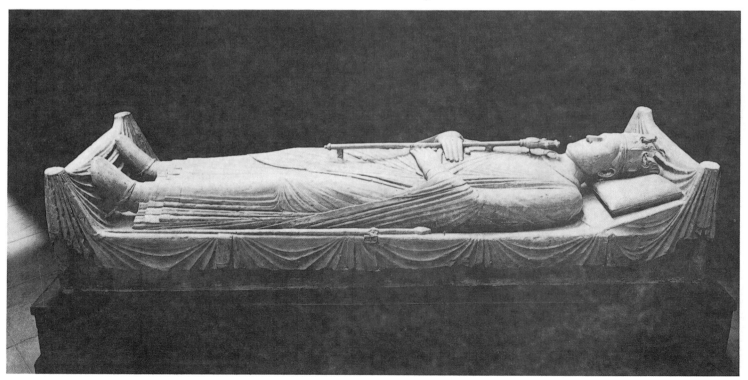

languages, and practised a pragmatic kind of charity – a tenth of the food and drink brought into the palace was given to the poor. But he was not an easy friend. Thomas à Becket had been a close companion, but after Henry had made him into what he thought would be a respectful archbishop of Canterbury, Thomas suddenly turned to the defence of all the Church's privileges, especially the right to trial by canonical court rather than by the king's men. Their quarrel was bitter and violently public. When Thomas was murdered in his cathedral by four of the king's knights, Henry insisted he had not given the order, although he eventually took responsibility and did penance both publicly and privately for the rest of his life. Perhaps unfairly, that one act has been the most enduring in the popular view of Henry's reign. Thomas became a martyr, revered even up to the present time, and the separate responsibilities of Church and state which Henry championed have been established since Henry VIII's time.

Left: Engraved capitals at Langon, France, depicting Henry and queen Eleanor.

Below: Seal of Henry II.

Then went wise men between the king's friends and the eorl's friends, and settled it so that the king should be let out of prison for the eorl and the eorl for the king, and they so did.

Later thereafter, the king and eorl Rannulf made a settlement at Stamford, swore oaths, fastened troths that neither should betray the other – and it availed nothing, for the king, through bad counsel, later seized him in Northampton and put him in prison. As soon again, on worse counsel, he let him out, on the condition that he swear on relics and find hostages, that he would give up all his castles. Some he gave up, some he did not give up, and then did worse than he should here.

Then was England greatly divided. Some held with the king and some with the empress. Because, when the king was in prison the eorls and the powerful men believed that he should never more be allowed out, and settled with the empress, brought her to Oxford and gave her the borough. When the king was out, and heard that said, he took his troops and besieged her in the tower. She was let down at night from the tower with ropes, and she fled, and went on foot to Wallingford.

Thereafter she fared over the sea, and the people of Normandy all turned from the king to the eorl of Anjou, some willingly and some unwillingly, for he besieged them until they gave up their castles, and no one had help from the king.

Then fared Eustace the king's son to France, and took the sister of the king of France to wife. He believed that he would obtain Normandy thereby, but he prospered little, and quite justly, for he was an evil man; wherever he came he did more evil than good. He plundered the lands and laid heavy taxes on them; he brought his wife to England and put her in the castle at Canterbury. A good woman she was, but she had little bliss with him. Christ would not have it that he should reign long, and both he and his mother died [1152].

The eorl of Anjou died, and his son Henry took the kingdom. The queen of France parted from the king; she came to the young eorl Henry, and he took her to wife, and all of Poitou with her. Then he

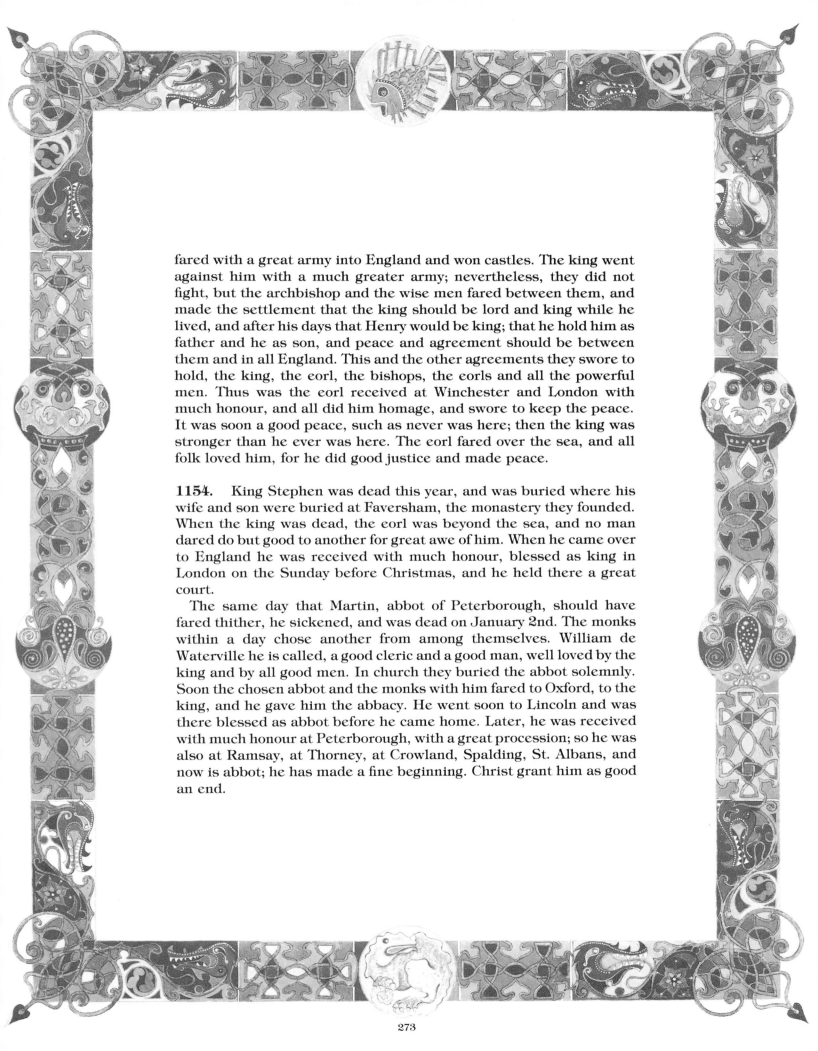

fared with a great army into England and won castles. The king went against him with a much greater army; nevertheless, they did not fight, but the archbishop and the wise men fared between them, and made the settlement that the king should be lord and king while he lived, and after his days that Henry would be king; that he hold him as father and he as son, and peace and agreement should be between them and in all England. This and the other agreements they swore to hold, the king, the eorl, the bishops, the eorls and all the powerful men. Thus was the eorl received at Winchester and London with much honour, and all did him homage, and swore to keep the peace. It was soon a good peace, such as never was here; then the king was stronger than he ever was here. The eorl fared over the sea, and all folk loved him, for he did good justice and made peace.

1154. King Stephen was dead this year, and was buried where his wife and son were buried at Faversham, the monastery they founded. When the king was dead, the eorl was beyond the sea, and no man dared do but good to another for great awe of him. When he came over to England he was received with much honour, blessed as king in London on the Sunday before Christmas, and he held there a great court.

The same day that Martin, abbot of Peterborough, should have fared thither, he sickened, and was dead on January 2nd. The monks within a day chose another from among themselves. William de Waterville he is called, a good cleric and a good man, well loved by the king and by all good men. In church they buried the abbot solemnly. Soon the chosen abbot and the monks with him fared to Oxford, to the king, and he gave him the abbacy. He went soon to Lincoln and was there blessed as abbot before he came home. Later, he was received with much honour at Peterborough, with a great procession; so he was also at Ramsay, at Thorney, at Crowland, Spalding, St. Albans, and now is abbot; he has made a fine beginning. Christ grant him as good an end.

Norman and Plantagenet Kings

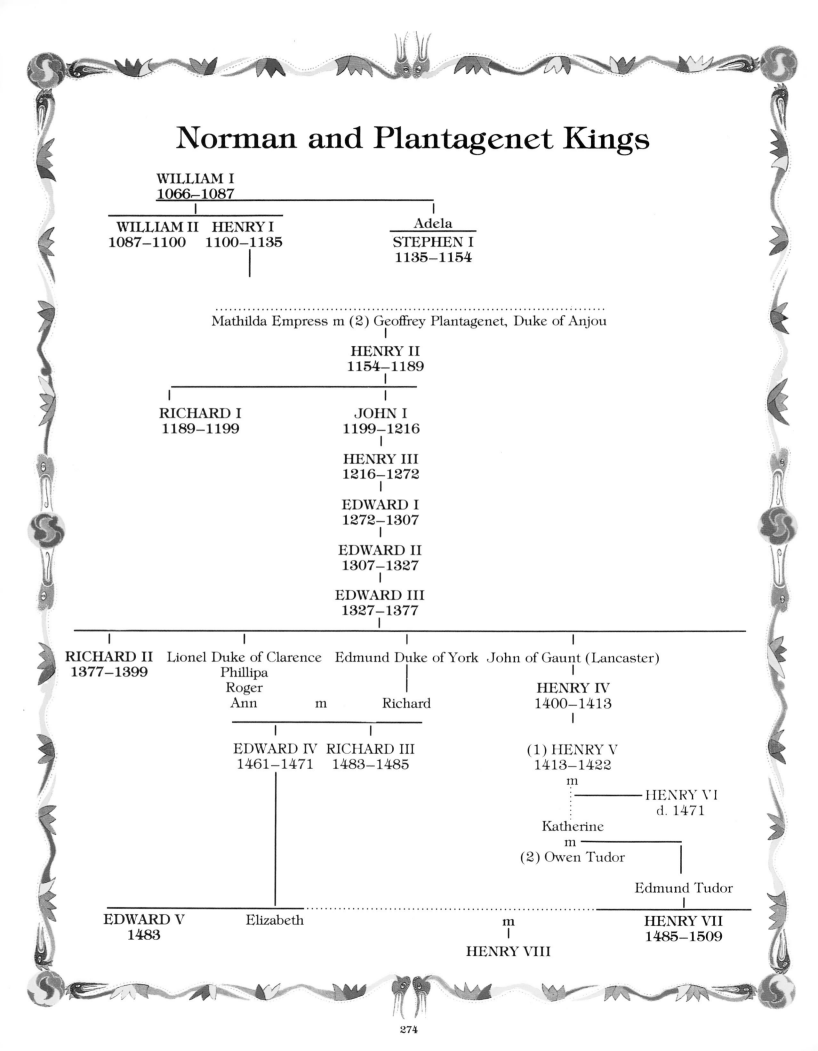

WILLIAM I
1066–1087

WILLIAM II   HENRY I   Adela
1087–1100   1100–1135   STEPHEN I
                                                   1135–1154

Mathilda Empress m (2) Geoffrey Plantagenet, Duke of Anjou

HENRY II
1154–1189

RICHARD I   JOHN I
1189–1199   1199–1216

                       HENRY III
                       1216–1272

                       EDWARD I
                       1272–1307

                       EDWARD II
                       1307–1327

                       EDWARD III
                       1327–1377

RICHARD II   Lionel Duke of Clarence   Edmund Duke of York   John of Gaunt (Lancaster)
1377–1399   Phillipa
                  Roger   HENRY IV
                  Ann   m   Richard   1400–1413

                  EDWARD IV   RICHARD III   (1) HENRY V
                  1461–1471   1483–1485   1413–1422
                                                                        m
                                                                             ————— HENRY VI
                                                                                   d. 1471
                                                                   Katherine
                                                                        m ————————
                                                                   (2) Owen Tudor

                                                                                   Edmund Tudor

EDWARD V   Elizabeth   m   HENRY VII
1483   1485–1509
                                          HENRY VIII

Appendix

Anglo-Saxon Poetry

About 30,000 lines – approximately the number in a long best-seller – survive from what must have been a much larger collection of poetry from the Anglo-Saxon period.

In addition to the poems in *The Anglo-Saxon Chronicles*, there are long, heroic-religious saints' lives, biblical stories and interpretations, shorter, more lyrical poems, riddles, prayers, others that defy classification – and, of course, the 3,182-line heroic *Beowulf.* All these bear witness to an ancient tradition: Anglo-Saxon poetry existed in oral form long before it was written down, and also probably continued to exist alongside inscribed verse.

The poetry in the Chronicles is unusual in that it is an integral part of a set of historical annals. Poems celebrate, dignify or lament battles, important deaths and injustices so that they stand out in relief against the general background of events. The two on these pages – a metrical calendar (the *Menologium*) and the verses that follow it – are in fact a preface to the Chronicles. Their theme is what time means to mankind, its effect on his creations and the Creation.

CHRIST WAS BORN,   KING OF GLORY
in midwinter,   mighty prince,
eternal, almighty,   on the eighth day,
Healer, called,   heaven's ward;
so at the same time   singing praises
countless folk   begin the year,
for the awaited time   comes to town,
the first month,   famous January.
Five nights later   the Lord's baptism,
and eternal God's   epiphany comes;
the twelve-days' time   to blessed men known,
by us in Britain   called Twelfthnight.
Four weeks later   February falls,
Sol-month brighter   settles in town,
a month   minus two days;
so February's way   was reckoned by the wise,
One night more   is Mary's mass,
the King's mother;   for on that day Christ,
the child of the Ruler,   she revealed in the temple.
After five nights   winter has fared,
and after seventeen   he suffered death:
the Saviour's man,   great Matthew,
when spring has come   to stay in town.
And to the folk   after five nights
– unless it is Leap Year,   when it comes one
night later –
by his cold clothes   of frost and hail
wild March is known   throughout the world,
Hlyda-month,   blowing loud,
Eleven nights later,   holy and noble,
Gregory shone   in God's service,
honoured in Britain.   So Benedict,
nine nights passing,   sought the Preserver,
the resolute man   celebrated in writings
by men under his rule.   So the wise in reckoning
at that time   count the equinox,

because, wielding power,   God at the beginning
made on the same day   sun and moon.
Four nights   after the Father
sent the equinox,   his archangel announced
the mighty salvation   to great Mary,
that she the Shaper   of all should bear,
bring to birth   the best of kings,
as it was widely   told through the world;
that was a great destiny   delivered to us.
So after seven nights   the Saviour sends
the month of April,   most often bringing
the mighty time   of comfort to mankind,
the Lord's resurrection,   when joy is rightly
celebrated everywhere, as that wise one sang:
"This is the day which the Lord hath made;
we will rejoice and be glad in it."
Nor may we hold   that time by tally
of a length of days,   nor the Lord's
ascension to heaven,   for always it changes
within the rules   known to the wise man,
old in winters;   in the cycle
he can with craft   find the holy days.
The martyrs' memory   we must yet recount,
say in words,   sing with wisdom,
that after nineteen   nights and five
from Easter's blessed   coming to us,
men begin   to raise the relics,
holy treasures;   that is a high day,
when Rogation is held.   Quickly to men's homes,
six nights further   in the fine gear,
in groves and flowers   comes glorious, shining,
strongly to men   as it must,
the fulness of May   through many lands.
On the same day   the noble disciples
Phillip and James   gave up their lives,
mighty warriors,   for the maker's love.

After two nights   was taken by God
to blessed Helen   the noblest of beams,
on which lay suffering   the Lord of angels
for love of man,   the maker on a gallows
by the Father's leave.   After the first week
minus one night,   to men are brought
sun-bright days   by summer to town,
warm weather.   Woods and fields as soon
bloom and blossom;   so beauty is called up
over middle-earth, as in his manner
each kind of creature   declares the King's love,
the Almighty's.   After eight nights
and days turning,   the Lord took up
Augustine   into the other light,
embraced the blessed   man who in Britain
gladly inspired   men's obedience
within the will of God   as wise Gregory bade.
Nor have I heard before   of a better man
anywhere bringing   better teaching,
a more celebrated bishop   over the sea;
by the king's seat in Kent   he rests near the church
after six long days   the month draws near,
earlier by us   called *Litha*,
now called June,   and the gem rises
in the heavens   the highest in the year,
then sinks from his place   and sets;
he will not for long   travel late,
the fairest light   over the fields.
After thirteen nights and ten   the glorious thane
loved by the Lord,   John the Baptist, was born,
whom we celebrate   in midsummer.
And widely it is held   throughout the world,
widely honoured   as well it should be,
that holy day   in the homes of men,
when Peter and Paul   the apostles,
loyal servants,   suffered in Rome
five nights on   from midsummer's day
glorious martyrdom;   miracles they worked,
many for men   among the nations,
countless, manifest and clear   through the Maker's
    Son.
Then after two nights,   timely to us,
comes July,   in which James
on the twenty-fourth night   took up his life,
wise and truthful,   teacher of the people,
Zebedee's son.   Summer on the seventh night
brings the weed-month   brightly to town;
everywhere August   comes to the earth,
and Lammas-time.   Later coming,
one week   minus one day,
is high autumn,   heavy with harvest;
then wealth is found   that is fair on earth.
On the third day   the glorious deacon
was martyred and went forth,   mighty man,
Lawrence,   who now has life

with the wonder-Father   in reward for his works.
After five nights   the fairest of virgins,
the wondrous woman,   went to the God of hosts
for her son's mothering,   to the victory-seat,
a home in heaven;   the Saviour has so
repaid forever   that perfect fostering.
Then on the tenth night   in the turning of time,
Bartholomew   here in Britain
is honoured far   and wide for his fate.
So also   after four nights,
the noble's death-day   is known to men:
he who baptized   the glorious Boy,
the worthy warrior   of the Word,
of whom God said   no greater man
was born on earth   between man and woman.
And after three nights   throughout the nations,
the month that is held   by men as holy
fares to the people   as it was foreseen,
as the old astronomers   ere found,
September's way;   and it was on the seventh day
that the best of queens   came to birth,
the Lord's mother.   Then more days pass,
thirteen in number,   and the blameless thane
clear-sighted in God's word   sent up his spirit:
Matthew   to his Maker
went in eternal joy.   Then arrives
after three nights   to the nations,
the day of equinox   to the children of earth;
and here we count worthy,   far and wide,
the archangel's time   in the autumn,
Michael, known to the multitude,
five nights after   the equinox-day.
Two nights later,   the tenth month
comes to men   with wise counsel,
October arrives   among men with abundance:
Winterfylleth   was the old word
among the island-dwellers,   Angles and Saxons,
men and women.   So the warriors' time comes
on the twenty-seventh, and the two noble ones
on the same day   are celebrated:
we have heard   how long ago
Simon and Jude,   shining with glory,
did great deeds.   For that their doom
was a blessed uplifting.   Then arrives quickly,
after four nights,   to the folk with plenty,
Blotmonath   in town, and brings feasting to men:
November,   a time of blessedness
like no other month,   by the Lord's mercy.
The same day we celebrate   the feast of All Saints,
who worked in the world   the will of God.
Then winter's day   opens wide
in six nights,   seizes the sun,
ravages the harvest   with rime and snow,
chains them with frost   at the Lord's command;
the green meadows   may not stay with us,

the fields' covering.   And four nights later
it was that the mighty one,   Martin, departed,
the stainless servant   sought the Lord;
and on the twelfth night   Clement was taken,
sunk in the grey sea,   strong in victory,
called on by name   by many in need.
On the seventh night after,   dear to the Saviour,
noble Andrew   arose into heaven,
gave his ghost   into God's keeping,
eager to depart   in earthly death,
Then morning to men   brings in the month

called December   by the Redeemer's children,
the old Yule.   So in eight nights and twelve
the Saviour himself,   strong in purpose,
gave with difficulty   an eternal kingdom to Thomas,
and to the bold man   his blessing.
Then after four nights   the Father of angels
sent his Son   into creation's expanse
to comfort mankind.   Now you can find
the holy days,   that man shall hold
throughout Britain   at the bidding
of the Saxons' king   at the same time.

King shall hold kingdom.   A castle is seen from afar,
artful work of giants   yet on earth
wonderful wall-stone work.   Wind is swiftest in sky,
thunder betimes most loud.   Many are Christ's powers.
Wyrd is strongest.   Winter is coldest,
Lent frostiest   and longest cold,
summer sun-brightest,   when sky is hottest,
and autumn most glorious,   giving to men
the year's fruits   which God sends.
Truth is clearest,   treasure dearest,
gold to each man.   The greyhair is wisest,
ancient in years,   who has much endured.
Grief clings;   clouds glide.
Young chief shall   encourage good companions
in grim war   and ring-giving.
Courage shall be in eorl, edge shall in battle
meet helm.   Hawk shall on glove
stay wild.   Wolf shall on hill
be lone.   Boar shall dwell in holt
with great tusks.   Good man shall in homeland
work judgement.   Spear shall in hand
be gold-adorned.   Gem shall in ring
stand broad and brilliant.   Brook shall in wave
mingle with sea-flood.   Mast shall in ship
swing sailyard.   Sword shall lie on breast,
lordly iron.   Dragon shall in barrow dwell
old, proud of his treasure.   Fish shall in water
beget his kind.   King shall bright ring
give in hall.   Bear shall on heath
dwell old and dangerous,   river come down
from hill flood-grey,   armed force together
stand firm, victorious,   good faith in eorl
and wisdom in man.   Woods shall on earth
bloom with flowers,   hill on plain

stand green.   God shall be in heaven
the judge of deeds.   Door shall on hall
be house's wide mouth.   Boss on buckler
shall shield the fingers.   Flying bird
shall soar in sky,   salmon in pool
slide swiftly.   Shower in heaven
mingled with wind   shall come in this world.
Thief shall go in dark weather.   Demon shall in fen
live alone inland.   A lady shall with secret arts
seek her friend,   if she would not be fulfilled
and bought in marriage with rings.   Sea shall well with
      brine,
circling sky and wave   be round all land,
mountain-streams course.   Cattle shall on earth
conceive and bring forth.   Star shall in heaven
brightly shine   as its maker bade.
Good shall with evil,   youth with age,
life shall with death,   light shall with dark,
army with army,   enemy with another,
injury with injury   oppose round the land,
accuse of wrong.   Always the wise man
shall think on this world's contention,   the criminal
      hang,
fairly repaid   for wrongdoing
against mankind.   The Maker alone knows
where the soul   shall afterwards shift,
and all the ghosts   who turned to God
after their deathday,   awaiting their doom
in the Father's lap.   The future
is locked and lightless.   The Lord alone knows it,
saving Father.   No one steps back
hither under roof   who could reveal
truly to men   the Maker's design,
the home of the triumphant,   where He himself dwells.

Bibliography

Select Bibliography

The Anglo-Saxon Chronicle according to the Several Original Authorities, (2 vols), edited by B. Thorpe, Rolls Series, 1861

Anglo-Saxon England, 3rd edition, F.M. Stenton, Oxford University Press, 1971.

Two of the Saxon Chronicles Parallel, with Supplementary Extracts from the Others, a revised text edited by Charles Plummer, on the basis of an edition by John Earle, Clarendon Press, 1892

The Anglo-Saxon Chronicle, translated with an introduction by G.N. Garmonsway, J.M. Dent, 1953; E.P. Dutton, New York

Further Reading

The Anglo-Saxons, edited by James Campbell, Phaidon, 1982

The Anglo-Saxon Chronicle, a revised translation, edited by Dorothy Whitelock, with David C. Douglas and Susie I. Tucker, Eyre & Spottiswoode, 1961

Anglo-Saxon England, 3rd edition, F.M. Stenton, Oxford University Press, 1971

The Anglo-Saxons, David Wilson, Penguin, 1971; Barnes & Noble, New York

An Introduction to Anglo-Saxon England, 2nd edition, Peter Hunter Blair, Cambridge University Press, 1977

Anglo-Saxon England, David Brown, Bodley Head, 1978

Anglo-Saxon England, Lloyd and Jennifer Laing, Routledge & Kegan Paul, 1979; Granada, 1982

Saxon and Norman Kings, Christopher Brooke, Fontana, 1963; Franklin Watts, New York

Anglo-Saxon Poetry, edited and translated by S.A.J. Bradley, J.M. Dent, 1982

The Lindisfarne Gospels, Janet Backhouse, Phaidon, 1981

A Guide to the Dark Age Remains in Britain, Lloyd and Jennifer Laing, Constable, 1979

Exploring Saxon and Norman England, P.J. Helm, Robert Hale, 1976; Newbury House, Rowley, Mass.

Life in Anglo-Saxon England, R.I. Page, Batsford, 1970

Anglo-Saxon Architecture, (2 vols), H.M. Taylor and Joan Taylor, Cambridge University Press, 1965

The Vikings and their Origins, David Wilson, Thames & Hudson, 1980

The Northern World, David Wilson, Thames & Hudson, 1980

Scandinavian England, Wainwright and Finberg, Phaidon, 1975

The Viking Achievement, 2nd edition, Peter Foote and David Wilson, Sidgwick & Jackson, 1980

The Vikings in England, Else Roesdahl et al, Anglo-Danish Viking Project, 1981

The Anglo-Saxon Chronicle, a revised translation edited by Dorothy Whitelock, with David C. Douglas and Susie I. Tucker, Eyre & Spottiswoode, 1961

The Genealogical Preface to the Anglo-Saxon Chronicle. Four texts edited to supplement Earle-Plummer, by Bruce Dickins, University of Cambridge, Museum of Archaeology, Occasional Papers (No. II, printed for the Dept. of Anglo-Saxon), 1952

Studies on Anglo-Saxon Institutions, H.M. Chadwick, University Press, Cambridge, 1905

The Concise Oxford Dictionary of English Place-Names, revised edition, Eilert Ekwall, Clarendon Press, 1960

The Sutton Hoo Ship Burial, R.L.S. Bruce-Mitford, Gollancz, 1968

Late Saxon and Viking Art, T.D. Kendrick, Methuen, 1949; Barnes & Noble, New York

Edward the Confessor, Frank Barlow, Longman, 1970; University of California Press

Kings and Queens of England Series, Lady Antonia Fraser, Weidenfeld & Nicholson, 1972

Anglo-Saxon England and the Norman Conquest, H.R. Loyn, Longman, 1962; Saint Martin's Press, New York

The Normans and the Norman Conquest, R.A. Brown, Constable, 1969; Thomas Y. Crowell, New York

The Normans and Their Myth, R.H.C. Davis, Thames & Hudson, 1976; Thames & Hudson, New York

The Conquest of England, Eric Linklater, Hodder & Stoughton, 1966

From Domesday Book to Magna Carta 1087–1216, 2nd edition, A.L. Poole, Oxford University Press, 1955; Oxford University Press, New York

Domesday Book – A Guide, R. Welldon Finn, Phillimore, 1973

The Feudal Kingdom of England, Frank Barlow, Longman, 1961

Henry II, Wilfrid Warren, Eyre, 1973

Eleanor of Aquitaine, Desmond Seward, David & Charles, 1978

The Crusades, Vol 1, Sir Steven Runciman, Cambridge University Press, 1978; Cambridge University Press, New York

Life in Norman England, O.G. Tomkeieff, Batsford, 1966; Putnam, New York

English Medieval Monasteries, Roy Midmer, Heinemann, 1980

English Drawings of the Tenth and Eleventh Centuries, Francis Wormald, Faber & Faber, 1952

Manuscripts

Details of manuscript illustrations are given below. Page numbers, and the position of the illustrations on the pages, are in italic.

28t   Bodleian Library, MS Can. Misc. 378, fo.150v.
30L   Trinity College Dublin Library, MS Al.6, fo.200.
38bL   Trinity College Dublin Library, MS 57, fo.21v.
38br   Trinity College Dublin Library, MS 57, fo.125v.
38bc   Corpus Christi College Cambridge Library, MS 286, fo.129v.
45   Corpus Christi College Cambridge Library, MS 173, fo.13v.
54c   British Library, Add MS 39943, fo.2.
54   Cambridge University Library, MS Kk.v.16, fo.70v.
55c   British Library Add MS 39943, fo.26.
55   Cambridge University Library, MS Kk.v.16, fo.70v.
67   British Library, MS Cot. Nero D IV, fo.139.
70   British Library, MS Cot. Nero D IV, fo.26v.
71tL   British Library, MS Cot. Nero D IV, fo.90.
90L   Pierpont Morgan Library, MS 736, fo.10.
90r   Pierpont Morgan Library, MS 736, fo.14.
94t   Corpus Christi College Cambridge Library, MS 26, fo.129.
94br   Bodleian Library, MS Hatton 20, fo.1.
101br   British Library, MS Cot. Claud. D II, fo.8.
103tL   Bodleian Library, MS Junius XI, fo.65.
103c   Bodleian Library, MS Junius XI, fo.81.
105   Stockholm, Royal Library, MS A.135, fo.11.
109tL   Florence, Laurentian Library, MS Amiat. I, fo.5.
120   Corpus Christi College Cambridge Library, MS 183, fo.1v.
121tr   British Library, MS Cot. Claud. D II, fo.13.
124   British Library, MS Cot. Tib. A III, fo.2v.
125br   British Library, MS Roy. 10 A XIII, fo.2v.
130   British Library, MS Cot. Vesp. A VIII, fo.2v.
131L   British Library, Add MS 49598, fo.99v.
131r   Bodleian Library, MS Auct. F IV 32, fo.1.
139   British Library, MS Harl. 2278, fo.98v.

143   Chantilly, Musée Condé, Registrum Gregorii.
162t   Iceland, Manuscript Institute, Flateyjarbók, col.310.
163L   British Library, MS Stowe 944, fo.6.
163tr   British Library, Add MS 3341, fo.1v.
170t   Public Record Office, Doc. E36/284.
171L   British Library, MS Cot. Vit. A XIII, fo.3.
177t   Cambridge University Library, MS Ee. III. 59, fo.9.
186br   Bodleian Library, MS 569, fo.1.
191   British Library, MS Cot. Vit. A XIII, fo.3v.
203tL   British Library, MS Roy 2 B VII, fo.172v.
203tr   British Library, MS Cot. Claud. D II, fo.33.
203br   British Library, MS Cot. Jul. E IV, fo.2.
206   British Library, MS Faust. B VII, fo.72v.
210t   British Library, MS Cot. Tib. B V Pt 1, fo.5v.
210bL   Public Record Office, Domesday Book Vol I, fo.64v.
211t   British Library, MS Cot. Tib. B V Pt 1, fo.3.
214t   Public Record Office, Doc. E372/1 M4d.
215t   British Library, MS Cot. Claud. B IV, fo.59.
227t   British Library, MS Cot. Jul. E IV, fo.2v.
227b   Bodleian Library, MS 271, fo.2v.
234b   British Library, MS Roy 2 A XXII, fo.220.
238   Corpus Christi College Oxford Library, MS 157, fos. 382 and 383.
239   British Library, MS Roy. 20 A II, fo.6.
243   British Library, MS Cot. Claud. B IV, fo.19.
253b   Durham, Dean and Chapter Library, MS B II 13, fo.68.
253t   Trinity College Cambridge Library, MS B.5.26, fo.1.
255bL   Corpus Christi College Cambridge Library, MS 4, fo.241v.
256L   Bodleian Library, MS Auct. E. inf 2, fo.67v.
266tL   British Library, MS Cot. Claud. D III, fo.72.
266tr   British Library, MS Cot. Nero D VII, fo.7.
266bL   British Library, MS Cot. Nero D VII, fo.87v.
270t   British Library, MS Cot. Claud. D II, fo.70.

(b = bottom; c = centre; t = top; L = left; r = right)

Index

Page numbers in *italic* refer to the illustrations and their captions.

Picture acknowledgements

Ashmolean Museum, Oxford 34b, 91tL, 94, 100r, 100L, 136tr; BBC Hulton Picture Library 170bL; John Bethell 22t, 22b; Bibliotheque Royale, Brussels 235tL; Bodleian Library, Oxford 28t, 94br, 103tL, 103c, 131r, 186r, 227b, 256L; Janet and Colin Bord 64L, 64r, 64b; British Library 54c, 55c, 67, 70, 71t, 101br, 121tr, 124, 125r, 131L, 139, 163t, 163bL, 171L, 191b, 203tL, 203tr, 203br, 206, 210t, 211t, 215t, 227t, 239b, 243bL, 266tL, 266tr, 266bL; British Library/loan from Stonyhurst College 69tr; British Library/Phaidon Archives 130; British Library/Weidenfeld and Nicholson Archives 234b, 270t; British Museum 26, 31br, 77bL, 94bL, 104L, 113, 121br, 136tL, 138, 142tr; British Museum/ Bridgeman Art Library 42, 43b, 43t; 46t; British Museum/M. Holford 47b; British Museum/Phaidon Archives 22c, 31t, 69b, 142br; British Museum/Photoresources 34tL, 34tr, 46b, 47t, 47c; British Museum/Weidenfeld and Nicholson Archives 271br; Burrell Collection, Glasgow Museums and Art Galleries 187; Cambridge University, Committee for Aerial Photography 39br, 103b, 114r, 207b, 210br, 266br; Cambridge University, Corpus Christi College 38bc, 45, 94t, 120, 255bL; Cambridge University Library 54, 55, 171t; Cambridge University, Trinity College/ Courtauld (photo: O. R. Dodwell) 253L; Chantilly, Musée Condé/Photographie Giraudon 143; David Collison 101tr, 101bL; Country Life 243t; Dean and Chapter Library, Durham 57L, 57tr, 57br; Dean and Chapter Library, Durham/

Weidenfeld and Nicholson Archives (photo: Edwin Smith) 253b; Department of the Environment 39t, 243br; Department of the Environment/Phaidon Archives 28b; C. M. Dixon 23, 24t, 30r, 63, 68, 78, 86t, 104L, 174t, 174bL, 175, 222r, 223tL, 242t, 255br; Dublin, Trinity College Library 30L, 38br; Dublin, Trinity College Library/Phaidon Archives 38bL; Fotomas Index 182L, 182r, 183t, 183bL, 183br, 190t, 190c, 190b, 207t; Guildhall Museum, London 159t; Clive Hicks 38t, 125tL, 125bL; Historical Museum, Bergen 110tr, 110b; Michael Holford 39bL, 222L, 223tr, 223b; P. Hunt 27, 162b; A. F. Kersting 62bL, 153br, 242b; Kunsthistorische Museum, Vienna 123; Landesmuseum fur vor-und Frühgeschichte, Keil 32t, 33b; Laurentian Library, Florence 109tL; Le Mans, Musées du Mans/Weidenfeld and Nicolson Archives 267; Leicestershire Museums and Art Galleries/Thames and Hudson Archives 31bL; Manuscript Institute of Iceland/Werner Forman Archive 162t; Metropolitan Museum of Art, New York/Weidenfeld and Nicolson Archives 271L; National Monuments Record 62t, 62br, 77br, 153tL, 153bL, 170br, 174br, 224t, 226, 234t, 235b, 255t; National Museum, Copenhagen 33t, 86b, 137; National Museum, Copenhagen/ Ray Sutcliffe 108L; National Museum, Copenhagen/Werner Forman Archive 136b, 156; Olsen, Ann-Mari 100tr; Oxford, Corpus Christi College 238; Phaidon Press Ltd Archives 42, 43t, 57L, 57tr, 131r; Photographie Giraudon 270b; Photoresources 158b, 271t; Pierpont

Morgan Library, New York 90L, 90r; Popperfoto 32b; Public Record Office 170t, 210bL, 214t, 215b; Royal Library, Stockholm/Phaidon Archives 105; Walter Scott 56, 224; State Historical Museum, Stockholm 163br; State Historical Museum, Stockholm/Antikvarisk Topografisk Archiv, Stockholm 75tr, 87br, 109b; State Historical Museum, Stockholm/British Museum Publications 75bL; State Historical Museum, Stockholm/Werner Forman Archive 74b, 75br, 91b, 108r, 159b; Universitetets Oldsaksamling, Oslo 79, 109tr; Universitetets Oldsaksamling, Oslo/ Phaidon Archives 158t; University of London, Courtauld Institute 186br, 254tr; University of London, Courtauld Institute/ O. R. Dodwell 253t; University of London, Senate House Slide Collection 186bL, 186tr; University of London, Warburg Institute 211b, 239t; Victoria & Albert Museum, Crown Copyright 256r; Victoria & Albert Museum, Crown Copyright/ Photoresources 254bL, 254br; Viking Ships Museum, Oslo 79, 87tL; Viking Ships Museum, Oslo/Photoresources 74tr; Viking Ships Museum, Oslo/Werner Forman Archive 74tL, 87tr; Weidenfeld and Nicolson Archives, 235tL, 254tr; Weidenfeld and Nicolson Archives/H. Roger-Viollet, Paris 202; Werner Forman Archive 114L, 155; Winchester City Museums 142bL; Woodmansterne Ltd 91tr; York Archaeological Trust 24b, 152, 214b; Yorkshire Museum/ Woodmansterne (photo: Jeremy Marks) 71; G. Zarnecki 254tr.

(b = bottom; c = centre; t = top; L = left; r = right)